CHERIE QUARTERS

# CHERIE QUARTERS

## THE PLACE AND THE PEOPLE THAT INSPIRED ERNEST J. GAINES

RUTH LANEY

Louisiana State University Press
Baton Rouge

Published with the assistance of The Noland Fund

Published by Louisiana State University Press
lsupress.org



Manufactured in the United States of America
First printing

Designer: Barbara Neely Bourgoyne
Typeface: Arno Pro
Printer and binder: Sheridan Books

Front jacket photograph: Reese Spooner at his home in Cherie Quarters, February 1982.
Photo courtesy Philip Gould. Copyright © Philip Gould.

Back jacket photograph: Ernest Gaines and Reese Spooner, Cherie Quarters, February 1982.
Photo courtesy Philip Gould. Copyright © Philip Gould.

Library of Congress Cataloging-in-Publication Data
Names: Laney, Ruth, author.
Title: Cherie quarters : the place and the people that inspired Ernest J. Gaines / Ruth Laney.
Description: Baton Rouge : Louisiana State University Press, [2023] | Includes bibliographical references.
Identifiers: LCCN 2022017753 (print) | LCCN 2022017754 (ebook) | ISBN 978-0-8071-7802-7 (cloth) | ISBN 978-0-8071-7892-8 (pdf) | ISBN 978-0-8071-7891-1 (epub)
Subjects: LCSH: Louisiana—Social conditions—19th century. | Louisiana—Social conditions—20th century. | Louisiana—Intellectual Life—19th century. | Louisiana—Intellectual life—20th century. | Gaines, Ernest J., 1933–2019.
Classification: LCC HN79.L8 L36 2022 (print) | LCC HN79.L8 (ebook) | DDC 301.09763—dc23/eng/20220422
LC record available at https://lccn.loc.gov/2022017753
LC ebook record available at https://lccn.loc.gov/2022017754

*For Ben, who remembered*

You don't just learn to interview overnight. You've got to feel it in your bones. You're trying to walk in their shoes; you are trying to be them for a while. You don't tell about them; you try to *be* them.

—SUE EAKIN, editor of *Twelve Years a Slave*

Be just like wrapping a chain round a tree and jecking and jecking, and then shifting the chain little bit and jecking and jecking some in that direction, and then shifting it some mo' and jecking and jecking in that direction. Jecking and jecking till you get it loose, and then pulling with all your might. Still it might not be loose enough and you have to back the tractor up some and fix the chain round the tree again and start jecking all over. Jeck, jeck, jeck. Then you hear the roots crying, and then you keep on jecking, and then it give, and you jeck some mo', and then it falls. And not till then that you see what you done done. Not till then you see the big hole in the ground and piece of the taproot still way down in it—a piece you won't never get out no matter if you dig till doomsday. Yes, you got the tree—least got it down on the ground, but did you get the taproot? No. No, sir, you didn't get the taproot. You stand there and look down in this hole at it and you grab yo' axe and jump down in it and start chopping at the taproot, but do you get the taproot? No. You don't get the taproot, sir. You never get the taproot. But, sir, I tell you what you do get. You get a big hole in the ground, sir; and you get another big hole in the air where the lovely branches been all these years. Yes, sir, that's what you get. The holes sir, the holes. Two holes, sir, you can't never fill no matter how hard you try.

—AUNT CLO, "Just Like a Tree"

# CONTENTS

# A NOTE ON USAGE

The word "quarter" means workers' quarter, that section of a plantation complex in which workers were housed. The term originally referred to slave quarters.

In most of his books that are set in a plantation quarter, Ernest Gaines used the word "quarters," plural; but in his fifth novel, *A Lesson Before Dying,* it has become "quarter," singular. In this book, when referring simply to the quarter, I also use the singular form.

But when I use its full proper name, I go with the traditional Cherie Quarters, using the plural form. To be grammatically correct, it should be Cherie's Quarters, using the possessive form; the name was taken from that of Pervis Cherie Major, who was known by his middle name, Cherie. Major purchased the plantation in 1892 and owned it until he died in 1934, when ownership passed to his children. But perhaps because of lingering holdovers from French usage, the name became Cherie Quarters, and it stuck.

There are disparities in the spelling of the name River Lake Plantation, where Cherie Quarters is located. I have seen it spelled as a single word, Riverlake, in some documents. But having also seen it spelled as two words, and having been told by owner Madeleine Caillet that she preferred it as two words, I have chosen to go with that form.

I refer to the main residence on the plantation as the Big House, using capital letters. Calling the main house the Big House is common on southern plantations, and it has been incorporated into the name of at least one book, *Back of the Big House,* which explores the structures and spaces that formed the environment of slavery in the antebellum South. My choice of capital letters here is reflected in the psychology of those who used the term. The Big House was a big deal. It was physically much bigger than the workers' houses, and it was a place of power and control. To the residents of the quarter, most of whom never entered the Big House, and who went in through the back door when they did, it was a place that merited capitalization.

Another discrepancy exists in the spelling of the first name of Gaines's beloved great-aunt Augusteen Jefferson. "Augusteen" is the way he spelled the name in 1971, when he dedicated *The Autobiography of Miss Jane Pittman* to her memory, along with others. When speaking about her, former residents of Cherie Quarters referred to her as "Aunt Teen" or "Miss Teen." But in census records, her name is recorded as "Augustine," as is the name of her grandmother Augustine Brigitte Vincent, for whom she was named. Again, it seems to be a matter of choice; I have chosen to go with "Augusteen," the name memorialized on the dedication page of *Miss Jane.*

Use of the word "crippled" to describe Aunt Augusteen is outdated; today we would describe her as having a "disability." But Ernest Gaines consistently used the word "crippled," from the first time I interviewed him in 1972 right through to a 2013 interview.

Although Gaines has referred to his mother as Adrienne, and used the name St. Adrienne in his fiction, most documents list her first name as Adrean, and those who knew her pronounced her name *Ah-DREEN*. Gaines used that form when he dedicated *Mozart and Leadbelly* to her memory in 2005.

Although the term "enslaved person" has gained favor in recent years, Ernest Gaines always used the word "slave." I have elected to stay with that usage because, in writing about slave cabins, it is simpler, more concise, and reflects the usage of the time.

# CHERIE QUARTERS

# INTRODUCTION

In late October 1972, I was a copy editor at Louisiana State University Press in Baton Rouge. I was sitting at my desk on the second floor of the Hill Memorial Library on the LSU campus, working on a manuscript, when Charles East, director of the press, rapped on the doorjamb.

With Charles was a tall, shy man in a brown suit who held a brown beret in his hand. Charles introduced him as Ernest Gaines and said he was in town from San Francisco to help select sites for the filming of his novel *The Autobiography of Miss Jane Pittman.*

I had never heard of Gaines, but my life would be entwined with his from that day forward.

Gaines, thirty-nine years old, was giving a reading that afternoon on campus. If we wanted to hear him read, Charles said, we were welcome to take off from work to do so. At the appointed hour, chief editor Beverly Jarrett and I strolled the few hundred feet to Lockett Hall and took seats among the small audience of creative writing students and English teachers.

Professor Warren Eyster introduced Gaines, who seemed a bit ill at ease as he stood in front of us. Eyster said Gaines had written three novels and a book of short stories. Then Gaines read his story "Just Like a Tree."

He was not a showy or dramatic reader of his own work, but his quiet voice underscored both the humor and the pathos of his characters, who range from a young boy to an old woman. He didn't need pyrotechnics; his words were enough. I think everyone in the room that day knew we were in the presence of a master storyteller.

Like most of Gaines's fiction, the story is set in a plantation quarter. It focuses on Aunt Fe, an old woman who has lived there all her life but must now leave because civil rights activities and growing racial tension have made it dangerous for her to stay.

Just as interesting to me was Gaines's own story, which he sketched for us. He had grown up in Pointe Coupée Parish, Louisiana, leaving at fifteen to join his mother and stepfather in Vallejo, California. He had stood out on the highway near False River, and when the Trailways bus appeared he flagged it down by waving his handkerchief. The bus pulled over, and Gaines climbed aboard and rode it to New Orleans. There he caught a train to California.

I was so intrigued by his story that I turned to Beverly and said, "I'm going to try to interview him for *Gulfstream,*" a little magazine recently started by graduate students in LSU's English department. I asked Gaines for an interview, although I had no real idea whether *Gulfstream* or any other magazine might publish it. But he agreed to talk to me, and we made a date to meet a few days later at the LSU Student Union.

I had never interviewed anyone, but now I had to get ready to meet that challenge. At the Union bookstore I found a Bantam paperback of *The Autobiography of Miss Jane Pittman,* which had been published a few months earlier. I speed-read it and made notes.

That Saturday morning, I met Gaines in front of the Union. We went inside and sat at a table in the Tiger Lair food court. Armed with a pen, a notebook, and a borrowed tape recorder, I asked him about his book and his life.

We spent two or three hours drinking coffee and talking. He told me about his "crippled" great-aunt who had raised him, about his childhood on the plantation, and about his life in California. And he told me about the graveyard where generations of his ancestors were buried. "I just hope that the place where I was born and raised, that I can be still be buried there."

The following week, I told Charles East about the interview, which I had transcribed longhand into an examination blue book. Charles told his friend Lewis Simpson, coeditor of LSU's literary quarterly, *The Southern Review,* and Simpson asked to look at it. I typed up the interview and submitted it.

"A Conversation with Ernest Gaines" was published more than a year later as the lead article in the winter 1974 issue of *The Southern Review.* My brief introduction concluded, "In conversation, Ernest Gaines's simplicity and humanity shine steadily; he considers his words carefully, and beside him more facile talkers sound shallow. It is this quality—his essential human-ness—which I hope is conveyed here."[1]

That Saturday over coffee was the first of my many interviews with Gaines,

Gaines and Ruth Laney at Northwestern State University, Natchitoches, Louisiana, February 1977. Gaines read from *Miss Jane Pittman* as part of the Distinguished Lecture Series. Photo courtesy of Tom Whitehead.

the beginning of an association that lasted until his death in November 2019. Publishing that first interview encouraged me to later embark on a career as a writer and reporter. It was not always a smooth road, and the need to earn a living took me down varied paths. For a while I pursued poetry, attending the Bread Loaf Writers' Conference and working as Poet in the Schools in Louisiana's rural Avoyelles Parish. I even tried novel writing, taking classes with Walker Percy and Ellen Douglas. I veered off into covering sports for newspapers and magazines, specializing in track and running events. But I felt most at home in feature writing. I enjoyed hearing people's stories and relating them to readers, and I recognized the importance of oral history. These interests culminated in my work on a television documentary about Gaines—and ultimately in this book.[2]

Meanwhile, I read the novels *Catherine Carmier* and *Of Love and Dust* (the latter remains my favorite) and the short story collection *Bloodline,* from which he read the day I met him. In October 1973, I went out to the St. Francisville set of the CBS television movie of *Miss Jane.* That night, I wrote in my notebook:

I spotted Ernest Gaines in the ever-present brown beret, red shirt, and green baggy pants. He was shooting some film of his own with an 8 mm Viennette camera. He recognized me at once (I was surprised) and was terribly cordial to me.

Again I was struck by his essential humanity. He introduced me to everyone who came up to speak to him. . . .

We talked about writing; he asked me when was I going to write my own novel? I said when I could afford to quit working—"It's hard to come home after eight hours working and write." He said, "Yes, but not for those possessed people."

He said his first job after he graduated from San Francisco State College was in an insurance firm—he was the mail man. Had to open & sort the mail. He said he used to sneak into the bathroom and write—the story was "A Long Day in November." He said he'd write on the rough paper towels in the bathroom until they [his coworkers] came to drag him out. He wrote on his lunch hour and coffee breaks, too. At night, he'd go home and redo what he'd written that day.

He is totally modest and self-effacing. I think he is the most natural person of any achievement that I've ever met. I wish that I could become his friend, but I suppose that is too much to ask. I know he'd be a good friend.

In fact, we did become friends, although ours remained a professional relationship. Over the years, I received letters and Christmas cards from him as well as inscribed copies of his books. I met his agent and editor, and got to know his colleagues at the University of Louisiana at Lafayette.

In subsequent interviews, I learned more about Gaines's life. But it was not until 1982 that I visited Cherie Quarters. I was on assignment for *Louisiana Life* magazine, and photographer Philip Gould wanted to shoot Gaines at his "home place." On a cold, gray February afternoon, Philip and I accompanied Gaines to the quarter. We parked in a clearing near a small wooden church and strolled up Major Lane, the road that divided the quarter, passing the old cypress cabins with wood smoke curling from their chimneys. Cherie Quarters was still home to many residents then, most of them old people and children. Several came out onto their porches to greet Gaines.

At the last cabin before the lane gave way to sugar cane fields, Gaines spotted a familiar face. "Reese!" he called. An elderly man blinked uncertainly in our direction, and Gaines added, "It's E. J." Reese Spooner broke into a smile of recognition as we entered his yard. He was a tall, rail-thin man in his eighties,

Gaines at Cherie Quarters, February 1982. Many families were still living there and several people came out to greet "E. J.," as he was known in the community. Photo by Philip Gould. Copyright © Philip Gould.

ramrod straight, dressed in work pants and shoes, a red plaid wool shirt, and a cap. At his heels, tail wagging, was a small dog that was missing a leg. Spooner referred to him as "that little sweet-legged dog."[3]

We talked of one thing and another, and I felt fortunate to meet this man who had known Gaines's family for generations. Reese Spooner was a source of many stories about Cherie Quarters' past, stories Gaines had borrowed for his books. Just three years later, he would collapse while testifying at a service in the Cherie Quarters church; he died a few days later. He was laid to rest in the graveyard a hundred yards or so from his cabin.

That day in 1982, Spooner talked to us about his fourteen hogs and his garden. He moved rather stiffly in front of the camera, patiently cooperating as Gould asked him and Gaines to walk toward him down the gravel driveway, over and over. Gould lay in the gravel to get the shot he wanted. Then he asked Spooner to walk down his front steps, over and over. Efforts to call Spooner's little dog into the pictures proved fruitless.

Gaines at False River, February 1982. Photo by Philip Gould. Copyright © Philip Gould.

Gaines told us that the cabin where he grew up was gone, but others like it were still standing. He spoke about smoke rising from chimneys, Spooner's butchering hogs—scenes he wished he had photographed.

We said goodbye to Spooner and drove into New Roads to visit Gaines's great-uncle Horace McVay. Gould asked Gaines how his people reacted to him when he came to visit. "They're proud of me; they love me," Gaines said without hesitation. "And I love them." He said of Spooner, "I talk to him just like I talk to anyone. We could sit down and talk all day."

At his great-uncle's house, we were greeted by McVay, a light-skinned man in his seventies who welcomed the bag of cracklings his nephew had brought. (As was common in country communities, he called them "cracklin.") We sat in the kitchen, cozy and warm despite the raw day.

Gaines drank a beer and then a glass of Scotch. He talked about the girl he was sweet on when young, who was *passe blanc*. He said she had married a light-skinned man and they moved to Baton Rouge. She "registered her children as white," he said. Later, he heard that she had drowned herself, unable to cope with the fear of being revealed as mixed race. I wondered if this story had been on his mind when he wrote his first novel, in which Catherine Carmier's sister Lillian plans to turn her back on her family and pass for white. This may have been the first time I realized how much he drew on his own experiences in his writing. In time, as I learned more of the backstories, I would make more such connections between his life and his art.

As I continued to write about Gaines, I met other family members and friends. But it was not until 1992, while working on a television documentary about him, that I truly began to grasp what a remarkable community Cherie Quarters was, and what a force it had been in Gaines's work. The place in which he was born and grew up, the place he wrote about, the place where he is buried—in many ways, Cherie Quarters defines Ernest Gaines.

While working on the documentary, I interviewed many important people in Gaines's life and the life of the quarter. In addition to Gaines himself, I spoke to his mother; his sisters Lois and Deborah; brothers Lionel, Norbert, Mack, and Michael; sister-in-law Ada Mae; friends James Brooks and Bill Robillard—and especially with David Biben, who recalled in great detail life in Cherie Quarters.

When I interviewed Gaines's friends and relatives for the documentary, I learned more about the place. They told stories of a life often harsh but filled with love and an enviable sense of community. They talked of house fairs and fistfights, cane fields and mule-drawn wagons, tea cakes and clabber (sour milk in which the whey has not separated from the curd). They talked about people long dead, such as Gaines's grandmother "Zuma," the cook at the Big House; his great-aunt Augusteen, who raised Gaines and his younger brothers; and his great-grandfather James McVay, who had fled the plantation during the night.

The world of Cherie Quarters unfolded bit by bit. One of the first to paint a picture of life there was Gaines's contemporary James Brooks, who took the meager education he had received in the little schoolhouse at Cherie Quarters and built on it, eventually becoming a high school principal. Brooks was retired when I met him in 1992, and almost totally deaf, but he told wonderful stories and drew a crude map of the quarter as it had looked when he lived there—a little dirt road lined with "tin-topped" houses. I learned about the sugarhouse, where cane was processed for nearly a century. Behind it were more houses, where the Robillards and other families had lived. "It was just love," is how Cherie Quarters was described by Ada Mae Gaines, née Robillard, who married Ernest Gaines's brother Lionel. "One gon' do for the other."

Later I met David Biben, known as Ben, a tall, thin man with gray-green eyes and a dapper mustache. A contemporary of Gaines, he made a much

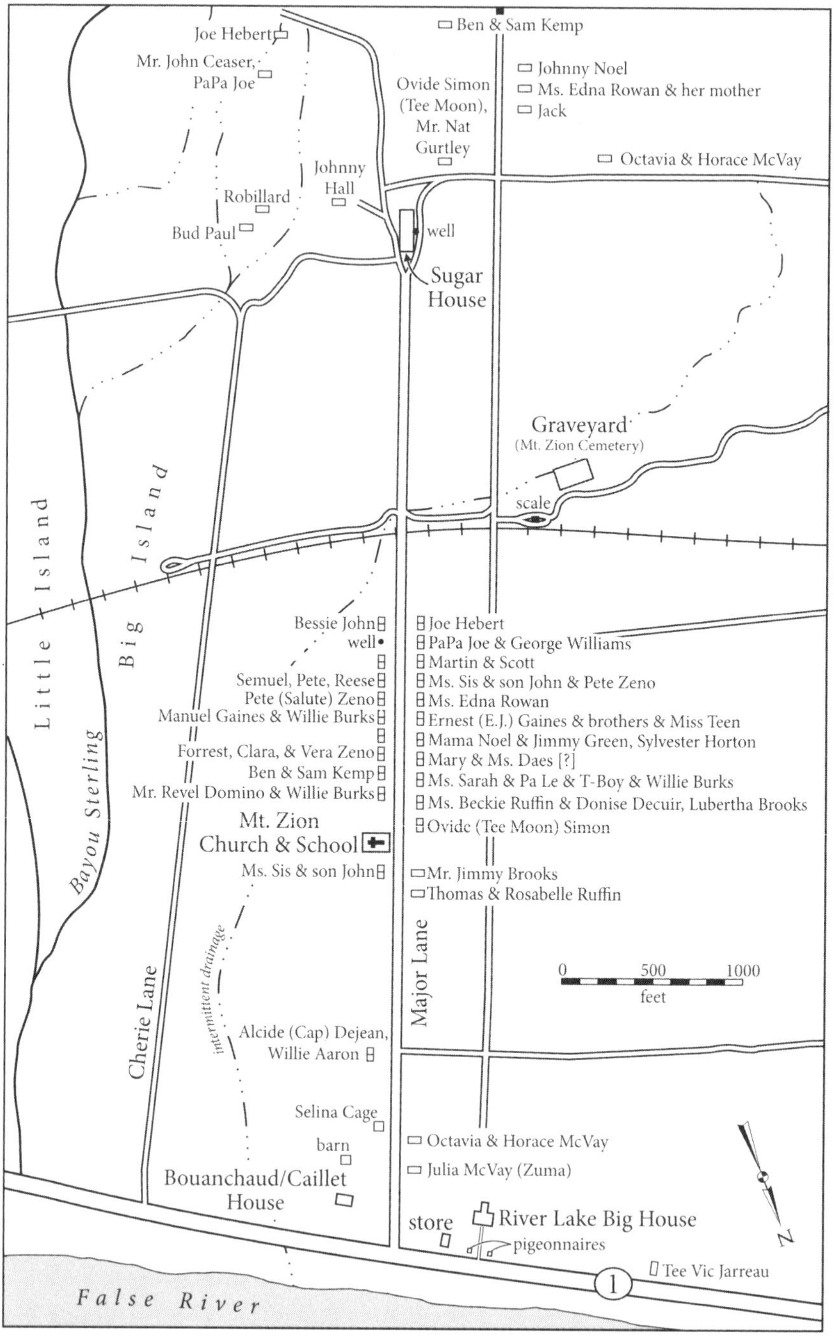


Cherie Quarters

more detailed map of the quarter, told stories even richer in detail, and showed me how the children of Cherie Quarters made their own toys. Biben said he recognized home in the works of Ernest Gaines, especially Gaines's second novel, a plantation romance set in the 1940s, the period when he and Gaines were growing up there. "*Of Love and Dust*—that's the quarters," said Biben of the 1967 novel.[4]

But all of that—the world I would come to know as Cherie Quarters—was far in the future that day in 1972, when I sat in a classroom at LSU and listened to Ernest Gaines read "Just Like a Tree." All I could divine of Cherie Quarters then were the descriptions in the story, which like nearly all of Gaines's fiction, was set in a plantation quarter. Aunt Fe is being uprooted, and that is the metaphor that was so moving in the part of the story told by Aunt Clo.

I have read the Aunt Clo passage many times since. As I came to know and care about Cherie Quarters, I couldn't help thinking how eloquently Gaines's words speak to the urgent need for preservation—particularly the need to preserve landmarks in African American history. Aunt Clo's metaphor of a tree being ripped from its landscape could serve as a call to arms for preservationists. As I learned from Cherie Quarters, it isn't just people who are uprooted but also whole sections of the landscape that holds our collective history.

We can't know the people from the past, those who lived and died in Cherie Quarters, who worked so hard, suffered so deeply, loved each other so fiercely, and kept their remarkable faith against so many odds. The people are gone. All that is left are a few possessions—furniture, letters, an old radio. The place itself—the houses that once were home to the people of Cherie Quarters—is gone. In memorializing the place, we come as close as possible to bringing back its lost people. The place holds the story of the people.

# 1

# THE LAST ONE LEFT

## THE AUTOBIOGRAPHER OF *MISS JANE PITTMAN*

> I did it for them back there under them trees. I did it 'cause that tractor is getting closer and closer to that graveyard, and I was scared if I didn't do it, one day that tractor was go'n come in there and plow up them graves, getting rid of all the proof that we ever was. . . . [B]ut they ain't go'n do it while I'm still here. Mama and Papa worked too hard in these fields. They mama and they papa worked too hard in these same fields. They mama and they papa people worked too hard, too hard to have that tractor just come in that graveyard and destroy all proof that they ever was.
>
> I'm the last one left. I had to see that the graves stayed for a little while longer. But I just didn't do it for my own people. I did it for every last one back there under them trees. And I did it for every four o'clock, every rosebush, every palm-of-Christian ever growed on this place.
>
> —ERNEST GAINES, *A Gathering of Old Men*

To get to River Lake Plantation, you drive thirty-five miles west from Baton Rouge, across the Mississippi River, cruise along Highway 190, turn right onto Highway 1, and follow it to the little town of Oscar, Louisiana. Back before the tractors, you would turn left on Major Lane to get to Cherie Quarters, but the quarter is gone, all traces wiped away. A newly constructed house sits far back on the road that once was the quarter. Now all that's left is the graveyard, encircled by an ever-thinning ring of trees.

River Lake was one of several large plantations that flourished in Pointe Coupée Parish during the 1800s. Even after the Civil War, plantations along False River continued to grow and harvest sugar cane, cotton, and corn with the labor of emancipated slaves. The name Cherie Quarters was first used after Pervis Cherie Major bought the plantation in 1892. His descendants still own River Lake, making it one of very few Louisiana plantation houses to remain in the same family for more than a century. The family now leases the land to sugar cane farmers, so the familiar activity of "grinding" season—cutting the cane, loading it into trucks, and hauling it to a nearby sugar mill—still goes on as it always has.

When Ernest Gaines lived there, from 1933 until 1948, Cherie Quarters was a vibrant community of sharecroppers and tenant farmers who worked the land and "shared" the fruits of their labor with the owners. But the predatory nature of sharecropping and tenant farming—including high interest rates, unpredictable harvests, and unscrupulous landlords and merchants—often kept families severely indebted to the landowners.

The world Ernest Gaines was born into was little changed from that of slavery days. Agriculture remained much the same; Jim Crow laws and Black Codes replicated the race relations of the pre–Civil War South. Landowners kept the workers in debt. Debt peonage was an intrinsic part of the Jim Crow system of racial repression in the Reconstruction era.

Change came in the early 1940s, when young men left to fight in World War II or to work in wartime factories, where they earned far more, reducing the plantation's labor force. Real change came after the war, when the men returned, having experienced other countries and cultures with very different attitudes on race. Many people—including members of Gaines's family—left in search of education and jobs. But the quarter was home to old people and children for many years after that. The last three tenants left in 1993, when the four remaining cabins on the west side of the road were removed, leaving only two cabins on the east side.

Although emancipation had come nearly seventy years before Gaines was born, life at Cherie Quarters continued much as it had during slavery. During grinding season, roughly from early October until Christmas, the workers chopped cane, threw it onto mule-drawn wagons, and loaded it onto a train that carried it to Alma Plantation in the nearby town of Lakeland to be made into sugar. At other times of the year they planted and picked cotton or corn. The plantation store on Highway 1, between the Big House and the quarter, supplied groceries and dry goods The workers used color-coded scrip money; the storekeeper jotted down their purchases in a large ledger book.

Times were hard all over the country during the Great Depression, especially in cities and towns. Farming communities fared better, as they could at least grow their own food. Life for Gaines's family and their neighbors in

Cherie Quarters went on much as it had during slavery, when their ancestors built the small cabins their descendants still occupied. "After emancipation, [the freed slaves] remained there to work," Gaines explained. "It was not until the late 1920s or early 1930s that they went to sharecropping." Their work was backbreakingly hard and its rewards were meager. "With sharecropping, whites also began to work the land. The whites got the better land, grew better crops, and got better equipment."[1]

Separated from white society by the laws of Jim Crow and the remnants of slave codes, the residents' lives were bounded by the plantation.[2] That life centered on False River, an oxbow lake formed when part of the Mississippi was cut off by a change in the river's direction. The people of Cherie Quarters fished and bathed in the river, hauled buckets of water from it for cooking and washing, and were baptized in its waters.

Gaines's family lived in workers' quarters—a dirt road lined with two rows of twelve to fifteen houses each, two-room cabins built by and for their slave ancestors. The cypress wood houses were whitewashed, the front yards filled with flowers—especially four o'clocks and roses—and nearly everyone grew a vegetable garden, as Reese Spooner still did nearly fifty years later. Many kept chickens and hogs penned behind their houses. There was no running water; residents hauled water from the river, or later from wells, and used privies set back behind the houses. Trash was thrown into ditches and buried or burned.

Gaines was born in a cypress cabin in Cherie Quarters on January 15, 1933, delivered by a midwife. Adrean Jefferson Gaines was sixteen years old when she gave birth to her first child. Her husband, Manuel Gaines, was twenty-one. Adrean named her firstborn Ernest James, presumably after her maternal great-grandfather, Ernest Vincent, and her maternal grandfather, James McVay. As a child, he was called by his initials, E. J., sometimes shortened to Jay. He was born on a Sunday, and he said that his mother was back at work in the fields the following week.[3] (In late January, following grinding season, the workers would probably have been planting Irish potatoes and onions.)[4]

Adrean left her infant son in the care of her paternal aunt Augusteen Jefferson, with whom she sometimes lived. Within the next seven or eight years, Adrean had given birth to two more sons, Lionel and Eugene; a daughter, Lois; then three more sons, Charles (Mitchell), Norbert, and Joseph, known as Mack. Augusteen Jefferson cared for the boys, while Lois lived up the road

Adrean Jefferson Gaines, the mother of Ernest James Gaines, as a young woman. She was sixteen years old when she gave birth to Ernest in January 1933. Photo courtesy of Deidra Biben-Glynn.

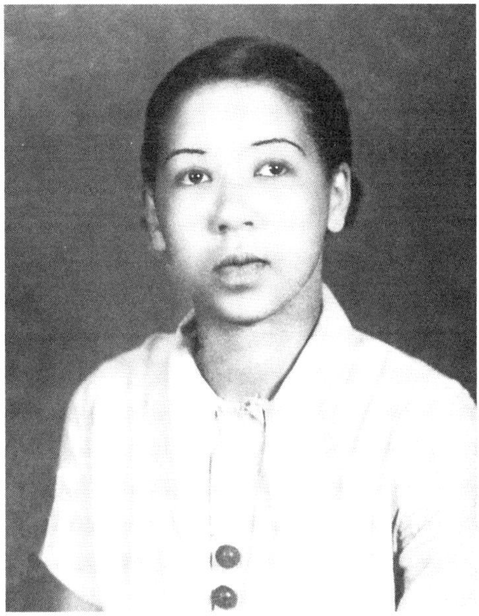

near the Big House with her maternal grandmother Julia McVay, whom the children called Mama Julia.

Gaines described life in the rude cabin that he called home. "A cane knife would always be stuck in the wall. Some people had wallpaper, some had pictures on the walls. The long-handled equipment [hoes and rakes] was all kept under the house. The ax could be stuck in a log outside." There was a privy out back, water hauled from wells, baths in tin tubs, a kerosene or coal-oil lamp at night. The family ate mostly cabbage ("three or four times a week"), rice, Irish potatoes, sweet potatoes, and occasionally chicken or pork from hens and hogs they raised. Chewing on a knob of cane was a treat. "To keep sugar cane fresh, we'd bury it under the house and cover it with hay." They washed dishes in a pan placed on a shelf in the kitchen window. The shuttered windows were not screened, so they used mosquito netting over the beds at night. Tin roofs had replaced the original cedar shingles, probably in the early 1940s.[5] Gaines's brother Norbert Colar, who was born in 1940 and moved to California around 1951, said the sound of rain on the tin roof was "like a tranquilizer."[6]

Colar recalled that he and his brothers slept in one bed, although the youngest would usually share a bed with "Aunty." Ernest Gaines said his aunt had a photo collage of Abraham Lincoln, Booker T. Washington, and Frederick Douglass on the wall in one of the rooms.

> The front room was for socializing. The front porch was also. The side room was for sleeping. Both back rooms could be used as kitchens. In ours, the kitchen

> was on the left. We had a wood-burning stove, a [food] safe with a screen. No refrigerator—later we had an icebox. A big old washtub hung against the wall on a huge nail. In the corner were an ax and a broom. We had handmade tables and chairs—or maybe they were bought. The chairs had rattan or wood bottoms. The pots and pans were hung on the wall with nails. There was a water bucket on the table or the wall—usually the table—with a long-handled dipper. We all had our little personal cups and pans to eat out of.[7]

E. J. lived in that cabin not with his parents but with his aunt and his brothers. Both Adrean and Manuel Gaines were working, at first in the plantation fields and later in New Orleans. Their absence in E. J.'s early life was filled by female relatives of his mother, particularly his great-aunt Teen.

Augusteen Jefferson, who was born circa 1894, was disabled from a very young age, probably from birth. Gaines said that no one knew the cause of her handicap. "Some people have said that she had been dropped on the floor by another child when she was small; others have said that she was born with that affliction. . . . I do not know which story is true." Augusteen had a wheelchair delivered by a social services agency, but it sat in a corner, unused. Ben Biben referred to her as "a lady on the floor."[8] But Augusteen Jefferson never lived as a stereotypical "disabled" or handicapped person. Given the restrictions of her disability, she lived a surprisingly normal life.

Aunt Teen, or Aunty, as Gaines and his siblings called her, crawled over the floor like "a child six or seven months old," according to Gaines.[9] Biben recalled that Miss Teen had legs that were "completely useless, they just dragged." She got about by supporting her body with her arms, letting her legs hang in a semikneeling position—in effect, walking on her hands.[10]

"Her arms were very strong," Gaines said.

> She'd cook for us—we'd bring the [ingredients] to the stove for her and set it on a little table in front of her, and she'd mix the [food] up. She could make bread, bake our bread—we had the old wood stoves then. She could wash our clothes: she sat on a bench and leaned over the tub and used the washboard, [one of] those old tin things. She could sew our clothes. She used to use the sewing machine. She could not use her feet, but she could use her hands—how she ever did this, I really don't know. You know those old things with the pedal down here—she would reach down and do this with her hands, because

there was no other way to run it. It was one of these old machines, probably one of the oldest ones. I wish I knew where it was today—if I could find it, I'd keep it forever. Besides that, she used to go into the little garden to work among her vegetables. She'd crawl over the floor, out of the house, down the steps, into the yard, into the garden. . . . She never felt sorry for herself a day in her life. I never heard her complaining about her problems. And as a result nobody felt sorry for her.[11]

Aunt Teen even disciplined the children, having them cut a switch and hand it to her when the occasion demanded. "If the switch was too small, she sent you right back out for another one," Gaines said.

His sister-in-law, Ada Mae Gaines, who married his brother Lionel, likewise recalled Miss Teen disciplining the children of the quarter if she caught them misbehaving. "If she called, you went to her and fell on your knees [for a switching]. You accepted it. That wasn't just Lionel and E. J.; that was any child playing marbles in her yard."[12] After administering a switching, Miss Teen would send word to that child's parents, who often repeated the punishment. Biben said that as an adult he still had scars on his legs from being switched by Miss Teen.[13]

Aunt Augusteen was very involved in their lives and the life of the community. "This lady wasn't walking around, but she was saying a lot," said Gaines's brother Norbert Colar Jr.[14] His sister Lois Young (who lived up the road with her maternal grandmother but visited often) likened Aunt Augusteen to "an army sergeant" for the way she issued orders to the children.[15] Biben recalled Miss Teen having a strong voice. "It was loud, it was up there. It wasn't a sick-sounding voice. She had sort of a French accent." She usually wore dresses made of blue denim and "socks but no shoes." Biben remembered Miss Teen smoking a corncob pipe. "She would save the pompee [scrapings from smoked tobacco] and give it to other people in the quarters," he said. "They would tuck it into their lip and get drunk on it."[16] Lois remembered her great-aunt "making the pompee into little packages and selling it to the people in the quarters."[17]

Barbara Bibbens Overstreet Hardy, who was born at Cherie Quarters in 1945, said Miss Teen kept an immaculate house. Barbara's mother, Albertha Kemp Bibbens, was particular about whose house Barbara could eat in, telling her to only accept food from people whose houses were clean. Miss Teen's house passed that test. "I remember her sliding on the floor. I was at her house once and saw a fly on the screen and tried to hit it with my bare hand. She told me don't ever hit a fly with your hands. 'Oh, no, baby, that's nasty!' That stayed in my mind. She'd houseclean. I remember her house being clean."[18]

Because her disability made even limited travel next to impossible, Aunt Augusteen's house—especially her porch and her front yard—became a gathering spot for the families of Cherie Quarters. Gaines said that in the winter his aunt sat on the floor by the fireplace and in the summer on her front porch or "gallery."[19] The porch was one of the most important places in quarter life, where people often sat when the weather was warm. "We'd go sit on the porch and talk, let our legs swing," said Biben.[20]

Gaines's work has many scenes that take place on porches. In my October 1972 interview, he said that his earliest education was sitting on the porch listening to the older people talk:

> I come from a long line of storytellers. I come from a plantation where people told stories by the fireplace at night, people told stories on the ditch bank—especially this time of year, when you have the sugar cane shuck that you can burn, mix it with some firewood. People sat around telling stories. I think in my immediate family there were tremendous storytellers or liars or whatever you want to call them. My aunt was not a storyteller, she was more of a recorder; she could tell about what happened in the past. She remembered quite well. Since Auntie could not go to their place, the old people used to come to ours. They would talk and talk and talk, and I listened to them. . . . Say there was a funeral today, or a wedding, the old people would sort of gather in a little room and talk about things, you know. They might start with the wedding, or they might start with that particular funeral, but by the time they end up, they've talked about everything that had happened the last twenty years.[21]

While the storytellers spun their tales, E. J. was on hand to serve coffee or ice water, and he soaked up the words. When the adults spoke of matters they didn't want the children to know about, they spoke a French patois they called Creole, or they sent the children off to play. James Brooks recalled hearing many times the phrase "Don't dip in the older folks' business. Don't stay and hear our conversation, boy."[22] Biben remembered Augusteen Jefferson in these porch sessions as a woman with a strong presence, very much involved in community life. "Miss Teen was nosy. She gathered information. A lot of people would go talk to her and she'd pass it on. . . . She was an interesting person when she talked. She was a gossip. She'd laugh and talk and [in the case of naughty children] whip your butt."[23]

Gaines's brother Lionel summed up the role Aunt Teen played in the lives of her niece's children, "She was like Mama to us. She *raised* us."[24] Ernest Gaines said that Augusteen Jefferson, who was thirty-eight years old when he was born, was the person he loved most in his life. "She made me what I am, as a writer and as a man."[25] In 1971, he dedicated *The Autobiography of Miss Jane Pittman* to the memories of her; his maternal grandmother Julia McVay; and his stepfather, Raphael Norbert Colar. His dedication read in part, "To the memory of my beloved aunt, Miss Augusteen Jefferson, who never walked a day in her life but who taught me the importance of standing."

The word "standing" in that dedication is meaningful. Some of Gaines's strongest characters are men and women who defy the order of things and choose, even under threat of death, to take a stand. Take a stand, stand up for yourself, stand on your own feet—the word, with its implied deeper meaning, appears repeatedly in Gaines's work. Often his books turn on a central scene in which a Black character stands up to the white plantation owner. Jim Kelly, in *Of Love and Dust,* refuses the offer of a job recommendation and leaves the plantation. Copper Laurent, in "Bloodline," demands to be recognized as the son of the white landowner and an heir to the family fortune.

In other works, the decision is one of personal pride, what Gaines often referred to as grace under pressure, a concept he had encountered in the work of Ernest Hemingway. Procter Lewis, in the short story "Three Men," says, "I didn't want to have to pull cover over my head every time a white man did something to a black boy. I wanted to stand." Phillip Martin, the agonized civil rights leader of *In My Father's House,* describes the lingering aftereffects of slavery: "I was paralyzed. . . . I wasn't a man. I was just some other brutish animal who could cheat, steal, rob, kill—but not stand." In *A Lesson Before Dying,* when Miss Emma visits the Big House to ask Mr. Henri to help her get permission for Grant to visit Jefferson in jail, her friend Tante Lou accompanies her to lend moral support; she puts her arm around Emma "to comfort her and to help her stand."[26]

Other Gaines women also take a stand. He said that the character Miss Jane was not entirely based upon his great-aunt, but his great-aunt's will to survive was embodied in Miss Jane. Aunt Teen's strength, dignity, and courage surface in other characters, such as Aunt Charlotte in *Catherine Carmier,* Miss Julie Rand in *Of Love and Dust,* and Aunt Fe in "Just Like a Tree." Gaines called his great-aunt "the person I respect above all others" and noted that her memory "does give me encouragement and strength [when] I think about the obstacles [she] had to face each day."[27]

When E. J. was six years old, his Aunt Teen sent him a few hundred yards up the quarter to the plantation church, Mount Zion Baptist. During the week, the building served as a school, at least during the four, five, or six months when the children could be spared from digging potatoes or pulling corn. They crowded on to wooden benches and tried to learn, taught by a succession of female teachers who came across the Mississippi River from Baton Rouge, boarding during the week with Gaines's grandmother Julia McVay, who cooked for the owners and lived in the first house on the west side of the lane, to give her quick access to the Big House.

The students had no desks but used the pews in the church, writing on tablets held in their laps or kneeling on the floor and using the seats of the pews to write on. Once or twice a year, the white public school superintendent would pay a visit. Gaines drew upon memories of the school in his fiction, most memorably in the short story "A Long Day in November" and the novel *A Lesson Before Dying,* which depicts the children's inadequate schooling and the bigoted superintendent's annual visit.

Gaines, who began attending around 1939, said students did not usually get their full allotment of six months of school; more often they got only five. "We had cotton until the first of October. Then by the middle of April, we began to plant and harvest . . . potatoes and whatever you had in the field. And children whose fathers were sharecroppers had to go into the fields."[28]

At school, the children were respectful. "Discipline at school was no problem," said James Brooks. "All the teacher would have to say was 'I'm coming to your house to tell your mother about your behavior.' All you had to do was point, and the kids would stop [misbehaving]."[29] Ada Mae Gaines said that she, Lionel Gaines, and schoolmate John Ceaser were made to kneel as punishment for not doing their lessons. "We stayed on our knees for a week." They kept that a secret from their parents for fear of additional punishment.

E. J. liked school and quickly mastered reading and writing. His sister-in-law Ada Mae recalled him as a boy who loved to read. "He always read a lot of books," she said. "He'd sit under the porch and read, or in the back room."[30] While still a child, he outdistanced most of his elders at those skills, and he soon became the official scribe of the quarter, writing letters for "the old people," or reading to them from the Bible, the newspaper, or the Sears catalog. The adults would give him a nickel or a tea cake as payment. His intelligence and ability quickly distinguished him. "I felt that people treated me as someone who was very smart," he said. "I knew I was doing things that other kids were not doing at that age."[31]

From the time he learned to read and write, Gaines served as eyes and ears for "the old people," giving them both a voice and a link to the world beyond Cherie Quarters. They expected him to make something of himself. It was as if someone, or some force, had singled him out. "I suppose that's where I got my first education, by sitting out there on the gallery. That's where I wrote my first letter. I'd sit on the steps, and they would sit on the porch in a chair and dictate the letter. That was the beginning of understanding my place in the world."[32]

As the oldest child in his family, E. J. took on grown-up responsibilities, hauling water from the well or leaving his warm bed on icy mornings to chop wood for the stove. At the age of eight, he went to work pulling corn, digging potatoes, chopping or hauling sugar cane, or cutting trees for firewood. "My first job was picking up Irish potatoes. We'd go into the field with water buckets and bring them to the headland and dump them in a sack. I can remember picking cotton," being paid fifty cents a day for his work. The work was hard, but it gave him entrée into the grown-up world, which could be exciting. During grinding season, he watched workers load cane onto a train that carried it to nearby Alma Plantation. "It was amazing to watch as a small child," he said. The sugarhouse at River Lake, which had been built around 1850, was no longer used and would be torn down in the 1950s. "It was a big brick building. We'd play in there and run through it."[33]

E. J. learned at an early age "how to survive," which included basic skills a country boy needed to master, such as how to kill animals for food. But he could never bring himself to wring the neck of a chicken. "My aunt used to tell me to go out and catch a chicken," he said. "I'd catch it, but somebody else would have to kill it. My aunt would wring the neck." Later, at *boucheries,* or pig butcherings, as one of the older boys he was expected to help hold down the pig while the adult men slit its throat and drained the blood to use for

Gaines's maternal grandmother, Julia McVay, circa 1945, on the front steps of the Big House at River Lake Plantation, where she worked as the cook for thirty years. Around 1950, she moved to San Francisco, where she worked as a domestic. When she died, in 1970, her body was returned to Oscar; she is buried in the graveyard in Cherie Quarters. Photo courtesy of Deidra Biben-Glynn.

"blood pudding." Gaines confessed he hated this chore and looked away over his shoulder while the pig was slaughtered. He preferred catching and cleaning fish, a less violent way of dealing death.[34]

The children of Cherie Quarters learned early that life could be harsh. Midwives sometimes delivered babies who died in childbirth or shortly after. Medical treatments were catch-as-catch-can, some based on folk medicines concocted from plants. Gaines recalled being plagued with toothaches as a child and traveling to New Orleans to have a tooth pulled;[35] this experience no doubt colored his short story "The Sky Is Gray." He was treated with "salt meat tied on your foot" to draw out the infection after stepping on a sharp object. "I don't know where they got the idea from."[36] Freddie Kemp, who was a generation older than Gaines and lived in the quarter much of his life, remembered fevers being treated by the laying on of large "elephant ear" leaves.[37] Malvina Pickett, the granddaughter of plantation owner P. C. Major, remembered that the people of the quarter "would boil leaves and make tea to reduce blood pressure."[38]

E. J.'s grandmother, who was born in 1896, was called Mama Julia by her grandchildren, but she was known to the adults of the quarter by her nickname, Zuma (pronounced *Zoo-MAH*) and to the other children as Miss Zuma. She worked as a cook in the Big House for about thirty years. Gaines referred to her as a "conduit" between the white owners and the Black workers. Using information she overheard in the Big House, for instance, she would caution a neighbor to do or not do a particular thing. (Although his grandmother worked there, E. J. did not spend much time at the Big House and was expected to enter through the back door when he went there. He recalled having attended a wake there as a child, possibly that of George Major, one of the owners, who died in February 1946.) Miss Zuma was unanimously recalled as a great cook, who often made pies and cakes for the children of the quarter. But she also kept a strict eye on them. If she spotted a child en route to the plantation store on Highway 1, she would stop him and demand to know who had sent him. Gaines said that, in her rare leisure time, she loved to fish in False River, smoking cigarettes as she waited for a tug on the line.[39]

Zuma's brother Horace McVay and his wife, Octavia, lived far back behind the quarter in one of four or five houses

Octavia Jack McVay, Gaines's great-aunt. Married to his great-uncle, Horace McVay, Octavia sold Avon products throughout two parishes and often took young Ernest along in her Ford to help. Photo courtesy of Ruby McVay Simmons.

"in the field," past the sugarhouse. "That was about two miles back from the quarters," Gaines said. "The houses were like ours in some ways, but with some differences. Horace's house did not have double doors." E. J. "used to hang around . . . and drink clabber" in Horace and Octavia's kitchen. "I had many meals at their house." Aunt Octavia would "try to teach me to milk cows, which I could never do." Horace and Octavia held fish fries or gumbo suppers on weekends to raise money for the church. About 1940, they acquired one of the few automobiles in the quarter, a dark-colored Ford that Octavia used to run errands and buy groceries for people; she also sold Avon cosmetics throughout Pointe Coupée and West Baton Rouge Parishes. E. J. was one of her favorites, and she often took him along to help her.[40]

Although he had been "christened in the church as an infant," E. J. was about twelve when he was baptized in False River, and he regularly attended Baptist services at Mount Zion. But when he was thirteen, he was sent to St. Augustine, a Catholic school for African American children, which was one of the few options open to E. J. because public schools in the area did not admit Black children. (He said that this choice also owed something to the influence of his stepfather Norbert Colar, a Roman Catholic.) St. Augustine school was in the town of New Roads, about ten miles north of Oscar. E. J. was taught by a white priest whom he had to address as "Father." "The lay teachers were all women and all unmarried: Miss Hurst, Miss Walker, and Miss Richard."[41]

"The school had a bus, but it was for Catholic school children," said James Brooks. "It didn't come to our plantation. We'd walk out to the highway, about half a mile, and wait for the regular Trailways bus. We had to pay the bus to get to New Roads."[42]

The children of Cherie Quarters had to cross Highway 1 and stand on the bank of False River to catch the Trailways bus. Ben Biben said it cost each child $3.60 a week to ride back and forth to school. The children bought coupon books from the driver, who tore out a coupon each time they rode. "The bus had a curtain with a window in it [to separate the races]," Biben said. Sometimes they hitchhiked or caught a ride with Alcide "Bub" Bouanchaud, the sheriff of Pointe Coupée Parish, whose wife, Eloise Major Bouanchaud, had inherited a portion of the plantation from her father, Joe Major, a son of P. C. Major.[43]

Gaines recalled Bouanchaud as a man with abnormally large hands and feet, who perhaps suffered from elephantiasis or pituitary dysfunction. The children of Cherie Quarters called him "Mr. Foots." But he stood out in Gaines's memory as one of the few white people who treated him with respect—and who perhaps recognized him as a gifted child. "I used to shine shoes to earn money to pay my tuition. One day he gave me a ride and I asked him if I could shine his shoes. He told me, 'I don't want to see you shining shoes.' He was one of most decent men I ever knew, Black or white." By contrast, the bus driver commented occasionally about "drowning me a little nigger."[44]

The Trailways bus dropped the children a half mile from the school, and they walked the rest of the way. At lunchtime, they walked some more. "There was no lunchroom," James Brooks said. "There was a little store on the corner. We'd buy bread, sausages or sliced ham, and a soft drink." Brooks remembered taking the school bus for the trip home—or most of it. "It would put us off almost two miles from home. When it finished [dropping off] the regular Catholic students, it turned around. Sometimes it would be snowing, sometimes it would be raining, sometimes it would be very, very cold." The children trudged the two miles back to the quarter.[45]

Gaines had a few "romances" as a teenager. "I was often unhappy about my relationships to girls," he said. "I never knew what to say to them, and I envied boys who did. I was always having little flirtations." One girl who attended St. Augustine school with him was *passe blanc,* light enough to pass for white. They rode the school bus together in the afternoon, and flirted shyly, but when the bus passed beyond a certain point, he said, she would stop talking to him.[46]

"She liked me, maybe because we were both outsiders. She was blonde, with white skin and freckles. Kids were always kidding her. They did me the same. I was dark and didn't speak Creole, I was Baptist. We were twelve years old. I'd see her in New Roads at the parish fair, but she could never speak to me. When we came near her house, she'd clam up."

Gaines said the girl grew up passing for white. "She married a light guy. She moved from place to place every time Blacks moved into the area. She had nervous breakdowns. She committed suicide because of these pressures. She walked into False River and [drowned] herself."[47]

Even many years later, this discrimination persisted. In 1993, he told me, "These people can use excuses not to be part of a darker community. There are some in Louisiana who want nothing to do with darker ones. . . . I walked around Girard Park [in Lafayette] today and saw a guy of mixed blood. He avoided eye contact with me. There are brothers right here in Lafayette—it's a common thing for one to speak and one not to speak to me." Gaines said such self-segregation was on his mind when he created the character Mary Agnes LeFabre, the Creole teacher in *Miss Jane,* beloved by the white owner's son, who "would bend over backwards to make up for these things." And in *Catherine Carmier,* originally titled *The Comeback,* "Jackson and Lillian are coming back home. That's what it was really about. Lillian was white and had to go one way. Jackson [who was dark-skinned], who's been educated in the North, has to go another."[48] No doubt such memories also informed his later unpublished novella, *Daughters of the Creole Lady.*[49]

At St. Augustine, E. J. saw a play for the first time. Gaines recalled it as a sort of minstrel show, staged by a troupe of performers from New Orleans. Captivated by the entertainment, he was inspired to write his own skits, which he staged in the church to entertain the people of Cherie Quarters. These "little plays" were the first expression of his creativity. E. J. wrote the scripts, cast his friends and siblings in the roles, applied shoe polish to blacken their young faces, borrowed sheets from the adults to use as a stage curtain, made posters to advertise them.[50] His dramas were often mock weddings in which E. J. played the minister, a convenient position from which to hiss reminders when his actors forgot their lines.[51] Frank Spooner, a few years younger than Gaines, was in one of the plays. "He had me playing [the cartoon character] Dagwood," said Spooner. "I was a comedian type of person."[52] James Brooks said that Gaines's mother, Adrean, once got angry at seeing her light-skinned daughter Lois in blackface, demanding, "Take all that stuff off your face!"[53] Adrean herself never attended the plays.[54]

E. J. took an after-school job as a dishwasher, working from 4:00 until 10:00 p.m. at the Triple Arch nightclub and restaurant on False River. He earned three dollars a night at Triple Arch, which served only white patrons. (Black customers bought takeout from a side window.) When he graduated from the eighth grade in 1948, his education was finished as far as Pointe Coupée Parish was concerned. There was no Black high school in the segregated parish; the closest was in Baton Rouge. Many places were off limits to him, including the public library in New Roads, which was in an antebellum house. "It never occurred to us to go there," Gaines said.[55]

By 1948, E. J. had seen some changes in Cherie Quarters. The dirt road that raised clouds of dust during the hot summers and turned into wagon-trapping muck when it rained had been overlaid with gravel in the 1940s. He also saw the advent of electricity after the war. "Electricity came in 'forty-six or 'forty-seven," he said. "I remember people watching the light; they just looked at this darn thing. There was a string to pull. The bulb hung from the ceiling by a cord. We used to sit there and just stare at that lightbulb." Until then, Gaines had studied his lessons by the light of a coal oil (kerosene) lamp or the fireplace.[56]

Around the same time, owner George Major had water lines installed on the west side of the quarter, piping in water from a well on the grounds of the Big House. "All the houses had a pipe and a faucet right by the back door," said Ben Biben. "George Major dug a well in the yard of the Big House and ran the pipes from there and had some for his cattle."[57]

"We'd take a bucket, cross the road, and go to the pipe with the faucet. Every house on the right side of the lane had one. You carried two buckets, one for water to cook and one to drink. For washing water, we'd take a tub and fill it; it took two people to carry it."[58]

During World War II, Manuel Gaines served in the US Army while Adrean struggled to support her children. After Manuel returned to Pointe Coupée, the couple divorced, and Adrean moved to New Orleans to find work, leaving the children in the care of Aunt Augusteen and Mama Julia. Gaines said that neither his mother nor his father was present in his life after 1945. (While he would eventually move to California to reunite with his mother, Manuel generally disappeared from his life after 1945.)[59]

Adrean filed for divorce in December 1945, and the divorce was granted in June 1946.[60] Soon after, she married Norbert Colar, whom she had known since childhood. Colar lived at Cherie Quarters and walked daily to work at neighboring Parlange Plantation, a distance of about two miles. Ben Biben said Colar was a big man, authoritative and strong willed, of whom many people were afraid.

"Norbert was bossy, big, his voice would roar like a lion. He'd walk from Cherie Quarters to Parlange Lane. We'd offer him a ride, and he'd say, 'No, I'm gon' walk on.' He had big old feet on him. He was kind of a loner, liked to be by himself.[61] "Norbert was a bully," Biben said. "You listened or else. . . . [He] was somebody to fear. You just feared him."[62] "He was a big mule of a man. He wasn't mean, he just looked mean. [He] kind of bossed the kids around. You respected him."[63]

Colar came from a family of French-speaking Catholics, and Gaines remembered his speaking in a thick Creole accent. The Colars owned land in the area—as Gaines put it, "They were property people."[64] Even before they were free to marry, Norbert and Adrean moved to New Orleans to find work. According to Adrean, Norbert worked as a longshoreman "until he got his papers for the merchant marine. He was a merchant marine in 1943." In 1947, Norbert and Adrean moved to Vallejo, California, a small seaport town across the bay from San Francisco. "I didn't want to live in the South any longer," said Adrean Colar in a 1992 interview. "I wanted to come here so I could start a life and make a life for my children—go to school, go to college, get a trade. If I had stayed there [Louisiana], we wouldn't have got it."[65]

## LEAVING CHERIE QUARTERS

When Ernest Gaines left Pointe Coupée Parish in 1948, he was young and gifted, but he was also Black. In the Louisiana of the 1930s and 1940s, that combination would, at best, get him ignored. At worst, it meant being branded dangerous. In a 1983 interview, Gaines bluntly assessed his chances of surviving on the plantation. "I would have been one of the dead ones. Sooner or later, I would have said or done something, and I would probably have been killed." He would see many boys his age brought down by the life he left. "Another five years and I could have been broken, bitter. So many kids are dead now. Half of the boys I grew up with are dead—violent deaths, heart attacks, whatever. So many hurt miserably and became alcoholics. Violent, violent death. It's a good thing I left when I did."[66]

One by one, Adrean and Norbert sent for the children, starting with E. J. in 1948, when he was fifteen and a half years old. One day a train ticket arrived at the post office in Oscar. A few days later, he climbed aboard a bus that took him to New Orleans, where he boarded a Southern Pacific train for Crockett, California, just across the bay from Vallejo. He recalled that the cars were segregated until the train got to Los Angeles, after which "everybody was together."[67] Gaines wrote about the hot August Sunday when he left, his last day as a resident of Cherie Quarters:

> It took me all day to pack, unpack, and repack the old brown leather suitcase. I didn't have many clothes, I can assure you, but for some reason I could not get it done. Maybe it was the bag of oranges, or the shoebox of fried chicken and bread, or the tea cakes and pralines wrapped in brown paper, or the bag of unshelled pecans—maybe it was one of these or all of these that kept me opening and shutting the suitcase. But, finally, I got it done and came out onto the

> porch. Everybody was there: the old people on the porch talking to my aunt and the children in the yard waiting for me to come down the steps so they could follow me to the road. I went to each one of the old people, shook their hands, and listened to their advice on how to live "up North." Then I went to my aunt. She sat on the floor—just inside the door. "I'm going, Aunty," I said. I did not lean over to kiss her—though I loved her more than I have loved anyone else in my life. I did not take her hand, as I had taken the other people's hands, because that would have been the most inappropriate thing in the world to do. I simply said, "I'm going, Aunty." She looked up at me from the floor. I saw the tears in her eyes. She nodded her head and looked down again. When I came out into the road, I looked back at her. I waved and smiled; she waved back. The old people were silent all this time—but I'm sure that before I reached the highway to catch the bus, they were talking again.[68]

Many themes in Ernest Gaines's fiction can be traced to that scene of leave-taking: grace under pressure, the child's acceptance of responsibility, feelings of love and duty so strong they defy expression in words, journeys, roads, porches, the setting free of the young by the old. All are found repeatedly in his powerful stories about the place and the people he left behind.

In "The Sky Is Gray," for example, eight-year-old James has already been well schooled in behaving like a man—denying his toothache, checking the impulse to hug the mother he loves because "that's crybaby stuff," denying the cold and hunger that assault him as they walk through town in the sleet while waiting for the dentist's office to reopen.

When E. J. arrived in Vallejo in August 1948, Adrean and Norbert Colar were living in Carquinez Heights, a government project that housed a variety of races—Black, white, Asian, Hispanic, Native American.[69] Shortly after E. J. joined his parents, they moved to 219 Florida Street in downtown Vallejo. He enrolled at Franklin Junior High School, where classmate Pearl Jones Tranter remembered him as a diligent student. "Coolness. Calm. Quiet. Didn't fidget. Didn't vie with others for attention. Paid attention to the teachers."[70] Years later, Gaines recalled

> a little teacher, Miss Legg, a little short woman. [Classmate] Gilbert Crane, he looked like a crane. White boy with a long nose and hair swooped back. He'd put a tack in some girl's seat—Jane. He'd buy all these little trick things.

> He had a pile of rubber dog doo-doo he put in the teacher's seat. The teacher came in, and just as he was getting ready to sit down, he saw it. He pushed it off. He didn't want to dignify anybody [by calling him out]. This was around 1949. I was just coming from the South. I thought he was one of these crazy white guys.[71]

Franklin was so different from the Catholic school in New Roads. "When I was going to St. Augustine, the priest called on me, white priest. He said, 'You,' and I jumped to my feet and said, 'Yes, sir.' He said, 'Say "Yes, Father."' When I jumped to my feet in California, everybody cracked up. They'd be all stretched out in their desks."

Not long after the family moved to Florida Street, E. J. began hanging out on street corners in the naval town, which was filled with sailors, pool halls, and nightclubs. "I got caught up with some pretty rough guys," Gaines recalled. "And my stepfather told me, none of that. These guys would go into movies without paying, or pick up comic books, or just stand on the corner and make noise—as any boys would do. But my stepfather didn't want me to be part of it."[72]

Adrean Colar agreed that her husband was "a very demanding person. He would show you the liberry in a minute." The library was only a few blocks from their house on Florida Street, and she, too, often walked there.[73] "A huge old fashioned [building] with cobwebs and all that good stuff. Old people working there who made sure you brought those books back."[74]

Gaines described his stepfather as "a very strict person with me. Very strong. A very handsome man, a big man. Most of my strong characters, I think, are built around him."[75] Later, he said that Colar was "physically very big and very opinionated. A strong male symbol. Phillip Martin [protagonist of *In My Father's House*] is based physically on him."[76] When Norbert Colar ordered him off the street, he suggested three options for the teenaged E. J.: the movies, the YMCA, or the library. Lacking money to go to the movies, sixteen-year-old E. J. chose the Y, but he was quickly discouraged. "One day someone asked me to put on some boxing gloves. I didn't know that his sparring partner hadn't shown up. He hit me everywhere. I was in such a hurry to get those gloves off I was using my teeth to untie them. A couple of days later I went to the library."

In the spring of 1949, Ernest Gaines climbed the marble stairs and pushed open the double doors of the Carnegie Library in Vallejo, an imposing two-story building with the words "Free to All" chiseled into its marble facade. He stepped through those doors into another world—the world of books and ideas—and, ultimately, another life—the life of a writer.

Gaines was so nervous on his first trips to the library that he pretended to read newspapers and magazines until he got the lay of the land and was sure it was okay for him to be there. Once he was certain he wouldn't be thrown out, he said, "I noticed that some people left with books under their arms." Soon he had his own library card and gathered his courage to climb the stairs to the second-floor fiction section.

"I felt like I was taking a trip to a foreign country," Gaines wrote. "I walked the length of the room, looking at each rack of books. I don't think I checked out a book that day. I was too overwhelmed with this new world." Eventually he chose a few books, randomly selecting colorful dust jackets or interesting-sounding titles. "The librarian checked me out without looking at me," he said. "If she had looked at me, I might have told her that this was my first time ever to check out a book."[77]

Seeking to connect with his roots by reading books with rural settings, Gaines said he "looked for certain words in the titles: road, tree, water, field, country. I was looking for a book about my background. I had worked in the fields from the time I was eight, fished in bayous and rivers, cut wood with a handsaw from the time I was eleven." He remembered reading Willa Cather and John Steinbeck, even *A Tree Grows in Brooklyn.* "I did not find me or the people I knew—my aunt who raised me, my brothers, my uncles—in the stories by white writers. Their black characters were one-dimensional. They were either too good or too evil. They sang all the time, or they did not sing at all. I continued to walk down the aisles, searching for me."[78]

E. J. was particularly disenchanted with the Black characters, stereotypes who spoke in the "darky" dialect found in *Gone with the Wind* (both book and movie) and the Stepin Fetchit films. White writers, he found, didn't get at the truth of their Black characters, and the work of Black writers was largely unavailable in libraries then, even in California. E. J. wanted to see the people he knew from his childhood in Cherie Quarters; he wanted to hear their voices. "It was through loneliness for my brothers and sister, my aunt, my friends, that I began to write," he said. In the summer of 1949, at sixteen, he decided to write his own book. "I thought, 'Well, all these books are here, and somebody must have written them, so why can't I do the same?'"[79]

"I was not so much trying to tell the rest of the world about my people as much as I was trying to tell myself, to record it, to say it was beautiful."[80]

# 2

# I WANTED TO READ ABOUT THE SOUTH

## BECOMING A WRITER

*It's tempting to speculate about why his introduction to the library inspired the young Ernest Gaines to write a book. Perhaps it was the fact that he was older than most children entering a library for the first time. He might have looked around and decided books were not for him. He might have simply checked out books and read them, perhaps establishing a lifelong love of reading. But as he described it, he was on a mission. He had left the South and found himself in Vallejo, a strange new world where he wasn't quite sure how he fit in. Part of him clung to Cherie Quarters, and the library enabled him to bridge those two worlds. Like so many things in Gaines's life, that moment seems touched by magic.*

. . . .

E. J. decided to write about a quarter community much like the one he had recently left. His main characters were a man and a woman who were in love but separated by skin color—not Black–white but Black–mulatto. The darker-skinned Jackson is seen as an unacceptable suitor for the light-skinned Creole woman Catherine, whose father abhors anyone with dark skin. E. J. titled the book *A Little Stream,* for the body of water separating the houses of the main characters. Writing it was complicated by the fact that he had to fit it in while babysitting for his new brother Michael.

"All I had to do was keep Michael asleep," he said. "I did that by keeping my fingers lightly pressed against his eyelids until he got tired and fell asleep. My stepfather would come home from his merchant marine trips, look at me down there on the floor writing in longhand, and tell my mother I must be going crazy."[1] But the teenaged Gaines took such pronouncements with a grain of salt. "I really loved him," he later said of Colar. "He had a strong influence on my life."[2]

After completing a handwritten draft, Gaines persuaded his mother to rent a Royal portable typewriter so he could get the novel ready to submit to a publisher. "My stepfather thought I was crazy because I was spending twelve, thirteen, fifteen hours a day typing with two fingers," he said. "I cut my sheets of paper in half so they would be book size. I typed on both sides of the paper, single-spaced, because that's how books were printed. I wanted to make it easy for the publishers."[3] Adrean Colar said her son stacked his typewritten pages and "would put them on the side and tell the [other] kids they better not touch them."[4] Driven by dreams of fame and wealth, he wrapped the novel in brown paper and mailed it to a New York publishing house. "The way that package looked, I'm sure they thought it was a bomb," said Gaines with a reminiscent smile. "They sent it back to me and I threw it in the incinerator."[5] Discouraged, he stopped writing.

In 1950, E. J. enrolled at Vallejo High School; for the first time, his classmates were not only white students but also Chinese, Filipino, Japanese, Mexican, and Native American teenagers. He made the track team, specializing in the 440-yard dash,[6] and also played football. "I played end for one semester. I was the worst player to ever put a helmet on."[7] He also took a typing class. "Miss Olsen had us typing on manuals. I think they were Royals." He mimed putting his fingers on the keys, reciting them from memory. "ASDF, JKL semicolon.

"Miss Olsen walked behind you with a ruler. You had to have your hands on the keys. You couldn't rest your hands on the typewriter. *Whop, whop,*" he imitated Miss Olsen slamming his hands with the ruler. "When I had to walk to school, I passed by her home every morning. She'd want to walk to school with me. Then, in second period . . ." He made the strict-teacher face Miss Olsen had used.[8]

In the summer of 1950, about two years after he had moved to Vallejo, E. J. returned to Louisiana for a visit. At Cherie Quarters, he persuaded the boys his age to join him on training runs up and down the gravel road. By that time, he was a dedicated track runner, specializing in the quarter mile. "He was trying to teach us how to start, how to pace your running, how to stride," recalled Ben Biben.[9] "He'd come down the quarters with the dust flying," said James Brooks. "We'd ask him why, and he'd say, 'I'm on the track team.' We'd try to keep up with him, kick up dust on the gravel road. He'd encourage us to keep up with him, but I'd always give out."[10] E. J. also spent time with Aunt Teen, who by then was in her midfifties. When it was time for him to return to California, he said goodbye to his beloved great-aunt for the last time.

By now Gaines was seventeen years old. Even at this young age, he must already have been different from his friends in the quarter. He had two years of California living and schooling under his belt, and he had become an athlete recognized for his talent. Did he talk to them about California and his life there? Was his reunion with Aunty equally joyous and sad? She must have been proud of him, and she must have realized that his leaving had been the right thing, but it's easy to imagine her pain at seeing him leave again. Later, when he wrote about Jackson and Aunt Charlotte in *Catherine Carmier,* did thoughts of that visit come to mind?

After graduating from Vallejo High School in 1951, he attended Vallejo Junior College for two years. "Junior college was free if you lived in . . . Vallejo, but it was not top education, just an extension of high school really," Gaines said.[11] Brooks recalled getting a letter from Gaines around this time. "He said he was majoring in journalism. I wasn't surprised, because he was always interested in books. I used to sit and think, 'What is he going to write about?'"[12]

In 1953, Gaines clocked 48.8 seconds in the 440-yard dash, placing third in the California junior college track meet. He also set a record of 21.9 in the 220-yard dash, a mark that would stand for twenty years.[13] "I was impressed with all those medals," said his brother Norbert Colar, who recalled "a whole wall full of medals" in his brother's bedroom. "He was a real good quarter-miler. He won a lot. Don't think his chest wasn't stuck out."[14] Gaines finished junior college that same year, with an associate of arts degree in journalism, but "I did not have a penny in the world to finish college."[15]

In February 1953, Augusteen Jefferson died at about the age fifty-nine. Her death certificate notes that she was attended by Dr. Eugene Durel for eight days, from February 5 until her death on February 13. Cause of death is given as "gangrene of both feet" due to "abnormally small crippled legs since birth."[16] Ada Mae Gaines, who lived with her husband, Lionel, on the other side of Miss Teen's double house, recalled that "she stayed sick off and on for about a month," and that neighbors came by to check on her daily, often bringing fruit, which Augusteen loved.[17] Ben Biben, who was still living at Cherie Quarters, was surprised to learn of Miss Teen's death; he did not recall her having been sick. Although Adrean traveled to Louisiana by train, taking four-year-old Michael with her, the family could not afford to send E. J. home for his great-aunt's funeral.[18] She is buried in the graveyard at Cherie Quarters, where she lies in a grave as yet unmarked.[19] About the same time, the early 1950s, Gaines's grandmother Julia McVay moved to California, settling in an apartment on Lyon Street in San Francisco and going to work as a housekeeper.[20]

Gaines's lack of funds for college was a problem temporarily solved when he was drafted into the army. After basic training, he was stationed in Guam. He continued to run track in the army, and he also enjoyed socializing and drinking at local clubs. But eventually he returned to writing, scribbling away in the post library. One of his stories was selected for second prize in a short story contest, and he won fifteen dollars. The same story earned him ten dollars for honorable mention in a GI competition sponsored by the US Far East Command in Japan.[21]

Gaines cashed the ten-dollar check but saved the fifteen-dollar one. He put it in a little glass bank that had belonged to his Aunt Teen; it had been given to him after her death, along with the few coins it contained. "I put the check in the bank when I was discharged from the army in 1955, and it's been there ever since," he said. "Because in order to get it out I would have to break the bank open, and that I'll never do." The prizes had rekindled his interest in writing. Discharged from the army, he returned to California intent upon going to college to study writing. "After Ernie went in the service and came back, he just kept writing on his mind," said his mother. "His determine [*sic*] was to be a writer."[22]

## SAN FRANCISCO

With $110 a month from the GI Bill, Gaines enrolled at San Francisco State College in 1955.[23] He majored in language arts and minored in English literature, studying under such teachers as Stanley Paul Anderson and Mark Harris.[24] "Real encouragement began . . . when I enrolled at State," he said. "I got concrete criticism and concrete recognition."[25]

But first he was assigned books to read—works by Mark Twain, Guy de Maupassant, Anton Chekhov, Ernest Hemingway, Gertrude Stein, James Joyce, William Faulkner, Eudora Welty. Gaines particularly liked Ivan Turgnev's *A Sportsman's Sketches.* "That was about hunting and meeting people in rural life," he said. "And then, the clarity and the beauty of his writing, even in translation."[26] "I fell in love with the Russian writers, especially Turgenev," he said. "But those Russian peasants were not my people.[27]

Gaines's patchy early education showed as he struggled to write essays, and his compositions earned poor grades. "I was very bad at expository writing," he said. "My professor [Stanley Paul Anderson] said, 'How did you get into college?' He gave me a D on my first assignments. I asked him to let me try creative writing instead. . . . I don't know that I would have graduated from San Francisco State if I hadn't gone into creative writing."[28] Anderson agreed to let Gaines write short stories instead of essays, and Gaines submitted a story called "The Turtles," about a young Louisiana boy's sexual awakening.

In 1956, State began publishing a campus literary magazine, *Transfer,* with a staff of twenty-five people who edited and designed issues containing student works of art, literature, and philosophy. Anderson was faculty adviser to the magazine. Published twice yearly, with a circulation of a thousand copies, it was more ambitious in scope than the typical student publication. The first story in the first issue was "The Turtles."[29] It was a stroke of good fortune that the teacher who allowed Gaines to write fiction instead of essays was in a position to recommend his work for publication.

Another of Gaines's teachers, Mark Harris, was best known for his four baseball novels; he wrote the screenplay for one of them, *Bang the Drum Slowly,* published in 1956 and filmed in 1973. He, too, would play a crucial role in Gaines's career.

Dorothea Oppenheimer had recently moved to San Francisco and was working as a literary scout. "She asked Mark Harris if he knew of any other talented writers and he told her that I was a good 'potential,'" Gaines said.[30] After reading his story in *Transfer,* she contacted the English department at San Francisco State and asked to meet him.

Gaines met Oppenheimer in the student union, and she told him, "I think you have great talent." Gaines recalled, "She told me, 'Whenever you have written something, let me see it.' My instructors had seen my stories, but no one else had ever said to me, 'Let me see whatever you write.' It was the greatest thing that could happen to a young writer."[31]

Born in Berlin in 1918, Oppenheimer, who was Jewish, had come to the United States from Germany during World War II.[32] According to Gaines, her family was wealthy, and she had attended a private school in England. When she arrived in New York as a teenager, she enrolled at Radcliffe College. She had worked as an editor and then a literary agent in New York.

That day in 1956, the aspiring Louisiana writer and the sophisticated German expatriate—both recently arrived in San Francisco—began a relationship that would last for thirty-one years, until Oppenheimer's death in 1987. More than an agent, she would be Gaines's friend and teacher—and, for a time, a romantic partner.[33] She introduced him to classical music, contemporary art, and European films. An astute editor, she read his work and suggested changes, challenging him to do better. She insisted that he put his work first, and she nagged him about his health. With her encouragement, and sometimes financial support, he continued to write. "Dorothea was not just looking at a black writer writing a black story," Gaines said. "She knew what literature was about. She had done a lot of editorial work. She knew music. She knew the arts. She knew all the great painters' work. She taught me all these things. . . . She traveled a lot. And she knew all the people in New York. . . . She knew literature and saw what I could do."[34]

In 1957, Gaines again published a short story in *Transfer.* "The Boy in the Double-Breasted Suit" is about Max, who is given a suit by a woman who hopes to marry his widowed father. Perhaps its most memorable character is the preacher, Reverend Johnson, who "could pick up a fifty-pound sack of rice with his teeth and swing it like a pendulum for a minute every weekday, and go to church on Sunday and preach two full hours without stopping."[35] Once again, Gaines's setting was a south Louisiana plantation inspired by Cherie Quarters.

While working hard to master the short story form, he was discouraged when a visiting lecturer told one of his classes at San Francisco State that there was no money to be made by writing short stories. Gaines immediately decided to switch to writing novels. Casting about for ideas, he remembered the book he had written at sixteen, about a Black man, a Creole woman, and the strict barriers between their two cultures.[36]

When not in class or writing, Gaines enjoyed the cultural life of the city, so different from the South he had left. "San Francisco was a moveable feast," he said, borrowing the phrase from Hemingway's book about his early years in Paris. "The small bookstores would let you come in and sit and read. You could go into record shops and they'd let you play [a record] or take it home and play it. It [the city] was much more safe. I used to hitchhike to school."[37] He heard beat poets Kenneth Rexroth and Lawrence Ferlinghetti read their work.[38]

He graduated from San Francisco State College in 1957. "When I graduated from State in 'fifty-seven, I gave myself ten years," he said. "I said, in ten years, I must be a writer, or I don't know what else I'll do with my life. I didn't know what I'd do—become a farmer?" But he had a plan. "I had heard about the creative writing fellowship at Stanford," he said. "So when I got out in 'fifty-seven I went to work for one year." His plan was to support himself and save a little money while writing short stories that might help him win a fellowship.[39]

In 1957 and 1958, he worked as a mail clerk at an insurance company. Despite having been told there was no money in stories, he was still naturally drawn to short fiction. He began writing "A Long Day in November," which depicts a day in the life of a plantation quarter as seen through the eyes of a six-year-old boy whose parents' marriage is troubled. At the insurance company, "I used to sneak into the bathroom and write on paper towels, and laugh at the dialogue I was writing," Gaines said. "My boss would kick the door and yell, 'Get back to work!' And I'd say, 'Don't you know there's a genius at work in here?'"[40] "I thought it was one of the funniest things I'd ever read."[41]

He submitted three short stories to Stanford, and later learned that Wallace Stegner had awarded him a fellowship. He was not surprised to win, he said, because he had known one of the judges. "He told me I had a good chance. I was always sort of cocky, I suppose, and thought, 'I'm just as good as the other guy.'"[42]

Gaines remembered that his application for the Stegner fellowship was Dorothea Oppenheimer's idea.[43] By the time he arrived at Stanford in the late 1950s, Stegner had been head of the creative writing department since 1946. Already an accomplished author and professor, he had been lured away from Harvard by Richard Foster Jones, head of Stanford's English department, who hired him to teach fiction writing and American literature. Stegner, an early environmentalist who would become renowned for writing about the American West, asked for several guarantees: a full professorship with tenure, no committee work, and no morning classes. "He always needed the mornings to write," his wife Mary explained. "He would come in from his study about 11:30 to shower and shave and have lunch, and then tear down to Stanford for a one o'clock class."[44]

At a meal hosted by R. F. Jones, Stegner mentioned that returning GIs who had served overseas had stories to tell but needed financial help. "He said they needed a place where they could write and talk, like a coffee house in Europe," Mary said.[45] Stegner was seated next to Jones's brother, Edward H. "Ned" Jones, who asked him to describe his ideal writing program. Stegner did, and Jones responded, "I would like to fund that." In addition to being a Greek scholar and a physician, Ned Jones was also a Texas oilman. His $75,000 grant enabled Stegner to start the creative writing program.[46]

Mary Stegner, a licensed interior decorator, furnished the Jones Room on the fourth floor of the library with a specially built table imported from Denmark. The room, where the fellows and other students met weekly to discuss their work, included well-stocked bookshelves, a coffee machine, and even a record player.[47]

Fellowship winners for the 1958–59 academic year were Gaines, the first Black writer accepted; Kentucky native Wendell Berry, who was working on his first novel *Nathan Coulter;* and Chicagoan Mitch Strucinski, who had published stories in *The Atlantic.*[48] The fellowship paid $2,500 for the academic year, at a time when the average salary in the United States was $3,000 a year. The money gave Gaines the freedom to concentrate on writing alone.

The spacious campus, its sandstone buildings roofed in red tile, was about thirty miles south of San Francisco, in Palo Alto. It was an intellectually stimulating but somewhat intimidating environment for Gaines. His fellow students included Berry; a rather arrogant Ken Kesey, who would go on to write *One Flew Over the Cuckoo's Nest*; and Larry McMurtry, who would win the 1986 Pulitzer in fiction for *Lonesome Dove.* Berry is considered an agrarian writer and McMurtry has also been called a regionalist, associated with the Texas where he grew up. (McMurtry would also become a client of literary agent Oppenheimer.)

Novelist Richard Scowcroft, whose fiction reflected his Mormon upbringing, taught Gaines's classes in the fall and winter quarters, and Stegner taught in the spring quarter. Scowcroft, who joined Stanford as an assistant professor of English in 1947, contributed immensely to the development of the writing program, where he served as associate director, and then as director after Stegner retired in 1971. He was widely liked for his acerbic wit. "If you went to a party, you could find most of the people there trying to get up close to him," said Nancy Packer, a former student who recalled him as "extremely witty and a marvelous raconteur."[49]

Gaines stood out as the only Black student among the fifteen or twenty people in the class—and one of only half a dozen on the entire campus. "That was 1958, four years after the Supreme Court decision [*Brown v. Board of Education*]," recalled Berry, a native of Port Royal, Kentucky. "Ernie was the first real Black classmate I'd ever had." According to Berry, the class met for three hours in the early afternoon. "We sat at a long, oblong sort of Danish-type table, with tolerably comfortable chairs, at least for young people." On one occasion, "We were all sitting around the table one day and an earthquake happened. A huge fluorescent light fixture began to oscillate and rattle a little bit. We looked up, but nobody said anything, and Scowcroft went on with the class."[50]

Rather than having the students read aloud from their work, the teacher read their work. Because of the size of the class, said Berry, "You weren't getting your work read every week. Maybe one or two times during the quarter. The criticism would be pretty vociferous, strong, good. There were some pretty bright people in there." Berry himself also talked a lot. "I remember saying quite a lot because I was afraid not to; [I had] the fear I wouldn't measure up. I was really pretty green, doing my best to hold my own among people I assumed were devastatingly brilliant."

Gaines, on the other hand, spoke little. "Ernie was very quiet," said Berry. "My take on him was that he was not overly confident at that time." Nonetheless, Berry sensed that Gaines was committed to his work. "Ernie, I think, already understood what his burden was, his obligation was [as a writer]. I think Stegner and Scowcroft both took Ernie very seriously and were being very careful of him and very kind to him. I picked that up. They thought well of him."

Gaines wrote in the mornings, met the Stanford group for lunch, then wrote in the afternoons. "[Stegner] always liked to let the writer do what he wanted. and he'd check it every so often," he said. "At that time there were very few blacks on the campus, hardly anyone as poor as I. I was pretty much alone—I didn't mind that; to write you have to lock yourself in a room to work. But I was sort of out of place there. It's not my kind of world."[51] In a 1983 interview with University of Southwestern Louisiana colleague Jane Bonin, he went a bit further. "I'm happy here. I was unhappy at Stanford," he said.

He did establish a friendship with Berry, who recalled a "confrontation" in which they acknowledged that, as southerners, they had a more intense relationship than Gaines might have with others in the class. "Ernie and I knew from our first glance at each other that we'd have to deal with each other in some way," Berry said. Finally, at a party in Palo Alto, they did. "We walked outside together and talked it over," Berry said. "I remember Ernie and I going out into the back yard and coming to light to each other, speaking to each other of this thing we both had on our minds, about the affection between the races. Both of us had this feeling that we needed to talk. There was no use pretending we didn't know about the racial difference. We weren't color blind, and there was not a chance either one of us ever would be."

Gaines himself spoke of the confrontation when he was interviewed by Stegner's biographer. "He just called me into the back yard . . . [and said] we have to talk this over. . . . After talking we realized we had more in common, I had more in common with him than I did with most of the white people in the class; after that we became close friends."[52]

"When I read that, it pleased me," said Berry. "That was probably the most important social event of the year for me. That it was important to Ernie, too, was pleasing to me. We have been friends ever since. I admire him without reservation and love him."[53]

While Berry was revising his novel, Gaines was struggling with his own first novel, the same one he had first tried to write a decade earlier. He was influenced by Turgenev's *Fathers and Sons,* which may have been recommended to him by Stegner. "It was a simple, small book," Gaines said. "I know I could never write a big book. . . . And, too, at the time I discovered Turgenev, I could almost see myself in Bazarov's position, you know. When you go back, *what?* Not that I'd become a nihilist, but I could understand the nihilistic attitude after someone had been away awhile." Yevgény Bazárov, a central character in the novel, is a medical student and nihilist who challenges the traditional Russian Orthodox beliefs of his own parents. "But I think the major thing I liked about [Turgenev] was the structure of his small novels." While reworking his early novel, Gaines used Turgenev's book as a model. "My *Catherine Carmier* is almost written on the structure of *Fathers and Sons,*" he said. "As a matter of fact, that was my Bible. I used it on my desk every day."[54]

Berry admired Gaines's work for not "demonizing" white characters; he believed that Gaines struggled to accommodate the complexities of white–Black relationships. "I remember Ernie acknowledging [affection between the races], and with difficulty. I remember his talking about his grandmother ironing, with great love and affection, an apron or pillowcase that the white lady of the house [River Lake Plantation] had given her. She spoke of it with affection, and he found this difficult to deal with."

Malcolm Cowley, who had written *Exile's Return,* about Paris in the 1920s, also taught at Stanford. Both he and Stegner recommended that Gaines cut the background material in *Catherine Carmier,* in which he tried "to show these old Creoles as I knew them as a child," because "it doesn't move the story along." Both men told him "the action of the book was not moving, with all the things I wanted to include."[55]

In 1959, Gaines submitted his in-progress novel, now titled *Comeback,* for the San Francisco Foundation's Joseph Henry Jackson award, and he won a grant-in-aid of $2,000. Established as a memorial to a distinguished San Francisco literary critic, the award was designed to encourage and recognize fine literary work by young writers between the ages of twenty and thirty-five who were residents of Northern California or Nevada. The competition was open to unpublished works of fiction, nonfiction prose, or poetry. Gaines was only the third recipient to win the award, which had been established in 1957, after Jackson's death.

While he struggled to write the novel that would be *Catherine Carmier,* he worked at a series of jobs. "I wrote in the mornings and took odd jobs in the afternoons and evenings," said Gaines, who shined shoes, washed dishes, and worked in a post office. While clerking in the post office, he began his lifelong habit of wearing a beret, a ritual adopted by several workers there as a sign of solidarity.[56]

These were lean times. He lived in a one-room apartment with a Murphy bed and no phone, subsisting on hot dogs and pork and beans, "stuff I bought from a Chinese grocery." Sometimes he went across the street for a home-cooked meal with his grandmother, Julia McVay, who had moved to San Francisco in the 1950s. "Here I was, the first male in my family to go to college, and I was living like a bum," said Gaines.[57] For several years he could not afford to buy his mother a Christmas, birthday, or Mother's Day present; a girlfriend broke up with him because he could never take her out. His agent, Dorothea Oppenheimer, frequently paid his rent when he was broke, and even cooked for him. "She was much more than an agent," he said. "She was there. I needed a person like that at the time."[58]

With Oppenheimer's help, he was publishing. She sent his stories to little magazines, fielding the rejections and rarely taking her percentage of the tiny fees. Gaines's short stories recalled his plantation childhood but also reflected the growing unrest of the civil rights era. In 1962, he wrote "Just Like a Tree,"

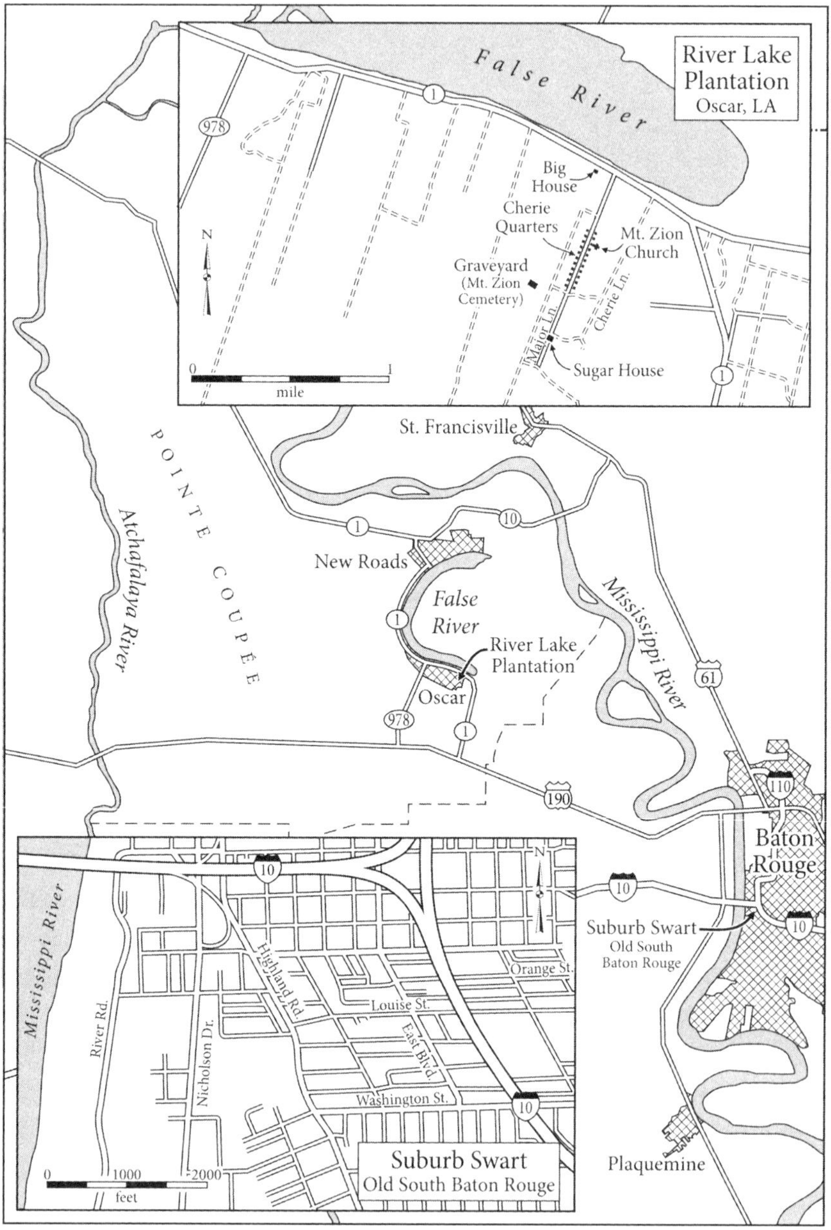


River Lake Plantation and Baton Rouge

and in 1963, partly influenced by Eudora Welty's "A Worn Path," he wrote "The Sky Is Gray," which has become a much-anthologized classic. As Gaines later wrote in the essay "Miss Jane and I," he was, in these stories and in the novel *Of Love and Dust,* consciously trying to re-create the landscape of his childhood in Cherie Quarters.[59]

In the early 1960s, Gaines considered traveling to Europe or Mexico, but he changed his mind. He said that he was inspired to return to the South by the bravery of James Meredith, who had to be protected by armed guards when he arrived at the University of Mississippi in September 1962. Gaines also realized that he needed to return to Louisiana, to soak up its atmosphere, in order to finish his book. He contacted relatives in Baton Rouge, who agreed to let him stay with them for a while. He gave up his San Francisco apartment and on January 3, 1963, packed a bag and left for Louisiana by train.[60]

He moved in with his great-uncle George Williams (a half brother of his grandmother Julia McVay) and George's wife, Mamie, who lived on Louise Street in a primarily Black area of Baton Rouge known as the Bottom, just north of Louisiana State University. By 1963, their daughter Lee had left home to attend college in California, but their teenage son Joe was still living at home, attending McKinley High School just around the corner. The four-bedroom house was crammed with people. "We had a house full," recalled Ben Biben, who lived with the Williams family after leaving

George Williams and Mamie Kemp Williams in a photo booth at the Pointe Coupée Parish fair in New Roads, circa 1952. The couple welcomed Gaines to their Baton Rouge home for six months in 1963 when he was writing *Catherine Carmier.* Several former residents of Cherie Quarters lived with the Williams family after leaving the quarter, until they could afford to rent or buy their own place. "We called it the Underground Railroad," said Sam Bibbens, who lived with the Williamses in the early 1960s. Photo courtesy of Tony Cador.

Cherie Quarters. "Mamie wanted everybody around her; she loved having people around her."[61]

Shared housing was not uncommon among Cherie Quarters residents who left for Baton Rouge. People moved in together and found work, paying minimal rent and grocery money and saving up until they could afford homes of their own.[62] The community spirit of the quarter was very much alive. Sam Bibbens, Ben's brother, had lived with the Williams family for a year and a half, from 1959 until 1960, before moving to San Francisco. "We called it the Underground Railroad, where you went to [transition] from the farm to the city," he said.[63]

George Williams worked as a janitor at the Copolymer rubber plant in Baton Rouge and Mamie worked in the cafeteria at a school for the deaf. Ben held two part-time jobs, working for a drugstore and a health club. Ernest Brooks, nicknamed Booster, delivered groceries by bicycle and shared a bedroom with Little Joe, age fourteen. Roosevelt Brooks, Ernest's brother, was also in residence. Every night, Mamie Williams cooked dinner for the extended family. "We had so much fun in that house," recalled Biben.[64]

Into this already full house in January 1963 came Ernest Gaines, who was given a room of his own. Every day, after Little Joe had set off for school and the others for work, Gaines would go to his bedroom and work on his portable Royal typewriter until three in the afternoon. "That was his magic hour" to quit work, Biben recalled. Closed in his room, Gaines re-created the novel he had begun at age sixteen. He got angry if anyone disturbed him, even for meals. Often, Mamie Williams left a tray outside his door. Biben realized that Gaines's determination was solid. "He told me, 'I *will* be a writer,'" said Biben. "Not, 'I'm going to *try* to be a writer,' but 'I *will* be a writer.'"[65] Gaines's brother Norbert agreed. "I always thought he was going to be a writer," he said. "One thing he didn't like was working for other people."[66]

Biben was impressed that Gaines's agent sent him money in Louisiana. "Some lady who lived in California, she somewhat supported him financially," he said. "If she had that much confidence in him—we saw that she had faith in him—we just felt good about him leaving the country and going to the city and making something good of himself."[67]

On January 15, 1963, shortly after his arrival in Baton Rouge, Gaines celebrated his thirtieth birthday. After nearly fifteen years in California, he had to readjust to the indignities of Louisiana: segregated bus stations, "colored" eating sec-

Gaines, about age twenty-seven, and his cousin Joe Williams, about eleven, in a photography studio on East Boulevard in Baton Rouge, circa 1960. Photo courtesy of Tony Cador.

tions in restaurants, stores where he had to buy clothes without trying them on, white cabdrivers who refused to pick him up. On visits to False River, he realized that life on the plantation had changed drastically since he had left. After the war, many young men had not returned. Families had scattered, some moving to California in search of a better life, some to New Orleans, and others across the river to Baton Rouge. Most of the young adults were gone, leaving old people and sometimes children behind. The "Cajuns" had taken over the good farmland, squeezing out the Blacks. The bonds that held the people of Cherie Quarters together were dissolving.

But there was still plenty of fellowship to be had, still plenty of stories to hear on his trips to the home place. One of the more colorful characters still living at Cherie Quarters was Walter Zeno, also known as Salute or Pete, who told Gaines stories about his family for generations back. Gaines also talked to Reese Spooner, another man who seemed to recall everybody who had ever lived at Cherie Quarters and everything that had ever happened there.

On weekends, Gaines went out drinking with buddies. "We went to some dives in Baton Rouge and New Roads, Port Allen, Erwinville," he said. "There was all this dancing going on. Ben [Biben] and I, every Sunday night we'd go to the White Eagle in Port Allen. We'd park half a block away and could hear the music."[68] Biben recalled the bar, across the river from Baton Rouge, as a pretty rough place. "We used to get in fights to get a table," he said. "We'd pretend to fight so the people would clear the tables."[69]

On a much earlier trip to the White Eagle, Gaines had witnessed a knife fight between two men. "Around 'fifty-six or 'fifty-seven, I was in a pretty rough bar in Port Allen called the White Eagle," he said. "I saw a knife fight there; it was broken up. As a child, I remember, there were two kinds of Blacks, the good nigger and the bad nigger. If the good one killed the bad one, he could get out of jail. They might put him on a plantation to work." That event meshed in his mind with the words from a Lightnin' Hopkins blues song, "Tim Moore's Farm." The words that played over and over in Gaines's mind were "If you stay out the graveyard, nigger, I'll keep you out the pen." From that combination would eventually result both a short story, "Three Men," and a novel, *Of Love and Dust.*[70]

Gaines's life to date had been marked by turning points: the move to California, the discovery of the library, meeting his agent Dorothea Oppenheimer. An equally crucial turning point was his journey home in 1963, where he saw the place of his youth through a sensibility matured and broadened by his years away. As civil rights demonstrations raged throughout the country and Black people died in an effort to win freedom, Gaines was revisiting a Louisiana plantation still mired in the Jim Crow past. His love for his home was tempered by frustration at the need for it to change. He saw that the mechanized farming of the "Cajuns" with their tractors had pushed Black sharecroppers even lower on the economic ladder. (Although he calls them Cajuns in his books, not all whites in the area were of Acadian descent. "We used to call them Cajuns," Ben Biben said. "This was a degrading word, like 'nigger.' That's what we thought of it as.")[71]

Gaines had found the source of his restlessness and frustration as a writer—he needed to connect with and make sense of his past. In this time of inner and outer turmoil, he confronted a painful reality: for change to happen, some things must be destroyed. But what was worth saving and what was worth throwing away? When was the time to be silent and when was the time to take a stand? He wrestled with questions that would later form the philosophical underpinnings of his work. Searching for purpose and meaning, he realized that his sojourn in Baton Rouge was a defining moment in his life.

> I do feel deep down in me that the six months I spent in Louisiana definitely saved my writing and quite possibly my life . . . in that I could never have written *Catherine Carmier* if I had not gone South, and maybe I would never have written any other book . . . because my writing is my life. For me not to write is for me not to live. So I went there, put up with many things I hated, but I learned much, much about the people and the place that I wanted to write about.[72]

His trip to Louisiana not only allowed Gaines to soak up the atmosphere of home but also provided him with room and board—and company when he wanted it. He was completely free to focus on his work. By July, he felt that he had the book well in hand. He bade his relatives goodbye and headed west.[73]

Tragically, in the summer of 1965, Mamie Williams, in whose house Gaines had lived two years earlier, died. She, George, Joe, and three others had been traveling to California by car when Mamie, whom Gaines described as "short and very heavy," suffered a heart attack and died in Needles, California. Gaines attributed her death partly to the racism of the time, which pervaded not only the South but also much of the country. "They did not know how they could stop at motels and rest," he said. "It was the kind of thing that happened to our people, afraid to go in, afraid to be insulted, afraid they'll say you can't have that water or food. So they tried to drive [straight through], just stopping to rest a little bit."[74] Years later, he would partially dedicate the novel *In My Father's House* to the memory of George and Mamie Williams: "They gave you whatever they had; they asked for nothing in return."

## GETTING PUBLISHED

When he returned to San Francisco in the summer of 1963, Gaines rented a three-room apartment on Divisadero Street in a section known as the Western Addition. Six months later he finally finished the novel he had been trying to write for nearly half his life. "The only reason I got it finished was coming home [to Louisiana] in 'sixty-three," he said. "I rewrote and rewrote and rewrote that book. Dorothea sent it all over the place. Atheneum finally accepted it."[75]

Gaines named the central figure after two girls he had known. "I had a girl at St. Augustine—I loved her, but she didn't love me—named Catherine. At [Vallejo] high school in typing class was a pretty girl, Lolita Cormier. She was a beautiful girl. She never had typing paper. Every morning she'd borrow it from me."

While awaiting the publication of his novel, Gaines had continued to write short stories and to do whatever jobs he could find to support his work. After several publications turned it down, *Negro Digest* published "The Sky Is Gray" in August 1963.[76] That fall, the *Sewanee Review* published "Just Like a Tree." In its summer 1964 issue, *Texas Quarterly* at the University of Texas published an abbreviated version of "A Long Day in November."

Oppenheimer helped Gaines secure a job setting type for a printing company, a position he would hold for about three years, until 1966. "I used to take these little tweezers, and piece by piece by piece, I was setting those durned things," he said. "I knew all about the types and sizes, the different shapes of them. I used to love to do it."[77] Away from work, he wrote for hours at a stretch, sitting at a little kitchen table in his apartment.

In October 1964, Atheneum published *Catherine Carmier,* which earned scant acclaim and less money. "Nobody ever heard of the book, nobody ever read it," Gaines said.[78] But at last he had published a book. He dedicated it "For S______," later explaining that S stood for "Stinker," a nickname he and Dorothea called each other.[79] He took any opportunity to promote the novel, even appearing on a call-in radio show in the Bay Area. "The announcer started talking about feeding chickens and corn [plugging a sponsor]," Gaines said. "When you're starting out, you do these things. I went through a lot of that stuff. I'd do whatever I had to do [to sell books]."[80]

*Catherine Carmier* contained the essential elements he would build on as a writer. The strongest was a sense of place. "The quarters were extremely quiet. There was a moon, very high and very bright. Shadows from the trees, from the weeds along the ditch bank, from the old warped picket fences, lay across the road in front of him. Every house was quiet, looking gray and ghostlike. A dog barked at him every now and then, but other than that, absolute silence."[81]

Gaines's Louisiana was a different world, a somewhat foreign land where mixed blood and forbidden kinship complicated the social hierarchy. Even in his first novel, he used the life of the quarter to reflect broader themes. The quarter is seen as a place of scenic tranquility and community closeness fraught with tension brought on by interaction with the outside world. The old ways, the old values, are always being questioned. Often the natural elements reflect the human forces at work, as when Jackson, the protagonist, ponders telling his Aunt Charlotte that he will leave the quarter: "The half-dozen rows of beans that run beside the house were nearly dry. Everything else in the garden had that half-green, half-yellow color. I should have told her, he was thinking. I should have told her then that I'm going back. How can anyone stay here? Just look at this place. Everything is drying up; everything is half dead."[82]

By this time, Gaines's short stories were beginning to be recognized by important writers and editors. In 1966, "The Sky Is Gray" was included in the anthology *American Negro Short Stories,* edited by John Henrik Clarke, a respected historian of African and African American history. Langston Hughes, a leading voice of the Harlem Renaissance, selected "A Long Day in November" for inclusion in *The Best Short Stories by Negro Writers,* published in 1967.

That same year, Gaines met his self-imposed ten-year deadline to make it as a writer when the Dial Press published his second novel, *Of Love and Dust,* which examined a complicated social hierarchy and the consequences of breaking unwritten rules. With the release of this quietly told tale of tangled Black–white relations on a Louisiana plantation, critics began to pay attention to Gaines's work. The book, which had grown out of the meshing of the knife fight at the White Eagle and the Lightnin' Hopkins blues song, was highly praised. James Baldwin, whose work was also published by Dial, called it "a really fine and truthful study of the black–white madness."[83]

"*Of Love and Dust* wasn't the easiest book to write," Gaines said. "The first draft was sent out and the editor said, 'The two parts have nothing to do with each other. Make it comic or tragic.' I made it tragic. [Editor Bill Decker, who was also a novelist,] said, 'Run it back through the typewriter one more time and I'll publish it.' The reason I tried to write that book was that I wanted to publish [the short story collection] *Bloodline.* A novel introduces the writer. I based *Of Love and Dust* on [his short story] 'Three Men.' Procter and Marcus are the same people."[84]

The protagonist in *Of Love and Dust,* Marcus, is far from a typical plantation worker of the 1940s. He insists on wearing silk shirts, dress pants, and hard-soled shoes while pulling corn, and he romances Louise, the wife of white overseer Sidney Bonbon. Their dalliance, and Bonbon's trysts with the plantation worker Pauline, are the interracial relationships at the heart of the novel. Both begin as sexual alliances and become love affairs—and both end tragically. Nonetheless, around the time he published the novel, Gaines began an interracial relationship of his own.

### "MY LADY LINDA"

Linda Lawrence, a white woman in her late twenties, married, with a four-year-old child, would not seem to be the ideal candidate for a love interest, but she and her daughter, Rosalind, were part of Gaines's life for the next sixteen or so years—years when he was writing *The Autobiography of Miss Jane Pittman, In My Father's House,* and *A Gathering of Old Men.*[85]

Linda Bryant, a native of Santa Barbara and a graduate of Whittier College, had married David Michael Lawrence, known as Mike, in June 1962, when she was twenty-two; their daughter Rosalind, called Rozzie or Roz, was born in July 1963. By 1967, when Linda met Ernest Gaines, her marriage to Mike Lawrence was rocky.

"Ernie had a new book out," recalled Lawrence. "We met just before it [*Of Love and Dust*] was published.[86] I worked in a little storefront in a federally funded program administered by the state of California. They wanted young, idealistic people, and that was just the kind of work I had been looking for. Ernie was temporarily hired to work in the office to do a survey. I noticed this really tall man with a recent haircut. He had dressed for the occasion."[87]

In the office, "Ernie and I began talking to each other. We saw each other every day, but I was busy with my work." Still, her encounters with Gaines, then about thirty-four, caught the attention of the willowy blonde Lawrence, who had occasionally worked as a model while studying political science. "He was very sweet, very shy, quiet."

While they were working in the same office, Gaines and Lawrence were guests at a party thrown by their boss. Gaines took the woman lawyer he was dating. "My husband wouldn't go to the party," said Lawrence. "But my dad and mom were visiting, and my dad came with me. He loved to talk about sports. He buttonholed Ernie, who patiently stood there and listened."

After Gaines finished his client survey, he was no longer an employee, but he often dropped by the office. Lawrence eventually caught on that the purpose of those visits was to see her. On one occasion, she left early with a headache, and Gaines walked her to her car. "I offered Ernie a lift home, and he said, 'Would you like to have a drink?'

"We went to a place called Sugar Hill. We were the only people in there; it was dark. I had crème de cacao. At some point I said, 'Ernie, I don't have a headache anymore.'"

A few days later, Gaines invited Lawrence to his apartment for lunch. He was leaving the next day to visit relatives in Louisiana. "He was really excited about it," said Lawrence. "When he walked me to my car, he kissed me on the forehead and I started to cry. He said he wanted to be friends. He told me later how lonely he had been."

During the two weeks he was gone, Gaines found time to write to Lawrence. "I got a letter from him delivered to my job. He asked me to be his woman and said 'I'll call you when I get back.'"

Lawrence's marriage ended, and Mike Lawrence seldom saw Rosalind after he and Linda split up. To Roz, Gaines quickly became the father she longed for. Photos from that time show Gaines holding young Roz in his arms. "I'd sit on his knee and say, 'Oh, you're like a big brown horse,'" said Roz Arbel. "I loved horses. I was fascinated that the backs of his hands were dark and the palms were pink. He was a very playful person. I loved Ernie. He was a very important part of our lives. He was really tall and strong. He taught me to jitterbug in the kitchen when I was ten. I remember him throwing me up in the air."[88]

Because Arbel had darker skin, some people assumed that Gaines was her biological father. "I was told that word '*mulatto*' when I was a kid," she said. "Everybody thought I was a mulatto. They assumed I got really good [straight] hair and I was brown because Ernie was my dad. We had so many friends where the mom was white and the dad was Black. A lot of the children were lighter skinned than me, with curly blond hair. I always thought they were the most beautiful kids." In an earlier conversation on the same subject, Arbel observed, "Ernie said that in the future that's what everyone will look like."[89]

Gaines's family readily embraced Roz. "I liked his mother, Adrean," she said. "She was super mellow, very chill. Deb [Gaines's younger sister Deborah

Gaines with Linda Lawrence's young daughter, Rosalind, around 1968. Roz considered Gaines her stepfather and grew up seeing his photos of Cherie Quarters on the walls. Photo courtesy of Roz Arbel.

Colar] was for me the cool aunt, very fashionable." Linda, too, quickly became part of the family. In August 1968, when *Bloodline* came out, she was mentioned in an article in the *San Jose Mercury News.* Gaines's sister Lois hosted a book-signing party at her home in Campbell, near San Jose. According to the newspaper, an "ethereal blonde [Linda] flitted from room to room" and "Mama [Adrean Colar], dressed for a party, was hiding out in the kitchen."[90]

That book party was particularly meaningful to Gaines. *Bloodline* was the book of short stories he had persuaded Dial to bring out in addition to his novel. "I always knew my stories were better than anything else I had written. When *Of Love and Dust* was published, I told the publishing house, 'Give me a two-book contract, because these stories are going to make it for me. They might not make money, but they will make my name.' So they gave me a two-book contract. And they have been successful."[91]

Gaines knew the dangers of interracial relationships. They underpinned every aspect of the lives of Black males in the South. Raise your eyes to a white woman and lynching would surely follow, as it had for Emmett Till, the fourteen-year-old who was lynched in Mississippi in 1955 for allegedly flirting with a white woman. Interracial or light–dark relationships were at the heart of Gaines's two novels. Yet here he was, deeply involved with a white woman—a blonde, no less—and her daughter. This could not have happened in the South of his childhood, or even the South of the current civil rights era.

In fact, another famous writer with whom Gaines would become friends experienced a "mixed marriage" in the South. In 1967, Alice Walker married Mel Leventhal, a Jewish civil rights lawyer, in New York City. Later that year they moved to Jackson, Mississippi, becoming the first legally married interracial couple in Mississippi since miscegenation laws were introduced in the state. They were harassed and threatened by whites, including the Ku Klux Klan.[92]

The image of white women as pure and vulnerable, in need of protection from rapacious Black men, was as cherished by white men as it ever had been in the antebellum era. But Gaines was in San Francisco, a cosmopolitan city that tolerated lifestyles that were unacceptable in other parts of the country, from the gays on Castro Street to the hippies in the Haight. Here Ernest Gaines, a lonely man far from home, could risk loving a white woman and her child.

In May 1969, Gaines was invited to give a reading at the Black Culture Lounge at Denison University in Granville, Ohio. Lawrence went with him. "The campus gave us a lovely, stately home to stay in, complete with a couple who maintained the place and cooked for us," she said.[93] *The Denisonian* student newspaper quoted writer Ralph Ellison calling Gaines "one of the most promising young Negro writers" of the day.[94]

While Linda and Ernie were away, Roz stayed with Gaines's grandmother Julia McVay. "She lived in the Western Addition in her own house," said Arbel. "I was about six or so. They dropped me off, and she said, "Come on, honey, I'll make you some grits.' I said, 'What's a grit?' Ernie would tell this story constantly. He thought it was the funniest story. He would even open book lectures with it, especially if I was there. Sometimes he'd introduce me. He'd be like, 'My stepdaughter Rozzie, when she was a kid . . . What's a grit?'"[95]

In an interview about his new book, Gaines enumerated the sacrifices he had made for his writing: "Sure I would like to have a television set, a nicer place to live, a wife, children, a stereo, a car—I have never owned a car—and all those other things. But more than that, I want to write. If you want to do something, you have to sacrifice some other things."[96]

Dial's publication of *Bloodline* solidified Gaines's critical reputation. The book contained three previously published stories—"A Long Day in November," "The Sky Is Gray," and "Just Like a Tree"—along with two new ones—"Bloodline" and "Three Men," the second of which was based on the knife fight Gaines had witnessed in Louisiana. The stories focus on progressively older characters, beginning with six-year-old Sonny in "A Long Day in

November" and ending with elderly Aunt Fe in "Just Like a Tree." Many critics commented that the book read like a novel.

Gaines's next book project, *The Autobiography of Miss Jane Pittman,* would take him back to the library to research a period of more than one hundred years, from slavery to the civil rights movement, embodied in Miss Jane, who lives to be 110 years old. Gaines incorporated many of his own memories, such as the oak tree that Miss Jane talks to, which was based on an enormous live oak shading the highway between Oscar and Lakeland, a small town about two miles from Cherie Quarters. He had often passed the oak when he walked to the Little Zion Baptist Church in Lakeland. "There was always someone sitting under the tree, usually an old lady," he said, noting that people used the tree for shelter from both sun and rain.[97]

Gaines also returned to Louisiana to do research for *Miss Jane.* In conversation one day with his friend Alvin Aubert, a poet who taught at Southern University in Baton Rouge, he came up with a list of things Miss Jane might talk about, things he imagined the old people of the quarter talked about when he was a child: slavery, the Civil War, Reconstruction, the floods of 1912 and 1927, the construction of spillways to control floods, the reign of governor and senator Huey Long, the civil rights movement, and athletes Jack Johnson, Joe Louis, and Jackie Robinson. "Al Aubert was not the only person of whom I asked these questions," Gaines noted. "I went to several other people, older than Al, and uneducated, and asked them the same thing."[98] Poet Pinkie Gordon Lane, who taught English at Southern, met Gaines when he visited the school. "I knew him before he was famous, before he wrote *Miss Jane,*" she said. "There was a lot of humility there because he really didn't know his own potential."[99]

## A DEATH IN THE FAMILY

Gaines's comfortable life with Linda and Roz, interspersed with visits home to research his next novel, was disrupted by a shocking event that has been largely absent from accounts of Gaines's life: the murder of his stepfather Norbert Colar.[100]

In 1969, Colar was killed in front of his house on Sutter Street in Vallejo. Newspaper accounts reported that he was shot by an unknown assailant, or possibly the Zodiac Killer. But court documents and news articles show that Gaines's younger brother Leonard Colar, then sixteen, was charged with the shooting and served time for it. "There were rumors that he did it," said Roz Arbel, who was six years old at the time. "He went to prison. I remember them talking about it. Norbert was walking to his front door and someone came out of the shadows and shot him."[101]

On November 24, 1969, the Monday before Thanksgiving, Norbert Colar, age fifty-six, was returning from a two-week stint at sea, having worked as an assistant cook on the SS *California.* Newspaper accounts state that he was struck in the head, stomach, and legs by bullets from a nine-millimeter pistol at a range of about twenty-five feet. He underwent brain surgery at Queen of the Valley Hospital in nearby Napa but died the following morning.[102]

Norbert and Adrean's son Lavern and grandson Ernest, both teenagers, had just come in from playing basketball and were eating dinner with Adrean when they heard gunshots about 9:00 p.m. "At first we thought it was firecrackers," said Ernest Gaines II, then fifteen, who was named for his uncle the writer. They summoned help and "sat praying at the hospital" until Norbert died.[103]

Norbert's death certificate states that he died at eleven the next morning of "cerebral edema, contusions, lacerations with Skull Fracture secondary to trauma consistent with gunshot wound (bullet removed by surgery)." His death was attributed to "Homicide" at his home. "Deceased was walking from car to house when he was shot by unknown person."[104]

Linda Lawrence was supposed to meet Norbert Colar for the first time over the Thanksgiving holiday. "But that evening he was ambushed and killed." She was amazed that Gaines showed no signs of trauma when, a few days after the murder, he helped her move from her apartment on Collins Street to a larger place on Masonic Avenue. "Ernie was helping, and Jules, Norbert's brother—they were both merchant seamen. Both of them [Ernie and Jules] were helping me move. I was astounded that there was no sign of any atrocity having happened."[105]

Police investigated for more than five months before arresting Leonard Colar on May 8, 1970.[106] Although juvenile records are sealed, newspaper accounts state that he served time at the California Youth Authority and was later transferred to a facility in Oakland. By 1974, he was out of prison.[107]

Despite the horror of losing his beloved stepfather and having his young brother tried and imprisoned, Gaines kept working. In his cramped third-floor walk-up on the corner of Divisadero and Golden Gate, he wrote *Miss Jane,* which he would partially dedicate to the memory of his stepfather.

"Ernie's focus was on writing," said Lawrence, who had settled into a routine with Gaines, both keeping their separate residences. She and Roz lived in a spacious apartment in Ashbury Heights. "He went to Bayonne [his fictional name for the town of New Roads] every day when he sat down to write. He was in his apartment, and he was working. He had a very strict schedule, and he adhered to it. But then he loved to get together with friends."[108]

Linda embraced Gaines's circle of friends, including photographer Edward "Ned" Spring and his wife, Betty, and Francisco "Fran" Ortiz, the first Black photographer at a major Bay Area newspaper, who worked for the *San Francisco Examiner.* Like Ernie, he had attended both Vallejo High School and Vallejo Junior College. (Both men took early book jacket photos of Gaines.) They also hung out with Black poet Michael Harper and with James Alan McPherson, the first African American writer to win the Pulitzer Prize for fiction. "James McPherson—Ernie loved his work," said Lawrence. "*Elbow Room, Crabcakes.* Jim was a pretty weird guy. He'd tell me, 'Be patient with Ernie.'" She introduced Gaines to her friend Tom Uriarte, who later became co-owner of a sailboat with Gaines and taught him to drive a car. "Tom used to tell amazing jokes," said Linda. "Ernie and I would be rolling on the floor laughing."

Gaines did not discuss his work with her. "Our days and nights were mostly about our life and the outer world," said Lawrence. "He didn't tell me a lot about his work." She remembered one exception, when Gaines told her about the character Ned in *Miss Jane.* "He was writing about the little boy carrying the rock and the flints, and he realized that it was the little boy's masculinity."[109]

"We'd have wine and talk about stuff every night after dinner. I was working in the justice system in California and was very angry about the politics of it. I remember him telling me once, 'You complaining about your job really bothers me because I can't help you.'[110]

"Ernie did not have a lot of distractions. He was totally focused on writing. He was not concerned with all the phenomena we wade through in life. He kept his own counsel. I think in some ways he protected his genius by not squandering himself. I'd see women give him the eye, but I never ever felt like Ernie was gonna trot off and be distracted. He had only so much energy to give."[111]

They saw each other several nights a week and every weekend. "Every Friday night we'd go to Ernie's for dinner and watch *I Love Lucy* and *Sanford and Son,*" said Roz Arbel. "On Saturdays, he'd come to our place and we'd watch *All in the Family* and the Saturday night lineup. It was our ritual."[112]

In his three-room apartment that one interviewer described as a "book-and-record-cluttered bachelor apartment [penetrated by] the relentless throb of traffic,"[113] Gaines hung photos of Martin Luther King, William Faulkner, novelist Walter Van Tilburg Clark, and Aunt Teen. Arbel described the neighborhood as "like a ghetto. There were no non-Black people in the neighborhood. If you were not Black and in the area you were out of place. My mom would get all dressed up to go over there, and I was afraid people would think she was a prostitute. Once she stepped on a bullet in Ernie's apartment and she freaked out and said, 'You have to move out!' We concluded it must have ricocheted off something and landed in the apartment."[114]

They spent lots of time watching television, and Gaines indulged his love of film. "We'd stay up late, watching movies," said Arbel.

> Ernie knew all the guys in the movies. I had a crush on Elisha Cook Jr., the first person killed in *The Maltese Falcon.* Ernie would always say, "There's your boy!" He had a TV stand with a couple of books on it. One was a kids' book of *Black Like Me* [written in 1961 by white journalist John Howard Griffin, who passed for Black to write about life on the other side of the racial divide] that I would look at all the time. Another was *Who's That Face?,* a book of actors from the 1920s to the 1950s. I would pore over this book. Ernie would talk about Elisha Cook Jr., Herb Lom, Rondo Hatton, all these bit players. We made a game of spotting them in old movies.

They went to the occasional film festival. "Ernie was obsessed with Humphrey Bogart," said Arbel. "I'd be dragged along to Bogart festivals and fall asleep."

Arbel and Gaines also bonded over music.

> Ernie was always super into music. He'd always buy me records. I was a classical musician for many years. I played violin from seven to eighteen. He liked Chopin, especially the nocturnes. He liked the Romance composers. He had a huge classical collection. We used to go to a place called Doughty's Records on Geary Street. That was *the* place to go. They'd let you listen to records. We went to Tower Records, Odyssey Records, which had three or four floors of classical. He was very supportive of any music I wanted to listen to. He was constantly buying stereos and speakers. On Divisadero he had speakers in

every room. For my twenty-first birthday, he bought me speakers and wired them for surround sound.

In newspaper and magazine articles, Gaines occasionally referred to "Linda," without identifying her further. A 1970 article mentions that he walks several times a week and spends time on Sundays in the park "with the pretty girl named Linda he's been dating regularly. Sometimes they picnic. Sometimes they walk."[115]

In the same interview, Gaines talked about how hard he had worked to keep writing and not take a nine-to-five job or a teaching job. "When I was at San Francisco State, everyone said, 'Get a teaching credential or you'll starve.' I was prepared to starve and to have my way. I didn't want a way out, what to me would be an easy way out—like teaching. The day I knew I couldn't write, I'd teach. But I'd have to write or fall flat on my face or go mad. I hoped it wouldn't come to that." He admitted, "The first ten years were total hell. The first ten years are the hardest, when you need help but haven't produced enough so anybody knows what you can do."[116]

He also mentioned his compulsiveness about time. "I stick to schedules. I like to know what to expect. I don't like people who say they'll be here at eleven to show up at twelve." He told the interviewer he walked seven miles two or three times a week. "Gaines has realized lately that the children in his stories walk a lot. All his people walk. There's a restlessness about some of them."[117]

With help from a Rockefeller Foundation grant-in-aid that he won in 1970, Gaines returned to Louisiana to research the book, again staying with relatives in Baton Rouge. Twice a year, through 1970, he returned to Louisiana to do research. Head librarian Sallie Farrell and her colleague Edith Atkinson at the state library helped with information about the 1912 and 1927 floods. At the LSU library, Evangeline Lynch in the Louisiana Room found books and opened the vertical files to him. "When I came to Louisiana, I'd always visit Miss Lynch," he said. "We would eat cookies and drink coffee from those little tiny cups. She always asked how I was getting along with Miss Jane Pittman."[118]

He read *Lay My Burden Down: A Folk History of Slavery,* absorbing the reminiscences of former slaves, and he looked at photographs of former slaves taken in the 1930s by the Works Progress Administration. He studied the book and the photos until "I knew those faces and those voices."[119] When he needed additional information, Louisiana's lady librarians would copy materials and send them to him. He also read Booker T. Washington's *Up from Slavery* and learned that slaves did three things after emancipation: change their names, move away, and get an education. "So I knew I had to have movement, she had to change her name, and she would try to educate Ned [her adoptive son]."[120]

Throughout the 1960s and 1970s, Gaines made annual or biannual pilgrimages to Louisiana, often at Mardi Gras. He visited relatives and also used the trips to stay in touch with the sights, sounds, and smells of home. "I come back to Louisiana not to look at it under a microscope but to observe it from a distance," he said. "I like the feel of things here: the oak trees, crossing Henderson swamp. I love driving over the swamp. I have a feeling for it without even stopping the car and really looking at it."[121] Each time he returned, he noticed that Cherie Quarters had died a little more. White farmers with tractors were driving out the Black sharecroppers. The oil-and-gas boom came and went. More and more people were leaving.

In the 1960s, Gaines bought a camera and began photographing the quarter—the men and women, the houses, the store, the highway. His black-and-white photographs suggest that he realized the life he had known at Cherie Quarters was dying. The old way of life was fading, like a photograph that slowly loses clarity.[122]

Between trips to Louisiana, Gaines returned to his small San Francisco apartment and wrote about Miss Jane. He originally told the story from multiple points of view. But then, he said, "I fell in love with my little character. I thought she should have more to say about herself." He rewrote the book in Miss Jane's voice.[123] "I had to go back, dig her up, breathe life into her nostrils, and let her tell her own story. I didn't get her voice until I read *Lay My Burden Down*," learning such words as "secesh" and "pater-rollers."[124]

Gaines sought to incorporate into his title the rhythm in the title of Gertrude Stein's *The Autobiography of Alice B. Toklas*. "*Miss Jane* was very consciously constructed," he said. "She doesn't have to be involved in everything [in order to talk about it]. I got that idea from *Alice B. Toklas*." He said Stein, whose work he had first read in college, had influenced his use of repetition. "You find the same sort of thing in jazz, especially Black music," he said. "Her work has made me concentrate on music much more. . . . Stein made me see how I could write what people actually said."[125]

In January 1971, a few months before *Miss Jane* was published, Gaines was invited to spend three weeks as writer in residence at Denison University in

Granville, Ohio. In an article published in the *Denisonian* on his thirty-eighth birthday, Gaines talked about teaching a creative writing class with seven students. "I like it and find it quite interesting—though I don't really think I can teach students to write stories in three weeks—or even three years." The article, accompanied by a photo of a smiling Gaines in a white shirt and tie, noted that his next novel, "a folk autobiography," would be published in April.[126]

The school gave Gaines an apartment for the term. Herman Nibbelink, who taught in the English department at Denison, lived upstairs with his wife, Ellen, and their two young sons. Ellen Nibbelink recalled:

> We had [Ernie] for dinner a few times. . . . He was so easy to have around. I found him unassuming and kind. We had two boys who were two and a half and one at that time. . . . . My most powerful memory is how sweet Ernie was with the little boys. He was very natural with them. The youngest, Karl, was sitting next to him at our kitchen table for one of the meals. Ernie was wearing a long-sleeved shirt that was the same color as his skin. Apparently this intrigued Karl, who at that point had likely not seen a person of color. He reached over, touched Ernie's shirt and then his hand and said, "Same." Ernie just looked at him and smiled with such tenderness. It warmed my heart.[127]

William Nichols, who also taught in the English department there, recalled Gaines as "a charming, wonderful guy to talk with." He had fond memories of Gaines's "joyous laughter" when he was a dinner guest at the home of Nichols and his wife, Nancy.[128] Nichols was teaching a class on Native American and African American folklore that term, and he was especially impressed by student Wrisë Dugger, who interviewed her own family members and wrote up their stories for class assignments.

"Wrisë [pronounced *REES-ah*] and Ernie were the guests of honor that night," recalled Nichols. After dinner, he asked Dugger to read one of her pieces aloud as they sat in the living room. "There was something so powerful and authentic to Wrisë's reading," he remembered. "She performed it, really." In an article he wrote fifty years later, Nichols recalled that night vividly. "[Wrisë] told one of her family's best stories, leading Gaines to laugh so heartily he rose and, bent over, backed down the hall away from us as though getting away from the story might be the only way he could control his laughter."[129]

In his article, Nichols described how reading aloud *The Autobiography of Miss Jane Pittman* to his wife led them to recall that 1971 dinner. "Hearing [Miss Jane's] voice as I read, we both realized how much our shared memory of Ernest Gaines was tempered by the laughter we heard so long ago," he wrote. "We knew her quiet, justified anger must have been alive in the imagination of Gaines, her creator, even on the night he laughed so wonderfully in our house."

Although Nichols did not meet Linda in 1971, she visited at least once. Her presence at Denison was documented by Ellen Nibbelink, who took photos of Lawrence and Gaines, bundled up against the cold, standing on a street covered with snow "in front of our house looking down toward Granville's main street."[130]

Inspired by Gaines's 2019 death and by his recollection of Gaines's visit to his house, Nichols dug through his papers and found a journal entry he had written on January 25, 1971, the day after he, Gaines, and Denison philosophy professor Ronald Santoni had talked about life in Louisiana.[131] Nichols wrote in his journal,

> We talked for a long time last night about the South. Ron Santoni asked Gaines about his attitude toward a place where Black people have been lynched and oppressed. How could he continue to love it?
>
> Gaines began with a sort of theoretical. statement: Black people have been disappointed in their moves from the rural South. In the North their families are fragmented, and they usually feel no relationship with the land at all.
>
> For Ernie, it is terribly important that generations of his people have been buried in Louisiana. Just recently, his grandmother died in California, and her body was shipped to Louisiana to be buried.[132] At the funeral a white woman who had been raised by his grandmother asked permission to take a ring off her [own] finger and leave it in the coffin.
>
> Ernie added to this, however, that no member of his family and no close friend has been lynched; and it may be that fact, in part, that makes it possible for him to return. Also, he added, writing about childhood as he has done might have effects similar to psychoanalysis. He has been able to call back his childhood in great detail, and that experience may have made the South more important to him.[133]

This information from Nichols offered an interesting insight into how Ernest Gaines thought about his home place. Although he said no member of his family had been lynched, he did reveal later that his great-grandfather James McVay "had to leave the plantation during the night" following a confrontation with white men.[134]

I was fascinated by the mention of psychoanalysis. Was Gaines's writing a form of what today we would call (that awful word) "journaling"? Did writing about the injustices of the past help him to somehow come to terms with them? Was he able in some way to "defang" such experiences? Was this conversation a key to what some critics have found to be his overly benevolent view of the past and his refusal to villainize any of his characters?

With the publication of *The Autobiography of Miss Jane Pittman* by Dial Press in 1971, Gaines finally tasted popular success. Her narrative voice was so convincing that many reviewers believed Miss Jane was a real person.[135] Gaines felt vindicated in his decision to write about his plantation past. "In 1968, when I began working on *Miss Jane,* all those big demonstrations were going on on college campuses," he said. "Cops were bashing in heads. And there I was at home writing a story about a little old lady."[136] He later supplied more details.

> I'm not less angry than militants, but I am looking at different aspects of life, at all aspects. . . . When I'm angry, I have a different response. I sit down and try to write the perfect paragraph, the perfect sentence. That's how I strike back.
>
> In 'sixty-eight, I was writing *Miss Jane Pittman* in San Francisco, and there were lots of demonstrations going on at San Francisco State. Cops were brought in. [S. I.] Hayakawa later became a senator because he broke up that demonstration.[137] State is my alma mater, and I was asked to carry a placard. I said, "I can do this better if you let me write this book. It lasts a little bit longer than what I would do on the picket line." In the late fifties and the sixties, there was violence in the South. When I would hear about it, I'd promise myself that the next day I'd write the best page I ever wrote in my life. I fight my battles with the pen and the paper.
>
> Everyone was telling me, "Put away your writing and carry a placard—or write something for the press now, a magazine or a newspaper." I was telling them that I was writing about this little old lady who lived to be 110 and they said, "We don't want to hear that kind of junk. We're talking about action, now. Pick up the gun now."[138]

Gaines summed up his resistance to marching, "I felt that anyone could carry a placard, but not anyone could write a book."[139] He described going to a Black Panthers meeting and getting angry when he was challenged to state the ten points.[140]

Gaines said that although some critics and fellow writers found fault with him for not being militant enough, "I believe it was a very radical thing to write about Miss Jane instead of a woman who was a junkie or a prostitute."[141] Most critics agreed. *Time* magazine's Melvin Maddocks said, "Ernest Gaines may just be the best black writer in America. He is so good, in fact, that he makes the category seem meaningless."[142] The book was nominated for a Pulitzer Prize and won a gold medal from the Commonwealth Club of California.[143] Gaines also won the Louisiana Library Association award for *Miss Jane* (the first time in twenty-five years that the award had been given to a work of fiction) and was pleased to note that Evangeline Lynch, the librarian who had helped and encouraged him, was in the audience. Ultimately, *Miss Jane* would be translated into more than a dozen languages and readers worldwide would find wisdom, humor, and truth in the story of her journey from slavery to the civil rights movement.

After *Miss Jane* came out, Gaines's life got much busier. "Being with Ernie was exciting," recalled Linda Lawrence. "He was a celebrity; there were always things happening." Her daughter, Roz Arbel, said, "They were like party animals, gone all the time. . . . The fame, book tours."[144]

Lawrence hosted a book party at her apartment. "We had so much booze," she said. "We asked a friend to be the bartender, and Ernie's sister Lois made turkey sandwiches. We sent out an invitation with a picture that Fran [photographer Francisco Ortiz] had taken of Ernie and me. People thought we were getting married!"[145]

Gaines's short story "A Long Day in November" was published as a standalone book in December 1971, when Roz was eight. Told in the voice of six-year-old Sonny, the story depicts a day in the life of a plantation quarter in every way like Cherie Quarters, including the church/school. Sonny's mother, Amy, disgusted by her husband, Eddie's, neglect of his family after he purchases a car, takes her son and moves into her mother's house. After trying various ways to win back Amy, Eddie follows the advice of Madame Toussaint to "burn it," and Amy and Sonny return home with him.

"I was thrilled when he came out with a children's book," Arbel said, adding that her relationship with the author impressed her teacher at her school in the Tenderloin district.

> I had a teacher who was very Afrocentric, Mrs. Livingston. She had a big Afro, wore dashikis, tried to teach us Swahili. She found out that Ernie was my dad, and she was insanely excited. She begged me to bring him in to talk to the class.
>
> He came in and read from *A Long Day in November.* When he got to the part about "I had to pee-pee," the whole class busted out laughing. I was mortified. Ernie laughed and waited for them to stop giggling. It's not really a children's book.[146]

Not long after *Miss Jane* was published, Gaines's agent Dorothea Oppenheimer was contacted by a CBS Television representative who wanted to buy the film rights. "They offered $12,500," Gaines recalled. "I said, 'Tell them to go to hell.' I decided not to take less than $50,000." He got it. "According to the producers, that was big money," he said, although he had to pay Oppenheimer her 10 percent and "Uncle Sam got part." But Gaines "did not get one cent in royalties" because the producers "say they never made their expenses back." He had learned from the experience. "I will never deal with net again. I'll deal with gross. Net means when everything is paid off, then they pay you."[147] But the money gave him a measure of financial stability for the first time in his career.

Gaines returned to Louisiana in late 1972 to help select sites for the film starring Cicely Tyson. Although he visited the set in St. Francisville in West Feliciana Parish, he hastened to point out that he was there merely as a guest, not a consultant. "I was offered the position of technical adviser on the film, but I turned it down," he said. "I wanted to officially have nothing to do with the film. My job is to write fiction the best way I know how."[148] Gaines said he had since been offered other script-writing projects but had refused them, too. Years later, he would tell an interviewer that he turned down Hollywood offers because, "I've read about what happened to F. Scott Fitzgerald, and it worries me."[149]

Linda and Ernie threw a party at her apartment to celebrate the television film of *Miss Jane,* which first aired on January 31, 1974. "I love parties where every room is filled and it spills out into the streets and the cops come," she said. "At this party, everybody roamed the whole place. Everybody came happy.

Gaines and Linda Lawrence in San Francisco, 1975. He and Lawrence were involved for sixteen years, although they maintained separate residences. Photo courtesy of Linda Lawrence.

We had great parties. We'd sit there and look at each other and say, 'This is so amazing!'"[150]

In May 1974, Lawrence accompanied Gaines to the Emmy Awards at the Pantages Theatre in Los Angeles. *Miss Jane* won nine Emmys, including best actress for Cicely Tyson, best director for John Korty, and best screenplay for Tracy Keenan Wynn. Linda dressed up for the occasion. "I remember the dress she wore; she cut a very elegant figure," said Arbel.[151] Gaines said of watching the film, "I cried like everybody else."[152]

The CBS movie was seen by 85 million viewers. One of the first made-for-TV movies to treat African American characters with depth and sympathy, it preceded the groundbreaking miniseries *Roots* by three years. Gaines was pleased with the program, considering that the director had to squeeze one hundred years into a two-hour program. But he found fault with some of the production values. "Lots of small details were wrong, like showing Miss Jane in a bed with no mosquito netting," he said. "Or showing a clothesline pulled taut instead of slack."[153]

He thought that *Miss Jane* and Alex Haley's *Roots,* published in 1976, had had a positive influence. "We've given young black writers a new approach," he said. "They don't have to just write about ghettoes and playing jazz." He was also pleased that youngsters could identify with him. "I visited half a dozen elementary schools in Louisiana," he said. "Everywhere I went, kids would come up to me and talk about the film. For the first time, they could come up to a black writer and say, 'I know that person!'"

Around 1974, Linda and Roz accompanied Gaines to Washington and Oregon. At a panel discussion at Lewis and Clark College in Portland, said Roz, "Ernie got confronted by two African students who called him an Uncle Tom. They said that because he wrote about slave times, he was promoting the story of Blacks being downtrodden. Ernie handled himself really well."[154]

Just after Easter, in April 1976, Lawrence attended a conference in New Orleans, and Gaines met her there for a few days. "Ernie was really apprehensive about the two of us being in New Orleans [as an interracial couple], but we had a better time there than we did in San Francisco," she said. "I booked us a room on Dauphine Street and we had a few days together."[155]

After Gaines left for a speaking engagement in Texas, Lawrence visited his birthplace in Oscar, which she had never seen. "For me, it was where Ernie was from—and especially Miss Teen," she said. She called Gaines's great-uncle Horace McVay, who agreed to meet her at the bus station in Baton Rouge. "I took the Greyhound bus from New Orleans," Lawrence said. "Horace was standing there with his arms folded across his chest. I had never met him, although I had met his wife, Octavia [who had died in January 1975]."

Horace took Linda to his house in New Roads, where they lunched on chicken and drank whiskey. Then they drove to Oscar.

> He took me to the quarters. People were doing fieldwork. Pete Zeno [Walter Zeno, the model for the character Mathu in *A Gathering of Old Men*] was there. I swear that guy had some amazing mojo. In his yard there were blossoms on the trees. There were plants coming up. There was life teeming everywhere at his place. I remember going up on the gallery to look inside, and Horace said, "Don't do that."

> [We] went way out to the cemetery. He wanted to show me where Augusteen Jefferson was buried. He went to a tree and then counted out so many steps and stopped. We stood there together and thought about her. It was just before a storm; there was a lot of wind. It was monochromatic except for the daylilies, orange and deep pink. Ernie was so much from that land.

In 1976, Gaines was interviewed by a *San Francisco Chronicle* reporter, who noted that he "divides his time between his apartment and that of a woman friend and her twelve-year-old daughter." While talking over sherry, Gaines "self-consciously fiddles with his new carved ebony walking stick, a gift from the woman he calls 'my lady Linda.'"[156]

"I had got a walking stick for Ernie that needed a top on it," Lawrence said. "Ernie and Rozzie and I designed a silver cap for it. Ernie wanted a poppy on one side for California and an oak leaf for Louisiana on the other. On top was a little crown that Rozzie designed."[157]

"Some of his writing reflects not only past and present Louisiana attitudes but his own experiences in San Francisco," noted reporter Blake Green. "When he writes of the problems of interracial relationships, for example, he has his own with Linda to draw upon. This may well be one of the reasons Gaines has not gone back to Louisiana to live, but it is not, he insists why they have never married."

Gaines told the *Chronicle* reporter, "I'm a lonist [*sic*]—so much of a loner, so caught up in my work that I could not be at all times what I should be. There are so few of us [Black writers] and we have so much to do. I feel I have to do my share and I put that before things, people, family. Even, sometimes, before myself."[158]

Five years earlier, shortly after the publication of *Miss Jane,* Gaines had told another interviewer, "The South is where I'd live if I could, if it were possible to live and write as I want, to have Linda, my white woman, with me." [159] Arbel said that the situation, even for California, "was kind of groundbreaking stuff. She [Linda] actually got some shit from the sistas [Black women]: 'You and your kind' [stealing hardworking Black men from Black women]. He's a good-looking, smart, potentially successful Black man."[160]

"It wasn't easy being a Black man with a white lady," Lawrence said. "There were articles that would mention 'pictures on the wall of his white girlfriend.'

Ernie and I just passed it off. . . . My relationship with Ernie wasn't that easy for him."[161]

Eventually, the fact that they didn't get married upset Lawrence. "He didn't want to marry," she said. "He used to say, 'I don't want to leave somebody with nothing.' All our friends were married, and they all split up. I think we should have married, but it was up to Ernie. We would just *say* we were married. It was not something we had arguments or fights about at all. Many people wanted to marry him."[162]

In a 1982 interview, Gaines made comments that seemed to reflect his deteriorating relationship with Lawrence. "[I've] never been married, but women have tried," he said. "But I've fought it." He added that he was attracted to "women who love bars. Fast women. I love them and they love me." Asked if he had any regrets, he told interviewer Jeanie Blake, "I regret that I don't have a twenty-five-year-old daughter, someone to take care of me when I have a cold. A daughter would make me coffee and put a scarf around my neck."[163]

"They were basically common-law husband and wife," said Arbel, who would have been happy to play that caring daughter role. "It's quite a tragedy that they never got married. They even talked about having a kid. They had a name picked out—Wesley. Kind of a cool name, Wes Gaines. They talked a lot about Wesley." An only child, Roz liked the idea. "Yeah, I wanted a sibling, of course," she said.[164]

# 3

# THE HOUSE AND THE SCHOOL

## WRITER IN RESIDENCE

*The next few years would be years of change for Gaines. He found a new, larger place to live in San Francisco, saw the publication of* In My Father's House, *and his long-term relationship with Linda Lawrence ended. He still considered San Francisco home, but he would spend more time in Louisiana, traveling there more often, thanks to a new connection with a city some fifty miles west of the plantation where he grew up—the town of Lafayette in the heart of "Cajun country." He began a relationship that would be central to his life—as writer in residence at a Louisiana university. Cherie Quarters was still home to several of the "old people" who told him about the past, and he returned to the quarter as the setting for his next novel,* A Gathering of Old Men.

. . . .

In 1978, Gaines moved from his cramped apartment to a sunny eight-room flat a couple of doors down on Divisadero Street in the primarily Black, working-class neighborhood where he had lived since 1963. He filled his new place with books and phonograph records—jazz, blues, and classical discs.

Linda Lawrence explained that his decision to move was based on economics: the landlord at his original apartment was raising the rent. "Ernie got a notice that they were doubling the rent. He wasn't going to pay that kind of rent. He was very upset. We looked and looked. I tried to talk to my parents about a down payment."[1] But although most of Gaines's family had readily embraced his love and her daughter, Linda's parents resisted meeting Gaines out of prejudice, despite the fact that her father had chatted with him amiably at a party years before. "Ernie never got to meet my family," said Lawrence. "That was sad, heartbreaking."[2]

Gaines had left the segregated South and found success in California, but he was still running up against the wall of prejudice. “My parents refused to meet him,” said Lawrence, whose mother died in 1981 and whose Boston-born father died in 1995. “I was aghast. We would have had such fun together. I feel sad for them. They missed out.” In his way, Gaines exacted revenge. “My maiden name is Bryant. Ernie gave my parents’ last name, Bryant, to the slave-owning couple in *Miss Jane Pittman*.”[3]

Roz Arbel recalled, “They had almost enough to buy a house but asked my grandparents for a loan to finish the rest. My grandparents refused because, well, my stepdad was Black. Also my mom felt weird about me having to walk through the neighborhood by myself, which at the time was ghetto.”[4]

Gaines’s southern good manners helped him find his new place. “Ernie would always help the ladies in the neighborhood carry their groceries,” said Lawrence. “Many of them had worked as domestics, and many were paid in property given to them by the people they worked for. When they learned he was looking for a place, they spread the word. The landlady lived on the same block.

“A gay couple had skipped out on the rent, so Ernie moved in,” she continued. “They left a lot of their furnishings there, very nice Danish modern. He bought a leather couch. I made curtains for his studio. Two guys who worked for the landlady helped him fix it up, and he had it painted.”[5]

Gaines worked hard on his new place, which was much roomier than his old one. “He had a little room set up as a bar,” said Lawrence. “He had snapshots on the walls. In the front room he had shutters built. Of course it had no heat, maybe [space] heaters. Ernie said I had to realize that he had a place for the first time that he could do something with.” Having grown up in Cherie Quarters, where he had shared a bed with his brothers, then living in crowded housing complexes and duplexes in Vallejo, in barracks in the army, and in tiny apartments in San Francisco, Gaines relished being able to spread out, buy furniture, and display his collections of books and records.

The move prefigured the eventual breakup of Gaines and Lawrence. “As soon as he moved in, he and my mom started fighting,” said Arbel. “He would get on my mother about not having dinner ready when he walked in the door. Sometimes he’d just leave. My mother was so late for everything, and Ernie’s whole thing was being on time.”[6] “Ernie would get upset if dinner was slightly late. He would abort. If dinner was late, he would just leave. We’re talking like five or ten minutes late. He'd say, 'Woman, where's my dinner?' He'd call her 'woman' all the time. My poor mom was working full time and racing home to cook. Cooking takes a long time. He was cool about it, usually, but he was very, very into being punctual. My mother has never been on time in her life."[7]

"We split up around 1983, but we had a really bad time before then," said Lawrence. "He'd be angry just out of the blue."[8] Gaines was also critical of what he called Arbel's lack of discipline, having been brought up strictly himself. "Ernie takes no prisoners," said Arbel.

> He was not always a nice person. Growing up, I'd see how he'd treat my mom, and so as not to be in the same boat, I'd be the supplicant, the clown. As problematic as he was, I was always the one who could make Ernie laugh. When I was a kid, I'd say, "Artistic temperament is just an excuse for being an asshole." That's because I grew up with someone who everyone said had an "artistic temperament."[9]
>
> There wasn't a big blowup. He was just really hard to live with. My mom ended it. He was very difficult. He did a lot of passive-aggressive stuff. He could be really cruel. In some ways we were scared of him. He'd have temper flares. . . . He'd be a jerk sometimes. He made her feel less than worthy. She was very sad about it.[10]

In the mid-1980s, Lawrence left for an extended hiatus in Asia, spending time in India and Nepal. "I wrote Ernie a couple of letters from there," she said. "He said he didn't read them because he couldn't read my writing. I would spend a day writing a letter meant to be a very loving communication. Everybody else saved them and gave them back to me."[11]

The breakup was hard on Arbel, too. "I'm pissed about it," she said many years later. "I'm like the only kid that guy's ever gonna have. It boggles my mind. It caused a lot of sadness for me. I'm bitter about it."[12]

After Gaines and her mother broke up, Roz stayed in touch with Gaines, and even stayed at his flat for a time when he was in Louisiana. "It must have been 1987-ish that I last spoke to him," she said. She understood why he would lose touch with her mother. "I tell her, 'You're the ex.' But not talking to somebody who was basically your only child? I'm probably the closest thing Ernie will ever have to a kid."

I had seen other examples of Ernie's ability to walk away from people. Early in our professional relationship, I met his friends Aubrey and Mary Ricard, who were among the first people to hold book signings for him in Baton Rouge. Aubrey, friendly and engaging, sold clothing at one of the city's quality men's stores. Mary, quiet and ladylike, was a librarian. At one point, when Ernie was living in Lafayette, they lent him an automobile for a year. In the mid-1980s, Ernie's sister Lois, her husband, Chet, and another California couple visited Louisiana. Aubrey and Mary hosted them, Ernie, and two other friends, first for drinks at their house and then for dinner at one of Baton Rouge's fancier restaurants, where they had reserved a private dining room. Ernie announced that night that he would be awarded an honorary doctorate at LSU that spring. I have a photo of him with Aubrey and Mary at the reception afterwards.

Sometime in 1992, however, the Ricards and Ernie had a falling out. I never was clear about the reasons, but Ernie stopped seeing them. I had become friends with them myself by the time I completed the documentary, and I called to invite them to the premiere. Aubrey answered the phone and told me they wouldn't come because of hurt feelings over the misunderstanding. "If you won't come for Ernie, please come for me," I asked him. They did.

Later I got a note from Ernie thanking me for "the film [and] Aubrey and Mary," and I understood there had been a rapprochement. But I don't think the relationship was ever again as close as it had been. Knowing how good-hearted the Ricards were, I never really understood the breach. But I saw that Ernie had an ability to compartmentalize his life. No doubt that was what enabled him to focus so clearly on his work, but it could be hurtful. It was that ability to turn his back and walk away that probably inspired Roz Arbel's comment that he "takes no prisoners."[13]

Ironically, the protagonist of Gaines's next book was a father who abandons his child. While supplementing his income with visiting professorships at campuses throughout the country, Gaines had struggled for seven years to write *In My Father's House,* about the gulf between African American fathers and sons.

"We know that on the slave block . . . families were separated," he said. "I feel that because of that separation they still have not, philosophically speaking, reached each other again. I don't know what it will take to bring them together again. . . . I don't know that the father . . . can reach out and bring his son back to him again."[14] The novel differs markedly from *Jane Pittman* in a

Gaines in front of the house on Louise Street in Baton Rouge, where he lived while writing *Catherine Carmier*. This photo was taken in September 1978, following an interview by the author. Photo by Ruth Laney.

number of ways—its contemporary and largely urban setting, its middle- and upper-class Black characters, and its focus on contemporary issues such as civil rights, leadership, and moral/ethical responsibility.

When the book was published in 1978, reviews were mixed. It was favorably reviewed by the *New York Times,* the *Washington Post,* and *Newsweek.* But writer friends James Baldwin and James Alan McPherson both declined to review the book. "I think the people who criticized it feel that the book is not vintage Gaines," Ernie told me. "For example, Jimmy Baldwin thought that it was a farce, the entire thing. He wrote me a personal letter to tell me why he would not make [public] comments on it." Baldwin, Ernie said, had written, "It seems like you just put it together in six months, just threw it together to get something out there to the public" to follow up on the success of *Miss Jane.* "I think from his letter that's what he thought I had done," said Ernie, noting that in fact he had "worked and reworked and reworked" the book. Jim McPherson, who won the Pulitzer Prize that year for his collection of short stories, *Elbow Room,* also "said he could not make a comment on it either." Ernie paused a few seconds and added, "They *were* friends."

“I had some bad news yesterday,” he added. Dorothea Oppenheimer had told him Knopf had not sold paperback rights to the book and she wasn’t sure if they would. “That book has been a jinx from the beginning,” he said. “So maybe I’ll have to hurry up and get something on this one. I can probably get an advance on this one any time.”[15]

“This one” was his next novel, tentatively titled *The Revenge of Old Men.* For the first time, he was telling his entire story in the voice of a white person—Lou Dimes, a Cajun newspaperman engaged to the daughter of wealthy plantation owners. In the beginning of the book, Gaines said, a white man has been killed and Dimes is interrogating the Black people on the plantation. “Everyone is going to tell him ‘I did it.’” Gaines said his choice of a white narrator was giving him problems. “If that book was not being told by my quote Cajun quote, I could finish it off in six to eight months. But since it is going to be told by a guy I created and whom I’m beginning to like, I’m going to have to get involved with the Cajuns—and I don’t know a thing about them. I think I know some of the dialect.”[16]

He eventually decided not to make Dimes the narrator but to tell the story from multiple viewpoints. He retitled the book *A Gathering of Old Men.* The basic plot remained the same: a white man is found shot to death in the front yard of a Black man on the plantation. “Fifteen or sixteen old people gather there. They have never really stood up for anything. This is their last chance to do anything.”[17]

In 1980, the Public Broadcasting System released a film of Gaines’s short story “The Sky Is Gray.” Set during World War II, the story is told in the voice of James, an eight-year-old boy with a bad toothache. In many ways, James reflects the young Ernest Gaines. He lives with his mother, aunt, and brothers in a plantation quarter and is trying to be the man of the family because his father, a soldier, is fighting overseas. James and his mother catch the bus on a bitterly cold day and ride to town to see the dentist. At noon, forced outside until the office reopens after lunch, they walk up and down the streets, with no money to go inside and eat. They are befriended by a white woman who serves them a meal in exchange for James’s carrying her trash cans, which are clearly empty, to the curb.

Gaines was disappointed with the film, whose thirteen-year-old lead actor was too old to play eight-year-old James. He noted that the landscape was all wrong, because the film had been shot in California instead of Louisiana. In a biographical sketch appended to the film, Gaines said that the story "was not autobiographical, but I had myself and my mother in mind when I was writing. I had gone to the town [New Roads] quite often. I know the river well." He also cited Hemingway's influence, particularly his notion of grace under pressure. "The child must not complain about the pain of his tooth, about hunger, about cold," he said. "Also from Hemingway I learned understatement. For example, only white people [in the story] are very nice [to James and his mother]. They offer food and warmth and shelter. Yet you know that it is because of race relations problems in the South that they must go back of town [to the Black section] for a cookie or a glass of water."[18]

In the fall of 1981, Gaines taught a class in creative writing at the University of Southwestern Louisiana in Lafayette. He had avoided teaching, fearing it would take time from his work, but economic necessity finally forced it upon him. Interestingly, the school that hired him was not the state's flagship university, Louisiana State, but USL, the first white university in the state to admit African Americans, though it was still known as Southwest Louisiana Institute when its administrators admitted Black students in 1954. The school provided Gaines with a tiny apartment in married students' housing. The following year, he returned and taught a class in the spring semester. I sat in on one class and laughed when he addressed plotting problems. "The third chapter is the hard one. Chapter one, the cowboy rides into town. Chapter two, he meets the bad guy. Chapter three—I don't know what the hell's going on."[19]

In the spring of 1982, I met his English department colleague Jane Bonin, who was working on a "critical biography" about Gaines for the Twayne series on American authors. A small, energetic blonde woman with a great sense of humor, Jane invited me to her "little cottage" for lunch. Sitting in her colorful garden, we chatted about our mutual interest in Ernie's work. Jane, who had recently published a Twayne book on Italian playwright Mario Fratti, suggested that I write the first three chapters of the Gaines book, the biographical portion, while she focused on critical analyses of his work. "There has been no full-length critical treatment," she said.

I happily agreed, and we began meeting almost weekly in Baton Rouge, and sometimes in Lafayette. As we tried to work out a chronology, we sat down with Ernie for an interview. We soon realized that he was reluctant to go into detail about his life. Even the simplest questions were sidestepped: How many of his brothers and sisters were born in Louisiana and how many in California? Who was the father of which children? We were a bit stymied by his reluctance—by his, in Jane's words, "rolling out the myth, which is enchanting, instead of [giving us] hard data."[20] But we kept plugging away, exchanging notes on a chronology and editing each other's drafts.

There were fun times, too. One of Ernie's colleagues at USL was English professor and poet Darrell Bourque. One night Ernie, Jane, and I gathered at the home of Darrell and his wife, Karen. As Ernie sat on the couch with his glass of Courvoisier, Darrell put some jazzy tunes on the phonograph and asked the ladies to dance, one by one. Ernie didn't dance, but he approved of others doing it. I once took him to Tabby's Blues Box in Baton Rouge. We sat at a small, tipsy table, drinking dollar beers, and he chuckled at the antics of a decked-out woman and her young partner who stepped to the blues on the tiny dance floor.

Jane wrote to me in May 1982, lamenting Ernie's departure from USL after a semester of teaching. "He contributed so much to our department, raised the general consciousness, caused hardened bigots to fall in love with him, etc. Thank God it's been arranged for him to come back from time to time. We need him to keep the level of civilization up."[21]

Back in San Francisco, Gaines's work on *A Gathering of Old Men* was interrupted by an unfortunate accident. In June 1983, he fell down the stairs at his friend Sam Bibbens's apartment, damaging the patella tendon in his left knee, which required a two-hour surgery to repair. For the next six months, he would undergo physical therapy to rehabilitate his knee.[22] Linda Lawrence recalled it as "a very bad fall. He stepped on a magazine and went right down the stairs. He said it was hard to do any activity with that knee. Walking up and down stairs was really hard."[23]

Late that summer, still not fully recuperated from his knee surgery, Gaines flew to Lafayette to prepare for his fall semester creative writing class. He was met at the airport by his friend Carl Wooton, who taught English at USL. While driving Gaines to his student apartment, Wooton detoured to an elegant subdivision called Arbolada, near the USL campus. He pulled up in front of a brick house with a neatly manicured lawn and magnolia trees shading the side yard. "Let's go in for a minute, Ernie," he said. "There's a lady here who has read all your books, and she wants to meet you." Gaines demurred. The long flight from San Francisco had left him tired and rumpled, and his knee hurt. "I just wanted to go to my apartment, get cleaned up, and get some rest," he said. But Wooton persisted, pleading, "It'll just take five minutes." Reluctantly, Gaines limped up the walk to the house.[24]

As he stepped into the living room, his eyes were drawn to an oil painting of himself hanging over the fireplace. *Why is that here?* he wondered. Then he spied an enormous photograph of himself on the opposite wall. People began drifting into the room—Lafayette friends and fellow teachers from USL. Albert Fields, chairman of the English department, stepped forward and handed the stunned Gaines a set of keys. "This is your home now, Ernie," he said.[25]

The house, a gift of Lafayette attorney Ray Mouton and his wife Janis, had two bedrooms, a study, a glassed-in porch, a formal dining room, and a breakfast nook. Mouton, who had persuaded local merchants to donate furniture, estimated the value of the house and furnishings at more than $265,000. Both graduates of USL, the Moutons gave the house to the university in Gaines's honor, to be used by him whenever he returned to Louisiana. In a welcoming letter, Mouton wrote, "Please accept the gift of this home in honor of Miss Jane, Catherine, and the Old Men." Mouton stipulated that the house was to be always available to Gaines.[26]

Explaining his motive, Mouton said that, after watching the 1974 television version of *Miss Jane Pittman,* his seven-year-old son had "talked about it for five days. For the story to have that type of impact on a young white boy in the South, it had to be exceptional."[27]

On a weekend in late September 1983, the annual Deep South Writers Conference was held at USL, with several sessions devoted to Ernie. The big event would be on Sunday—a formal presentation of the house to him. Ernie's agent, Dorothea Oppenheimer, flew in from New York for several days. My notes describe her as a rather dour woman in her sixties who had "escaped with her family from Nazi Germany." I added, "She is a difficult woman, with what private demons one can only guess, but it is clear that in her way she loves Ernie. He responds to her with affectionate tolerance. She hints at dark secrets she knows about him—family matters—but does not divulge them." Jane Bonin and I told Dorothea about our planned book. I noted that she was "difficult about dealing with both of us."

I was curious about Dorothea, who even now is a somewhat mysterious figure in Ernie's life. When I met her she was sixty-four, likely already suffering from the pancreatic cancer that would claim her life just three and a half years later. I knew that she also represented novelist Larry McMurtry, who had been in Ernie's class at Stanford. McMurtry described her as "a wonderful if eccentric woman who got through life on an intricate balance of beauty and bravura. [She] was born in a castle on the Danube and died in a one-room apartment on York Avenue in New York City. . . . Dorothea Oppenheimer had 'quality,' even in the dusty apartment on York Avenue, and unto the hour of her death." Although Irving "Swifty" Lazar was in fact representing him, McMurtry wrote, "A dying, impoverished European woman got the credit . . . for selling *Lonesome Dove*."[28]

Ernie's Knopf editor, Ashbel Green, also flew to Lafayette that weekend. Saturday night, he accompanied Ernie and Dorothea to Jane's house for dinner. Ernie clearly enjoyed Ash's company, and a good bit of the conversation was about sports. Over a meal of pâté, cornichons, fresh French bread, green salad, and Jane's specialty crabmeat dish, we drank white wine, talked, laughed, and had a merry time—at least four of us did. I later wrote in my journal, "Dorothea refuses to be happy. She appears to be one of those persons determined to look on the negative side of life."

Years later, when I spoke to Gaines scholar and friend John Callahan, he described his own encounters with Dorothea. "She was a pretty strange woman," he said. "I spoke to her on the phone once. She was very much a prickly pear." When he met her in person, he said, "She seemed pretty frail. She may have already been ill. A strange woman. I often wondered whether she was a bit overly protective. He was her special writer. I thought we could get a Norton critical edition of *Miss Jane,* get the book wider play. As soon as she understood that I was interested in including the movie, she was rude and unhelpful. I've got to wish he had had a real pro. I found her impossible, insistent on being catered to."[29] After dinner at Jane's, we repaired to Ernie's new house for a party with lots of people and free-flowing liquor. "Toward midnight, Ernie could be found seated, resting his leg," I wrote.

Sunday, Ernie gave a reading from *A Gathering of Old Men* at the final day of the Deep South conference. He ended with the moving passage "I'm the last one left. I had to see that the graves stayed for a little while longer. But I just didn't do it for my own people. I did it for every last one back there under them trees. And it did it for every four o'clock, every rosebush, every palm-of-Christian ever growed on this place."

Then it was announced that Ray and Janis Mouton had donated the Arbolada house to USL for Ernie's use. He accepted "in honor of all the Jane

Pittmans . . . and Old Men of the world who have worked hard and suffered." To express his gratitude, he gave the Moutons autographed first editions of all his works, which Dorothea had tracked down in New York bookshops. Jane and I had wrapped each one individually.

The Moutons invited all present to a jazz brunch at their new house in the nearby town of Carencro. After a thirty-minute drive, we arrived at a house I described as "impressive," with "eighteen-inch floorboards, thick white walls, and lots of doors and windows open to the insects." There was champagne, catered food, and a jazz quartet. Guests roamed over a spacious lawn with a gazebo and a fishpond. Ernie was gracious to everyone who wanted to chat with him, but he showed signs of fatigue. It had been a jam-packed weekend, and his knee was still painful.

As we left the party, with Jane driving and Ernie in front, his stiff leg stuck straight out in front of him, Jane gave him a sidelong look. "Well, Ernie," she said. "You've come a long way since they wouldn't let you into the public library." She said it with affection, and he took it that way, laughing and shaking his head.

### "NOTHING PRIVATE AND PERSONAL"

In late November, Jane and I got a bit more insight into Ernie's agent, when Dorothea sent a letter throwing cold water on our projected book.

> November 21, 1983
>
> Dear Jane,
>
> You've been such a good friend to Ernie—a real guardian angel, and I'm so grateful. When Ernie said on the phone not long ago, "I *love* Jane" (he said it twice), I wasn't even jealous, or at least not very jealous.
>
> Now comes the bad part: Ernie said yesterday that you and Ruth Laney asked him questions about his life and he didn't like it. (This is in confidence. He doesn't like people to discuss him either and would probably be annoyed at me for telling you.) This brought up a whole complexity of problems all having to do with the fact that I said I would make my Gaines files available to you. I did not realize when I said this to what extent my files contained a lot of very personal material. Also, perhaps more importantly, I thought then that your book was going to be of a scholarly nature dealing very largely with his work. Now I realize with a shock that it is turning into a biography rather

than a scholarly study. I love biographies. But I've always felt that a person's life should not be pried into in his/her lifetime and not after, until some distance can be achieved. All this apart from the fact that Ernie has specifically asked me not to open up my files to anyone in his lifetime.

All is not lost, however. You can have all the information you want and need for a work of scholarship—even it if it has biographical elements provided nothing private and personal is revealed. This leaves a whole lot that you can get a head start on for your project. We can discuss the various aspects when you come here [New York City] next month, to which I have been looking forward very much. I think at this point, perhaps, Ernie and I (as his agent) ought to be given an idea about the specific nature of your project, so that I, in particular, can start looking for the information you want. I have (sigh) 27 years of filed material (not counting several hundred unfiled letters).[30]

I would like to make you my "literary executor" if there is such a thing for literary agents. We can discuss that too. If you live long enough, perhaps you'll be the one to do the definitive biography. So be patient!![31]

Once I like a person I very rarely change, as Ernie already told you.

Besides the lunch, I'd love to go see a play with you. Do you have any particular one you long to see?

Fondly,

Dorothea [signed by hand][32]

In December, Jane flew to New York, where she saw both Dorothea and Ashbel Green. In mid-January, she called to tell me: "Dorothea worked me over. I can't decide whether to make her a key figure [in the book]. We had a long talk over lunch at her apartment. She professes deep, undying affection for me. She said, 'Ernie isn't going to tell you anything he hasn't already told you.' I told her I was just getting chronological lineage. She doesn't know a lot of it herself."[33] Jane also told me that when they talked in New York, Dorothea had confided that she and Ernie had been romantically involved for a time, when both lived in San Francisco.

I was dismayed to hear Jane say of our book, "It's not trade, not academic. The combination of journalism and critical study is not workable. I'm thinking now that two people writing the book is scaring them. We could work around it by doing short pieces separately."

Despite Dorothea's lack of enthusiasm for the project, Jane and I kept working on the book; we even talked about traveling to California for research. But eventually, having encountered so many roadblocks, we abandoned the idea, and our planned book never materialized.[34]

Gaines's fifth novel, *A Gathering of Old Men,* was published in late 1983. Reviews were enthusiastic, and the book won Gaines a second gold medal from the Commonwealth Club of California. He had based the protagonist, Mathu, on Walter Zeno, the man who had told him stories about the plantation's past. (He also dedicated the book to the memory of Zeno.) He admitted to borrowing traits from others, such as the character Dirty Red, based on "a brother who smoked like that, letting the ash get really long, and liked to tell long stories."[35] Asked about his keen ear for dialect, reflected in the voices of the characters who tell the story—ranging from old African American men to children, Black and white women, white men, and Cajuns—he said, "When I was writing about Miss Merle, I'd become this elderly white woman. When I was writing about Snookum, I'd become that little boy. You live with that character for a week. You have to listen very well. You have to be aware of people. They speak differently."

### TENURE

In 1983, USL offered Gaines a lifeline—tenure and a contract to teach creative writing every year during the fall semester. "USL came through when I was just about down and out," he said later.[36] Still, his feelings about teaching, and about being a lionized Black author on a mostly white campus, were always mixed. "I think anyone who has some reputation, some influence, causes change just by being there," he said. "I think my being on the campus does have some effect. . . . I can tell both Black and white students things about conditions which they will never experience." But he also saw the irony in the fact that most of his students at USL were white.

> I don't have Blacks in [my class]. I know the reason they're not in the class. Writing takes a lot of time, and as a kid [in my class] said, "Suppose I don't make it." If I don't make it as a writer, what do I do with this time? Because most of them will not make it. I tell those middle-aged and middle-class white women, "I know you have the time. Your husband can afford to pay your bills. You don't have to go to work, or if you go to work, you still have time to write, because you have someone else keeping the house, to clean up the house. So

> you put your couple hours a night into your work if you want to." But making a living at it is not the easiest thing in the world. It's really tough. When you're writing the novel or the short story today, it's almost a love or maybe it's something driven in you to do it. But I would not recommend anyone to go into writing today. . . . The serious story or novel, it's impossible to make money on it.[37]

In December 1984, Ernie asked me to accompany him to Lee High School in Baton Rouge, where he had been invited to give a reading. As we drove up to the school, he cast a wary eye on the sign with the school's name. "*Robert E. Lee* High School, huh?" he muttered.[38] Inside, a large Confederate flag was displayed in the main hallway; the school's football team was the Rebels. The white principal stepped forward to grasp Ernie's hand. "Mr. Gaines, we're so pleased that you could come to our school today," he said reverentially. A female student rushed up and threw her arms around Ernie.

Carlette White was the daughter of family friends. A pretty, light-skinned girl, she clung to Ernie's arm lovingly. "This is my daddy," she said, rubbing her head against his shoulder. Ernie chuckled fondly.

Carlette wore a tan pantsuit and a tan beret that Ernie had given her. She ushered us into the school library, where about forty students and teachers had gathered. She had decorated the bulletin board with copies of Ernie's book covers and red letters that spelled out "Welcome to Lee High School Ernest Gaines / We Appreciate Your Coming." The books displayed on a table were her personal copies.

Carlette introduced Ernie, reading from small note cards, then yielded the lectern and microphone. Ernie immediately glared at a young man in the audience who was chatting audibly to a friend. "Either I talk or you talk," he told the offender. Then, a minute later, "I mean it." Having been raised strictly himself, he didn't tolerate disrespectful behavior.

After reading from *A Gathering of Old Men,* Ernie told the class about his life. Some of the boys in the room looked as if they'd rather be anywhere else. "As a child I loved reading," Ernie told them. "At sixteen, I discovered libraries, books, all these kinds of things. I just fell in love with them. The more I read, the more I loved books."

He told them he had rewritten *Catherine Carmier* twelve, maybe twenty times. "Rewriting is necessary so you have something you can be proud of ten or twenty years later. It pays off in the end, if you do your work well." Even after becoming a writer, he told them, "I wondered if I had made the right choice. But there was nothing else in my life I'd be. I made that decision at sixteen, that I would be a writer, and I'd just have to suffer the consequences."

He admitted, "The books have not been supporting me that well. Even as famous as *Miss Jane Pittman* is, no one out there knows my name, as that American Express card commercial says."[39] He mentioned that *A Gathering of Old Men* had excited interest from movie producers, but "no one has his name on the dotted line yet."

### SHOOTING *A GATHERING*

Soon enough, CBS made an offer, and by November 1986 a film crew came to Louisiana. Richard Widmark, then seventy-two, came out of retirement to play Sheriff Mapes, and Louis Gossett Jr. played the book's hero, Mathu, the only Black man on Marshall Plantation who has consistently stood up to white people. Holly Hunter, just starting out in films, played plantation owner Candy, whose devotion to Mathu is so strong she is willing to take a murder rap for him.

On a sweltering November day, I drove out to the set with Ernie, who told me they were filming in Thibodaux, ninety miles south of Oscar, because "there isn't enough cane in Pointe Coupée Parish."[40] At Melodia Plantation, the cane was twelve feet tall and stretched for what seemed like miles. We drove up to a weather-beaten cabin that had been moved there from another nearby plantation. (Workers' houses were already beginning to disappear from the Louisiana landscape.)

Ernie, who described his role as "unofficial consultant," was warmly welcomed by director Volker Schlöndorff and the crew. We were invited to step inside the two-room cabin to watch a scene being shot. Inside, we saw torn linoleum, ripped wallpaper, an unmade iron bed, a battered chiffarobe, and two ancient oscillating fans. Cameras and lights filled every inch of available space. Crew members greeted Ernie with silent smiles as they squeezed around corners and tiptoed over wires. The climactic scene being shot was the gathering of old men inside Mathu's house.

Gossett, made up to look much older than his fifty years, with white hair and beard, came up and told a risqué joke, at which Ernie laughed heartily. Then, with cameras rolling, Gossett exuded quiet intensity as he addressed the old men, each of whom was clutching a shotgun. Their eyes were fixed on Mathu as he told them, "This is the proudest day of my life," because they had stood up to the white sheriff. Many crew members had tears in their eyes as Volker, a short man with a cigar clenched in his teeth, yelled, "Cut!"

Schlöndorff called a break and we strolled over to a huge striped tent with ten long tables inside. Craft services had prepared a lunch of steak and baked potatoes. A crew member approached Ernie in an almost worshipful manner and asked him to sign his copy of the book.

I chatted with some of the actors, experienced and sophisticated men, an interesting contrast to the roles they played. Musician and songwriter Danny Barker, seventy-seven, had just published his autobiography, *A Life in Jazz.* Actor/musician Tiger Haynes, seventy-three, whose Scottish wife, Joy Hatton, was an actor and singer, told me they lived in Greenwich Village and were demons for the *New York Times* crossword puzzle. Papa John Creach, sixty-nine, had played jazz violin with Jefferson Airplane and Jefferson Starship.

When filming resumed, the crew shot a scene in the front yard of the cabin with Widmark, Hunter, Will Patton (as Candy's boyfriend, Lou), and the old men. Widmark was being difficult, demanding that "Mr. Gaines" be removed from the area near the set. Everyone had to move back by the trucks in the driveway so Widmark couldn't see us. Gower Frost, the British producer, told me that the actor "gets crazy when people are in his line of view."

Frost said he had read the book in 1984 and had phoned Ernie's agent the next day. Others wanted to make a movie of it, he said, but Dorothea liked him and awarded him the contract. "I've read it half a dozen times," he said. "Sometimes you can just visualize something as a film." He said the production had been denied the use of a bar in nearby Napoleonville because the owner was afraid they would bring a lot of Black people into the bar and his white customers wouldn't like it. "We even had your 'leftenant' governor talk to him," to no avail. Ernie had experienced this sort of thing himself and used it in his fiction. In fact, the novel includes a scene in a segregated bar. This real-life event revealed how little had changed.

After a couple of hours, I ventured forth with my camera. Randy, a Black man on the crew, warned me, "Richard Widmark is very temperamental, and if he sees you'll he'll raise hell." At the time, I was fifty feet away from the actor, behind a truck. A bit later I wandered a little farther, and as I wrote in my notes, "Widmark glared at me with laserlike intensity." Ernie and I spent the rest of the afternoon sitting with our legs dangling from a Ryder truck, unable to see anything. "That bastard Widmark!" Ernie grumbled. I got sunburned and nearly fell asleep.

That evening, Ernie and I joined Volker, Holly Hunter, and a couple of crew members for dinner at the popular Lafitte's Landing in Donaldsonville, a forty-five-minute drive away. Over redfish with hollandaise sauce (Hunter chose dolphin), we chatted about the movie. Friendly and down-to-earth, Hunter peppered Ernie with questions about her character. On the trip back to the crew hotel in Thibodaux, she rode with Ernie so they could continue their talk.

Ernie told me later that on a recent Saturday night, the cast and crew had reserved the bar at the Sheraton and thrown a party. Barker, Haynes, and Creach played music, and another of the old men, Sandman Sims, sixty-eight, tap-danced.

Just days before the premiere of the movie in May 1987, Dorothea Oppenheimer died of pancreatic cancer at the age of sixty-eight. At the gala premier at USL, Ernie asked for a moment of silence in memory of his agent, whose thirty-one-year professional association, support, and friendship had helped his career immeasurably.[41]

Since Oppenheimer's death, Gaines has been represented by Jeff Gerecke (pronounced *Jer-EEK*), who began work in New York as a scout and joined the JCA Literary Agency when Oppenheimer "was looking to be bought out because of her terminal cancer diagnosis. . . . I [went] up to her apartment once a month to talk over the agency history with her and find out . . . [about] her client list, which . . . had dwindled to just a few major authors," including Gaines and Larry McMurtry. After working with Gaines for a few years, Gerecke attended the 1993 American Bookseller Association meeting in Miami. Gaines, who had just published *A Lesson Before Dying,* attended as a guest of his publisher, Knopf, to meet media and booksellers. Oprah Winfrey was there, and Gaines asked to be introduced to her. "A publicist led him over and introduced them and put a copy of the book in her hands. . . . Four years after that, in 1997, Oprah made the book a selection of Oprah's Book Club."[42]

## DOCUMENTING ERNIE

I had first mentioned the possibility of a documentary to Ernie in 1985, and he had responded positively. When he was named Humanist of the Year by the Louisiana Endowment for the Humanities in December 1989, Louisiana

Public Broadcasting producer Rick Smith and I got serious and started applying for grants and lining up a panel of scholars to help us chart our course. We received support from the Louisiana Endowment and the California Endowment for the Humanities but were denied grants by national organizations. One agency responded that Gaines was not an important enough writer to warrant a documentary.

We asked Ernie for the names of friends and family members whom we could interview. When I called his friend Ben Biben, he told me, "He [Gaines] was aggressive. Nobody else left the place and progressed like he did. No father, no mother around, raised by a lady on the floor."[43] On a Saturday afternoon at the LPB studio, we met Ben, Gaines's brother Lionel, and Lionel's wife, Ada Mae. We interviewed them that day; their faces and voices appear in the documentary, powerful testaments to the life of Cherie Quarters. Ben was so helpful throughout the two-and-a-half-year process—recalling details, suggesting interviewees, and finding old photographs—that we gave him a special thank-you in the credits.

At Cherie Quarters, we shot video of Ernie pointing out the house where his grandmother had lived, and the Big House: "These were the people who owned you." We filmed him at the church where he went to school, and in the graveyard where he hoped to be buried some day. "There were people who said I shouldn't write about this kind of life," he said. "But what other life did I have?"

In Lafayette, we filmed him at home and on campus and talked to his colleagues at USL. One memorable afternoon, Ernie was in the back of his house, getting dressed for that evening's presentation of awards to honors students. Rick, photographer Charles Bush, and I were in the sunroom at the front of the house, setting Ernie's framed photos of Aunt Augusteen, great-grandfather James McVay, and other relatives on an easel and filming them. Somebody jostled the easel and a photo toppled to the tiled floor, shattering the glass. I grabbed a phone and located a store that could quickly replace the glass.

Ernie heard the commotion and came into the living room in his stocking feet, scowling. We cautioned him to be careful not to step on the glass and apprised him of the situation. He was clearly displeased. Charlie and I spent an anxious hour carefully shooting more video while waiting for Rick to return with the reframed photo. Ernie, Charlie, and I and were on the front stoop when Rick drove up. He got out of the van with the photo and, in an attempt at levity, pretended to trip on the curb. Ernie was not amused.

By the time we flew to the Bay Area in the spring of 1992, Ernie was clearly growing weary of having us follow him around and ask him questions. He was already in San Francisco, but I was on the phone with him almost daily as we planned a tightly scheduled week doing interviews with him and family members, shooting B-roll of him strolling in the park and sailing on his sloop the *Curmudgeon,* and filming old photos of the public library in Vallejo, which had been torn down in 1969.[44]

I had told Ernie I'd call him the afternoon we got in, adding that we landed at 3:30. We had set up an interview at his flat the next morning at 9:30. By the time Rick, Charlie, and I had rented a car, driven downtown to rent lights for the filming, and checked in to our hotel, a couple of hours had passed. I called Ernie as soon as I got to my room and was chagrined to discover he had canceled our interview in favor of a dental appointment. We knew he was a stickler for punctuality, but wow! I told Rick about this snafu, and we were still trying to figure out what to do when Ernie called back and said he had changed his appointment and to come on over as scheduled the following morning.

We were practically tiptoeing when the three of us showed up the next day—right on time! Ernie seemed to be in a good mood as he showed us around his flat, its shelves loaded with books and LPs, a bead curtain in one doorway, and a well-appointed study with a terrific view of the city. There were many photos on the walls, including one of Aunt Augusteen. We videotaped his agent Dorothea's passport photo, and other photos of her. She was stunning, with movie star looks—probably as she had looked when he met her; he was twenty-four then and she was thirty-eight. Seeing the photos, it was easy to imagine a romantic entanglement between them. Perhaps it explained her possessiveness and protectiveness, her refusal to reveal any personal information about him; she may have been protecting her own privacy as well.

Gaines's own writing supports this idea. In *Mozart and Leadbelly,* in an essay titled "Bloodline in Ink," Gaines wrote that "a woman," unnamed but clearly Dorothea, said she would help him buy and select clothes, would cook and bring him food, but "she wouldn't give me money for whiskey or for other women." He wrote that they drank Stolichnaya vodka and orange juice, went to foreign films, symphonies, museums, and bookstores. She had a big German radio that always had classical music playing. He wrote that she would read his work and say, "Yes, but not quite yet," and that he'd get angry and then get over it.[45] Perhaps most telling, he dedicated his short story collection *Bloodline* "For Dee with my deepest love." He later confirmed that "Dee" was Dorothea.[46]

As the day went on and the camera rolled, Ernie said that he could gaze out of his window in San Francisco and recall perfectly details from his childhood in Cherie Quarters. He talked about the plays he had put on in the church. After interviewing him, we asked him to read from an essay he had written about his first venture into the public library in Vallejo. That library, built in 1904, was now gone, but we had called ahead and found that its replacement had large framed photos of the original, both interior and exterior, with "Free to All" carved into its facade. A day or so later, we removed the photos from their frames and Charles shot them carefully, panning up, down, and across—shots that would be accompanied by Ernie's voice talking about climbing the stairs to the second-floor fiction section.

We drove to San Jose to interview Ernie's mother and siblings at the home of his sister Lois Young and her husband, Chet. Ernie's mother, Adrean Colar, talked about having to sit behind the WHITE/COLORED sign on a bus, "as if you might rub off on somebody," her anger still strong. Like Ernie, she said that she *had* to get out of Louisiana. "I know I'd have been dead a long time ago [if I had stayed]," she said. "I got out of there as quick as I could. I know just how much I could take." Her decision to leave, she said, was because "I never thought that minorities had a chance [in the South]."[47]

Lois talked about how much Ernie's brothers and sister had missed him after he left in 1948, when she was ten. "We felt lost without Ernie," she said. His much younger sister Deb—like Lois, married to a white man—told us she used to fling herself off the porch into his arms when she was small. "He always caught me." On his regular visits to Vallejo from his home in San Francisco, "he always brought ice cream."

Ernie's brother Norbert Colar Jr., who was born in Louisiana and left for California a few years after Ernie, recalled the sound of rain on the tin roof and also talked about the differences in skin color among members of the same family.

On a memorable afternoon, we filmed writer Alice Walker. Her three-story row house across from Alamo Square was, quite simply, one of the most beautiful interiors I had ever seen. From the large burlap bag of Georgia pecans just inside the front door, to the pale apricot–colored walls and elaborate woodwork, to the light-filled rooms, to the art on the walls, it was fabulous. A gracious interview subject and host, Walker spoke movingly about *Miss Jane Pittman*: "That book is the equivalent of a really huge, beautiful, massive, gigantic tree—that's what that book is like."

Afterward, Ernie met us there. Charles, with handheld camera, caught him as he walked into the front room, looked around, and said, "Wow!" Later, he and Walker—both born in the rural South during Jim Crow and now living as "expatriates" in the city—posed for photos on the front steps. They seemed to be genuinely fond of each other. Walker had been an early advocate of Ernie's work, observing in 1970, "He can write about whites and blacks exactly as he sees them and *knows* them, instead of writing of one group as a vast malignant lump and of the other as a conglomerate of perfect virtues."[48]

Ernie was relaxed and cheerful when we went out on San Francisco Bay with him and one of his *Curmudgeon* buddies. We shot video of him in the sailboat, beer in hand, laughing with his friend. Later we docked at a marina and consumed a few more beverages.

Gaines and Laney in his sailboat, the *Curmudgeon*, on San Francisco Bay in May 1992 during the filming of the television documentary *Ernest J. Gaines: Louisiana Stories*. Laney wrote the script and coproduced with Louisiana Public Broadcasting's Rick Smith. Photo by Rick Smith. Courtesy of Rick Smith.

When we returned to Louisiana, Rick and I were constantly busy—reviewing interviews for the best quotes, organizing photos, recording actors reading from his work. I wrote the script. We hired Ed Shannon, who drove over from Texas to record the narration, coaching him on how to pronounce "Pointe Coupée" and "Guy de Maupassant." We often had to work after hours, when nobody else was using the Louisiana Public Broadcasting facilities. One memorable night in November, we pulled an all-nighter to select the music, picking pieces we knew were meaningful to Ernie, such as blues songs and Modest Mussorgsky's *Pictures at an Exhibition,* which he had listened to while writing *Miss Jane.* We worked from 6:00 p.m. until 1:00 the next afternoon, fortifying ourselves with chips, candy bars, and cold drinks from the vending machines.

On a rainy night in February 1993, LPB held a premiere of the one-hour documentary in Lafayette. Ernie said a few words after the viewing, which was attended by about two hundred guests and local media. "I've seen it three times, and each time it's brought tears to my eyes," he said. One local newspaper ran a photo of him with his brothers Lionel and Eugene, who had driven over to see it. The documentary was shown throughout the state and picked up via satellite by public broadcasting stations around the country. Louisiana native Rod Dreher wrote in the *Washington Times* about its "unsentimental yet touching reminiscences of Quarter life" and noted, "With the Quarter now abandoned[,] the numerous shots of the humble cabins decaying under the oak branches are poetic and heartbreaking."[49]

# 4

# THE RELATIONSHIP I DREAMED OF

## GETTING MARRIED, COMING HOME

*Gaines returned to his home place, Cherie Quarters, as the setting for his novel* A Lesson Before Dying. *Within the next few years he would establish the importance of home to him, taking steps to ensure the graveyard would remain untouched by "the tractor" and building a house on False River. He would bring his life full circle, ending where he had begun.*

. . . .

In April 1993, Gaines published his first novel in ten years, *A Lesson Before Dying*. Critics praised the story of a Black man wrongly condemned to Louisiana's electric chair by a white jury in the late 1940s. "Gaines has written a moving and truthful work of fiction" (*New York Times*); "enormously moving. . . . Gaines unerringly evokes the place and time about which he writes" (*Los Angeles Times*); "reconfirms [his] position as an important American writer" (*Boston Globe*); "this majestic, moving novel is an instant classic, a book that will be read, discussed and taught beyond the rest of our lives" (*Chicago Tribune*); "invests the story with emotional power and universal resonance" (*Publishers Weekly*); "by containing unbearably painful emotions within simple declarative sentences and everyday speech rhythms, Gaines has written a novel that is not only never maudlin, but approaches the spare beauty of a classic" (*Kirkus Review*). The novel would win the Louisiana Library Association award; once again, librarian Evangeline Lynch was in the audience.

In May 1993, Gaines married for the first time, at age sixty. He had met his future wife when he appeared on a panel at the Miami International Book Fair in 1988. A native of New Orleans, Dianne Saulney Smith was an assistant district attorney in Miami and the mother of four grown children. She attended Gaines's reading, bought a copy of *A Gathering of Old Men,* and had him autograph it for her son. Later, Smith and Gaines crossed paths at a party and talked at length. When Gaines returned to San Francisco, they began corresponding but did not see each other again for eighteen months.

"He sent me an autographed copy of *Catherine Carmier,*" recalled Dianne Gaines, during an interview at their Lafayette house a few weeks after their wedding. "I was just tickled. He blushes now, because it was a very flirtatious inscription and he's not that way. I may have called him to say thank you, and I sent him a Christmas card. He did send me all of his books over the next year, and we did discuss them [over the phone], without seeing each other. Of course, I'd devour them, and I'd tell him what I thought. He just kind of chuckled." There were gaps in their communication because "I never knew whether he was in California or Louisiana," but "we started talking a little more often. I was an English major. I love books." Dianne said that as she read Gaines's books, "I came to realize how much his writings give to people—understanding each other, developing a sensitivity. His books are so special. What stood out for me was his treatment of women was so positive, unlike so many Black male authors whose treatment is negligible to hostile. His women characters are all treated so gently. To find women treated with that much respect was special." [1]

In the spring of 1990, Gaines invited Dianne to be his guest at a wedding in New Orleans. She was helping her daughter move, but she agreed to stop in New Orleans on her way back to Miami. In New Orleans, she stayed at the house of her ninety-year-old mother. "That was in May of 1990, the first time we had met in a year and a half," she recalled.

> By that time, I had read a lot more of his writings and articles about him, but they were separate from the person I knew as a human being and friend. . . . We were supposed to go to dinner, but my sister insisted we come to her house to see pictures of my niece's wedding. I didn't think he'd want to, but he said, "Fine." So our first date was at my sister's house with my mom, my sister and her husband, and my daughter, watching videos of the wedding for two hours. It was a nuptial Mass! Everybody liked him. After dinner, we went to the French Quarter for coffee and beignets at Café du Monde and walked around the Quarter. It was just so comfortable.

As for Gaines, he had found his soul mate. "I keep telling Dianne we've been married for thirty-three years," he said. "This relationship is the one I dreamed of when I was writing *Catherine Carmier*." They married on May 15, 1993, at Gaines's house in Lafayette, with only Dianne's children and a few close friends present. He explained why he had waited so long to marry.

> Many of . . . the kids I went to school with at San Francisco State or at Stanford . . . couldn't take it. They got married, had families, started teaching, went into business, traveled. . . . But maybe, at the same time, they didn't have a damned thing to write about in the first place. . . . Because I think if you have something to write about and really want to do it, you'll start giving up everything. . . . If you want to be a writer, you don't love anybody else but your writing. You're married to it. . . . You have to have that kind of ego, to believe that you have something to say that no one else can say. . . . You will not let anything in the world get in the way of it. . . . I had lots of regrets when I went to spend Christmas with my brothers and sisters and their children. Regrets that I didn't have a little child there of my own. But I knew darned well I had to be a writer. . . . I could not afford to have a child around, because I would not have been able to support that child. I had to write.

In the summer of 1993, the MacArthur Foundation honored a lifetime of achievement by awarding Gaines a "genius grant" of $355,000. "I knew people who had won MacArthurs, but I never thought I'd win," he confessed. "I assumed they were political." The MacArthur may have been the highlight of a year crowded with milestones. That fall, he was happy to get back to Louisiana to teach a new crop of students at USL. "I used to think that when I was sixty, I'd like to live near a small university," he said. "Someplace where I could communicate with young people who like to write. Just sit around and talk to them maybe once or twice a week. And that was before I ever knew that there would be a woman in my life, or who that woman would be. And now there's Dianne. What frightens me is that so many things are falling into place." Gaines said that despite the MacArthur money, he had assured department chairman Doris Meriwether that he was still committed to teaching at USL. "I'd like to stay ten more years, if I live that long," he said—and, in fact, he taught his last class in the fall of 2003.[2]

But all was not perfect. Just a few weeks earlier, Gaines had undergone back surgery in Lafayette. He had needed it because he experienced numbness in his legs after walking any distance. He would not know if it was successful until he was able to walk a quarter mile. At the time, he could not walk unsupported. He planned to have a second surgery on his neck in early 1994.[3] He said,

> That's the most important thing in my life today, just being able to walk. To go to the bathroom or turn on the television or look out of a window or walk across the yard and throw peanuts to the squirrels. . . . I want to write as much as I can. But writing is not the most important thing to me anymore. My life with Dianne is much more important now than anything else. . . . It's made my life more whole now. Everybody loves her, my colleagues. My mother just loves her to death; she thinks Dianne is her thirteenth child. Dianne talks to her every other day. . . . Even people who don't speak to me here in Arbolada [subdivision in Lafayette] talk to Dianne. They tell her all the gossip that goes on in this place.[4]

For three years, Ernest and Dianne Gaines divided their time among Lafayette, Miami, and San Francisco. After Dianne retired, in 1995, they realized their dream of spending a year in France when he accepted a writer in residence position at the William Faulkner Foundation at the University of Rennes. He took copies of the films made from his books as well as a copy of the documentary. While in France, Gaines was named a Chevalier de l'Ordre des Arts et des Lettres (Chevalier of the Order of Arts and Letters). Established in 1957 by the French government, the award recognizes eminent artists and writers as well as people who have contributed significantly to furthering the arts in France and throughout the world.

In 1997, family and friends, many of whom had grown up with Gaines in Cherie Quarters, turned out to eat steak dinners and hear his keynote speech at an event benefiting the Pointe Coupée Parish Library—the very place he could not have entered when he left Louisiana nearly fifty years earlier.[5] That summer, in July, Gaines returned to San Francisco to move out of the Divisadero Street flat where he had lived since the 1970s, working as the sounds of street life floated through the windows. This was where he had written *A Gathering of Old Men* and *A Lesson Before Dying,* where he had watched movies with Linda and Roz, where he had entertained friends, where we had filmed him for the documentary.[6]

In September of that year, *A Lesson Before Dying* was picked for the Oprah Book Club. Gaines was at his Lafayette house when the phone rang. "This woman said she was Oprah Winfrey and I thought someone was pulling a trick," he said. "She told me my book had been selected, and then she said, 'You can't talk about it.' I told her, 'I have to tell my wife.' When the producers got in touch with me, they said, 'This is all hush-hush, but you'll have to tell your publisher and agent so we can get the books out.' . . . It was not hard for me. I can keep a secret."[7]

Oprah and her crew went to Louisiana to tape the show, shooting scenes at Cherie Quarters and the Big House. With cameras rolling, Gaines escorted her on a tour of the plantation, including the two remaining cabins and the church/schoolhouse. Inside, he explained that the children had no desks, so they knelt on the floor to write on the benches. Oprah got down on her knees to demonstrate. "It's a wonder anybody learned anything," she said. Although the show was taped in October, in the middle of grinding season, the cane fields immediately behind the Big House were not harvested until after her visit so the cane could be photographed. Strolling through the fields, Gaines made a sudden detour to break off a piece of cane, from which he whittled a knob or two with his pocket knife. "Chew it until you get all the juice, then spit it out," he instructed Oprah, who retorted, "I know how to do it!"

Oprah knew how to do many things. Her power and influence were front and center throughout the filming of the show. Four readers from across the country were flown to Louisiana for a book discussion. The group was served dinner in the main house. Producers had visited the area in advance to talk to owner Madeleine Caillet and secure permission to use the house. Her son Craig and his family moved out for several days so the shooting could take place. Winfrey commented that it was "really a big deal" to be at the Big House, "where we would not have been allowed a hundred years ago. If these walls could talk, I wonder what they'd say," she exulted. "They'd say, 'Surprise, surprise! Look who's in here tonight!'"

Gaines was pleased to be only the second male author chosen by Oprah. "And mine is the first book she has chosen that is about male characters," he said. "She's doing a great job getting those books attention. She's a fantastic little woman."[8] Before Oprah, the book had respectable sales, but the attention associated with the show resulted in the sale of 950,000 copies in paperback. Film rights were sold to HBO, which made a television movie of the book, starring Don Cheadle and Mekhi Phifer, which premiered in 1999. Cicely Tyson, who had skyrocketed to fame as Miss Jane Pittman twenty-five years earlier, played Tante Lou. The film won Emmys for writing and for best made-for-TV movie. Compared to the other films made from his work, said Gaines, "It's the most faithful to the book."[9]

## COMING HOME

In 2000, Gaines bought a fishing camp on False River, where he and Dianne often spent weekends. In late October, I went to one of the early graveyard cleanups that would become an annual event. It was rather sparsely attended, and after we completed our work decorating the graves, Ernie invited us to "come over to the camp for a few minutes." Along with me, there were Ben Biben and his wife, Carol, Ben's sister Barbara Overstreet Hardy, and Ernie's nephew Wilfred Hebert. Those "few minutes" turned into nearly five hours!

We drove our individual vehicles to the camp a quarter mile or so from the Big House. The driveway dipped steeply, and I feared I'd drive straight into the river. The camp was a trailer with a walkway leading to a covered pier. A screened porch attached to the trailer had a swing, comfortable lawn chairs, and a flowering vinca in a hanging basket, reflecting Dianne's love of plants. Dianne offered us a choice of burgers or fried chicken from Bonaventure's, a café and bait shop down the road. She, Carol, and Barbara picked up the food while the rest of us went out on the pier.

It was a beautiful late fall day, sunny, dry, in the eighties, with a nice breeze. Powerboaters roared up and down the lake. Ernie and Wilfred poured themselves glasses of Wild Turkey; the rest of us drank Cokes. It was interesting to see Ernie survey the river where he had spent so much time as a boy—indeed, where he had been baptized. From his seat in a porch swing on the pier, he directed us to get folding chairs off the porch. He seemed to be in a good mood, reminiscing about playing knucks, which was, as nearly as I could make out, a vicious game of marbles in which the goal was to hit the other person's knuckles with your marble, as hard as you could, and then take their marbles.

I had my first close-up view of *poules d'eau* (which my hosts pronounced *pool doo*). They looked like ducks floating in the water in pairs, from time to time making a little cry. Ben recalled a man who used to come to Cherie selling them for a quarter apiece. His mother, Albertha ("Bert"), would cook them like ducks, but Ben never liked them because they had a "fishy" taste. Wilfred said they were very dry when cooked.

After we ate, Ben, Barbara, and I fished with bait—crickets, worms, and shiners—that Dianne had brought back with our lunch. After about an hour, I gave up, but Ben caught a small catfish. Barbara caught a turtle and took a lot of teasing for snagging it by the foot. Ben unhooked it and threw it back.

We moved to the porch, and Barbara kept everybody laughing with her memories of life in Cherie Quarters. She talked about being chased by Shug Edwards's dog Clora Lee, a "junkyard dog" that was small but had sharp teeth and was very fast. Wilfred joked that Clora Lee was a coach and trainer who got all the kids in shape to run track. Barbara also said that as kids they relished throwing rocks at Willie Burks's and Reese Spooner's houses. Willie would come out and shoot his gun into the air, but Reese would never emerge or even turn on a light when they pelted his house. Next morning, he would go out and sweep away the rocks and dirt.

Barbara recalled a girl from a nearby plantation who always wanted to fight with her. Barbara took to carrying her little brother Albert James on her hip, telling the girl, "It's a good thing I got this baby," implying *If I didn't, I'd beat you up.* Once, another girl offered to hold Albert James so Barbara could fight. Barbara's inflections and facial expressions were funny, and Ernie laughed heartily. It was good to see him relaxed and enjoying himself.

Ernie subsequently bought land on Highway 1, across from the camp, and built a house about a quarter mile from River Lake Plantation's Big House. In 2003, he persuaded owner Madeleine Caillet to give him the church/schoolhouse in Cherie Quarters and had it moved to his property. He had come full circle, returning to live in the place he had left at age fifteen, although in vastly different style. He and Dianne continued to work with the Mount Zion River Lake Cemetery Association they had established to preserve the graveyard at Cherie Quarters. And, perhaps surprisingly, Gaines continued to write. He was working on a novella called *The Man Who Whipped Children,* but the writing went slowly. "I have five or six chapters, but the energy is not there," he told an interviewer. "The creative energy is not there." He also spoke of arthritis that kept him from being mobile.[10]

In 2005, the University of Louisiana at Lafayette threw a retirement party for Ernie. More than twenty years had passed since *A Lesson Before Dying* came out, and many readers and critics assumed that he had also retired from writing. But that year he published *Mozart and Leadbelly,* a collection of stories and essays, including his first published story set in San Francisco, "Christ Walked Down Market Street." Gaines, who steadfastly refused to ever name a favorite among his novels, would say in 2017 that his favorite short story was his only work of fiction not set in Louisiana. In an address at the Louisiana State Library in 2000, he again said it was "my favorite story," though he called it "Jesus Walked Down Market Street."[11] He was also working on two novels.

### A NEW PRESIDENT

In November 2008, my elation over the election of Barack Obama had cold water splashed on it by the comments of friends and relatives. One friend railed that we would be attacked by terrorists. A cousin asked sarcastically, "Now that we're all equal, can we do away with affirmative action?"

Frustrated with these reactions, I joined a weekly Dialogue on Race group, twenty people, Black and white. I was only two weeks into the six-week dialogue when I was asked to participate in a symposium called "The Sky Is Gray." A young museum professional, Leslie Charleville, had conceived an ambitious project to be held at the LSU School of Art's downtown gallery. Artists were invited to create works based on Gaines's fiction, high school students would give readings from his work, my documentary would be shown, and a panel discussion on race would relate to Gaines's fiction. Charleville asked me to be on the panel slated for late November.

At the opening reception in mid-November, I was fascinated to see what works of fiction the artists had chosen. I especially liked Michael Crespo's painting of Diamond and Job, the two mules recalled by Johnny Paul in *A Gathering of Old Men.* Bobby Hausey, who had remembered my documentary and suggested I be included, painted the stars and the crescent moon seen through the barred window of the jail cell by Procter in "Three Men." Malaika Favorite made a mixed-media painting on a washboard, inspired by Miss Jane's work as a laundress (among other jobs). "It was not difficult to translate his words into visual images because he gave me all I needed in his writing," she wrote in her artist's statement. "I was so inspired by this assignment that I bought several more of Mr. Gaines' books just for the pleasure of seeing more of the world he wrote about."[12] Melody Guichet painted Madame Toussaint's yard from "A Long Day in November." Kelli Scott Kelley painted the redbird and the black grass from "The Sky Is Gray." Morris Taft Thomas made a mixed-media piece of men chopping cane—a piece that Ernie purchased. Leslie Charleville, who had pulled it all together, contributed her own collage inspired by "The Sky Is Gray."

A few days before the panel discussion, the dialogue topic was white privilege. The Black people in the room grasped the concept much better than the white ones. At the gallery discussion, I connected the idea of white privilege to the short story "The Sky Is Gray." I quoted Gaines: "Only white people [in the story] are very nice [to James and his mother]. They offer food and warmth and shelter. Yet you know that it is because of race relations problems in the South that they must go back of town for a cookie or a glass of water."[13]

"Back of town" refers to the Black part of town, past the white downtown, which had stores and restaurants that James and his mother couldn't enter because of segregation. They walk several blocks in the cold to the part of town with Black-owned businesses so they can go into a café and eat. In the white part of town, they briefly go into a hardware store, where James's mother, Octavia, pretends to look at ax handles so that James can stand next to the heater. Only a white couple who own a grocery store invite them inside, feed them, and are kind to them.

I also read a quote from my first interview, when Ernie told me, "I'm not really involved in politics. There are certain governors and senators I think should be shot tomorrow morning. But when it comes down to writing, I feel that it has to work into a form of art. . . . If I cannot move you by dramatizing a situation . . . then I'm not going to try to move you by all the rhetoric in the world. I just am not that kind of person."[14] I quoted poet and novelist Clarence Major on *Miss Jane:* "There simply is no evidence that social propaganda has ever helped anybody toward a larger or deeper vision and sense of life. On the other hand, real art, such as [*Miss Jane*] does achieve this goal. Real works of art stand up and prove themselves over and over. . . . An artist such as Ernest Gaines is, in the most important . . . sense, our true revolutionary."[15]

I talked about giving my mother a copy of *Bloodline* and asking her to read "The Sky Is Gray." After she read it, she told me it reminded her of growing up in the small town of Donaldsonville, Louisiana, in the 1930s. On the downtown sidewalk, she said, if a Black person was coming toward a white person, the Black person would step completely off the sidewalk until the white person had passed. Some might take that as a sign of "respect," but to me the meaning was painfully clear: put as much daylight as possible between yourself and the white person so there can be no suspicion of contact. It was a matter of life and death.

I told the assembled group—which included Ernie and Dianne—that I had read the story dozens of times but it never failed to touch me. Even now, I can be driving down the street and think about the last scene in the story and be moved to tears. I'm especially touched by the words of Octavia to the white storekeeper who has called her inside from the cold and given her and her son James a hot meal in exchange for James's hauling empty trash cans to the curb.

> Mama opens the door to go out, but she stops and comes back in the store.
>
> "You sell salt meat?" she says.
>
> "Yes."
>
> "Give me two bits worth."
>
> "That isn't very much salt meat," the old lady says.
>
> "That's all I have," Mama says.
>
> The old lady goes back of the counter and cuts a big piece off the chunk. Then she wraps it up and puts it in a paper bag.
>
> "Two bits," she says.
>
> "That looks like an awful lot of meat for a quarter," Mama says.
>
> "Two bits," the old lady says. "I've been selling salt meat behind this counter twenty-five years. I think I know what I'm doing."
>
> "You got a scale there," Mama says.
>
> "What?" the old lady says.
>
> "Weigh it," Mama says.
>
> "What?" the old lady says. "Are you telling me how to run my business?"
>
> "Thanks very much for the food," Mama says.
>
> "Just a minute," the old lady says.
>
> "James," Mama says to me. I move toward the door.
>
> "Just one minute, I said," the old lady says.
>
> Me and Mama stop again and look at her. The old lady takes the meat out of the bag and unwraps it and cuts 'bout half of it off. Then she wraps it up again and juggs it back in the bag and gives the bag to Mama. Mama lays the quarter on the counter.

"Your kindness will never be forgotten," she says. "James," she says to me.

We go out, and the old lady comes to the door to look at us. After we go a little piece I look back, and she's still there watching us.

The sleet's coming down heavy, heavy now, and I turn up my coat collar to keep my neck warm. My mama tells me turn it right back down.

"You not a bum," she says. "You a man."

In the Dialogue on Race group, we were learning that racism is bigger than individual acts of hatred and violence. It is systemic, institutionalized. "Still," I said, "I can't help wishing we could reach across the divide, person to person, with random acts of kindness that may never be forgotten."

A few days later, I read a blog post by Carleen Brice: "What if every one of us bought a book by a black author and gave it to a white friend? So I'm naming December National Buy a Book by a Black Author and Give it to Somebody Not Black Month."[16] That Christmas I gave copies of *Bloodline* and *Miss Jane* to my freaked-out friends and relatives.

On January 20, 2009, Ernie and Dianne hosted a watch party for President Obama's inauguration. I was thrilled about his election, but I suspected that some of the guests—who included Madeleine Caillet and other older white residents of the parish—were not. Nonetheless, they were there, eating, drinking, chatting, and smiling.

Ernie and Dianne sat on a couch in front of the television set. Dianne kept her eyes and hands on her grandson Nicholas, a lively toddler. I asked about his older sister Annalisa, who was about six. "She's in Washington!' Dianne declared, beaming.

It felt like such a breakthrough, watching the young president take the oath of office on Lincoln's Bible, with his smiling family, the cordial former president and first lady, the crowd that stretched for miles. He was being called the first African American president, but he was also the first mixed-race president. The next day I wrote to Dianne and Ernie to thank them for including me in the party. I closed by saying, "Looking to the future with pride and hope."

Four years later, on July 10, 2013, at a ceremony in the East Room of the White House, President Obama awarded Ernest Gaines the National Medal of Arts, the highest award given to artists and arts patrons by the US government. Photos show Ernie in his wheelchair, smiling as the president drapes the purple ribbon around his neck. "To receive a National Medal of Arts from a black president of the United States at the White House was the greatest honor I think I will ever receive," he said.[17]

In late September 2013, Ernie gave a reading from his in-progress novella, *Daughters of the Creole Lady,* at the Gaines Center at ULL. The small room set up for the reading held about two hundred people. Ernie entered from the back in his wheelchair, with friend and colleague Darrell Bourque pushing it. On an elevated platform in the front of the room, Darrell helped him into a chair and handed him a bottle of water. Ernie wore what I had come to think of as his grumpy face. He just didn't look happy much of the time.

"I haven't published anything original since *A Lesson Before Dying* twenty years ago," he said, and I sensed this troubled him. "I submitted one [manuscript] recently to my agent in New York, but it's too small for a novel and many things needed to be corrected. I wrote another novella to go along with it, *Daughters of the Creole Lady.*"

As he read, Ernie was hard to understand at times, his voice weak. But I understood enough to realize that the piece seemed to be about his 1963 stay in Baton Rouge. The characters who welcomed him were named George and Mamie, just as his real-life relatives had been. The character apparently based on Ernie was called Octave. He arrives, puts his "carpetbag" on the floor and his typewriter on the couch. George drinks Old Forester while Mamie bakes a cake. The scene switches from their house to a party at a Southern University professor's house, where Octave admires women in colorful dresses and asks the beautiful Nita to dance. The narrator tells a woman who asks about Octave's marital status, "He has a wife—a typewriter." He adds, "Against that typewriter, I wasn't too sure she could win."

I hastily scribbled notes as Ernie read, highlighting the phrases "Old Creole lady of the old school" and "Light skin made all the difference."

After the reading, he took questions from the audience. He talked about the other novella he was writing, *The Man Who Whipped Children,* explaining, "The old people would do anything to keep their children from ending up in Angola [state prison] or the local jail. They got a man on the plantation to whip a child if the child did something wrong. He did it to make them good. They had nothing to believe in, nothing to do. The setting would be in the thirties or forties, just like this story here [*Creole Lady*] is in the sixties."

A woman in the audience said, "I'm a member of the Writers' Guild of

Acadiana. Would you come and speak to us?" Ernie looked skeptical. "They'd have to know who I am and what I wrote," he said.

Another woman noted, "It seems like skin tone plays a bigger role in what you read today" than it had done in his previous books. "You are right, it does play a very big part," Ernie said. "This is the first book that I've really concentrated on this kind of thing. I've touched on it in other books, [especially] *Catherine Carmier.* But in this one I'm dealing with it more."

A young woman said, "My family is twelve generations in Oscar. I'm a writer. What advice would you give to writers of color to heal the divisions in our own family with light and dark skin color?"

"I don't know, other than to be honest with yourself and try to see all sides of the problem," Ernie said. "Describe the situation as well as you possibly can. That's what I try to do." He leaned forward in his chair. "I'm still learning to write really," he said. "I'm still working at it. Every book is a challenge. *Daughters of the Creole Lady,* I've never done anything like that before. It's still out there. It's not only about light skin and dark skin. It's about other things. Painting our faces, doing all these different things to our hair."

My last interview with Ernie was in 2015, a week before his eighty-second birthday, on assignment for the online publication *The Root.* On a cold January day, with a freeze expected that night, I drove to his house on False River. Traffic was backed up on the Mississippi River bridge, and I arrived ten minutes late for our 11:00 a.m. appointment. Knowing Ernie's "insane mania" for being on time, I hoped that wouldn't spoil the interview.[18]

Dianne opened the door and ushered me into the warm kitchen. Ernie came in slowly, using his walker, and talked with Dianne about the mask for his CPAP machine, which helped him breathe.[19] Dianne suggested we sit in the library, a cozy room with comfortable chairs. She lighted the gas heater in the fireplace, brought in coffee, then left us alone to talk. Somewhat to my surprise, Ernie was in a good mood.

We talked about the upcoming Ernest J. Gaines Award ceremony honoring Mitchell S. Jackson, whose novel *The Residue Years* was based on his experience growing up in Portland, Oregon, in a neighborhood ravaged by violence and drug use.[20]

"This is the highest monetary award in the name of an African American writer," Ernie said. "Ten thousand dollars, that's a heckuva lot of money. When

I started out I got twenty-five hundred to go to Stanford. My first award, the [Joseph Henry] Jackson, was a thousand."[21]

"Everything has changed since 'sixty-four," when *Catherine Carmier* was published, Ernie said. "All publishing has changed. But it's always been hard for Black writers to get published." Just as in 2013, when I had heard him read from his novella at ULL, Ernie seemed distressed about his lengthy absence from the world of books.

> I don't know what's going on in publishing these days. I haven't published a novel in almost twenty-two years. I know I was never given a big advance. I think I got three hundred fifty thousand for *A Lesson Before Dying*. After Oprah picked it up, it moved to the best seller list in the *New York Times* for six weeks. That's still carrying me today. The book is being read all over the country—all over the world, in about a dozen or more countries. All my books are still in print. *Mozart and Leadbelly* is still in print.

He was still working on the two novellas he had talked about in 2013. "In *Daughters of the Creole Lady,* the daughter is not the major character now. A cousin took over. The female cousin is dark and the ladies are very fair-skinned. I know a family like that."[22] He had sent the second novella, *The Man Who Whipped Children,* to his publisher. "I've had no correspondence with anybody at Knopf since Ash Green left and then died [in 2012]. They're all younger now." He grimaced and added, "I'm not working at all anymore. To me, working is five hours a day five days a week. If I put in five hours a week, that's all I'm doing."

He worked at his fishing camp across the highway on False River. "It's a two-bedroom trailer. I use one for my office. It's quieter—no telephone, no one on either side of me. I can look out at the river, at the beautiful weeping willow moving in the wind." Frigid weather can feel even colder on the river, but Ernie said he had a heater in the trailer. "I'll put on a sweater and heavy jacket." He no longer drove, so Dianne would drop him at the office. "I can get from the door to the car," he said. He still wrote drafts in longhand, then typed them on his Royal electric or the computer. "I usually have music in the background, usually chamber music."

Talking about music led us to recall a favorite hangout, Tabby's Blues Box, which had been torn down in 1999. "I took my buddies from San Francisco over there once," he said. "This woman was dancing around us and she'd pull her skirt up a little. David Pellerido got up and started dancing with her."

As we chatted, a multicolored cat wandered in and sniffed around Ernie's chair. He told me his granddaughter Annalisa had named her Rainbow, but he preferred Fiona—FiFi for short. FiFi was shy but eventually came up and nudged my hand a few times. Ernie was impressed and later told Dianne about the encounter. "She's afraid of people and seldom comes around them," he said.

He told me the other cat, Thomas, had done something extraordinary. Their dog DeeDee had recently escaped from the fenced yard and ventured onto heavily traveled Highway 1, where she was run over. The veterinarian couldn't save her. Ernie said a local man had made her a "little cypress coffin. We wrapped her up well in a blanket. I put one of my berets in there and Dianne put a medal in. I put a letter in there with her. I kept a copy of it."

A friend dug a grave for DeeDee, and Dianne and Ernie buried her behind their guest house. "Thomas knows she's there," he said. "One day we looked all over for him; when we found him, he was looking at the mound of dirt. They have such a strong sense of smell. He knows DeeDee is in there. He misses her."

We wandered onto the subject of religion. I consider myself a fallen-away Catholic, disenchanted by too many school nuns. Ernie said he "took a lot of crap [at St. Augustine] because I was Baptist." He said he believed in God. "If there were no God, I wouldn't be here. I'd be dead or crazy or in prison. Guys I grew up with were all killed at an early age."[23]

By the time we finished talking it was two o'clock. I gathered my notebook and pens and prepared to leave. But Dianne, an excellent cook, invited me to join them for lunch. They belonged to a co-op that delivered fresh vegetables every week and they had just gotten a box. As she put the finishing touches on the hot dishes, I minced garlic for the salad and set the round table in the kitchen. Gazing into the back yard, where the Cherie Quarters church now stands, we feasted on flounder, spinach and beet greens with garlic, sweet potatoes, and snow peas—all delicious. They drank white wine; mindful of my drive home, I had ginger ale.

Ernie had bought the table and chairs in San Francisco as "raw wood" and stained them himself after sanding the wood with steel wool. He said it had made a nice change to do something with his hands after hours of writing. He had bought the daybed in the next room at a "garage sale" on the street.

We talked about race. Ernie said he and his nephew Wilfred Hebert were "laughing the other day," predicting that at some point, instead of the one-drop rule, white people will allow anyone who is 25 percent Black to be considered white, so whites can continue to be the majority.

I helped Dianne load the dishwasher, then asked them to use my phone to take photos of me with each of them. "Are you afraid I might die?" Ernie demanded. I told him about my recent health problems and said, "So, Ernie, I might go before you do." He said he hoped not, but "I don't want to go anytime soon."

### REACHING OUT

In 2016, Ernie phoned Roz Arbel, who had always considered him her stepfather. They had not been in touch since the late 1980s. "He was surprisingly up front about his feelings," Roz told me. She wondered if the recent death of their mutual friend, writer Michael Harper, had inspired him to call her. "Maybe it lit a fire," she said. "He really wanted to reminisce. He told me, 'I think about your mom and you all the time. Five years after I moved back to Louisiana I was really sad about what had happened. I just want you to know I care about you very much.' I started bawling. He just let me cry it out. We have a lot of history. I told him, 'You're my dad.'"[24] Roz said her impression from their conversation was that Ernie was depressed.

> I asked him, "What's your typical day like?" He said, "I don't do much, hang out at home." He mentioned the walker and the wheelchair. I've seen pictures of him using them. He told me he doesn't get out much. He used to walk all over San Francisco. For him to be in that situation is a real bummer.
>
> After our phone conversation I emailed him that it was wonderful to talk to him. Next thing I know, I get a package from Ernie, next-day delivery. It's beautifully packed, all of his hardback books. My mom has all the first editions, signed of course.

Encouraged by their recent connection, Roz went to Louisiana the following year and spent several days, bunking with Ernie's sister Lois in the guesthouse on his property. She attended the annual graveyard cleanup and the lunch afterward.

Roz sat next to Ernie in the carport where lunch was traditionally served after the cleanup. She enjoyed chatting with Wilfred Hebert, the nephew to whom Ernie had dedicated his last novel, *The Tragedy of Brady Sims.* "Ernie loved just sitting and drinking with the local guys," she said. "I think that fame annoyed him."

A highlight of her visit was going with Lois to see Cherie Quarters, or what was left of it.

> I'm really thankful that I got to stay with Lois, because we went all around, and she showed me all the different places, where different people's houses were in the quarters. I got to ask her what their life was like. I think it's such a horrible shame that there's only one or two of those quarters houses left. I think it would be the right thing to put a couple of them back on the property.
>
> I grew up seeing photos that Ernie had taken of all of those houses, a really long row of them. I was pretty shocked when I went there and saw one [cabin] completely overgrown and another maybe half a mile down the road.
>
> I'm glad I got to see that beautiful place. I can see why he would want to come back. It's a huge feat for someone who started out so indigent to have a successful life there.[25]

### SAYING GOODBYE

I hadn't seen Ernie in a year when I learned that he had died on Tuesday, November 5, 2019. Ben Biben called to tell me. His friend Leonard Edwards had seen "emergency cars" at the house that morning, and word soon spread. Ben called Dianne, who confirmed the sad news.

Ben was stunned. "We were over there Sunday, laughing and talking," he said. "He was in a good mood." E. J.'s death, said Ben, "is a low blow, because we were together. I'm next," he said, meaning that he was only eighteen months younger than his lifelong friend.

The next day, I called Ernie's sister Lois, who had moved from the guesthouse to her brother Norbert's house nearby. "My dear big brother," she said of Ernie. She was thankful that family members had visited recently, including her sister Sambra, brother Charles, and niece Wanda, Norbert's daughter.[26]

Michael, who was a baby when Ernie scrawled out his first draft of *Catherine Carmier,* had spent five days in Oscar. "Last Saturday, he picked Ernie up and brought him over here," Lois said. "Norbert fixed a special dinner. The last couple of years, Ernie would only eat two or three spoonfuls. We had a wonderful Saturday with him. Sunday Michael spent three or four hours with him."

Lois told me, "He was so unhappy. He was ready to go. He had this distant look in his eyes. He just got tired and let go."

The funeral would be November 16, a Saturday, to give people from out of town a chance to attend. The burial, at the Cherie Quarters graveyard he had fought to preserve, would be "just a small family thing."

I had last seen Ernie a year earlier, in a panel discussion at the annual Louisiana Book Festival at the State Capitol. My impression was that he was phoning it in. I had to strain to hear him, and he looked downcast, distant, disengaged. The man who had once walked all over San Francisco was now confined to a wheelchair, and he was writing much less. I thought about my last real conversation with him, on that cold, blustery January day. We had sat in his cozy library drinking coffee as the cat wandered in and out. Ernie was in good spirits, expansive and laughing. He seemed happier than I had seen him in a long time.

At the visitation on Friday night, I saw many old friends of Ernie's who had by now become friends of mine: Ben; his brother Sam, who had flown in from San Francisco; Mary Ricard, who with her late husband, Aubrey, had been such good friends to Ernie for so long.

Dianne told me Ernie had been in great spirits at the recent graveyard cleanup and at a meeting of the cemetery association, eating, drinking, and laughing. Monday night he had watched football on TV before going to bed and dying in his sleep.

Next day, Hall Davis funeral home in Scotlandville was packed with hundreds of people. Reverend Levert Kemp, who grew up spending summers with his grandparents at Cherie Quarters, officiated. Cicely Tyson, ninety-four, spoke about stumbling across a copy of *Miss Jane* in a California bookstore, being captivated by it, and later playing the role of Miss Jane. Ernie's brother Michael Colar, his stepson Stephen Smith, and his ULL colleague and friend Darrell Bourque gave tributes. I kept my composure until Darrell's personal and heartfelt words, which described the long-ago evening with Ernie and Jane Bonin, and then my tears flowed. I saved a copy of the program for Roz, along with a few rose petals from the casket spray.

A week after the funeral, I talked to Ben, who had gone to the cemetery to see where Ernie was buried. "I went back to E. J.," he said. "They didn't put him where he wanted to be. They buried him by the bayou, turned north. I could have cried. Only Dianne, Lois, Dianne's sister, and somebody else were there. I wanted to be there but they said 'only a few people.'" Years before, Ben had told me, "You're supposed to be buried with feet to the east, head to the west. When you rise up, you rise up to the east."[27]

Roz later told me that Norbert's daughter Wanda went to the burial by herself because her father, Norbert, wasn't feeling well. "Wanda said it was pretty emotional," Roz told me. "She said Dianne read a prayer that Ernie had written. She was looking through some boxes and she came across a little piece of paper with his handwriting on it. I guess it was kind of his way of letting her know he was still around. Wanda said that Dianne read it aloud, and then folded it up and put it away."[28]

I thought back to my conversation with Lois. "Ernie and I were so close," she had said. "He's in peace now. What's helping me is I know he was so sad. We want to remember him not in the casket but laughing in the sailboat."

# 5

# EVERYBODY WAS EVERYBODY'S CHILD

## THE PEOPLE OF CHERIE QUARTERS

The caravan of a dozen cars and vans cruised along False River, then turned off Highway 1 onto Major Lane and slid silently past fields of sugar cane. After traveling a mile or so, the automobiles turned right, off the asphalt and onto a gravel-and-dirt road. They snaked their way up to a grove of oak and pecan trees, where they stopped. Men, women, and children dressed in their Sunday best climbed out of the cars and strolled into the Cherie Quarters graveyard, a patch of ground surrounded by trees in the midst of cane fields. Hundreds of people lie buried there, most in unmarked graves. But on this hot and humid summer afternoon in 1996, members of the Kemp, Lovely, and Horton families didn't need markers to remember their dead.

Ben Biben pointed toward the tallest pecan tree. "Miss Teen is buried over there," he said. He turned 180 degrees and pointed at the trees that separated the graveyard from the surrounding fields. "Miss Zuma and Rang are back over there." (Miss Zuma was Julia McVay, Ernest Gaines's maternal grandmother, and Rang was her brother Griffin McVay.) Joe Williams, a stocky, round-faced man of forty-seven, pointed at a double tomb near the fence. "My grandmother and grandfather are buried there," he said. "Papa Joe Williams and his wife, Susan."

The trip to the graveyard was the culmination of a three-day reunion organized by Ben's sister Barbara Overstreet of Baton Rouge. One of seven children of Albertha Kemp Bibbens, she was the leader when it came to organizing gatherings of her siblings and cousins. Each of her reunions had a theme and a color. In 1996, the theme was "Gone But Not Forgotten" and the colors were black and white. All the women visiting the graveyard wore dresses in those colors, and the men were somberly clad in tones of black, white, and gray.

"Age," said Barbara, explaining why she had organized three family reunions in the past five years. "The older people. You begin to lose your ancestors, your grandmother, your mom. You want to do something. Let them see something of this. This is history."

Since the exodus from Cherie Quarters began in the late 1940s, various individuals have functioned as the hub of the group, and their houses have served as the gathering place. In the 1950s and 1960s, it was George and Mamie Williams's house in Baton Rouge, where Ernest Gaines stayed while writing *Catherine Carmier.* After Ben got married in late 1963 and moved to a house on Twelfth Street in Old South Baton Rouge, he and his wife, Carol, played host to the group. When Ben and Carol moved to a more remote area of town, Barbara took over the role. Her house on Evangeline Street in north Baton Rouge became headquarters for the circle of family and friends.

About fifty family members had come from across the country for the 1996 reunion. Relatives from San Francisco, Seattle, and Dallas had begun arriving two weeks earlier. Four of them stayed at Overstreet's house. A heavyset, perpetually cheerful woman of fifty with a sly sense of humor, Overstreet then worked for the East Baton Rouge Parish school system food service. She did much of the cooking for the three-day reunion.

Joe Williams, the son of George and Mamie Williams, was staying at Barbara's house. Born in Cherie Quarters in 1949, Williams had left Louisiana in 1973, eventually settling in San Francisco, where he lived next door to his cousin Ernest Gaines on Divisadero Street. "We've had a joyful time talking about the past," he said. "When we lived here, we didn't realize how historical it was. It's a great feeling to see the value Ernie placed on it in his writing."

Gaines wasn't at the reunion—he was teaching in France that year—but his presence was felt. His photograph of quarter cabins, taken in the 1960s, decorated the programs and T-shirts that Overstreet had had printed. The focus of the reunion was Cherie Quarters.

The reunion had started the previous Friday night, when forty adults and ten children gathered at the Baton Rouge Garden Center to eat, drink, and reminisce. Hanging from one wall was a large brown paper banner with a pastel drawing of the Cherie Quarter cabins. Across the bottom was printed

George Williams, *left*, and Lionel Rowan in front of the house where Gaines once lived at Cherie Quarters, January 1957. Rowan was the model for the character Marcus in *Of Love and Dust*. Williams had married Mamie Kemp and moved to Baton Rouge with their son Joe. Gaines spent six months living with them in 1963 while he worked on his first novel. Photo by David Biben. Courtesy of Deidra Biben-Glynn.

"Gone But Not Forgotten." Fifteen watercolor paintings of scenes from quarter life dotted the room, the work of Joe Williams. A graduate of Southern University with a degree in architectural engineering, and a resident of San Francisco for most of his adult life, Williams had reconstructed life in Cherie Quarters on paper, much as his cousin Ernest Gaines had done in his books. He had studied old photographs of the people and events of the quarter, copying some of them in watercolor. At Ben Biben's request he had even painted the sugarhouse that was once the center of the plantation. Unable to remember the building, which was torn down in the 1950s, Williams went to Wilson Domino, one of the oldest former residents of Cherie Quarters, and asked him to describe the tall brick mill where cane was processed. Biben said Joe's painting did not entirely jibe with his memory, but he later gave it a place of honor on a wall in his den.

Sam Bibbens, Ben's brother (the difference in their last names is discussed later in the chapter), flew in from San Francisco for the reunion. According to Sam, the sugarhouse was a dividing line between those who lived in the quarter and those who lived back in the cane fields. "There was 'up the quarter' and 'down the quarter,'" he said. "Sometimes there would be territorial feuds." Bibbens said people from back in the fields sometimes feared passing the sugarhouse and venturing into the quarter. "It was like crossing into enemy territory," he said.[1]

Bibbens spoke nostalgically of Julia McVay, who cooked for the plantation owners until leaving Cherie Quarters around 1950 to join her daughter and grandchildren in San Francisco. "She was the best cook I've ever known," said Bibbens, who often sampled Miss Zuma's cakes and pies as a boy in the quarter. McVay died in San Francisco in 1970; she is buried in the plantation graveyard near her mother, Susan Jones McVay Williams, her brother Griffin, and other family members.

On Saturday, the second day of the reunion, the families convened at False River for an all-day picnic and some fishing. On Sunday they attended religious services in Baton Rouge and in Lakeland, near Oscar, conducted by family members Levert Kemp and James Terrance. Afterward, they drove to Cherie Quarters to visit the graveyard and the two 150-year-old cabins that still stood. The white wooden church was also there, and next to it a shed built by Ernest Gaines's paternal grandfather Izel Gaines. Izel Gaines was a carpenter and handyman at River Lake, upon whom Gaines modeled his character Felix in the short story "Bloodline."

Standing in front of a cabin nearly obscured by vines and weeds, the group remembered Reese Spooner, who had lived there until he died in 1985. "We used to throw rocks on Reese's [tin] roof to tease him," recalled Frankie Christopher, another former resident of Cherie Quarters, with whom Ernest Gaines stayed during his research trips to Baton Rouge for the writing of *The Autobiography of Miss Jane Pittman.* (Christopher, the sister of Ben, Sam, and Barbara, now lived in the house on Louise Street that the Williams family once occupied.) "Reese would come out on his porch and tell us, 'Don't stone my house!'"

Reese was one of the best-loved elders of Cherie Quarters. Ben Biben remembered his kindness. "I had to get wood to burn in the fireplace," he said. "I couldn't always get a mule to take back in the woods. Reese would bring wood for me to use at night. Later, when I went back to visit, I told Reese I remembered that. He said, 'Your mama [Albertha Kemp Bibbens] worked at

Triple Arch [restaurant]. She'd bring us chicken necks and catfish rims. My children were starving to death and your mama would feed 'em.' We used to share everything."

Levert Kemp pointed to an empty spot across the road from Reese's house. "That's where Mama lived," he said. "Mama" was Emma Lovely Kemp, grandmother to Levert and many others at the reunion. Emma, whose name was pronounced *Em-MAH,* French fashion, used to grind her own coffee beans out on the front gallery. Her husband, Sam Kemp, was good at math. Other plantation workers would seek him out to learn how much they had earned on their crops.

Before heading to the last event on her reunion agenda, dinner at the Oxbow Restaurant overlooking False River, Barbara Overstreet gave a last glance at the curtain of green that covered nearly every trace of the community where she had once lived. "Gone, but not forgotten," said Barbara, who made regular expeditions to Cherie Quarters with camcorder in hand. "I videoed the cabins before they tore them down, I videoed while they were taking them down, and I videoed after they came down. That was it. It was all there at one time. You know we'll never forget it."

## THE GAINES FAMILY

The earliest known member of the Gaines family in Cherie Quarters was the Reverend A. A. Ginn. Little is known of Reverend Ginn, and it is not clear when or why the name was changed to Gaines; possibly the two spellings were simply the result of carelessness by census takers. Evidently, Ginn and his wife had died by 1900, when the census of the Eighth Ward of Pointe Coupée Parish reveals that his sons Isaiah (twenty years old) and Joseph (twelve) were living with their uncle Alfred Jackson.

Isaiah Ginn, who was born in 1880, was listed as "Isia" Gaines in the 1910 census, as "Izel" Gaines in 1920, and as "Iziah" Gaines in 1930. He married Rose Steeple, with whom he had eight children between about 1904 and 1919. Of the six boys and two girls, a son, Manuel, was the fifth child, born on November 22, 1911.

In the 1920 census, Izel, age forty, and Rose, forty-one, are listed with their eight children, ages sixteen years to seven months. Their son Manuel was nine. In the 1930 census, Izel, fifty, is listed with his wife Harriet and six children. Evidently, Rose had died between 1920 and February 1926, when Izel married Harriet Ranson or Ransom. A marriage certificate on file at the Pointe

Coupée Parish Courthouse shows that "Isiah Ginn" and "Harriet Ransomme" married on February 14, 1926. On his marriage certificate, Isiah listed his parents as Alex and Adline Ginn.[2] Harriet "Gains" is buried in the graveyard at Cherie Quarters; the gravesite locations of Izel and Rose are unknown, but presumably they, too, are buried there. Manuel, age eighteen, was living with his father and stepmother.

Manuel had only two years of schooling before dropping out to work at farming and sharecropping, work he did throughout his years in Cherie Quarters. He had just turned twenty when he married Adrean Jefferson, who was fifteen and a half, on December 3, 1931.[3] In January 1933, Adrean gave birth to a son whom she named Ernest James, or E. J. He apparently saw more of his grandparents and other relatives than his parents during his early years. Manuel Gaines was living in New Orleans when he applied for a Social Security card in February 1938 and when he enlisted in the army in November 1942.[4]

Ernest clearly remembered Manuel's father. Izel lived at Cherie Quarters until his death at age sixty-three on January 30, 1944, just two weeks after E. J. turned eleven. Gaines remembered Izel as the yardman, handyman, and carpenter for the white owners of the plantation. According to Gaines, his grandfather also built several structures in Cherie Quarters, including the shed that stood next to the church and served as a dining hall. (The shed still stood in late 2003, but by early 2005 it had collapsed or been torn down.) He also replaced worn-out building parts, such as piers and stairs.[5]

Ernest Gaines's brother Lionel was born in July 1934, followed by Eugene (October 6, 1935), Lois (December 28, 1937), Charles (1939), Norbert (1940), and Joseph Mack (June 4, 1946). Like their older brother E. J., the boys were raised by their great-aunt Augusteen. Their sister Lois lived with her grandmother Julia McVay.[6]

Lionel was fourteen when his older brother left for California, and he was extremely upset by his leaving, according to his wife, Ada Mae. "Everybody was sad," she said. "It was like he was going away and you'd never see him again. Lionel went and hid. He didn't want to see his brother go. He was very sad. That was like a link broken in the chain. When the word got around, it was just like somebody died."[7]

Lionel attended school through the eighth grade and then went to work at the Triple Arch restaurant in Oscar. Although his siblings left for California within a few years after his mother and stepfather moved away, Lionel and his next younger brother, Eugene, chose not to go, instead electing to stay home and "take care of Aunty." In May 1952, Lionel (age seventeen) married Ada Mae Robillard (eighteen), with whom he had grown up in Cherie Quarters. According to Ada Mae, she and Lionel moved in to the other half of the house occupied by Aunt Teen. They were living there when she died in 1953.

In 1938, when he filled out his Social Security application, Manuel Gaines was living in New Orleans. He and Adrean divorced in 1946, after separating about ten years prior to that, although they occasionally lived near each other in Cherie Quarters. In 1948, Manuel married Clara Zeno, the daughter of Walter "Pete" Zeno, a man to whom Ernest Gaines often went to hear stories about the old days. Manuel and Clara Gaines, who lived in Baton Rouge, had nine children together. Manuel worked for many years as a janitor at Louisiana State University. He died in 1999, at the age of eighty-seven, and is buried at Southern Memorial Gardens in Baton Rouge. Although he has said that Manuel was "very kind" to him when he was a child, Ernest Gaines was estranged from Manuel Gaines from the time he was a teenager and had little contact with him as an adult.[8]

## THE JEFFERSON AND VINCENT FAMILIES

Ernest Gaines's mother, Adrean Janice Jefferson, was born June 26, 1916, the older of two daughters of Julia McVay and Matthew "Man" Jefferson. Her sister, Bernice, nearly four years younger, "used to visit, but she was not raised with me," according to Adrean, who grew up in a household that included her disabled aunt, Augusteen Jefferson.[9]

Adrean Jefferson's paternal grandfather is thought to be Calvin Jefferson, but information about the Jefferson family is scarce. Ben Biben recalled that "Miss Teen" and "Man" were brother and sister; he said they had another brother named "Tee Boy," but that possibly Tee Boy was not a full sibling.[10]

More documentation exists for the family of Calvin Jefferson's wife, the Vincents, whose name was given the French pronunciation *VAH-son.* In his Social Security application, Matthew Jefferson listed his mother's name as Virginia "Vanson," but census records list her as Rosana or Rosina. Adrean recalled that her grandmother grew up in Cherie Quarters.[11]

Ernest Vincent (born circa 1845) and his wife, Augustine Brigitte (born circa 1852), were married in Pointe Coupée Parish in July 1873.[12] In the 1880 census for Ward 8, they are listed with two daughters, Bebe and Marna, ages seven and nine. Since the 1890 census is unavailable, there is a twenty-year gap until we find the family in the 1900 census. Ernest, age fifty-five, and Augustine, forty-seven, are living with their daughter Rosana, thirty, and four grandchildren: Edward Lemon, thirteen; James Browsas, ten; Augustine Jefferson, six; and Matthew Jefferson, three. By 1910, Ernest, sixty-four, and Augustine, fifty-one, are listed with their daughter Rosana, thirty-nine, and six grandchildren: Simon and James Dickerson, Augustine and Matthew Jefferson, and Georgia and Andrew Cooper. In 1920, Ernest is listed as age eighty-five, undoubtedly an error, and Augustine as sixty-seven, which also does not jibe with her age in earlier censuses. They are living with their daughter "Rosina," forty-nine; granddaughter "Augustin" Jefferson, twenty-five; grandson Landro Charley, seventeen; and great-granddaughter "Aderine" Jefferson, age three. (Rosana, who was probably Augusteen and Matthew Jefferson's mother, apparently always lived with her parents and not with Calvin Jefferson, her children's father.) Ernest Vincent died before 1930; the census for that year lists a widowed Augustine Vincent, seventy-seven, living with her granddaughter and namesake "Augustine" Jefferson, thirty-five, and her great-granddaughter "Edwina" (doubtless Adrean, pronounced *Ah-DREEN*), age thirteen.

Adrean was raised by her aunt Augusteen and her great-grandmother Augustine Vincent. She recalled Augusteen Jefferson, who was twenty-two when Adrean was born in 1916, as "a very pleasant person. She was handicapped, but she was very good at getting around. She was a very good cook, and she cleaned very well." But while Aunt Augusteen kept the home fires going, her grandmother, Adrean's great-grandmother Augustine, was very much involved in the life of the community. "She was a doctor, a midwife," Adrean said, noting that her great-grandmother not only delivered babies but treated a variety of ailments. "She would do several different things, [treat] anything you had; in those days, they made tea for everything [as a medicine]. It was quite a ways before you could get to a doctor. She was the only midwife for at least twenty or twenty-five miles. She was there immediately [when needed], day or night. They didn't have plenty of money to pay her, so they gave her chickens or pigs. She always wanted me to be a doctor."

Adrean's father, Matthew "Man" Jefferson, was a rather shadowy presence. Ben Biben met him once or twice at Cherie Quarters but did not recall his living there. "I remember him coming there once, and another time I saw him at the store." Jefferson, who was born in 1896, was living in New Orleans when he applied for Social Security in 1936. Biben said Man Jefferson was "bald-headed," a trait that would surface in several of his descendants. He also was "sort of smart aleck; he'd bite you real quick." Biben had heard members of the previous generation say that Man Jefferson had gone to prison for murder.[13]

Although Adrean recalled herself as "a very happy kid," her life was still bounded by the harsh reality of life in Cherie Quarters. She went no further than the fifth grade in school, hampered by the lack of educational opportunities and the need to work. Before she was seventeen, she was a mother herself. While she apparently lived with her aunt Augusteen and her children for a while, Adrean also left the plantation sometime in the 1940s and found work in New Orleans, along with her second husband, Norbert Colar, whom she married in December 1946.

Although she was not home with her children full time, Adrean was a strict parent. "That's the way I was raised: mean what I say and say what I mean." She and her aunt Augusteen "pulled together," with help from all the other adults in Cherie Quarters. "We wanted our children to be the best. You can't see your children all the time. Help from people means a lot." She ticked off the rules her children were expected to follow: "When you're out of school, come home. I don't want you breaking fruit off people's trees, throwing rocks, picking no fights. I don't want no foul words spoken. Respect elderly, as I want to be respected." Her children were expected to come straight home, change out of their school clothes, and do their chores. When they went outside to play, "I will show you the sun, and I want you back before dark." The rules were clearly understood. "You learn right, you don't have to remind but once."[14]

Like her son Ernest, Adrean felt that she had to get out of Louisiana. Many interactions with the white world made her angry.

> You can go to a restaurant, but you have to go around the back. Or go to a movie and have to go in another door. Children get on a bus and have to wait for all the white children to get on first. And there's a board between you and the white person, like it was gonna rub off. Who wouldn't be mad? You learn to live with that anger until you can get out of it. . . . If I hadn't left when I did leave, I know I'd have been dead a long time ago. That's why I got out of there and that's why I got my family out of there. The best thing for me was to get away. I could be pushed just so far. I'm glad I got out when I did.

Education was high on Adrean's list of priorities. "I always thought education was the most important thing you could get," she said. "If we didn't get it, we wasn't going to get anywhere. They [children] had to be in school. You had to make a grade each year. . . . I couldn't afford to raise dummies. You was gon' get somewhere. Pass a grade every year, and I don't mean maybe. Pass it, no failing. . . . You have nothing to do but eat, sleep, and study, so do that. . . . If you don't want to do that, get a job. . . . If I'm the breadwinner, you gon' make the grades."

Adrean completed only the fifth grade at Cherie Quarters, but she never lost sight of her dream of finishing school, something she had promised herself and her great-grandmother she would do. After her husband died, in 1969, she enrolled in the fourth grade at a school in Vallejo, California, at the age of fifty-three. She attended either night or day school for the next eight years, while also working at various jobs. After graduating, she became a licensed practical nurse and worked until she was seventy-five. She died in 2003, a month shy of her eighty-seventh birthday.[15] Unlike her mother and sons, who are buried in the Cherie Quarters cemetery, she was laid to rest in All Souls Catholic Cemetery in Vallejo alongside her husband, Norbert.[16]

Ernest Gaines paid homage to his mother's family name in his books, most notably in his fifth novel, *A Lesson Before Dying;* its protagonist, a young man wrongly executed for murder, goes by the single name Jefferson. A variation on his mother's first name appears as the town of St. Adrienne in several of his works, including *In My Father's House.*

## THE McVAY AND JONES FAMILIES

Ernest Gaines said that his great grandfather James McVay was "half white." A photograph of McVay that hung in his study in Lafayette, and later in Oscar, revealed a handsome man who "looked like William Faulkner." Both census information and oral history suggest that McVay's father was from Ireland. His father was likely James McVea, a white man born in Ireland in 1826, listed in both the 1870 and 1880 censuses. Census data suggests that James McVea fathered two sons by a Black woman named Julia Harris—James, in 1874, and Henry, in 1877, both born in Louisiana. "Horace and Griffin [McVay] both told me that their father was Irish," Ben Biben said. "His father was white, I'm almost sure."[17]

Susan Jones, Gaines's great-grandmother, as a young woman. She married James McVay, with whom she had five children, and she later had four children with "Papa" Joe Williams. She is buried in the graveyard at Cherie Quarters in a double tomb with Williams. Photo courtesy of Ruby McVay Simmons.

James McVay married Susan Jones in Pointe Coupée Parish in 1894.[18] According to Biben, Susan Jones, born in September 1877, was the daughter of Margaret Jones and Jean Baptiste Major, making her a half sister to plantation owner Pervis Cherie Major.[19] In a photograph of Susan in her twenties or thirties, she has very light skin. Biben remembered seeing Susan's sister in Cherie Quarters when he was a child. "She was real white, with long hair down to her behind," he said. Adrean Jefferson, who was eight years old when Susan died, remembered that her light-skinned grandmother was distant toward her. "I was dark, and my grandmother didn't want to have much to do with me," she said.[20]

Ernest Gaines's maternal grandmother Julia McVay was the second of five children born to Susan Jones and James McVay. Preceded by a sister, Sarah (1894), Julia was born in 1896, followed by a sister, Margaret (1898), and brothers Griffin (1903) and Horace (1904). When Julia McVay was a child, her father left the family. His departure is shrouded in mystery, but Gaines said that James McVay had to leave the plantation because of a confrontation with white people.[21]

Census records support the idea McVay left the plantation. He is present in the 1900 census of the Eighth Ward of Pointe Coupée Parish, where Cherie Quarters residents were listed, but he does not show up in the 1910 census. Assuming he was still present when his youngest child, Horace, was born on December 10, 1904, it seems likely that he left the plantation between 1905 and 1910, when Susan Jones is listed as living with Joseph Williams and her children by McVay.

Oral tradition has it that McVay killed a man, perhaps in a dispute involving his wife, Susan, or another woman, but no documentation of that event has been found. Family members believe that McVay moved to Chicago and communicated with his family in Louisiana from time to time. Horace's adopted daughter, Ruby McVay Simmons, said Horace told her that James McVay had owned a tannery. "Some white people wanted to buy it. There was an argument and they started shooting. [James McVay] shot one and killed him. They [white men] tried to burn the [McVay] house down."[22]

"I think James McVay killed a white man," Ben Biben said. "Horace said he wanted them to come up to Illinois or someplace. James McVay tried to make contact with [his family], but he was afraid to let them know where he was. Susan must have known he was alive. I think he wanted them to know he cared, but it was impossible. A lot of 'em had to run."[23]

Ruby Simmons heard that members of the Major family helped McVay leave. If McVay's wife, Susan, was indeed a half sister to P. C. Major, that probably motivated Major to help her husband escape with his life. It may also explain why, later, Julia McVay was given a position of prominence as the cook at the Big House, where she remained for more than thirty years.

Julia also functioned as a surrogate mother or grandmother to the children of Cherie Quarters. From her house near the front of the quarter, which gave her easy access to the Big House, she could monitor the comings and goings of the children, who often passed her yard on the way to the store on Highway 1. "Mama Julia, any time you went to the store, she saw you," said Gaines's sister-in-law Ada Mae Gaines. "She knew how long you were gone. Everybody honored her. . . . She told every child what was right and wrong. Everybody obeyed her."[24]

Sam Bibbens recalled a long-running feud with his cousin Roosevelt Brooks, who was lying in wait for him because of a dispute over a game of marbles. "One day my mother asked me to go to the store," Bibbens said. "Roosevelt saw me walking and said, 'I got you now!' I took off running. When I got up by Miss Zuma's house, I was out of breath and I went up on her porch [to rest in safety]. She gave us a lecture and gave us each a piece of pie and made us sit and eat it. We left friends."[25] Bibbens, who moved to San Francisco in the early 1960s, graduated from San Francisco State College in 1972 with a degree in radio and television. In California, he saw a good deal of Julia McVay, who had left Cherie Quarters around 1950 and worked as a domestic. "Every holiday she'd invite me and Ernie over for dinner. She'd have a big spread—turkey, beefsteaks, vegetables, breads, the works."

Although Julia McVay's life seems to have been fairly straightforward, several mysteries emerge from the study of census records and other documents. Her younger daughter, Bernice Joyce Jefferson, born April 12, 1920, apparently lived with her mother, while Adrean lived with her aunt Augusteen Jefferson and Augusteen's parents. Census records make it clear where Adrean lived, but they are confusing when one searches for Bernice. In the 1920 census of Ward 8 in Pointe Coupée Parish, Bernice Jefferson, age one, is living with her mother "Julia Cross." In 1930, Julia and Bernice are missing from the Ward 8 census but are enumerated in Alexandria, ninety miles north of Oscar. Julia, thirty-two, is again listed as Julia Cross. She and her daughter Bernice Jefferson, eleven, are both listed as "roomers" in the household of Frank Johnson and his wife, Clara. One wonders why McVay, who worked at the Big House, would have left Cherie Quarters and moved with her younger daughter to a distant town. Possibly it had something to do with Matthew Jefferson—did she join him there, or did she flee from him? Was her time there a brief stay that happened to coincide with the census taker's visit? Another mystery of Cherie Quarters.

In 1940, "Julia Cron" and "Bernice U Jefferson" are in back in Pointe Coupée, ages forty-two and twenty-two, although Bernice was probably actually closer to twenty. It is unclear why Julia McVay, whose children were apparently fathered by Matthew Jefferson, would be enumerated with the last name Cross or Cron. ("Cron" may not be the name written by the census taker; the handwriting is hard to read.) Julia is listed as a "widowed" cook with a second-grade education, although Matthew Jefferson was still alive. Bernice has completed high school.[26]

According to Ben Biben, Bernice, like Biben's mother, had an "affair" with George Major. "Adrean's sister Bernice, that's one of those George Major stories. I think he used to run around with her. That scene in *Of Love and Dust,* when they [Bonbon and Pauline] go in the back while Aunt Ca'line and Pa Bully are on the porch, that's George Major and Bernice, I think." Biben said that when Major married Eola Bertonnier, around 1940, he gave Bernice money to leave Pointe Coupée Parish. "I assume Miss LaLa [Eola] knew about her. According to Reese [Spooner, who was an adult then], George Major sent her away after he married."[27]

Bernice married Ambrose Price Woodard soon after the end of World

War II and moved with him to Wichita, Kansas, where he pursued a career in the law, as his namesake father had. In the 1970s, Price Woodard served briefly as Wichita's first Black mayor.

Biben said Ernest Gaines resented his wealthier aunt, who paid little attention to him during his years of struggle. "I remember E. J. came to Louise Street [to visit] and said, 'God damn, she'll invite me to dinner now that I'm well known, but she wanted nothing to do with me when I was poor.' 'They only want me because I'm famous.'"[28]

According to Simmons, "E. J. couldn't stand [Bernice]. She shunned away from us as a family." Rather than embrace the mother who had worked hard to send her to college, "Julia said Bernice was not proud of her. She would correct her grammar in front of her uppity friends."[29]

Although Adrean and Bernice were not close, Adrean called her sister when their mother died in San Francisco. Adrean had promised Julia McVay that she would be buried in Cherie Quarters, even though Adrean herself wanted nothing to do with the home cemetery. "I called my sister and told her, and she said, 'Oh, no!'" said Adrean. "But I had promised her, because I knew she wanted to be buried next to her mother and Aunty."[30]

Bernice not only agreed, she apparently paid for a vault to cover McVay's tomb. Biben visited the graveyard with Adrean when she was in town for Thanksgiving one year. "I asked her, 'What about Miss Zuma's grave?' She said, 'It's in a tomb. Bernice had a vault made.'"[31]

Julia McVay worked cleaning houses almost until the day she died of cancer, in 1970. Ernest Gaines remembered his grandmother as a woman of iron will and credited her with his "insane mania" to be on time.[32] While most scholars name Augusteen Jefferson as Gaines's greatest influence and the model for his strong women characters, his grandmother was also a likely model for the resourceful elder women in his fiction, such as Tante Lou in *Lesson* and even Jane Pittman, who worked as a cook at Samson Plantation.

Julia's brother Horace McVay, a sharecropper, married Octavia Jack, or Jacques, in 1928. Horace and Octavia lived far back behind the quarter in one of four or five houses "in the field" near the sugarhouse. "That was about two miles back from the quarters," Gaines said. "The houses were like ours in some ways, but with some differences. Horace's house did not have double doors." Gaines recalled that he "used to hang around and drink clabber" at their house. "I had many meals there," he said. Horace and Octavia would hold fish fries or gumbo suppers on weekends to raise money for the church. Around 1940, they acquired one of the few automobiles in the quarter, a dark-colored Ford that Octavia used to run errands and buy groceries for people; she also sold cosmetics throughout Pointe Coupée and West Baton Rouge Parishes. E. J. was one of her favorites, and she often took him along in the car to help her. The character Olivia Antoine in *Miss Jane,* who travels to several parishes selling cologne and "making groceries" for other people, is clearly based on Octavia.[33] Gaines dedicated *In My Father's House* in part to Octavia's memory.

Horace and Octavia adopted two children, Ruby and Lawrence. Ruby moved to California and remained close to Ernest Gaines during his years in San Francisco. Horace and Octavia McVay moved to New Roads. Octavia died in 1975, at age sixty-eight, and Horace died in 1990, at eighty-five.

Horace's brother Griffin McVay served in the army, enlisting in 1942, and later moved to San Francisco, working as a janitor at the county jail. By the time he died, in 1976, he had returned to Pointe Coupée Parish. He is buried in the Cherie Quarters graveyard.

## THE WILLIAMS FAMILY

After Susan Jones's husband James McVay left Cherie Quarters, Susan married Joseph Williams (born 1873) and had four children with him: Evelyn (1913), Clinton (1915), Cecil (1917), and George, who was born on September 13, 1919. Susan's children by McVay and by Williams grew up together and considered one another brothers and sisters, not distinguishing between full and half siblings.

Papa Joe, as he was called, outlived Susan by many years. She died in 1924, at age forty-eight, from "chronic diarrhea."[34] After she died, Papa Joe married Louise Sturges, with whom he lived until his death in 1960 at the age of eighty-seven. Papa Joe and Louise had no children of their own, but Louise is remembered as a kind person by many of the children of Cherie Quarters—including Ernest Gaines, who based several minor characters in his books on her, including Madame Bayonne in *Catherine Carmier.*[35] "She was a very nice woman," said Sam Bibbens, who as a child lived with her for a time. "Tall, thin, concerned, caring."[36]

Clinton Williams would break horses for plantation owners George and John Major, sons of P. C. Major. Clinton later moved to Seattle, as did his brother Cecil; both lost touch with the people of Cherie Quarters. Evelyn married Herman Stallworth and moved to Texas and later California. George was the only one of the four Williams children to remain in Louisiana all his life. He married Mamie Kemp, the youngest child of Sam and Emma Kemp. George and Mamie had two children, a daughter, Lee Earl, born in 1943, and a son, Joseph, born in 1949.

His nephew Sam Bibbens described George Williams as "a cowboy." "He had two of the best horses in Louisiana, Tiger and Tony. Tony was a stallion and Tiger was a gelding. Tony loved to run. He was a big, tall, fast brown horse." George worked with his brother Clinton breaking horses for other people. "They'd mount up, load him with a sack of bricks, and let him buck until he got the wildness out." They also raised horses from colts, stabling them on a pasture behind George's house. The Williams brothers were doubtless models for Joe Pittman, the only horse breaker in Gaines's fiction.

Another of George's jobs was hauling cotton to the gin. "There were three cotton gins," said Sam Bibbens. "One was out past New Roads and two were on False River, up around Mix."[37] Ben Biben worked with George cutting cane reed, which could be dangerous work. "George used to haul 'em [reeds] in the truck. We got fifteen cents a bundle. My cane knife slipped once, and I cut Alcide Cage's toe almost off."[38]

Ben Biben said George owned two mules, Bird and Red, doubtless the models for Big Red and Mr. Bascom in "Just Like a Tree." "Bird was lazy," said Biben. "Red would pull. George whipped him, but Bird wouldn't pull. George wrapped moss around a piece of cane and lit it and put it under his tail [to make him go]."[39] In the story "A Long Day in November," which appeared in the collection *Bloodline* and later as a stand-alone illustrated children's book, Gaines created a character named George Williams who helps the car-crazed Eddie burn up his automobile to win back his wife Amy.

Several factors led George and Mamie Williams to leave Cherie Quarters in the early 1950s. "The sharecrop business petered out," Sam Bibbens said. "Mechanized farming came in. White farmers had first choice [of farmland]. George never did have the good land, which was near the sugarhouse. He had some farther back, by the bayou. It was worthless. Sugar cane wouldn't grow on it. His corn was full of weeds. He had a hard time. It stayed wet all the time because the land was in between the bayous. It got no sun, and there were lots of snakes. We killed so many snakes—rattlesnakes, water moccasins, cottonmouths."[40]

George also learned barbering skills and gave haircuts on the front gallery of his house. Later, after he moved his family to Baton Rouge, people continued to go to him for haircuts, some traveling across the river from Cherie Quarters and even from New Roads.[41] When George and Mamie moved to Baton Rouge, their daughter, Lee, was already there, living with her uncle Freddie Kemp's family so she could attend McKinley High School. Their son, Joe, stayed behind with Mamie's parents, Sam and Emma Kemp, until he was old enough to attend junior high school. George and Mamie eventually bought a four-bedroom house on Louise Street, which became headquarters for many people who left Cherie Quarters. "Most of us went there when we left," said Sam, who moved in with George and Mamie after graduating from high school and stayed for eighteen months, until he joined the army.

Lee moved to San Francisco after she graduated from McKinley, staying with relatives and attending college in San Francisco. After her mother died, she moved back to Baton Rouge to live with George and Joe. She graduated from Southern University, married Norman Cador, moved to Houston, and raised a son, Anthony. Joe moved to San Francisco as a young man but made frequent trips back to Cherie Quarters, which he memorialized in his watercolor paintings.

Mamie Kemp Williams died in 1965 en route to visit Lee in California, suffering a fatal heart attack at the age of forty-three. George Williams died of a stroke in 1972, at his house on Louise Street, at fifty-one. They are buried in Lakeland, just up the road from Oscar, at the Little Zion Church cemetery. Lee, who died of cancer in 1988, at forty-five, is buried in the cemetery behind the Catholic church in Lakeland. Joe Williams died of cancer in 2001, at fifty-one. He is buried near his grandparents Papa Joe and Susan in the graveyard at Cherie Quarters.

### THE KEMP AND LOVELY FAMILIES

The earliest member of the Kemp family known to live at Cherie Quarters was Loyd Kemp, who was born around 1840. Around 1864, Loyd married Charity Bashful, the daughter of Alfred Bashful (or Bashford) and his wife, Rose. Charity, whose descendants called her "Chatty," was born in 1843 in East Feliciana Parish. Loyd and Charity had two sons, Samuel (Sam) and Eddie. When Sam Kemp was born, in April 1865, right at the end of the Civil War, the family was living on Lorio Plantation in Lakeland, about three miles from Oscar.

In about 1903, Sam Kemp married Emma Lovely, the daughter of Anthony Lovely and Amanda Horton. Sam and Emma had six children: Charley (born circa 1906), Loyd (circa 1910), Freddie (1912), Albertha (1914), Lubertha (1916), and Mamie (1921). (Emma also had a son, Anthony Cochran, before she married Sam.)

Freddie Kemp, born February 18, 1912, remembered his grandfather Loyd Kemp falling off a barn at Lorio and breaking his back, around 1915 or 1916. Ben Biben, Loyd's great-grandson, said that Loyd later died from his injuries.[42] One of Freddie's proudest possessions was a branding iron with his grandfather's initials, which went to Freddie's son Levert Kemp after Freddie died in 1997. Loyd and Charity and their family remained at Lorio until about 1918, when they moved to Cherie Quarters. Sam's younger brother, Eddie, left Cherie Quarters as a young man, moving to Houston.

Loyd Kemp's exact date of death is unknown, but it was before 1920. In the 1920 census of the Eighth Ward, Loyd's widow, Charity, is living with her older son Sam, his wife, Emma, and their six children. Charity's death certificate reveals that she died in 1924, at the age of eighty-one, of "apoplexy," probably a stroke.[43]

At Cherie Quarters, Loyd and Charity's son Sam Kemp quickly became a leader in the small community. He was one of the few men of his generation, born at the end of the Civil War, who could read, write, and do sums. "I was told that he went up to the fourth grade," his grandson Ben Biben said of the man he called "Papa," the man who raised him. "Papa used to read a lot. I think he was just that kind of person. He picked it up. He just loved to read." (Census records reveal that Emma Kemp could also read and write, but Ben said she "wasn't too good at reading; she could sign her name, but that's about all.")[44] Freddie Kemp said his father Sam "would buy newspapers from the [plantation] store,"[45] though Ben Biben remembered the newspapers as "just a sheet," possibly a broadsheet. Another grandson, Ernest Brooks, said Sam owned many books, including a thick dictionary and a Bible in which he recorded births, deaths, and other important family events. Sam also kept records for the church. "He had the most beautiful handwriting you could ever want to see," Brooks said.[46] Sam's son Freddie said his father kept "an old book" in which he wrote down "when people died." He also recorded notes about his favorite athletes, "[boxer] Jack Johnson, baseball players."[47]

Biben said his grandfather kept records for a society, to which people paid "fifteen or twenty cents a month" toward burial insurance. Biben said Sam Kemp had a trunk full of books. After Sam died in 1950, the trunk disappeared. "I'd give anything to have it," Biben said.[48]

Biben said Sam Kemp and his friends "used to have night conversations around the fire." Semuel Gaines, Manuel's brother, often visited to argue and discuss the issues of the day. "I was too small to absorb it. You [children] had to sit back on the side. I had to get the water for them. They'd sit there and smoke cigarettes and drink water." Biben recalled that "Semuel could read and write; he went to school in New Orleans. They'd talk about books."[49]

Ben cited other examples of Sam's extraordinary abilities. When he needed to reroof his house, he would "walk it off," circling the outside of the cabin, studying the roof, and estimating how many cedar shingles he would need to do the job. Then, "He'd go cut 'em." After completing the job, Sam would "maybe have ten [shingles] left over."[50]

Sharecroppers asked Sam Kemp for help figuring out how much the Major family owed them for their crops. "My grandfather could read and write and figure," said Ben. "Even the white people would go to him and say, 'I had ten bales of cotton at forty dollars a bale, Sam—how much I'm supposed to make?'"

But Sam's abilities weren't appreciated by all the white men on the plantation. "Cherie Major didn't like that, so [Sam] got beat," said Biben, who was born in 1934, the same year P. C. Major died, but had heard stories of how his grandfather had been beaten for helping others. Ernest Books also heard the stories. "He got jumped on by some whites that beat him up real bad and he lost his eyesight that way. But I never heard him have anything bitter to say about anybody."[51]

During one beating, around 1934, Sam Kemp was yanked from his horse and fell to the ground, breaking his shoulder. Another time, someone knocked him in the head with an ax handle, a blow that gradually blinded Sam. The thrashing left "a big knot on the back of his head," said Ben. "He went through hell. . . . He'd try to read by lamplight. . . . He'd be straining by that lamp, trying to hold [a book] and trying to read." But even without sight, Sam could do sums in his head, and he kept using that skill to help other workers figure out how much pay they were due. And he was still resented for it. Ben was five years old in 1939 when his grandfather hid him under the bed as "night riders" gathered menacingly outside their house back in the cane fields. Sam Kemp was seventy-five years old at the time.[52]

Even blinded, Sam helped the children of Cherie Quarters with their homework. "I remember him being good in mathematics," said Ernest Brooks. "All the kids down in the quarter would come to him to get their lessons. You'd read a math problem out to him and he'd just rattle it off like that," said Brooks, snapping his fingers. "I've never seen something like that in my life. . . . . I think my grandfather was a genius."[53]

Freddie Kemp told his nephew Ben Biben a story that reveals the paternalistic attitude of the white owners of River Lake, who favored some Black families over others and bestowed "favors" on them. When Malvina Becnel, a granddaughter of P. C. Major, was born, in 1926, her father, Edgar Becnel, told fourteen-year-old Freddie to hold her. "He liked Freddie, because Freddie always dressed nice, with a clean shirt," said Biben. "Mr. Becnel told Freddie, 'You the first nigger to ever hold this baby.'"[54]

When the Mississippi River overflowed its banks in the great flood of 1927, Sam and Emma Kemp and their children fled their house in the field and moved into the two-story sugarhouse. Freddie, who was fifteen, recalled hauling beds, clothing, and other belongings up the stairs. The Kemps spent two or three weeks there before the flood waters receded. "Three families, I know, [stayed there] throughout the flood," Freddie said, naming the families of Johnny Noel and Frank Brown.[55]

Ben Biben remembered how remote the houses in the field were. "You'd cross the bridge, then cross the canal, then you'd come to our house. If you'd walk about a mile, there was another house back there. That's where Johnny Hall used to live."[56]

Around 1940, Emma and Sam moved from their house in the field to a cabin in Cherie Quarters, across from Reese Spooner. Ben was six years old when he moved with his grandparents. "Going to Cherie Quarters was like going to town," he said.

Most of Sam and Emma's children married someone from the quarter or nearby. Freddie Kemp married Ethel Ferdinand and had four children. Albertha Kemp (Bert) married Harklest Bibbens and had three children, including David Biben, Sam Bibbens, Frankie Christopher, and Barbara Overstreet Hardy.[57]

Frankie and Barbara remembered a George Cooper poem their mother, Bert, used to recite; it began "'Come, little leaves,' said the wind one day." Barbara, who organized all the family reunions, reprinted it in the first program.

Bert often told them stories and recited poems; one was about the most beautiful doll in the world. When Bert was sick at the end of her life, they asked her to recite it; she still knew every word.[58] Lubertha Kemp married Gable Brooks, the son of another family with a long history at Cherie Quarters, and had four sons, Ernest, Jerry, Roosevelt, and Gable Brooks. Mamie Kemp married George Williams, the son of Papa Joe Williams, who also grew up in Cherie Quarters.

Sam and Emma's grandchildren had fond memories of them. Joe Williams recalled being "spoiled" as a child. "I used to eat two breakfasts every day," he said. "I'd have breakfast with [Sam and Emma] and then go to my other grandmother's [Louise Sturges Williams] and eat again."[59]

Cherie Quarters residents Emma Kemp and Mary (Dora) Domino at the front gate to the Kemp house. Reese Spooner's cabin is in the background. Photo by David Biben. Courtesy of Deidra Biben-Glynn.

Sam Kemp died in 1950, at the age of eighty-five, and Emma in 1964, at seventy-four. They are buried at the cemetery on the grounds of the Little Zion Baptist Church in Lakeland, about three miles up the road from Oscar. When their daughter Albertha died, in 1986, she was buried in the same grave. "Where my mama's buried at Little Zion, Sam, Emma, and my mama all buried in that same grave," Ben Biben told me.[60]

In his eighties, Freddie Kemp talked about the old days in Cherie Quarters.

In 1996, when he was hospitalized for lung problems, Ben and I visited him. From time to time his daughter-in-law Verna, the wife of his son Sam, checked in on him. Freddie clearly remembered a white man named William Jarreau, the model for the assassin Albert Cluveau in *The Autobiography of Miss Jane Pittman*. Freddie said Jarreau had killed ten men, two white and eight Black. "He didn't have to be mad [to shoot someone]. He'd kill a Black man just like shootin' a rabbit."[61] One of Jarreau's victims was the teacher Petrus LaForest Albert Plantevigne, who built a school for Black children on False River at the turn of the century and was gunned down in 1903. Gaines based the story of Ned Douglass in *Miss Jane* on the Plantevigne story, which he heard as a child growing up. "He's buried on the banks of False River right now. . . . And my people knew the story quite well, which I'd always heard. So Ned was built around that man." [62]

Plantevigne was born November 23, 1869, in the Chenal area of Pointe Coupée Parish, followed two years later by a brother, Jean Justin. Their parents died young, and the brothers were raised by their paternal grandmother, a strict Catholic. Both sons worked to save money to attend Straight University in New Orleans, a school run by the American Missionary Association. At some point, LaForest anglicized his last name and became known as L. A. Planving. His brother, known as John Plantevigne, became a Josephite priest.

After he graduated from Straight with a degree in theology in 1897, L. A. Planving became a Congregationalist minister and was pastor at two New Orleans churches. He married around 1899; he and his wife, Bettie, had two daughters. In 1898, Planving bought land on False River; by 1900, with help from the association, he had built the Pointe Coupée Industrial and High School. He and his wife, who was also a teacher, lived on the premises with their young daughters. The school was unpopular among many whites of the parish. In 1902, a shot was fired into the window of their living quarters.

To help make ends meet, Planving did carpentry work. He was reportedly doing such work on the day he was killed, August 28, 1903. According to contemporary news accounts, he was on his way home on horseback about 7:00 p.m. when he and his horse were shot from ambush. Hit in the head by a bullet from a double-barreled shotgun, Planving reportedly died instantly. He was thirty-three years old. He was buried on the grounds of his school. His widow was one month pregnant when her husband was killed. Her son, whom she named Albert after his father, was born in April 1904.

In *The Autobiography of Miss Jane Pittman,* Miss Jane recalls,

> [W]e kept the place where his school was and where he is buried. . . . We want them to know a black man died many years ago for them. He died at the end of the other century and the beginning of this century. He shed his precious blood for them. . . . We have a marker there for people to stop by and see if they want to. No, it is not a tall and showy thing. It's nothing but a flat piece of concrete, but it's there for all to see if they just get out the car and look.[63]

The marker on the former site of the school reads: "Plantevigne / Professor / Nov 23 1869 / Aug 28 1903."

Freddie Kemp spent four years overseas during World War II, serving in the China–Burma–India theater from 1941 until 1945. One of the first things he did when he returned to Cherie Quarters was to give his mother, Emma, money saved from his paychecks. "He gave her five hundred dollars and told her to use it for the kids," said Freddie's son Levert, who learned of this event years later. "That was a lot of money in the 1940s. He always took care of his mother."[64]

Freddie briefly moved back in with his parents, Sam and Emma Kemp, until he could decide on his next move. He also met their next-door neighbor, Ethel Ferdinand, the mother of four young children. Freddie married Ethel, and they moved to Baton Rouge, where they lived in an apartment on Orange Street in the Bottom. Their three sons were all born in the apartment—Freddie Jr. in 1947, Samuel Charles in 1950, and Levert in 1951. They were delivered by a midwife, just as children born in Cherie Quarters had been.

"When I was six months old, in 1952, we moved across the street to 1419 Orange Street," said Levert. "My daddy had saved up so he could buy a house. He always saved his money and paid cash."[65] The shotgun house—comprising a front room, bedroom, kitchen, and back porch—was full. In addition to Freddie and Ethel's children, there were Ethel's sons Earle and Cecil. "We were piled up on each other. Daddy added three bedrooms and an inside bathroom to that house. I used to call it 'the dorm.'" Freddie treated Ethel's children as his own. "They always told us, 'There ain't no such thing as half; that's your brother.'"

Freddie, whom Levert described as "a common laborer and a union member," worked "digging ditches and pushing wheelbarrows," although he is listed in the 1956 city directory as a bricklayer. He always had an eye out for extra income. "Daddy learned to cut hair in the military. We had so many customers over there. He taught all of us to cut hair. We'd boil peanuts and fill bags with 'em and he'd sell them for twenty-five cents on his construction jobs."

Levert described his father as a "proud" man who would not dream of accepting a handout. "He came up hard, so he would never let us have holes in our underclothes, socks, or shoes. They used to make us eat before we left home. If anybody [offered us food], we'd say we already ate. They would say how well behaved we were."

Freddie bought his first car in 1969—"a brand-new blue Chevrolet Bel Air." Before that, throughout the fifties and early sixties, until his mother Emma died in 1964, Freddie would ride the Trailways bus to Oscar every weekend to visit her. "He'd check to see that they were combing her hair and keeping her house clean."

Freddie was strict, but "After you got a certain age, he was more bark than bite. He had a look he could give you. We'd say, 'Daddy lookin'!'"

While George and Mamie Williams were saving up to move to Baton Rouge, they sent their daughter, Lee Earl, to live with Freddie's family so she could attend McKinley High School.[66] "I was so crazy about Lee Earl," said Levert of his older cousin. "I was like her baby. She lived with us maybe three years. I remember she got a swimsuit so she could take swimming lessons at the Brooks Park swimming pool." The pool, built in 1949, was larger than Olympic size. It attracted people from all over Baton Rouge and from small towns as far away as Clinton, thirty miles north.[67]

Not long after Lee arrived, her parents joined her in Freddie's already crowded house on Orange Street, spending a couple of months there while looking for their own house. In 1957, George and Mamie rented a house on Georgia Street; a couple of years later they moved to 602 Louise Street, walking distance from Freddie's. At first they rented from Dr. Curtis J. Gilliam, a Black optometrist and civil rights advocate, but they eventually bought the house.[68]

Lee Earl Williams graduated from McKinley High in 1961 and moved to California, where she lived with relatives, probably members of the McVay family, while attending a community college and later San Francisco State.[69] After her mother's death, she moved back to Baton Rouge, enrolling at Southern University. She graduated in 1966 with a degree in business. In

Freddie Kemp at Cherie Quarters, 1993. Born in nearby Lakeland in 1912, he moved to the quarter as a child. He remembered moving into the sugarhouse in 1927 to escape floodwaters. In 1937, he helped build the church/schoolhouse. Photo by Sid Gray.

Baton Rouge she met Norman Cador, whom she married in 1968. They moved to Texas, where their son, Anthony, was born in 1972 just weeks after the death of his grandfather George Williams. George is buried beside Mamie in Lakeland.

Freddie and Ethel remained in their Orange Street house until they died, Freddie in January 1997 and Ethel in September of that year. The family held on to the house; in 2021, their youngest son, Levert, was living there. His older brother, Sam, died in 2021 and is in Louisiana National Cemetery for veterans in Zachary.

A few years before his death at the age of eighty-five, Freddie Kemp noted that although his family members were buried in Lakeland, his "four years and ten days" in the army during World War II had earned him the right to be buried at Port Hudson National Cemetery north of Baton Rouge. "I think the soldiers will take care of me," he said. "That's where I want to be, with the soldiers."[70] And, indeed, that's where he is.

### THE ROBILLARD FAMILY

The earliest known Robillard was William Robillard, who married Celestine (or Celesteen) Antoine. Their son Gustave Robillard (1888–1970) married Queen Victorine (1909–1974). They had four daughters and five sons.

One of those sons, William "Bill" Robillard, appears in the documentary on Ernest Gaines, talking about life in Cherie Quarters. "Like sometimes people would do something just sufficient to get by? No. It had to be done the right way. I guess that's why we love 'em in the grave. They was sincere. All the people the same way. We who remember the old ways of raising were grateful. There was no 'my child, your child.' Everybody was everybody's child."[71]

Bill's sister Ada Mae, who married Ernest Gaines's brother Lionel, also recalled the strict ways of the older generation. "Monday morning, you'd put your clothes in the tub and scrub 'em, then you hung 'em on the line. You scrubbed your porch with brick, crumbs of brick. Brick made the porch look much better. You scrubbed that house with a old piece of broom, a tub of water, and soap."[72] Ben Biben remembered a superstition. "You couldn't sweep salt outside at night. You'd let it stay on the floor until the next morning. It had to do with something in the Bible, about salt losing its strength."[73]

Gustave Robillard's brother owned a car that he often loaded with kids and drove to New Roads on Friday nights to see movies at the "colored" theater, the Star. Later, Bill Robillard bought a car from Sheriff Bub Bouanchaud and did the same thing, with everybody chipping in gas money. When Bill, who was born in 1927, left Cherie Quarters to serve in the army, Ernest Gaines, age twelve, was designated to help Bill's father, Gustave, cut wood and do other chores. Gustave paid E. J. for his help, and E. J. used the money to buy pencils and paper with which to write.[74]

Bill Robillard had vivid memories of Pa Bully and Aunt Ca'line, a married couple. Pa Bully was a short man who did not like to be teased about his stature. He also was talkative. Bill remembered getting in trouble as a child because he stopped on the way back from the store to talk to Pa Bully, who went on so long that Bill was late getting home with the groceries.[75] Freddie Kemp, who was fifteen years older than Bill, also remembered Pa Bully. "He used to live right here," he said on a visit to Cherie Quarters, pointing to a vacant spot next to Reese Spooner's house. "He was a little short fella. People used to say, 'Get off your knees!' and he'd get mad. Ca'line was his wife. She wasn't too short, for a lady."[76] Ernest Gaines used Pa Bully and Aunt Ca'line (or at least their names) as characters in his novel *Of Love and Dust.*

To Ada Mae, Cherie Quarters was "a beautiful, peaceful, dusty place to live," but also a place of hard work. "We picked cotton, pulled corn, cut cane, dug Irish potatoes. We just worked." Discipline was strong. "Boys will be boys, but not like today, [boys] who couldn't listen. We had no rogues among us, no dope, no access to no kind of weapons. Everybody was together. You were scared to even pick up a little piece of iron or a little piece of stick [to use as a weapon]."[77]

### THE ZENO FAMILY

The best-known member of the Zeno family was Walter Zeno (1895–1978), whose nicknames included "Pete," "Salute," and "Rider."[78] Zeno was something of a living legend in the quarter. Bill Robillard remembered him as "a man among men," who stood up for himself, demanding to be paid for his cane as soon as it was harvested rather than waiting until the plantation owner was ready to settle up.[79] Ernest Gaines recalled Zeno as physically tough, a man who could cut and load sugar cane, and fish and hunt, with the best of them. "Salute was a man among men," said Gaines, using the same expression as Robillard. "Strong and hard and tough."[80]

Gaines took a photograph of Zeno in his characteristic squatting position, which he reportedly could maintain for hours at a time. "He would squat for hours on the porch and talk to you. I always liked that."[81] Zeno was renowned for fathering numerous children (the count ranges from sixteen to twenty-five), with whom he was extremely strict. He lived to be eighty-two, dying in 1978. Gaines valued Zeno as a man who told him stories of the old days in Cherie Quarters. He dedicated *A Gathering of Old Men* to Zeno, whom he used as a model for the character Mathu, a man of pure African descent who scorned his mixed-blood neighbors and was the only one of the "old men" whom whites respected, willing to stand up to their unfair treatment and terrorism.

Gaines also modeled the protagonist of his final book, *The Tragedy of Brady Sims,* on Zeno. Sims was designated "the man who whipped children" in that novel. Parents sent their own children to him for corporal punishment, preferring that to having them go to Louisiana's notorious Angola prison.

Others saw Zeno as a menacing man who could be dangerous, not the romanticized version portrayed by Gaines. "I don't know why Salute was such a model for Ernest Gaines," said Ben Biben. "I don't think he was pure African. He had tiny lips, an Indian-looking nose, and his hair wasn't really kinky-kinky. He was Black, though. Salute did have a white horse, a white mare that was really fast. Very few people could ride her. At least that's what he said, that's the image. We used to call him Rider."[82]

"Salute was definitely a character," said Sam Bibbens. "I was nine years old the first time I got drunk. It was Christmas Day, about 1950. I went over to Pete's and he gave me some Gallo sherry wine. I got drunk and came back home drunk. My grandmother whipped my butt."[83]

Ben Biben remembered Zeno as a man who "didn't mind fighting" and was extremely aggressive toward women. "Pete used to take all his clothes off and walk down the quarters naked. When women went to the toilet he'd grab 'em, and they better not holler. He'd semi-rape [*sic*] 'em. That's why he had so many children. Salute was mean."[84]

Biben heard about Salute from older folks, including the story that he climbed in windows to accost women.

> He was walking [through] the quarters nekkid and grabbing women. They say it happened to Miss Louise Sturges and she beat him with a broom. But Miss Zuma [Julia McVay] told George and Mamie [Williams] and my mama [Albertha Kemp Bibbens] he came in her window nekkid and tried to get in bed with her. They used to keep the windows open at night. She told this story, and I heard it with my own ears: "That dirty, low-down nigger jumped in there with me." She used to sell suppers, and we was there eating with her. I was probably twelve or thirteen [around 1956 or 1957] when I heard that. She said [Salute] had been with Adrean, and Adrean was her own daughter. That was part of it.

Biben said Adrean's son Eugene was thought to be Walter Zeno's son, possibly as the result of rape. "Salute, he'd get up there and take a bath once a month, put on clean clothes and a hat, and go looking for women. We'd hang out at the Chustz store and he'd have a drink, laugh and talk, and then go walking on down Lorio quarters, checking out to see who was there so he could go [have sex with the man's wife while the husband was out drinking]."[85]

Biben said Zeno also committed murder at a nearby plantation. "He killed a guy on Lorio," Biben said, pronouncing the name *LOW-dee-oh*. "He hit him in the head with a singletree [a piece of equipment used to hook a mule to a wagon]. He got into the mule stall, sneaked in there while the guy was feeding the mules, hit him on the head with the singletree, and killed him. I think it was about a woman. He spent some time in Angola."[86]

I heard this story from Biben several times, and I assumed he had been alive when it happened. But later, Biben, who was born in 1934, told me he had heard about it from "the old folks." To verify such a serious charge, I needed to check records at the Louisiana State Penitentiary in Angola. I was a bit skeptical about the possibility of getting information from the prison, recalling

Ernest Gaines's comments about his failed attempts, during his research for *A Lesson Before Dying*, to find out whether a prisoner would have been allowed visitors in the 1940s.[87]

I telephoned the records department at Angola. Archivist Aftin Gaddy quickly located an index card stating that Walter "Zenon" from Pointe Coupée Parish had entered Angola on November 6, 1923, on a charge of "striking to murder." She wasn't sure whether that meant murder or attempted murder, and I wondered about the meaning too, but "striking" fit with Ben's story that Zeno had struck a man with a singletree. Gaddy emailed me a scan of the index card, which had the notation "Salute," in quotation marks. That was the nickname by which Zeno was commonly known in Cherie Quarters, which Gaines included in his dedication of *A Gathering of Old Men*.

The digitized Angola record book at the East Baton Rouge Parish Library shows that Walter "Zenon" was convicted on October 30, 1923, of "striking with intent to murder" (later known as "attempted murder" or "aggravated battery"). The term of imprisonment was six months and he was released from Angola on May 6, 1924, six months after he entered the state penitentiary. The record book describes him as twenty-three years old (estimating his birth year as 1900, although in fact he was born in 1895) and married. His height and weight are noted ("5-10 1/8, 153 lbs."), and under "Marks on Person" are noted "Good teeth, 1 front upper out, small normal nose, large ears, scar right corner mouth, [illegible] back neck, scar left elbow, numerous scars left shin, No. 9 shoe." Those remarks are starkly reminiscent of Angola's plantation past and of descriptions of slaves on the auction block. His mother and father were born in Louisiana and his occupation was listed as "Farm hand." His residence was Oscar, Louisiana.[88]

One of Salute's many children was a son, Forrest, who was born at Cherie Quarters in 1919. Forrest estimated that Salute had sixteen children, eighty grandchildren, and eighty-three great-grandchildren. Forrest was five years old when his father came home one day and told his wife and children he was leaving. "He moved in with a woman he was sweetheartin' with," said Forrest; the woman lived just two houses away. Soon after, Forrest's mother died. He and his sister Clara fended for themselves with the help of an aunt who took them food. "Outside that, we'd just do without," he said. "Me and my sister were twelve years old when we went to work." Walter Zeno's neglectfulness is reflected in Gaines's character Brady Sims, who also abandons his many children.[89]

Salute occasionally visited Forrest and his sister, usually to collect a check they received as a death benefit for their mother. "My daddy came back to us. That was to get that money. He always brought us a bag of cornmeal that cost ten cents. Sometime he would add a little piece of meat, [but he usually brought only] a bag of beans, cornmeal. That went on until we were grown." Forrest and his sister Clara (who would grow up to marry Manuel Gaines) did not protest the taking of their checks. "It was a training that came. It's right there in the Bible. We were raised: never talk smart to old people. John 3:16 [*sic*]."

Probably because of their orphan status, Forrest and his sister got little if any education. "I never went to school in my life," he said. "When you got twelve years old, you had to work or leave. School was one month for Blacks." But despite his lack of formal education, Forrest, a World War II veteran, became a minister when he was forty-eight years old. "I was baptized in 1965. I was an usher and then a deacon. They sayed you had to have an education to preach. But God called me to go."

Forrest described the vision that called him to preach.

> The voice said, "Today is your day." In a vision, I can picture myself driving a train on the track. The track was white as snow. Everybody on the train was dressed in white. Where I parked my car was white as snow. That was a vision. I ain't never preached in my life. I am that I am. Then everybody got on the train. I didn't listen to the voice because of the people.
>
> The second vision I had, I was called to go down to the river and get on a ship. You don't see nothin'. He told me to get on board. [I saw] nothing but sky and water. I said, "Tell me one thing—when do I get off?" [The voice said,] "When this ship stop." It pulled in to an island    trees, grass, sky. He told me, "You get off here. No, Forrest, you not by yourself. Follow me."

Forrest was led to "a big old brick church. He took me to the roster [*sic*] and said, 'I'm 'one give you this church.' They was shoes stacked this high. He said, 'That's your job; you fill 'em.'"

In 1994, in his seventies, Forrest began learning to read through a parish literacy program. He continued to preach, and he regularly spoke at funerals. He lived in a small frame house on the grounds of Austerlitz Plantation near River Lake. His only child, Forrest Zeno Jr., was a cook at the popular Joe's Dreyfus Store Restaurant in Livonia, about thirty miles away. Forrest had inherited

Salute's gun. "I got that gun at the house. It's a thirty-eight. Papa bought that gun from Tom's Hardware when he couldn't fight no more."[90]

### THE BROOKS FAMILY

The earliest record of the Brooks family can be found in the 1880 census of Ward 8, which lists Bill Brooks, his wife, Louisa, and their seven children, including a fourteen-year-old son named Manuel and a nine-year-old son named Gabriel. In the same census are "Gim" Brooks and his wife, Minerva, with their five children, two of whom are sons named Manuel and Gabriel. Possibly Bill and Gim Brooks were brothers who had named sons for family members. By 1900, Jerry Brooks is listed in Ward 8 with his wife, "Octavia," and his daughter, Olevia. In 1910, Jerry and "Octavine" are listed, with their son, Emmanuel, and granddaughters Lizzie Jones and Ida Cage. From this evidence we can deduce that the Brooks daughters had married Jones and Cage men. By 1920, Jerry and Octavine's household had grown to include six children, three grandchildren, and a lodger named Pearlie Scott.[91]

One of the sons of Jerry Brooks and Octavine Cézaire (the name was later anglicized to Ceaser) was James Brooks, who married his parents' lodger. By 1930, James Brooks, age forty-one, is listed as married to Pearlie and living with her, their six children, and his widowed mother, Octavine. James and Pearlie ultimately had eleven children: Gable, Ernest, Herman, James, Manuel, Frank, Beatrice, Leola, Dorothy, Gloria, and Eloise. James Brooks Sr., known as Jimmy, was a person of some importance in Cherie Quarters, being a deacon in the church.[92]

Jimmy and Pearl's oldest son, Gable Brooks, married Lubertha Kemp and with her had four sons, Ernest, Jerry, Roosevelt, and Gable, or Gabriel. Gable and Lubertha separated when Ernest was seven. The four boys grew up in Cherie Quarters, close to both sets of grandparents, the Kemps and the Brookses. Jerry Brooks said both his father and his grandmother, Gable and Pearl Scott Brooks, spoke French. "I spoke a little as a kid, but I forgot it," he said. Jerry said his grandmother Pearl, fifty-nine when he was born, was "a young grandmother" who was "jolly and liked fun. She used to kid a lot, always had something funny to say." (Jerry's wife was also named Pearlie.) All four Brooks brothers moved to Seattle. Ernest Brooks, known as Booster, was a faithful attendee at Barbara Overstreet's family reunions, never missing one. Later, his brothers also started coming home for reunions.[93]

In January 1957, this group gathered in front of the Cherie Quarters cabin, where Gaines had lived as a child. From *left*, front row: Charles Kemp, Louise Kemp, and Lionel Rowan. From *left*, standing: Sam Bibbens, Gabriel Brooks, Lionel Green, Rose Bibbens, Jerry Brooks, Lubertha Brooks, Mathilda Harrison, and Mamie Kemp. Photo by David Biben. Courtesy of Deidra Biben-Glynn.

Gable's brother James Brooks Jr. was a source of pride in the quarter. His parents were barely literate, but he graduated from high school in New Roads, served in the army, and then graduated from Southern University in Baton Rouge. He became a science teacher and eventually principal of Rosenwald High School in New Roads, where he served for many years.[94]

Widowed young, James Brooks raised three sons, only to die at the hands of one of them. In 1999, when he was sixty-eight, James was shot and killed by his youngest son, Dexter, following a dispute over the use of James's car. His friends mourned the loss of a well-liked person who had been a fount of interesting stories about Cherie Quarters.

In 1992, when we were working on the television documentary, James Brooks was one of the first people Gaines suggested we talk to. Coproducer Rick Smith, cameraman Charles Bush, and I went to the Baton Rouge apartment of Dexter Brooks to interview James, who lived in New Roads. Dexter told us he had once worked at Louisiana Public Broadcasting, which was producing the documentary. I took along a small tape recorder, but James Brooks, who had a prominent hearing aid on one ear, asked me not to use it. I took notes as he told us great stories about growing up in Cherie Quarters. We asked if we could interview him on video, but he declined, not wanting to be filmed with his hearing aid. We assured him that we could angle the camera so it wouldn't be visible, but he refused. A year later he came to the premiere of the documentary; he told me afterward that he regretted not appearing in it. I regretted it, too, because he was a wonderful storyteller.

Ernest Brooks said if he could choose where to grow up it would be "down Cherie. . . . People from Lakeland or St. Elmo [Alma Plantation], everybody always wanted to come to Cherie. It was nice and clean." People also envied the closeness of the community. "If my mother got sick, some friend of the family would wash and cook for her—Miss Octavia [McVay], Julia [McVay], or my godmother Evelina Brown."[95]

### THE COLAR AND BAYONNE FAMILIES

Raphael Norbert Colar, known as Norbert, was born in 1913 on Parlange Plantation, about a mile from River Lake. Colar, who would marry Adrean Jefferson and become stepfather to Ernest Gaines, was the fourth of eleven children born to Anatole Colas and Marie Edwige Bayonne. The Colar family was Catholic, and many of its marriages, baptisms, and funerals can be found in the Catholic church records of Pointe Coupée Parish, though records show several spellings of the name, including Colar, Colas, and Cola. Again, the variations may be attributable to careless annotation. All three are pronounced roughly the same in French: *Co-LAH.*[96]

It is interesting to speculate whether Norbert was related to Martino Colar, who is listed in the 1900 census of Ward 8, age seventy-nine, with his wife, Millien, age seventy-four. Martino and Millien, a farmer and a cook, lived next to Thomas Hewes, his wife, Anna, and their grown children at Pleasant View Plantation. They are apparently the Martino and Millien depicted in an album of photographs taken by Anna Hewes Denis in the 1880s, identified only by first names. (See chapter 8.)

The Colar family was living on Parlange Plantation at the time of the 1920 census, when Norbert was seven. In 1930, Norbert, age seventeen, was still living with his father, Anatole, and several siblings at Parlange. (Edwige Bayonne Colar apparently died before 1930; her husband is listed as widowed.) Although he grew up at Parlange, Norbert was well known in Cherie Quarters; Adrean said that she and Norbert "went to school together when I was a child."[97] Ernest Gaines described Norbert Colar as a family leader. "Although he isn't the oldest of his siblings, most of them looked up to him. He's the guy that took care of the responsibilities of the family."[98]

Although Norbert and Adrean would not be free to marry for six more years, they already had an infant son together when Norbert applied for a Social Security number on December 21, 1940. (Their son Norbert Jr. was born in 1940.) He named Adrean on the form as his wife, spelling her name the French way, Adrienne.[99] He gave his address as Parlange Plantation and stated that he was unemployed. Sometime in the 1940s, Adrean and Norbert moved to New Orleans in search of work. "He was a longshoreman until he got the papers for the merchant marine," Adrean said. "That's what he wanted to be. He was in the merchant marine in 1943. We went to California in 1947."[100] After moving to California, the couple had five more children together: Michael, Deborah, Leonard, Sambra, and Lavern.[101]

Ernest Gaines dedicated *The Autobiography of Miss Jane Pittman* in part to his stepfather, and he used many family names for characters in his books. Munford in the short story "Three Men" is named for Norbert's oldest brother. The name of another brother, Murphy, is reflected in the character Murphy Bacheron in *Of Love and Dust,* which also has a character named Burl Colar. A character in *In My Father's House* is named Virginia Colar.

Gaines used Bayonne, Norbert's mother's maiden name, to represent the town of New Roads in his fiction. In a 1964 letter to Atheneum editor Hiram Haydn about *Catherine Carmier,* he wrote, "My town Bayonne, in real life, is a little place called New Roads. Bayonne is the maiden name of my stepfather's mother. I like the sound of it, and since many of the people I write about are of French descent or speak the language, I think the name is quite appropriate."[102] In "The Sky Is Gray," Gaines used the name for both the town where James goes to the dentist and for the healer, Monsieur Bayonne, who prays over James to try to relieve his toothache.

## MIXED-BLOOD FAMILIES

Miscegenation is a topic often avoided in studies of Louisiana's plantation past, but certainly it existed. It seems safe to assume that many Louisiana natives with plantations in their past will find kinfolk of the other race, if they choose to look for them. During the nineteenth century, Black–white kinship was often acknowledged, as we shall see in chapter 8 in the case of Antoine Decuir and his mistress Sophie Deslondes, or of Antoine's brother Joseph Decuir and his mistress Françoise Beaulieu. The practice of plaçage (the custom among many white men in eighteenth- and nineteenth-century Louisiana of setting up a Black or mixed-race woman in her own household, in addition to or in place of a wife) existed at River Lake Plantation, and some of the children born of Black–white alliances lived at Cherie Quarters.

As we have already seen, oral tradition in the McVay and Jones families held that Susan Jones (1873–1924) was the daughter of Jean Baptiste Major (1834–1902), making her a half sister to River Lake Plantation owner P. C. Major (1859–1934). It is tempting to speculate whether that link was in any way connected with the sudden departure of Susan's first husband, James McVay. Did McVay perhaps confront P. C. Major, complaining bitterly about Susan's living in comparative poverty while her brother ran the plantation? Or did Major help McVay escape after he killed a white man?

Ben Biben said that P. C. Major's son Joseph (1891–1941) fathered a daughter by a Black woman; the daughter was a playmate to his two white children by his wife. Ben was the child of another of P. C. Major's sons, George, a fact acknowledged by many people, both Black and white.

Biben recounted dispassionately the story of how his mother, Albertha Kemp, came to bear a child by one of the plantation owners in 1934. According to the story Ben pieced together, the plantation's Black overseer, Cap Dejean, was the liaison who made the arrangement between his mother ("Bert") and George Major. Dejean also functioned as a distraction. Bert lived with her elderly parents, Sam and Emma Kemp, who would not have approved of her having relations with the white owner. Dejean would go to their house and chat with them in one of the front rooms while Bert left through the back door to meet George Major. Ben didn't know where these meetings took place—he suspected it was in Major's car. And he didn't know whether Bert was there by choice or by coercion, although the idea of free choice in this situation is debatable. "Cap Dejean told me, 'Your grandpa was sick, too sick to work.' George Major sent the overseer to tell my mother if she'd have an affair with George Major he wouldn't make my grandpa work. The overseer would go in the house. Bert would sneak out to a thicket and go back there with him [Major] in the car. Then after a while, the overseer would leave. He was there to keep my grandparents from seeing Bert leave."[103] At the time of these assignations, Bert was nineteen and George Major was about thirty-three. At twenty, Bert gave birth to Major's son, David. Biben wondered why George Major, who later married a white woman and had a daughter with her, chose his mother. He thought perhaps it was because Bert came from an intelligent, hardworking family. "Maybe they were trying to breed somebody to work in the yard," he said.

As Ben was growing up, he often saw George Major on the plantation. "I never thought of him as nothin,' just a white man passing through the quarters. If you got in trouble, he was there." Major was a man who "cussed a lot—'goddamn' this and 'goddamn' that." He also bet on the outcome of baseball games and fistfights in the quarter. "One time two guys were fighting and George Major put some money on a tree stump and said, 'The winner gets this.' Then he went on and fed his cattle and came back." Sometimes Ben was teased about the kinship; when Major passed, children in the quarter would tell Ben, "'That's your pa, boy,' or 'There your daddy go.' But I had no thoughts [that it might be true]. I'm sorry I didn't."

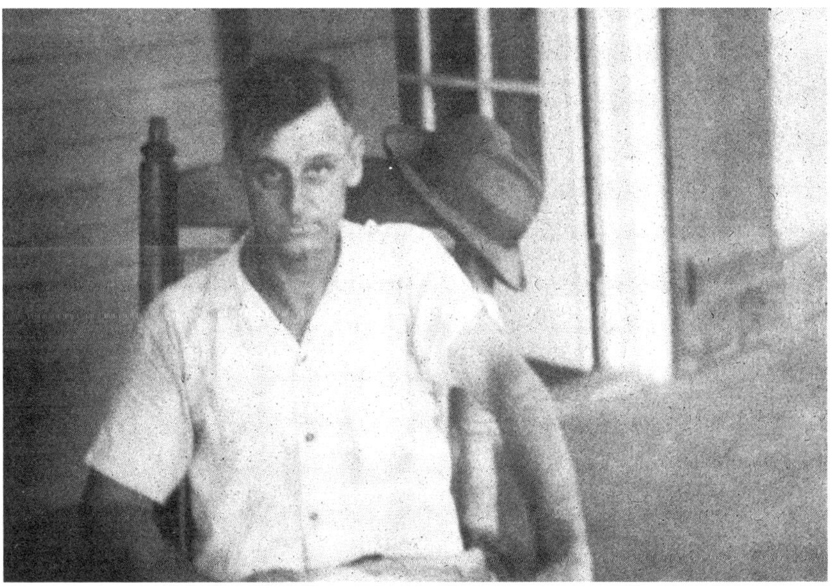

River Lake owner George Edward Major on the porch of the Big House, circa 1940. The son of P. C. Major, who bought the plantation in 1892, George fathered a child by Albertha Kemp, whom she named David (Biben). Photo courtesy of Deidra Biben-Glynn.

Once Ben started school, a teacher named Lillian White singled him out for special attention. "She used to push me so hard. In third grade, she . . . put me and Lionel [Gaines] up another grade. They'd get us to do fourth- and fifth-grade math." Miss White even doled out physical punishment. "She would whip me because I'd try to [play] with the other boys," he said. "As long as it was Lionel, E. J., and the Ruffins, that was okay. She told me, 'These are the kind of people we want you with.'"[104]

Ben believed Miss White knew George Major was his father, and that is why she made him spell his last name differently from the way his mother, and later his siblings, spelled theirs. "Since I was six years old I was Biben," he said. "Hark Bibbens is who my mother married. Bibbens was my sister Rose's name."[105]

"My name is Biben. My brothers and sisters are Bibbens. I couldn't figure out why she made me spell it like that. Miss White would never let me spell it with two *b*s. She demanded that I change my name from Bibbens to Biben."

Ben later realized that the altered spelling was a way of signaling that he was of mixed race. "I was thirty-five years old when [relative] David Lovely said 'Mixed breed spells it with one *b,* but all-Black spells it with two *b*s.' I never gave myself this [spelling]."[106]

Ben suspected that his father, George Major, had an affair with the teacher and perhaps urged her to take a special interest in him. "I think that's what he had in mind when he told her. I bet it was pillow talk. I'm almost positive he was having an affair with Miss White. People have said it. She was a pretty woman, beautiful." Miss White boarded with Ernest Gaines's grandmother Julia McVay during the week. "She had a room on one side and Miss Zuma was on the other side. He [George Major] could come from the Big House to that back door."[107]

Ben believed that even after his mother, Bert, no longer had a physical relationship with George Major, he acted on her behalf to lighten her workload. "She got to work in the restaurant [Triple Arch] instead of the field. She could bring home food. Not choice food, but food."

Ernest Gaines knew who Ben's father was and probably had him in mind when he wrote the short story "Bloodline," although the militant, strident, and ultimately mad character of Copper Laurent has little in common with Ben's genial personality. Likewise, Walter Laurent in "Bloodline" seems clearly based on George Major. Reflections of the real-life circumstances can also be found in the mixed-race relationships in *Of Love and Dust,* whose white overseer Bonbon has an affair with Pauline, a field-worker who secures a better job as a plantation cook because of her alliance with the married Bonbon—a relationship that produces twin sons.

Gaines said of River Lake Plantation, "That's as much Ben's place as anybody's. Everything about him is like [George Major]. He's tall, the way he walks, and all that. It belongs to him and he has a feel for it . . . If there were a possibility for Ben to make a legal claim, I'd pay for it."[108]

David Biben at Cherie Quarters, 1994. Biben shared many stories of growing up in the quarter and documented many scenes there with his camera. He was instrumental in trying to save the last two remaining cabins. Photo by Ruth Laney.

Occasionally, I'd half-jokingly suggest to Ben that he hire a lawyer and sue for his share of George Major's estate. He told me he would never do so, out of fear of retaliation against him or members of his family. Besides, said Ben, a wholly self-made man who earned a living by making and selling rust remover (a dangerous process) as well as by selling toys and fireworks, he took pride in the fact that he had never asked his white kinfolk for help.[109] He recalled only one conversation with Major, who died in 1946, when Ben was eleven. On the day in question, Ben was summoned to the plantation store.

George Major was standing there with a big grin on his face. He says, "How you doin'?" I said, "Fine." He says, "You want to be something when you grow up?" I said, "Yeah, I want to be a doctor." He says, "What kind of doctor?" I said, "One that operates." He kind of laughed. I told him, "I cut hair on the porch, and maybe if I can't do that I'll be a barber." He says, "Anything you want to be, you let me know, hear?" What did he have in mind when he told me to be anything I wanted to be?[110]

Through the haze of time, Ben remembered that the conversation took place on the very day George Major died of coronary thrombosis caused by arteriosclerotic heart disease, on February 23, 1946, after having several surgeries.[111] Major was forty-six. Ben, who believed that Major died of stomach cancer, fought his own battles with colon cancer. "Maybe it's a family thing," he said.

Ben eventually asked his mother if George Major really was his father, and she confirmed it. "My mama finally had to tell the truth to some white people. They wanted to know all the children's fathers. This was [connected with] welfare, to help me go to school. She told them George Major was my father. They went to John Major [George's brother]. He said he had nothing to do with that."[112]

Ben appreciated the irony of having a white father who didn't publicly acknowledge or support his child, a stereotype more commonly associated with Black men. "A lady in the quarters told me, 'We Black women are always quick to holler nonsupport, but we never ran to the white man and hollered nonsupport.'"[113] The irony is especially rich in light of the wealth of the Major family, one of the most prosperous families in the parish then and now.

But if the white owners didn't acknowledge their children, the facts were well known to the people of the quarter, and they were rich fodder for teasing. "They used to tell me, 'We ought to put you off here at Mulatto Bend with all your people,'" said Ben, who also endured the taunt of "half breed." Others were kinder. "My parrain [his godfather Clinton Williams] told me, don't feel bad about what my mama did. He said, 'I told your daddy to take care of you before I left.'"

Clinton Williams's departure from Cherie Quarters exemplifies the power of the white plantation owners. According to Ben, his parrain committed murder, went to Angola, and was released because of George Major's influence. "He went to prison, and George Major got him out and paid his way to Seattle."[114]

Some people from Cherie Quarters wondered how it felt to have mixed parentage, considering that some of Ben's white relatives knew he was kin to them. "Somebody asked me, 'Do you feel white or Black since your people [acknowledge you]?'" said Ben. "I said, 'All I want is for them to know it.' Heck, I don't know. What else can I be but Black?"

6

# GONE BACK IN TIME

## THE HOUSES OF CHERIE QUARTERS

> Just as historians consider primary source material, such as letters and fire insurance maps, so, too, is the building a primary source of information. The building contains a history of its evolution, a record of change. This change may be manifested in changing tastes, technology, or uses of a structure. Most important, the resource itself may be all that remains of the past—it may be the only tangible remnant of an era. Recorders are people who attempt to document cultural resources as accurately and extensively as time and money will allow. They develop written, drawn, and photographic information pertaining to the cultural resource involved. They produce the "as-found record." The golden rule of recording is to record a resource with as little disruption as possible. In carrying out recording, recorders become familiar with the resource and learn to know it better than anyone else. They are the ones who crawl under, through, and over a structure.
>
> —HUGH S. O'BRIEN, "The Building Speaks"

> He sat in the car looking into the yard at the house. The yard was clean and bare, except for a mulberry tree on the left side of the walk and a rose bush on either side of the steps. The house itself was exactly like every other one in the quarters. They all had the same rusted corrugated tin roofs with a brick chimney sitting in the center. They all had the same long, warped porches, with three or four steps leading up to the porch. Every house had two doors facing the road. All had been whitewashed at the same time, twenty-five or thirty years ago—none had been painted since—and the weather had turned all of them the same ashy gray color.
>
> —ERNEST J. GAINES, *In My Father's House*

It must have been serendipity, the random toss of the dice that took Sid Gray to Cherie Quarters. Serendipity with a sense of humor, because Gray seems like the last person you'd expect to find on a Louisiana plantation. A Yankee by birth, he came to Baton Rouge from Rhode Island in 1967 to study architecture at Louisiana State University. In the ensuing years, as he roamed the highways and back roads of his adopted state, he fell in love with the old houses, some of them just one room deep and one room wide, made of cypress, their walls filled with the mud-and-moss mixture known as bousillage.

Now seventy-plus years old, Gray is anything but a somber scholar. Wiry and intense, with piercing blue eyes, he is usually dressed in jeans, his shirt pocket sprouting roller-ball pens, his thick gray hair hidden under a fedora. He has traded the mud-splattered pickup in which he cruised back roads for an SUV crammed with books and tools. With his ever-present mug of coffee close at hand, he can talk for hours about old buildings. He talks about them passionately, almost as though they are people. And he does it in terms anyone can understand.

As an expert in old buildings, Gray has had clients ranging from homeowners to museum staffs, and his projects have ranged from analyzing paint remnants to moving buildings. Years of experience in the field enable him to offer practical advice, from how to make bousillage to how to get a fragile historic house from point A to point B.

Should he happen upon a house that intrigues him, Gray is ready. He pulls a jumpsuit on over his jeans, sticks a microcassette recorder in his pocket, and straps a spelunker's flashlight to his head. Then he ducks beneath the building and scoots around on his hands and knees, talking to himself as he records his observations of construction techniques and the condition of the building's materials. When he's finished doing that, he goes inside the house, if he's able, and climbs into the attic. "The attic is one of the more interesting things about an old house, because that's where you can see the alterations to the house over time," he says.[1] It was the attic construction of the St. Gabriel Church in Iberville Parish, for instance, that convinced him the eighteenth-century building is one of the rarest in North America. He has also learned a lot by examining the attic of the Big House at River Lake Plantation.

Gray first saw the plantation around 1986, when he accompanied LSU anthropology professor Jay Edwards on a visit to make drawings of the Big House for the Historic American Buildings Survey. While there, he got the owner's permission to inspect the Big House, including the attic. "The evidence is undeniable that the entire roof has been rebuilt," said Gray, who believes the Big House was built in 1795. "It was probably redone in the 1820s."

Several years later, Gray was hired to do work at nearby Pleasant View Plantation, which was built by the Hewes family, relatives of the Decuir/Denis family that owned River Lake. Gray thinks that the year 1820, when Pleasant View was built, is also the year River Lake was massively remodeled; a new roof was installed and twin pigeonniers were built in front of the Big House.

"I've always thought that 1820 was a period of significant remodeling and new construction throughout Louisiana," Gray said. "It has to do with the Americanization of Louisiana, which began in 1813. It was a period of prosperity."[2]

While sketching River Lake, Gray noticed that one of the pigeonniers in front of the house was "nothing but a pile of bricks." The wood from the top half of the pigeonnier was "long gone, either rotted or hauled away," and the remaining pigeon house was none too sturdy. "It looked like it was ready to fall over. It was leaning toward the ditch that runs along Highway 1." Gray knew that most French Creole plantation houses had been flanked by pigeon houses where the owners raised squab (considered a delicacy), and that few had survived—perhaps thirty in the entire state.

A believer in learning by doing, and a man who loves a challenge, Gray went to River Lake's owner, Madeleine Caillet, and offered to repair the remaining pigeonnier. She agreed, and Gray embarked upon a process that would take seven years, owing to difficulty in finding funding. "Finally Madeleine told me she wasn't going to spend another penny. She said she'd rather bulldoze the pigeonnier and let it fall into the ditch." To complete the project, Gray applied for a grant from the state Division of Historic Preservation, which awarded half of the total cost of $13,500. Gray completed the job in 1992.

Restored to its 1820s condition, River Lake's lone surviving pigeonnier stands about twenty-six feet tall. It features a ten-foot-high bottom half made of brick, a ten-foot-high top half of timber frame construction, and a six-foot-high tin roof. Gray stabilized the structure, a complicated process he documented on slide film. "First, I had to support the upper part in order to stabilize the masonry underneath—you put the support beams up tight underneath the top portion so it won't move." He hired a bricklayer to rebuild part of the masonry walls that made up the bottom half of the pigeonnier. "The brick mason was aware of the danger," he said. "He would ask me if it was okay to remove each brick. At one point, I walked around the side of the pigeonnier to talk to the owner, and the mason removed one brick too many.

The whole front wall of the pigeonnier fell into the ditch. The owners could see how fragile the whole thing was."

One day, while Gray was working on the pigeonnier, Madeleine Caillet's husband, Gerald, made a comment about "the cabins out back." "What cabins?" Gray asked. Caillet escorted him down Major Lane to "the back," stopping in front of a cabin that Caillet said had been built by slaves. Looking around, Gray realized that there were half a dozen such cabins, aligned in military fashion, nearly hidden by underbrush. "I was just amazed."

Caillet told Gray that a man named Ernest Gaines had written books about this place, which was called Cherie Quarters. The cabin they were looking at was the home of Reese Spooner, who was born on the plantation at the turn of the century and had lived there until he died in 1985.

Poking around in the underbrush on both sides of the narrow road, Gray discovered six cypress cabins with tin roofs—all that was left of the plantation quarter. Even more amazing, two of the six cabins were occupied, although only one had running water. "I really felt like I had gone back in time to nineteenth-century Louisiana."

During the seven years when he was rebuilding the pigeonnier (1986 to 1992), Gray slowly learned about the once-thriving community of Cherie Quarters, of which there was now only the barest remnant. Some people said there had been as many as thirty cabins there; others said perhaps eighteen. They had been built by slave labor some fifteen or twenty years before the Civil War. People had married, had children, and died in these houses, each home to six or seven generations of people. Most of them had crumbled with age; others had been bulldozed after their occupants died or moved away.

There were still three people living in Cherie Quarters. Joyce Edwards, known as Shug, and Carrie Hebert, two ladies in their sixties, lived in houses that faced each other across the road. Carrie, a quiet woman with a wistful smile, had been born in Cherie Quarters in 1925 and had lived there all her life. Her double house, where she had spent twenty years, was occupied on the other side by her friend Willie Aaron. Shug had moved to Cherie Quarters as a young woman with children and never left. Both cabins had only a central fireplace for heat.

Shug and Carrie not only lived there but also attended services in the church. Twice a month, a preacher from Baton Rouge drove over to conduct services. On those Sunday mornings, Shug and Carrie put on white dresses

The 1840s cabin last occupied by Joyce "Shug" Edwards, who moved out in early 1993. As evident in this photo from 1999, the house was still in good condition when the Friends of Cherie Quarters tried to save it. Photo by Ruth Laney.

and white hats. Just before ten o'clock, they walked out onto their front galleries, descended the wooden steps, crossed their front yards, and met in the road to stroll the hundred or so yards to the church.

Gray learned that the six remaining slave cabins, located on both sides of Major Lane, belonged to different owners, who were first cousins. Madeleine Bouanchaud Caillet, the woman for whom he had repaired the pigeonnier, owned the structures on the left, or east, side of Major Lane: a small shed, the church, and two cabins situated about four hundred yards apart. The first cabin was home to Shug Edwards, who had painted its facade white and planted the front yard with red gladiolas and other flowers and shrubs. That cabin had no running water. Shug used a slop jar or an outhouse behind her cabin; when she needed water for cooking or bathing, she crossed the road and filled a bucket from a faucet at the back of Carrie's house.

The second cabin on Madeleine Caillet's side had stood empty since Reese Spooner died in 1985, but it was filled with furniture and clothing he had left behind, and more furniture and clothing had been stored there by others. Its tin roof had massive leaks, so the clothing and soft furniture functioned as a giant sponge, soaking up and holding the moisture.

The slave cabin, built in the 1840s, where Reese Spooner lived for many years. After he died in 1985, residents used it to store clothing, furniture, and other items. Photo by Ruth Laney.

The second owner was Pervis Cherie Major II, Madeleine's first cousin. Major lived in West Virginia, and he was eager to get rid of the four cabins on the right, or west, side of the lane, whose ownership he shared with his sister Marjorie Major Broome. Major wanted to plant the land, which measured one arpent (192 feet) wide and five acres long, with sugar cane. And besides, he said, in the often-heard words of people burdened with historic properties, the cabins were "a liability." "Liability" was a word I heard a lot during the next few years. Briefly stated, liability meant the property owner's insurance coverage for claims for damage to persons or property. At one point, Madeleine told me, her insurance agent had urged her to get rid of her cabins. Malvina Pickett, Madeleine's aunt, said her uncle John Major had torn down the sugarhouse in the 1950s because he was afraid somebody would get hurt in it and sue him.[3]

Three of P. C. Major II's cabins stood empty and abandoned. Carrie Hebert and Willie Aaron lived in the fourth. Theirs was one of the few cabins in the quarter that had never been converted into a single-family house. (No doors had ever been cut into its central privacy wall.) Carrie lived on the right side of the house and Willie on the left. Theirs also was the only house remaining in the quarter that had a bathroom, which Willie had added to the back in the early 1960s. Their side yard boasted an impressive vegetable garden and even a tobacco plant.

When Sid Gray heard that the owner wanted to get rid of Carrie and Willie's house and the three empty houses on the right side of the road, he thought about Magnolia Mound Plantation in Baton Rouge. He had worked on many projects there and he knew that its director, Gwen Edwards, was searching for a slave cabin to move to the property. Gray negotiated an agreement among the owners, Edwards, and the Baton Rouge Recreation and Parks Commission (BREC), which owns Magnolia Mound.[4]

Once the deal was sealed, Carrie and Willie moved out of the house where they had lived for so many years, relocating to Baton Rouge. Shug stayed on in the quarter, but she was uneasy at night, knowing she was alone on the place. She stuck it out for a few weeks and then found another place to live, in nearby Erwinville.

Although it passed without fanfare, Shug's leave-taking was a momentous occasion in Cherie Quarters. For the first time since it had been built by slaves in the 1840s, Shug's house did not have people living in it. "That is the definition of a folk building," said Gray. "A building that has been continuously occupied by the same culture group for more than 150 years."

Shug was still packing up and moving out when BREC's trucks and men arrived on Major Lane in January 1993. As the workers began to dismantle the cabins, husband-and-wife archaeologists Paul Farnsworth and Laurie Wilkie of LSU hastily rounded up a crew of students and went to the site to do a series of excavations. Later, the archaeologists published a summation of their findings in the *African-American Archaeology* newsletter. From test pits behind Carrie and Willie's house, they recovered "artifactual materials" that included nineteenth- and twentieth-century ceramics and glass, numerous animal bones, iron nails, bone and shell artifacts, medicine bottles, and buttons.

From another site, where the next house in the row once stood, the excavation revealed the remains of a substantial brick foundation. "The foundation corresponds to the location of the chimney in the standing houses, and is half of the typical H-shaped chimney foundation pattern," wrote the archaeologists. "Materials recovered from the construction trench of the foundation date to the 1840s, corresponding to the approximate construction date suggested by the architectural style of the standing cabins. Unfortunately, before excavations could be completed, the area was bulldozed."[5]

In a second article, published in the journal *Louisiana Folklife,* Wilkie noted the discovery of fragments of school slates, pencils, pen nibs, and children's toys at River Lake:

> People stripped the abandoned houses of useful lumber, metal fixtures, and bricks, often leaving only the base of the fireplace intact. The rubble and clearing provided play space for plantation children; the flat brick surface of the fireplace foundation proved a perfect surface for marbles. Numerous marbles dating from the late nineteenth to mid-twentieth centuries were recovered from these areas. Children growing up in the mid to late twentieth century, when marbles seem to be less popular than earlier, brought toy cars and trucks to run along the brick surface. These toy vehicles lost wheels which [were] found archaeologically. . . .
>
> The material culture associated with children at Riverlake Plantation is very sparse. Marbles and truck parts were found, yet the absence of preservable toys is not surprising, in part, given the poverty of [the] quarters' population. Interviews with former tenants of the plantation demonstrate that children often depended upon their imaginations and ingenuity to fill play time. . . . [David] Biben remembered making toys by stringing a button on a cord to create a whirly-gig or type of slingshot. Likewise, dolls were easily made from cornhusks or fabric scraps. Buttons have been found in great abundance . . . at Riverlake. . . . Former tenants . . . did remember buttons being used as counters and markers in games.[6]

When they heard that the cabins were being torn down and moved, many former residents of Cherie Quarters drove over to take one last look and document the event. Eliza Robillard, camera in hand, reminisced about having lived in Carrie Hebert's house as a little girl. "I want pictures to show my children, where their daddy [Bill Robillard, from whom she was divorced] and mama was raised," she said. "My mother [Susan Campbell Sturges] used to live back there, too." Robillard, who was born in 1936, said her family left the quarter and moved to New Orleans in 1947. But she spoke nostalgically of picking blackberries and watching movies in "a big garage with no sound." "The quarters used to get full of water," she said. "After a rain we'd go out there and get as much crawfish as we wanted."[7]

Ben Biben also came out to observe. He too remembered catching crawfish, in ditches near the sugarhouse, on the side of the road, and in a canal near the graveyard. "We'd tie salt meat on a pole with string. The crawfish would take the meat with their claws, and we'd grab 'em and put 'em in a bucket. Sometimes Mama [his grandmother Emma Kemp] would clean 'em and make stew with the tails. Bert [Albertha Kemp Bibbens, his mother] used to make crawfish bisque, stuff the heads."[8]

Eliza Robillard, whose nickname was Too-Too, said, "Everybody had to sleep in the same room. Four people in one bed. I used to sleep on the floor in a shuck mattress. We would sit on the floor around the fireplace while our parents sat in the chairs." She expressed a sentiment I had heard from others who grew up at Cherie Quarters. "Some people don't want to remember that, but that's where I come from and I'm proud of it."

As she faced the removal of her childhood home, she quoted a hymn: "*I went to the house where I used to live / The grass had grown up to cover the do'*." Later I went online to find the hymn she had quoted, "Somewhere Around God's Throne." The lyrics include the lines

> Oh, I went to the house where I used to live
> The grass had grown up and covered the door
> When someone across the street said "Who do you seek?
> For no one, no one lives there anymore."

The hymn echoed the sadness Robillard and others felt at losing the last remaining buildings of the quarter.

> Then I went to the church where I used to go
> The preacher was still there and he met me at the door
> He said, "I know who you are, and I know who you're searching for
> Oh, but they don't, they don't come here anymore."

And finally,

> I went on down the road to my mother's dearest friend
> She met me at the door, she asked me to come in
> She said, "I was by your mother's bedside, when the doctor shook his head
> And now she's somewhere around God's throne."

Ben Biben showed up often to follow the dismantling process. Questioned by the archaeologists, he said most people in Cherie Quarters threw their trash in a ditch behind the house; the ditches ran into a canal. He also told stories about cooking in the chimneys.

Sid Gray noticed that in the four houses being dismantled, the ceiling boards merely rested on the rafters. They had never been nailed down. He asked Biben about that detail. Biben said that he and his grandparents had moved to the quarter from back in the field in 1940, settling on the left side of the lane, toward the front. The house had no boards on its rafters, just an open loft through which he could see the tin roof.[9]

Spurred by questions about ceiling boards, Gray was on a mission to find out as much as he could about slave quarters, especially the houses of Cherie Quarters. In addition to talking to Biben and other former residents, including Ernest Gaines, he began reading Gaines's books to get a sense of what life in the cabins had been like. He also read *Let Us Now Praise Famous Men,* lingering over James Agee's descriptions of rural Depression-era houses and the haunting photographs of Walker Evans. "Agee gave meaning to the beauty of simplicity," said Gray. "He gave humanity to what other people perceived only as poverty." Of course, the same can be said of Ernest Gaines's work.

Looking for details of construction, Gray searched for books about slavery. While prowling among the stacks at the LSU library, he found a book that answered many of his questions. Editor James Breeden had compiled *Advice Among Masters: The Ideal in Slave Management in the Old South,* published in

Beckie Ruffin at her house in Cherie Quarters. She married Donise Decuir, and those who lived next to them said they fought a lot. "That was a cursing lady," said Ernest Brooks. Photo courtesy of Malvina Becnel Pickett.

1980, from articles originally published in agricultural journals from about 1805 through the late 1850s. The book contained chapters on housing, clothing, food, and other concerns of slave masters.[10]

In the chapter on housing, one master stated that a slave cabin should be twenty-four feet wide by twenty-four feet deep, with an eight-foot-deep front gallery. It must sit two feet above the ground and be set forty feet back from the road. It should be fifty feet away from the cabin next to it. "That describes Cherie Quarters to a T," said Gray. "Of course, it is all written from the planter's point of view." That point of view included some bizarre scientific "facts," such as that Black people expelled "bad air" and did not "consume as much oxygen" as white people.[11] In the preface, Breeden states, "[This collection's] major shortcomings are indeed apparent: it presents a one-sided—and racist—view of slavery. . . . With scarcely an exception, the slaveholders who wrote for the southern farm journals believed that the black was hopelessly inferior to the white and, while deserving humane treatment, was created for the benefit of the superior race."[12]

An example of the racist views of the contributors is readily apparent in this excerpt by a Mississippi planter from 1851: "When the negro is treated with humanity and subjected to constant employment without the labor of thought and the cares incident to the necessity of providing for his own support, he is by far happier than he would be if emancipated and left to think and act and provide for himself."[13] But the book also answered Gray's question about the loose ceiling boards. "It said not to nail the boards down so they could be flipped over during the process of cleaning the cabins," he said.

Shortly after Gray discovered *Advice Among Masters,* he had a chance to test one of its dictates at Cherie Quarters. Archaeologist Paul Farnsworth was there to dig a test pit on the site where Carrie Hebert's house had stood. He brought along a hundred-foot measuring tape. Farnsworth stood at the central chimney that had served both sides of one of the dismantled houses and held the tape while Gray grabbed the other end and unspooled it as he strode to the chimney of the next house. Gray laid down the tape and saw that, sure enough, exactly fifty feet separated the chimneys. The houses of Cherie Quarters had been built fifty feet apart, just as the journal article mandated.

But when Gray measured the existing cabins at Cherie Quarters in 1995, he found the measurements slightly different from those advocated in *Masters.* The Cherie Quarters cabins were rectangular in plan, measuring approximately thirty-six feet wide by twenty-seven feet deep. Each cabin was two rooms wide, each room measuring approximately eighteen feet wide by eighteen feet deep. Each had a front porch, or gallery, that was nine feet deep. The cabins were raised about two feet off the ground on large masonry piers. The interior ceiling height was ten feet two inches. Each two-room cabin had a central chimney.

During the four months that BREC workers were dismantling the cabins (January through April 1993), Gray was at Cherie Quarters almost daily, studying the houses in detail. He estimated that they were built in the 1840s. "I base that on the materials used and the methods of construction. I look at the manufacture of individual parts and try to get a sense of the overall economy of the time. Then I bracket the likely dates."

When Gray nominated the two remaining cabins for listing on the National Register of Historic Places in 1995, he attached a document titled "Why I Think These Buildings Are Slave Cabins." He cited timber frame construction, sawing technology, nails and hardware, site plan, and floor plan. Timber frame construction "was used from the earliest period of occupation in Louisiana and continued through the early nineteenth century. The timber frame is evidenced by large timber pieces held together by mortise and tenon joints." Timber frame construction is generally considered to have fallen out of favor "well prior to the Civil War, when it was replaced by balloon frame construction, which is . . . employed on the shed additions to these cabins."

Steam engines had been used at large sugar plantations as early as 1825, which also encouraged Gray to believe the cabins were built in the 1840s. Steam engines were used to saw lumber. "Those 'marks' associated with the first sawn lumber are straight-up-and-down marks of a type called 'sash sawn.' This type is in evidence here." The nails, too, led him to date the cabins' construction to the 1840s: "The nail type found throughout [is] . . . found as early as . . . 1830." He noted, "The original extant shutter hardware, called strap hinges, is hand forged [iron]."[14]

Gray was even more comfortable with the 1840s date when he considered the layout of the quarter within River Lake Plantation as a whole. Referring to a dissertation considered authoritative on the subject of nineteenth-century Louisiana plantations, he noted, "The layout of the remaining plantation complex . . . is typical of the type described by Dr. John Rehder as a 'Linear Plantation Complex.' . . . The slave quarter location . . . conform[s] to this typical pattern."[15]

Gray also reviewed historic maps, including a 1906 map that "shows the plan of the entire complex . . . and shows the quarters in the same location . . . they now [occupy]." The cabins' "overall dimension and shape" was that of "typical two-family (double pen) cabins [that are] standard throughout the south. . . . The floor plan and dimensions of these buildings is typical of the standard slave cabin."

The cabins had not been significantly altered since their construction, making them rare. "Most slave cabins are gone, so these are rare just because they have survived. Parts of them, such as the front facades, which are protected by the galleries, have not been changed at all. They look just like the day they were built."

Having examined the Big House, which dates to about 1795, Gray was surprised to find the cabins as solidly built as the main residence. They had well-constructed mortise and tenon joints; tree nails or wooden pegs held the frame together. The shutters covering the doors and windows had sixteen-inch iron hinges, just like those in the Big House. "Hardware was expensive in those days," he said.

The cypress frames of the cabins were as well constructed as the frame of the Big House, Gray told me, "both in materials and in construction method. The method of construction is timber frame, even though there were other, simpler choices available. Plus the fact that the cabins were raised off the ground in the quarter, while down by the bayou, where some families lived, they had dirt floors." But after building the frames of the cabins, the workers had used "secondary wood, possibly hackberry, pine, or sweet gum" for the roof framing, which had deteriorated more rapidly. "The question that intrigues me is, why did they, at some point, begin using lesser materials?"

Each cabin originally had two rooms, making it "two rooms wide and one room deep," with the front gallery serving as an outdoor room. Ernest Gaines set many scenes in his fiction on the gallery. In *Of Love and Dust,* Marcus and Jim drink beer there at the end of their brutal workdays. Pa Bully and Aunt Ca'line pretend not to notice Bonbon and Pauline's lovemaking as they sit on their gallery fanning away mosquitoes. Mathu's front porch is a communal space in *A Gathering of Old Men.*

Because a cabin was built to house two families, both rooms were accessible only by front and back doors to the outside. There was no door cut into the central wall that separated the two rooms, which Gray dubbed the "privacy wall." In each cabin he studied, "it goes right up and touches the roof." He was intrigued with the privacy wall and how it related to life during slavery and later. "A lot has been written about slave life, but we're not restricting ourselves to slaves," he said, noting that the cabins were continuously occupied right up to 1993, when Shug Edwards shut her front door for the final time.

Over the years, some cabins had evolved into one-family dwellings, which Gray thought may have been mandated by Reconstruction laws. In those cabins, the privacy wall had a crudely cut door in it. In others, including the one shared by Carrie and Willie, no door had ever been cut.

Each dwelling had a central chimney that served both families, with a mantel and hearth on each side of the cabin. In his books, Gaines calls the hearth the "fire half."

Some tenants added rooms to the backs of their cabins, usually a kitchen and a bathroom. Ernest Gaines said the additions dated to about 1943, around the time the cabins got electricity. Running water was added then, too, but only on the right side of Major Lane, where George Major installed outside faucets. Those living on the left side had to cross the road and fill pails or buckets with water from the faucets, or they used a well.[16]

As BREC workers dismantled the cabins, Gray was intrigued by how the houses looked after the World War II–era additions had been removed. "The house takes on its original shape after the back is removed," he said. He also noticed some interesting "negative" information. "There's always a tremendous amount of trash when you take an old house apart. But many of these houses did not have a lot of trash because there was so little remodeling done to them over the years." One interesting discovery: as workers ripped away paneling or wallpaper in Carrie Hebert's house, they found inside the wall a man's sock filled with dimes.

BREC workers built a bridge across a ditch to move one of the disassembled houses, after packaging the wood into bundles and labeling them with a system devised by Gray. Each chimney was dismantled brick by brick and labeled for later reconstruction. Finally, in late April 1993, Carrie and Willie's cabin, stripped of its roof, porch, and chimney, reduced to a twenty-four-foot-square box, totaling 576 square feet, was loaded onto a steel-beamed building-mover's trailer and driven thirty-five miles across the Mississippi River to Baton Rouge. It sat untouched on the grounds of Magnolia Mound Plantation for two or three years and was eventually reconstructed, raised up on blocks that Gray said are "too high," its gray-brown cypress boards painted a glaring white, and opened to visitors, where it added a "slavery component" to the plantation's depiction of antebellum life.

The other three cabins—where once lived the immediate neighbors of Aunt Teen—were last seen as bundles of wood and bricks, sitting on the grounds of BREC headquarters in Baton Rouge. The original plan was to reassemble the dismantled cabins, but Gray suspects the boards have long since rotted on the ground and are beyond salvaging. In a sense, it seemed fitting—just as the people who once occupied the cabins had been devalued, so were the houses that for a century and a half had sheltered them.

The destruction and removal of the four cabins in the spring of 1993 was an epiphany for Gray. Seeing the houses reduced to shells or loads of lumber, watching trucks haul them away, he had a change of heart. Although moving them was preferable to seeing them destroyed, he realized that the cabins lost nearly all their historic value when moved off site. Certainly, they lost the value they had through their association with one of the great American writers of the twentieth century. Slave cabins are rare, Gray realized. Slave cabins associated with Ernest Gaines are even rarer. "His use of these old buildings as settings for his novels makes them worth saving, or at least documenting. They have never been documented . . . as buildings where people lived, died, and raised families. They've been considered adjuncts to the Big House."

Now that the four cabins on the west side of the lane were gone, Gray felt that the last two on the east side were more precious than ever. "They are some of the rarest surviving examples of early nineteenth-century construction in Louisiana," he said. The cabin recently vacated by Shug Edwards was in good shape, probably because it had been occupied from the 1840s until the 1990s. "It is rare to find a building that has been continuously occupied by the same culture group for that long."

The second surviving cabin was in much worse shape, having sat empty since the 1985 death of Reese Spooner, the tall, slender man who had told Ernest Gaines stories of the old days. When Gray first saw Spooner's cabin, it was still filled with furniture, soggy from rain that had fallen through holes in the tin roof. He recommended removing the soft furniture and clothing so that moisture would not collect in the cabin, further damaging the old wood. Birds nested in the rafters, and rats or possums had stored ears of corn in armoires that still held clothing. Out back were an outhouse, a warren of hog pens and overgrown gardens, and a rusted Volkswagen Beetle, barely visible among the undergrowth.

On one visit, Ben Biben pointed out the dismantled white picket fence resting on the front porch of Reese's cabin. In the 1930s and 1940s, the fence had surrounded the Big House. Later, Reese had used part of it to protect his vegetable garden. Inside the left front room, Biben pointed out benches built into the wall and said Reese once had a "bar" in his house, selling drinks through a side window and even holding dance parties. Gray noted that the floors had been replaced. "They are made of narrower planks than would have been used in the 1840s."

Just across the road from Reese's house was an empty space where once stood the house that Biben's widowed grandmother Emma Kemp had moved into around 1955. Next to it had stood the house where Ernest Gaines lived with his great-aunt Augusteen Jefferson. Like so many other structures, both had been destroyed. Now there were only two cabins left. Many past residents of the quarter seemed resigned to the surviving houses' fate, but Biben hoped both cabins could be saved; both had special meaning to him. "I grew up right across from Reese's house. And Shug's house is where we used to have receptions after a funeral."[17]

In 1995, Gray set the wheels in motion to have the last two cabins listed on the National Register of Historic Places. (The Big House had been on the register since 1983.) Eager to learn more about life in the cabins, he met with Ernest Gaines, who said the cabins originally rested on wooden blocks that were later replaced with brick piers, and even later with concrete piers. He said his paternal grandfather Izel Gaines, a carpenter, had replaced the piers on all the houses at some point. But Gray was convinced by the physical evidence that the houses were originally built on brick piers that were later replaced by concrete blocks.

Gaines clearly remembered houses in the field behind the quarter. His great-uncle Horace McVay and his wife, Octavia, had lived back there "by the sugarhouse. Those houses were still there when I left in 1948." He recalled an overseer's house on the east side of the lane, "one of the oldest houses there." It was torn down, he said, in the 1950s, as was the sugarhouse.[18]

"The old people who could not compete or farm were allowed to stay on the land as long as they wanted. As the older people died, the eighty-, ninety-, one-hundred-year-old houses were so dilapidated they'd be destroyed."[19]

Around the same time the quarter houses were dismantled, the owners also destroyed the house that had once been occupied by Gaines's grandmother Julia McVay when she was the cook at the Big House. It had been built later than the cabins, but it still had a good deal of history attached to it. When Gray sifted through the rubble, he discovered a pair of andirons. A delighted Gaines recognized them as having belonged to his grandmother and gratefully accepted them from Gray.

Besides Shug's house and Reese's house, there were two other buildings left on Major Lane: the church and the shed. The Mount Zion Baptist Church was a small, white wooden structure. Built around 1937, it had been the center of religious life in Cherie Quarters for nearly sixty years, until its last service was held in 1993. The building, which measured about twenty feet wide by forty feet deep, also served as a school for the children of the quarter. Ernest Gaines began attending classes there around 1939. The original pews, about twenty hand-built wooden benches painted brown, were still in the building. These pews had served double duty as desks, the students kneeling before them to write their lessons. Gaines said his paternal grandfather Izel Gaines changed the blocks, or piers, and built the wooden steps to the church. "At some point, he changed the blocks on all the buildings in the quarter," said Gaines, who still had tools that had belonged to his grandfather.

This one small building figures in almost every published work of fiction by Gaines. The schoolhouse in *A Lesson Before Dying* is based on the church/school that Gaines attended in the 1940s. In the short story "A Long Day in November," the narrator Sonny spends a good part of his day at the school.

Until 1993, a pastor from Baton Rouge drove over to conduct Sunday services twice a month. In the spring of 1992, coproducer Rick Smith and I had Louisiana Public Broadcasting cameraman Charles Bush record one of the last services for our television documentary. Shug Edwards and Carrie Hebert, who knew that their days at Cherie Quarters were numbered, asked their children and grandchildren in neighboring towns to come to the service so the church would once more be filled with people. Shug and Carrie wore white dresses and white hats. Their children and grandchildren were outfitted almost formally, the women in dresses, the men in starched white shirts and dark ties.

The Mount Zion Baptist Church building represented the only educational opportunity available to the children of the thirty or so Black families that lived in the quarter in the 1930s and 1940s. No known written records exist to document the exact date of construction or the reason it was built. Freddie Kemp helped build the church when he was twenty-five, dating it to 1937. The succession of P. C. Major reveals that a few months before his death he donated an arpent of land (about an acre) to the parish school board, suggesting that he intended to build a school there for the children of Cherie Quarters.[20]

To the left of the church stood a small shed, built around 1940 by Gaines's grandfather Izel. Ben Biben said the shed was used as a dining hall for students. It held a woodstove and a bench, and children often ate lunch there on cold days. Biben said the shed also functioned as a "social hall" for the church.[21]

In 1995, when he proposed the cabins for listing on the National Register, Gray hoped to save the last two cabins, the shed, and the church. The cabins were added to the register, but little else was done to save the quarter buildings. The owners delayed important decisions for years, citing concerns about liability. Meanwhile, Louisiana got sixty-five inches of rainfall a year, each rain like a deathblow to the cabins, particularly Reese's, which had gaping holes in its tin roof. By 1998, it had totally collapsed and was beyond salvaging.

Discouraged by what he called "demolition by neglect," Sid Gray made fewer and fewer trips to Cherie Quarters. Through the LSU Student Union's "leisure classes," he taught a course called "Old Houses of Louisiana," combining slide lectures with field trips to historic buildings. For a while, he took his class to Cherie Quarters twice a year. That was just often enough to notice the changes wrought by neglect—and worse. In the fall of 1998, as Gray was showing his class around, he noticed that the loose ceiling boards in Shug's cabin were gone, scavenged for who knows what use. The boards had been the subject of one of Gray's most exciting discoveries. They had rested upon the rafters since the 1840s, set there but not nailed down, so they could be turned over when the cabin was cleaned, following the dictates Gray had discovered in *Advice Among Masters.* "The ceiling boards were the most valuable thing in the building," he said. "When they cannibalize a building, that's the beginning of the end."

Gray deeply regretted the loss of the thirty cypress boards, which were sixteen feet long and twelve to sixteen inches wide. He mourned them both as physical objects and as clues to the construction of Cherie Quarters. "They had never had nails driven in them," he said. "They were nice boards, probably valuable boards."

"They were easy to remove," he said.[22]

Well, not that easy. Gray speculated that it probably took two men and a ladder to wrangle the boards down from the rafters they rested on, and a truck to haul them away. Where they are now, only the ghosts of Cherie Quarters know.

7

# OF LOVE AND DUST

## DAILY LIFE IN CHERIE QUARTERS

In 1992, when I was working on a television documentary about Ernest Gaines, I asked him for a list of friends and family whom I could contact. One of the first people I called was his brother Lionel, who had married Ada Mae Robillard when they were teenagers; they had grown up together at Cherie Quarters. As it happened, it was the ebullient Ada Mae who answered the phone. I asked her what Cherie Quarters had been like in the 1930s through the 1950s, when she lived there. "A beautiful, peaceful, dusty place to live," she told me. "It was just love."[1]

Caledonia Club on False River near New Roads, circa 1958. At *left,* at the jukebox, is Albertha Kemp. In *front* are Mamie and George Williams. At *right* are Freddie Kemp and Rosemary Spooner. Photo by David Biben. Courtesy of Deidra Biben-Glynn.

Love, embodied in a strong sense of community, animated the life of Cherie Quarters. The terms dictated by the white owners were brutally hard, and often unfair. Among the residents, however, while there may have been disagreements, fights, and even violence, the abiding image is of a community that survived by pulling together. Parents disciplined one another's children, neighbors cared for each other when they were sick. No one was in this alone.

When Gaines lived there, from January 1933 through August 1948, about twenty-five cabins lined both sides of the road, inhabited by about 150 people.[2] What was it like to live there—to actually inhabit the rough cabins that were bitter cold in winter and stifling hot in summer, to soldier through a life of hard work, to grasp what little education you could, to make a life for yourself and your family?

## WORK AND MAKING MONEY

In the 1930s and 1940s, most of the people of Cherie Quarters worked as sharecroppers or tenant farmers. Ben Biben recalled that River Lake functioned somewhat differently from other nearby plantations.

> What they call sharecropping, at other places, say you made a hundred dollars, you had to give twenty-five to your boss, and whatever you bought [at the plantation store] was taken out of your seventy-five dollars profit. But the way they done it [at Cherie Quarters], they charged 'em rent for the land and then [the workers] bought fertilizer, seed, plow, mule, whatever—that was taken out of your profit. I think it was a freer way; you were more of a manager. You didn't have to buy your supplies from the plantation store. You could go anywhere you wanted to for them.[3]

Biben said the sharecropping system changed after owner P. C. Major died in 1934. "During Cherie Major's time, it was sharecropping, because he owned the whole plantation," but after Major's death, the plantation was divided among his heirs.

Early rising was common, but "You could get up at different times. You didn't have to [rise at dawn] if you were a farmer. Most had their own mules. They got up early but were not obligated to." After working in the fields, men and women would go home for the noon meal, called "dinner," and a rest. Around 2:30 or 3:00 p.m., they returned to the fields and worked until dark. "The lady would leave out the field about four o'clock and come home and cook supper." Men, when they knocked off work, would "get home and feed the mules."

Biben recalled a schedule ruled by the seasons. In January, the workers planted Irish potatoes and onions. In mid- to late February, they dug sugar cane stubble. In March, they planted corn and prepared the land to plant cotton. In April, they were cultivating, hoeing, and thinning out corn and cotton plants; in May, they fertilized corn and cotton. "We called it [June] 'lay by,' pulling the dirt up around the cotton, cutting the grass and weeds, hoeing it out." July and early August was "sit-back time; I guess nothing special was going on. It was so hot." By the middle to the end of the August, they would "pull corn, cut weeds, clean the ditch bank."

In September, workers were "getting ready for cotton picking" by making their own sacks. "We were poor, so you couldn't buy the sacks," he said. "You'd take a feed sack or a croker sack [burlap or similar] and make a cotton sack from it. You'd make a strap from another sack cut into pieces and tie it to the sack. You'd make a loop to put your hand in. Everybody made their own sack, and you had to tailor it to fit you. Some people bought those long white [sacks] but we'd make 'em from [brown] feed sacks."[4] In October, the workers picked cotton, dragging the long sacks on their shoulders. October 1 was also the traditional date for planting sugar cane for the following season.

In October, November, and December—a season known as "grinding"—they harvested cane—cut it with cane knives, loaded it into mule-drawn wagons, and took it to the mill. After River Lake's sugarhouse was torn down in the 1950s, the cane was sent to a mill at nearby Alma Plantation. "Oh, boy, that sugar cane," said Biben, nearly fifty years after leaving Cherie Quarters. "Cutting it, loading it by hand, packing it on that wagon . . ."

Biben teamed up with his uncle George Williams. "George and me used to load together. I'd load the front [of the wagon] and he'd load the back." George's two mules, Red and Bird, pulled the wooden wagon. It was twelve feet long by five feet wide, with shallow sides eighteen inches high. The pair used stakes to hold the cane in and chains to tie it down. Williams had probably bought the wagon in nearby New Roads, and he customized it for various purposes. "The wagon was made somewhere else, but the bed was homemade. The wheels, the frame, the tongue all come in one piece. The bed, the thing you sit in, you had to make yourself. It was made of cypress. George made that, or Mr. Revel [Domino] or Mr. Isaiah [Izel Gaines, Ernest Gaines's grandfather], people [who were] like carpenters." When it was time to pull corn, Williams would again make adjustments to the wagon. "You'd build a higher side on it. You would add to the side, make it higher so you could carry much more."

The work was undeniably hard, but, Biben said, "You didn't know it was bad. You had fun. We'd sing, laugh, joke, talk about each other. Sometimes [couples] would sneak into the sugar cane patch for some hanky-panky. A lot of people would sing church songs: 'Satan, Your Wall Must Come Down' or 'Working on the Building.'" He sang a few lines from the hymn:

I'm working on the building  
It's a true foundation  
I'm holding up the bloodstained  
Banner for my lord.  
Well I never get tired, tired, tired of working on the building  
I'm going up to heaven to get my reward.

One song included the words "Oh, Lord have mercy, late in the evening sun going down." It was "the same thing like slaves used to sing. I found out later it was about getting away from the slave owner."

Children also worked at Cherie Quarters. Ernest Gaines became a wage earner at eight, earning fifty cents a day picking cotton, pulling corn, digging potatoes, chopping or hauling sugar cane, and cutting trees for firewood. Ben Biben picked cotton as a child, and Bill Robillard also worked as a child, in the 1930s. "I started loading cane when I was nine years old, and I was on the puny side. We had to survive. I started working for forty cents a day. Forty cents a *day*."[5]

Forrest Zeno went to work at twelve. "A child got forty cents a day for twelve hours' work. Ladies got sixty cents a day for hoeing sugar cane. Mens got eighty cents a day for hoeing cane. Men who plowed with the mules got a dollar a day—that was twelve hours a day. We started at six a.m., when day break."[6] Freddie Kemp started working at fourteen. "Farm work, hoeing, plowing. We kept hogs, chickens, mules, horses, cows. That was my job, milking cows. Cow done kicked me many times."[7]

In addition to sharecropping or tenant farming, most residents of Cherie Quarters found ways to make extra income. George Williams gave haircuts on the porch of the house he shared with his wife, Mamie, and their two children. Using a truck borrowed from his brother-in-law Freddie Kemp, he hauled cotton to gins for other farmers. He also broke and bred horses, renting out his stallion Tony as a stud. "George was the only one who had a breeding stallion back then," said Ben Biben. "They'd go back in the graveyard to keep people from seeing it [the horses mating]. The graveyard was surrounded by trees then. Nobody could hardly see it unless you were looking for it. Sometimes Lionel [Gaines] and Alcide [Cage] would sneak back there and get behind the bushes and watch."[8]

Ernest Gaines's maternal grandmother Julia McVay, who cooked for the white owners during the week, put her pots and pans to use on weekends, too. "She would give suppers every Saturday night," said Ben Biben, who often ate at McVay's house with his grandparents. "She'd feed 'em and charge 'em for it—fifty cents a plate for chicken and gravy, snap beans, peas, potato salad, rice, stewed chicken, fried fish."[9] McVay also made Mardi Gras costumes and took on other sewing projects.

Many residents of Cherie Quarters worked at the Triple Arch restaurant in Oscar, where Black people were allowed only as cooks and waiters. The restaurant was popular on weekends, especially when LSU was playing football in Baton Rouge. "Triple Arch, you almost had to have a membership to go there," said Joe Williams. "Wealthy white folks went there."[10] "A whole bunch of us worked there," said Ernest Brooks, who was in his first year of high school when he started at the restaurant, about 1950. He worked from nine in the morning until two the following morning for three dollars a day. He chopped onions, celery, and bell peppers; made hush puppies; and washed dishes. His seventeen-hour shift had few breaks. "We'd have a chance to eat, but our break wouldn't be that long." Brooks objected to the behavior of the white owner, Claude Melancon. "He always talked down to people, and I didn't like that. But I couldn't do nothing about it, being a kid."[11]

Although the kitchen workers were Black, the restaurant's patrons were all white. Brooks said, "There were no Blacks going in there. Anybody Black . . . had to be working." Black people were not allowed inside even to buy food to take out. "They had a little delivery side. You had to go to the side door if you wanted to buy something. You couldn't even go in there. You just had to knock on the door and order what you wanted and they'd bring it out."

Biben remembered an endless cycle of labor, both paid and unpaid.

> I used to watch people work so hard. People like Ovide Simon—we called him Tee Moon. He'd go into the field at daylight. His stepson would bring him breakfast and dinner [in the field]. He'd work until dark, feed his mules, then go home for supper. He'd sit and talk with us on the porch for a while, then he'd get his gun and go kill a possum. That's the next day's [meal]. They'd lay it out until the next morning, get up and skin him out, gut him and dress him, and eat him the next day. . . . We'd sit there talking and laughing, and he'd say, "Well, let me go see can I find something." He'd get a single-barrel shotgun and go out and hunt until he killed something. Get up in the morning and you'd see him with his wagon and his mule.[12]

## COOKING AND FOOD

Although the plantation store carried staples, money was scarce in the quarter and payment for work was often delayed until "settling up" time. Most people grew their own vegetables and raised their own livestock, particularly chickens and cows. "Everybody had a hog or two, chickens, a few ducks or geese," said Biben. "Back in the field we had guineas. Mr. Horace [McVay] had a couple of goats." They also picked pecans and blackberries, shot whatever game could be found, and fished in False River.[13]

Ernest Gaines said his family ate mostly cabbage ("three or four times a week"), rice, Irish potatoes, and sweet potatoes, and occasionally chicken or pork from hens and hogs they raised themselves. Chewing on a knob of cane was a treat.[14] His grandmother Julia McVay often made pies and cakes for the children of the quarter.

Ben Biben remembered his grandmother Emma Lovely Kemp as "a great cook." One of his favorite dishes was a stew she made from bream and rice. Biben often caught the fish that went into the stew. "They'd send us out and say, 'Go catch supper.' We'd come home with nineteen or twenty bream." Emma, he said, also made teas from orange peel and from mint that she grew.[15]

Emma's son Freddie Kemp recalled her making wine from berries and cooking rabbits seasoned only with salt and onions.[16] "She cooked a lot of wild game," said her grandson Sam Bibbens. "Raccoons, rabbits, robins, owls, killdeer, chicken hawks."[17] Her granddaughter Barbara Overstreet, who inherited Emma's talent in the kitchen, remembered Emma sitting out on her front

Freddie Kemp and his niece Barbara Bibbens Overstreet, 1970s. Photo by David Biben. Courtesy of Deidra Biben-Glynn.

gallery grinding coffee beans, chopping the ingredients for rice dressing on Christmas Eve, and making eggnog, beating the eggs with a fork and grating fresh nutmeg. "None of this canned stuff."[18]

Most families had woodstoves by the time Ernest Gaines lived there, but many people also used chimneys for cooking. "During our time, we had woodstoves," said Biben, who was born in 1934. "Before that, they would cook in the chimneys. They had the old iron pot, and they would set it on the fireplace, with a good solid piece of wood in back and another one in the front. They would set the pot on the wood." People used the iron pot to cook rice and various types of beans—red, white, pinto—and cooked cornbread in a skillet with a cover on it. "Way back when I was little, my grandmother had a way of hanging it on a hook over the fire, but I can't remember exactly how."[19]

Biben said the houses were lit by kerosene lamps, or people improvised. "My grandmother used to fill a wine bottle with kerosene and take a [piece of] sheet or a sock and wrap it real tight and put it down in the bottle and light it [like a wick], and that would be our lamp." Emma Kemp would set the kerosene lamp on the mantel, but even with a fire in the fireplace, "It was pretty dark. She'd take it in the kitchen and cook [by its light]."[20]

For food they couldn't raise, catch, or shoot, people relied on a Sicilian merchant who sold fruit. Giuseppe "Joe" Tuminello regularly drove a red truck with a canvas cover into the quarter and sold watermelons, bananas, oranges, and sometimes coconuts. Some children would sneak up while Tuminello was talking to customers, grab bananas off the wagon, toss them into a ditch, and retrieve them later. He also sold blocks of ice for people's iceboxes.[21] He owned a grocery store in New Roads. The people of Cherie Quarters knew him as Joe Dago, and his wife, who wore long black dresses, was called Madam

Joe. The Tuminellos, devout Catholics who attended Mass daily, were kind to Black people, allowing them to use the restroom at their store, a courtesy extended by no other white merchant. The couple were models for the grocery store owners in Ernest Gaines's short story "The Sky Is Gray." Madam Joe was also the model for Madam Orsini in *The Autobiography of Miss Jane Pittman,* who allows African Americans to use her restroom.[22]

## HUNTING AND FISHING

The nearby woods and bayous—not to mention False River—where the people of Cherie Quarters hunted and fished, were other rich sources of food. They regularly caught catfish and bream in the river. Gaines's grandmother, known as Zuma, went fishing every day after leaving the Big House about 3:00 p.m.[23] Freddie Kemp, who was born in 1912, recalled a childhood spent mostly outdoors. "I used to fish in False River, hunt rabbits in the woods. Take me a dog. Me and another fella would kill ten rabbits in one hour. Fishin', we used to put some asphidity [asafoetida] on that hook. It's a little cake of medicine. Put a little bit on the hook with the worm."[24]

Turtles were more troublesome. "I caught a turtle one time," said Kemp. "I was duckin' school 'cause they had a test. In the afternoon, I went and caught a little ol' turtle, a snapping turtle. That scoundrel caught me on my leg. Brother [Albert Cage, his friend] couldn't get him loose, so he light some fire in the stove and heated up a stick and stuck [the turtle] with it, and it opened its mouth. Then I got a whippin' after that." Ben Biben, too, vividly recalled catching a turtle when he was a teenager, in the 1940s.

> I had a horse named Dot, a little mare horse. I'd tie her by the railroad tracks so she could eat grass. On the [bayou] bank, I saw this big turtle, maybe a foot and a half across or bigger. I said, "I gotta bring this home." I took the rope off the horse's neck [and went after the turtle]. The turtle ran down to the water. I grabbed his tail—I guess it was a she, because she was laying eggs—and looped the rope around her neck. I dragged her up that bank.
>
> I didn't know how to take her home. I put my belt around the horse's nose and put the rope around the horse's neck and drug the turtle home by the rope. Everybody in the quarters was watching. "Boy, where you got that big cooter from?"
>
> I brought him home, brought him in the back yard. Mama [his grand-

mother Emma Kemp] said, "You got to kill it yourself." I got an ax and laid the turtle's head on [a piece of firewood]. I was trying to hold the turtle and chop its head off. The turtle kept pulling its head in. Mama took a broom handle and shoved it up that turtle's behind and the head came out and I cut it off.

To get the shell off you cut the [ligaments] on the side between the hard-top shell and the bottom of the turtle. We'd cut off the side and the skin, cut all that meat out, throw the shell away, throw the guts away.

We cleaned him, put him in hot water, took the skin off. When I finished, we had a dishpan full of meat, the legs and the back. The heart was still beating. We put it in an ant nest and watched until it stopped beating. We cooked it probably that night. I think she parboiled it then put it in the oven and baked it like a roast. We thought it was good. We didn't get much meat.

Biben, about sixteen at the time, felt like a hero for dragging the huge turtle home and providing such a meal. "Everybody watching. You feel big, like you done something."[25]

Biben said Walter "Salute" Zeno, who was a generation older, had another method for catching turtles. "Salute used to go in the bayou. If the water was low, like the last of June, he'd take a big stick and push it into the mud until it hit something hard and dig that turtle out and take him home to eat him. He'd bring home big old loggerhead turtles and snapping turtles."

Biben heard that Salute had tricked another man into eating what he thought was raccoon, considered a delicacy in the quarter. The man who told the story was Richard Isaac, from nearby Lorio Plantation.

He was a big, quiet man, big and strong. He'd come visit the quarters. He used to visit with Salute. One day Salute said, "Richard, you want a piece of coon?" He said, "Yeah, don't mind if I do." Salute gave him a plate and he ate it. "Man, that was good!" "You want another piece?" "Yeah, if you don't mind." Salute got him another piece [and he ate that]. Then Salute went and got his gun. He asked Richard, "You ever ate wildcat?" Richard said, "Man, nobody better ever give me wildcat!" Salute cocked his gun and said, "You just ate it." Richard looked at the gun and said, "Well, if it's that good, I guess I'll eat it then."

Along with wildcat, possum was considered off limits by many in the quarter, including Emma Kemp. "Mama would not eat a possum, no way," Biben said. "She'd cook it, but she wouldn't eat it." She was repelled by "the way he looks—and [the fact that] he'll eat anything."

Others preferred possum to the more popular raccoon. "Frank Spooner and I used to go hunting all the time together," said Biben. "We'd kill three coon and one possum and he'd take the possum. Everybody ate coon. They harder to kill, they climb much higher in the tree. Frank had a modern shotgun. I'd use a shotgun. If I didn't miss, that was it, he's coming down. The gun was old and long. I like coon; I still eat coon."

## SOCIALIZING AND ENTERTAINMENT

While work was the shaping force in their lives, the people of Cherie Quarters had plenty of good times, whether sitting on the porch telling stories or engaging in more sophisticated forms of fun. Conversation was definitely a favorite form of entertainment. Ernest Gaines spoke often of sitting and listening to "the old people" talk. His sister Lois Young said, "Visiting and talking was a very big part of our lives."[26] Gaines recalled James Brooks Sr., as "a great storyteller. He'd tell stories about Br'er Rabbit driving a tractor. Mr. Jimmy could tell a story. He told great ghost stories. It would be dark in the quarter and we'd be scared to walk home. Jim [James Brooks Jr., Gaines's contemporary] was just like his daddy. They had another brother, all great storytellers. Even Booster [Ernest Brooks], he was their nephew, he could make you laugh."[27] Ben Biben remembered that "foxfire reflected from old wood—we thought that was ghosts. We'd put horseshoes over our door, take flour and put it around a house, and they [ghosts] wouldn't come out. To cross it was voodoo."[28]

James Brooks said the quarter was a quiet place when he and Gaines were growing up in the thirties and forties. "There was no entertainment for us, no place to go. We'd gather in the afternoon in the street and just talk. There was no playground, so we'd just walk up and down and wrestle or tussle like boys do."[29] But others told of various forms of fun. The boys would squat in the dirt and shoot marbles—Ernest Gaines buried a large can of marbles he had won from other players. They also staged footraces, running a quarter or half mile up the lane to the sugarhouse. Both men and boys played baseball, often with homemade bats and balls, with a bit of wagering on the game's outcome. Ben Biben recalled making toys such as hoops and popguns from cane stalks.[30]

For the adults, and sometimes children, there were house fairs, or parties, and fish fries. On Mardi Gras, the people of the quarter would hold a *courir,* a rural celebration in which men rode horses while masked and costumed. Julia McVay, Gaines's grandmother, would make the costumes and *papier-mâché* masks. The men and boys would don costumes, masks, and cone-shaped hats and ride wildly up and down the quarter on horseback. One man, remembered only as Sabé (pronounced *sah-BAY*), frightened by all the commotion, would climb a huge oak tree to escape the festivities.[31]

Money was scarce, but most of the children of Cherie Quarters got presents at Christmas. "Boys got a new pair of pants or shoes. You might get a little toy gun, cap gun, and an orange and apple or banana. I remember getting a little red wagon when I was about five years old," said Ben Biben. The children believed in Santa Claus and accepted the tradition that he came down the chimney. "Oh, yeah! We went to bed early. But we didn't leave anything [food] out for him."[32]

A favorite form of fun in the quarter was teasing, and those who flared up when provoked marked themselves as perennial targets. James Brooks said a popular pastime among the children was "throwing rocks on old folks' houses at night to scare 'em. On the tin roof, they'd make a lot of noise. One man they'd always pick on, he'd always come out and shout. One night, he came out with a shotgun and made a blast. Everybody took off and dived in the ditch and the bushes."[33]

A man called Modo was picked on because his father had behaved in cowardly fashion during a fight. James Brooks relished that story, which bore some resemblance to the house party fight described by Gaines in his second novel, *Of Love and Dust.* As Brooks told it, Modo's father, Sylvester Horton, "would pretend he wanted to fight, but he wanted you to hold him back." On the night in question, "Syl Horton and a man named Jesse got into this argument. Jesse hit Syl and knocked him down. Syl said, 'I'm going home and get my gun, and when I get back, you better not be here and you better not be gone!'" Syl Horton left, the party continued, and a short time later, said Brooks,

> a shotgun went off in front of the house. Everybody started running, peeping out of every door and window. Jesse said, "Where he's at?" Everybody said, "Don't go out there, Jesse! The man's gon' kill you!" Jesse walked out into the yard. We heard the iron gate open and then slam shut. Syl came in the yard with his gun. They met each other in the yard. Jesse walked up to Syl and

took the gun from him and threw it in the yard and grabbed Syl and threw him down. Syl got up, picked up his gun, and went on home. Every time we'd see Syl's son Modo we'd holler, "Where he's at?" Modo used to hate to see us coming.

No one remembered Modo's real name, which is not surprising, because giving nicknames was another source of fun in the quarter. Many long-dead residents are remembered by nicknames only; others, whose real names are known, are still called by pet names. As noted, Ernest Gaines's grandmother Julia McVay was known as Zuma; Horace McVay was Mom-sun and his brother Griffin was Rang. Octavia McVay, Horace's wife, was Shall-doe. Gaines's brother Eugene was Gabby, his grandfather Matthew Jefferson was Man, and Man's brother or half brother was known only as Tee Boy—nobody remembered his real name. Tee Boy's mother is remembered only as Miss Coon. Augusteen Jefferson was Miss Teen, Emma Kemp was Miss Podnuh (Partner), and Emma's son Anthony Cochran was Scoo-Noo. Gustave Robillard was Fee-Non, and his daughter Eliza was Too-Too. Walter Zeno was most commonly referred to as Salute. Frank Spooner was Plut. Ernest Spooner was Snook. Rose Bibbens was Dal, and her brother Sam was Buckaroo. Ovide Simon was Tee Moon. Overseer Alcide Dejean was Cap. Children commonly called their parents by their first names, often because they lived with their grandparents and related to them as parents. Ben Biben called his grandparents Sam and Emma Kemp Papa and Mama; his mother, Albertha, was Bert. Ernest Brooks (Booster) also called his mother, Lubertha, by her first name.

Visitors to the quarter provided entertainment, such as cowboy movies. On weekends, a man known only as "Slim" would arrive with a projector and a cowboy movie, which he showed on a sheet hung in a shed or a tent. Gaines's mother, Adrean Colar, remembered a man who showed movies when she was a child, in the 1920s. Sometimes the children would go to New Roads, to the "colored" theater back of town, and then buy a treat. "There was an ice cream parlor. We'd go over there and get us an ice cream cone, then head on back to the country. We'd talk all the next week about the show and get ready for the next one."[34]

A man named Peter Brown, who owned a car, would pack it with kids and drive to New Roads to see movies on Friday nights. "We'd load the car down with thirteen people, little old stinky boys, sit on each other's lap," said Ben Biben. Later, Bill Robillard bought a car from Pointe Coupée Parish sheriff Bub Bouanchaud and did the same thing, with everybody chipping in gas money.[35]

The radio was a rich source of entertainment in the 1930s and 1940s. Julia McVay owned the only radio in the quarter, a battery-operated Zenith, around which people would gather to listen to Friday night fights (Joe Louis versus Max Schmeling in 1938 was a favorite) or baseball games. Ben Biben remembered the boys of the quarter listening to Major League games on the radio and later trying to imitate the plays they heard described on the air.[36] Ernest Gaines's brother Norbert recalled comedies and dramas such as *Amos 'n' Andy, Boston Blackie, Inner Sanctum,* and *The Great Gildersleeve.*[37]

"We listened to the radio a lot," said Gaines. "It was the heyday of radio, before TV came along. There were great plays—*The Importance of Being Earnest; Our Town.* A lot of short stories were dramatized, such as H. H. Munro's "The Monkey's Paw," with Peter Lorre. We used to listen to *Lux* [*Radio*] *Theatre* on Sundays. They had great plays, good actors. I remember lying there listening to those things. I still think *Gunsmoke* has the best dialogue." Gaines inherited the radio when his grandmother died, and he cherished it.[38] He paid tribute to the importance of the radio in quarter culture in *A Lesson Before Dying*—Grant gives Jefferson a radio to listen to in his jail cell.

## CHURCH AND RELIGION

In the 1930s, some of the men of Cherie Quarters built a church, originally intended as a school. The site selected was a vacant lot on the east side of Major Lane, about a quarter of a mile from Highway 1. Freddie Kemp was twenty-five years old when he helped build it, around 1937. "Before that, we used to go to a church on False River."[39]

Mount Zion Baptist was a small frame building, painted white, comprising a long, shotgun-style hall and a small entry foyer. It had doors at the front and back, windows on both side walls, and a small tower with a bell that was rung to notify residents that services were about to start. Ben Biben said, "They used to tone [toll] the bell when somebody died," as well.[40]

When the Baptist preacher christened the infant children, each baby had a *parrain* (*PAH-ranh*), or godfather, and a *nanan* (*nuh-NAN*), or godmother, chosen by the child's parents. The people of the quarter would say of their godparents, "He/she christened me." Most of the children of Cherie Quarters maintained a lifelong special relationship with their godparents.[41] Ernest

Gaines's parrain was Claiborne "Ussy" Horton and his nanan was Albertha Bibbens. Godparents figure prominently in his fiction, often serving as surrogate parents—Miss Julie Rand is Marcus's godmother in *Of Love and Dust,* Angelina Bouie is Reverend Phillip Martin's "nanane" in *In My Father's House,* and Miss Emma is Jefferson's long-suffering godmother in *A Lesson Before Dying*

Two Sundays a month, there were services that ran from noon until three or four o'clock, during which, according to James Brooks, the Baptist preacher would "talk, talk, talk, talk, talk." The little church was filled with people on those Sundays. Ben Biben said that on the second Sunday of the month, known as Determination Sunday, Reverend O'Neal Bouie would hold "a speaking meeting."[42] Every adult would leave his seat, walk to the front, stand before the altar, and "testify" about how he had been saved. "The service would go on for three or four hours," Biben said. Brooks said, "You would tell a determination, that you're doing the right thing and hope to go to heaven." The fourth Sunday of the month was called Sacrament Sunday, when the preacher gave Communion—a sip of wine (later grape juice) and a cracker. "You would emulate drinking the blood of Christ and eating the body." After the service, one of the deacons (four or five men of some standing in the community) would take Communion to the elderly, the sick, and shut-ins.[43]

Gaines's sister Lois Young remembered Reverend O'Neal Bouie's "exciting, electrifying sermons. . . . The children were there in their Sunday best, dresses starched and stiff, with a big white bow in your hair, little patent shoes if you had them. The ladies would wear white, especially the ushers, the ones that would usher people into the church, take them a fan or a glass of water if they started screaming, yelling, shouting too loud. They were so proud when they walked into the church."[44]

The preacher was usually invited to dinner after services. "When the preacher was coming, that's when we had a special meal," said James Brooks. "We'd eat red beans and rice or spaghetti during the week. But when the preacher was coming on a Sunday, that's when they'd kill a chicken."[45]

Reverend Bouie, who conducted services beginning around the 1940s, also lived in Cherie Quarters. Malvina Becnel Pickett, a granddaughter of plantation owner P. C. Major, who spent a lot of time at River Lake Plantation as a child, said that her mother, Mae Major Becnel, taught Reverend Bouie to read and write.[46] Ben Biben said Bouie used to tell the children that it was a sin to play marbles, to play ball, and to dance.[47] "You couldn't play on Sunday;

that was a sin," said Ada Mae Gaines. "Winning at marbles was a sin. Any stuff that consists of 'You gotta give me' or 'I gotta give you.' You could not let the pastor see you."[48] When they were about twelve years old, Biben and Lionel Gaines set a booby trap by pulling a wire between two gateposts, low to the ground. The gate was near the church, and they hid and watched as Reverend Bouie left the building and began walking to his car. He tripped over the wire and let loose a profanity.[49]

Children were baptized in False River around the age of twelve. Gaines was among about fifteen boys and girls baptized in a group that included Ben Biben. "You wore an old sheet wrapped around you, over your clothes, and a white rag on your head." The baptisms were considered entertainment, and spectators lined the riverbank to watch as boys and girls were dunked under water. "Ooh, my God, yes indeed! Everybody, white and Black, lined up along the river to watch, probably a hundred or more people. There was a line of cars; people would come out to see the baptizing." Boys were always given a new suit as a baptism gift, often ordered from the Sears, Roebuck catalog, and girls got "a brand-new dress."

Biben recalled hymns sung during services. "Reverend Bouie would say, 'We'll have a song by Brother [Willie] Burks, a prayer by Brother [Jimmy] Brooks, and a song by Brother [Revel] Domino.' One of them would sing, '*If I can't go forward,*' and point his finger, '*I'm not going back.*'" Another staple of the services was the song "This Little Light of Mine." "Revel Domino would sing that all the time. That was his song."

Women in front of the Mount Zion Baptist Church, 1950s, dressed for baptism in False River. Photo by David Biben. Courtesy of Deidra Biben-Glynn.

Jimmy Brooks, a deacon in the church and the father of James Brooks, sang a song that included the entire alphabet. "He would get up and say, '*Oh,* A *is Almighty, everybody knows* / B *is the Bible to comfort the dying souls* / C *is the Christ child sent from God* / D *is a doctor . . .* / E *is an eagle with watchful eyes . . .* F *is faith,* G *is God Almighty,* H *is the holiness . . .*" and so on through the alphabet.

Ussy Horton, Ernest Gaines's parrain, sang a song that went, "*Well I know the Mighty Rider got the reins in his hands,*" and the congregation would answer, "*All right.*" "He'd sing '*I went down in the valley,*' and he'd be preachin' and patting his feet like John Lee Hooker. Some people would dance. It would rock."

Biben said the deacons included Jimmy Brooks, Papa Joe Williams, John Ceaser, and Johnny Hall. "They would get the Communion ready and later they would call the collection," he said. "They would start the singing and you would get in line and walk up and put your nickel or dime on the table and then go back to your seat. They [deacons] would want more. Someone would start to sing something with a real rockin' rhythm to it."

As the deacons urged additional donations, the congregation sang songs such as "*You walk like your mama, shout for joy / You walk like your daddy, shout for joy.*" As each person walked up to put more money on the bare table, "They would try to walk like their mama or daddy. They'd get a little switch to 'em or a little twitch. My mama would walk with one hand still and one hand swingin'—her left hand would always swing. My sister Barbara would try to walk like her to the collection table."

Most services were daytime affairs, but sometimes a second one was held at night, from six o'clock until nine or even later. At night services, men Biben called "the sinner men" would not go inside because they were not dues-paying members. But they stood outside "with a bottle in their pocket" and listened to the preaching and singing, sometimes trying to catch a glimpse through windows painted blue to prevent anyone seeing in or out. Among the sinner men were Ernest "Snook" Spooner (son of the devout Reese Spooner), Brother Cage, George Williams, and even Reverend Bouie's son George. "They'd stand outside and listen, but they never joined. Eddie Phillips—I mean, a *real* sinner man. He used to fight so much. He was a little bitty man but a good fighter. He'd always be out there."[50]

Although churchgoing was important to many residents of Cherie Quarters, Gaines noted that neither his great-aunt Augusteen nor his grandmother

The Mount Zion Baptist Church in Cherie Quarters, built in 1937, also served as a school until about 1950. The last service was held there in 1992. The shed was built by Gaines's paternal grandfather, Izel Gaines. Photo by Ruth Laney.

attended—and neither did Miss Jane Pittman, if there was a baseball game to listen to. In his fiction, he treats preachers with more than a bit of skepticism. Jackson Bradley in *Catherine Carmier* and Munford Bazille in "Three Men" have little use for them, and the ministers in "The Sky Is Gray" and *A Gathering of Old Men* are portrayed as ignorant. (The minister in *A Lesson Before Dying* represents a stark departure from that view.)

## READING AND WRITING

During the week the church building was a school. Ernest Gaines attended during the four, five, or six months when the children of the quarter could be spared from digging potatoes or pulling corn. They crowded on to wooden benches and tried to learn, taught by a succession of female teachers who came across the Mississippi River from Baton Rouge and boarded during the week with Gaines's grandmother.

Former residents recalled especially one teacher, a Miss White, who later became Mrs. Green. James Brooks said Miss White had lent Ernest Gaines a book, possibly a book of plays. Malvina Becnel Pickett recalled a Miss Guerin who taught there. Others who may have taught at the school were Ada Paul and at least one man, Junius Hurst, who Ben Biben speculated was the model for Grant Wiggins in *A Lesson Before Dying.* Once or twice a year, the white public school superintendent would pay a visit.[51]

With no desks, the children sat on the pews, writing on tablets held in their laps, or they knelt on the floor and placed the tablets on the seats of the pews. Students did not always get their full allotment of six months of school; often they got only five. "We had to pick cotton until the first of October," Gaines said. Then, by the middle of April, we began to plant and harvest . . . potatoes. . . . Children . . . had to go into the fields."[52]

When the children were at school, they were respectful. "Discipline was no problem," said James Brooks. "All the teacher would have to say was, 'I'm coming to your house to tell your mother about your behavior.' All you had to do was point, and the kids would stop [misbehaving]."[53]

Ernest Gaines's generation was the first at Cherie Quarters to get much education. A generation earlier, children such as Freddie Kemp had to leave the plantation entirely to attend school on the highway. It is not clear how Freddie's father, Sam Kemp, acquired his ability to read and write, but it seems likely that there was little if any formal schooling available to him or his parents.

Freddie Kemp recalled "eight or nine" children walking two or three miles to attend school in a church on Highway 1 near North Bend Plantation, including his friend Brother and Brother's sister Odile Cage. "We'd go to school three months a year. We had to buy the little books we had. I loved school, but I had to work."[54]

Forrest Zeno got even less education, possibly because he and his sister Clara had been virtually abandoned by their father, Walter "Salute" Zeno, after their mother died. "I never went to school in my life. When you got twelve years old, you had to work or leave. School was one month for Blacks."[55]

Ben Biben said the people of Cherie Quarters benefited from the owners' laissez-faire attitude. "The people [on River Lake Plantation] were a little more lenient than the Lorios or the Majors farther up the river. They let you go to school if you wanted to." But Ada Mae Gaines noted, "At that time [the 1940s], schools were poorly [funded]. . . . It was a long time before education got better."[56]

Gaines's contemporaries differed in their memories of how many classes coexisted in the one-room schoolhouse. Some said grades one to five; others said grades one to eight. Possibly all were accurate to some degree, for the school may have added grades over the years. Memories also varied as to how long the school term was, with estimates ranging from four to six months, depending upon the demands of the seasonal work that took the children out of school.

Ernest Gaines said that as many as fifty children were in the schoolroom at one time, roughly divided into classes. Ada Mae Robillard Gaines remembered the school's encompassing grades one through five. "The highest it went was to fifth. The rest [of the children] was quiet while the first grade had their lessons. They were paying attention to what they had to do." James Brooks remembered, "We had one teacher for first through sixth grades, later we had two teachers, then later we had three teachers, from primer to eighth grade. We had two or three classes a day. The more advanced students would help the younger ones." Ben Biben said, "We had one teacher. Primer was first through seventh grade. She would teach one class so long, then go up to the older ones." "We were all huddled up in there together," said Bill Robillard.[57]

Brooks recalled the physical exertion required to get an education in Cherie Quarters. The children walked from their houses in the quarter, a distance of up to a half mile each way (longer if you lived back in the field, as the Robillard family did), along a dirt road that was later covered in gravel. A heater in the schoolhouse had to be stoked with wood. "We'd go into the woods and cut wood and bring it to the school. We would take turns chopping it for the wood heater—not stove, but heater." The windows had no screens. "If it was warm enough to open the windows, we had to be content with the mosquitoes."[58]

At recess, the children were sent outside to play on the grounds of the building, behind which stood a small graveyard with three or four tombs. "That yard seemed like the biggest place in the world to me," Ernest Gaines said. James Brooks thought "the church ground was too small for physical education. We mostly just stood around and talked." But Ben Biben remembered playing baseball and shooting marbles on the school grounds.[59]

Statistics about the education of Black children in Pointe Coupée Parish in the 1930s and 1940s are sketchy but telling, and they generally support the anecdotal information of the former residents of Cherie Quarters. The 1944–45 annual report of the Louisiana Department of Education compares average costs per pupil, Black and white. The average cost for attendance of a white elementary school child was $86.29, compared to $19.12 for Black elementary school children. The average cost for a white child to attend high school was $215.29; the average cost for a Black child is not given, because there were no Black public high schools in the parish.

During the 1938–39 school year (likely the first year Ernest Gaines attended school), there were 2,418 Black and 1,753 white elementary school children in the parish. There were fifty Black teachers and ninety white teachers—forty-eight students per Black teacher and nineteen per white teacher. Black teachers made an average annual salary of $321.66 and white teachers averaged $985.48.

By the school year 1941–42, there were 2,309 Black elementary students and 1,594 white students. The teacher numbers held steady at fifty-two and ninety-one, but the Black teachers were making only $339.98 per year while the white ones averaged $1,058.53. The report also notes that thirty-four supervisors were employed in thirty-six parishes in 1941–42, supervising "1,849 or 72.4 per cent of the 2,554 teachers employed in small rural schools, and 1,110 or 71.6 per cent of the 1,549 schools of this type in the state." By the year 1946–47, there were 2,164 Black elementary students, and 1,521 white ones. The Black teachers numbered fifty-two, while white ones numbered seventy-nine. Black teachers were now making $737.04 a year, while whites averaged $1,872.01.

Under the heading "Negro Education" in the 1940–41 annual report, it is noted that "the average length of term per teacher for the state . . . was 7.1 months." The report explains,

> The rural Negro is still handicapped in his efforts to justify a longer school term. . . . His low economic standards require the employment of children at home and on the farm, and too frequently they are too poorly fed and clothed for a long walk to school and a long day in a cold schoolroom. Absence from school is often due to ill health caused from lack of proper food and nutrition, and the prevalence of physical defects and the contagious and inherited diseases common to people uneducated and living under low economic conditions. . . . Teachers of small, isolated rural schools are rather limited in training and experience, educational facilities are limited, terms are usually short, grade and age levels within teaching groups vary widely, and many rural pupils are educationally retarded.[60]

In 1951, three years after Ernest Gaines had left Cherie Quarters, the first high school for Black students in Pointe Coupée Parish opened. A 1988 news story reported that parish school board minutes from April 7, 1948, read, "The secretary advised the board that a committee of Negroes asked him to inform the School Board that they have succeeded in raising about $4,300 to build a high school for Negro children. The superintendent advised this committee that the school board could give the framing for said project if they could use the above fund." The article also quoted from the July 1948 minutes: "The secretary presented a floor plan for the proposed Negro school . . . to be built on the Rosenwald School site in New Roads, La., with funds raised by the patrons. . . . NOTE: The aluminum to be supplied by the School Board and also some of the framing for the roof." (Ernest Gaines left for California the following month, August 1948.) Ultimately, the article reports, "The four-room high school for blacks—the first in the parish—opened for the 1951 school year, built, for the most part, with money raised privately by blacks. Although some public funds—in essence, funds from taxes collected from blacks and whites—were used to build the black high school, most of the final cost of $6,667.50, was raised by the black community."[61]

## HEALTH AND MEDICINE

Although doctors and hospitals entered the picture, folk remedies were still used up to the 1950s. Ben Biben recalled several treatments. "If you had whooping cough, they'd run a horse in the field until it was out of breath, then [let it] breathe in your face. [They made] goat [milk] tea for measles. Mare milk, I forget what we drank that for. Leaves of elephant ears, they'd put on your head for fever. They used cornmeal for measles; they'd rub it on you to bust the bumps. For colds, they used Vick [*sic*] salve with a piece of flannel or wool. Asphidity [asafoetida] for worms. Camphor and whiskey, we'd drink that for worms. We'd pass 'em. They'd have a BM [bowel movement that was] nothing but worms." Ben's sister Barbara Overstreet said her grandmother Emma Kemp "would rub our chests with tallow from cow fat" when they had chest colds.[62]

Seeing a doctor was a rare occurrence. Freddie Kemp broke his leg when he was ten years old. "My mother had told me not to leave the house," but he had sneaked out and gotten into a wrestling match with other boys. "A boy named Shingo Bell grabbed me, and I fell back. They put me on a horse to bring me home, and the bone was sticking out of my leg." Freddie's father, Sam Kemp, "went and got the doctor in Glynn [a few miles distant], and he came in a buggy." Since Sam and Emma Kemp lived "back in the field" behind Cherie Quarters, the doctor had to leave his buggy in the quarter and ride a horse through the mud to get to their house. "The doctor put a board on [my leg] and wrapped it with cloth. I had to lay down for twenty-six days. When I got up, I was scared to walk." With the help of crutches given to him by his friend Brother Cage, Freddie was able to get about. "Once I went to the bathroom [the privy behind his house], and when I came out, the crutches were gone. Brother stole the crutches [to force me to walk]. It took me about a year to get straight."[63]

Freddie's nephew Ben Biben remembered a time around 1939 when his mother, Albertha Kemp, fell ill. "Bert got sick when we was living back in the field below the sugarhouse. I was a little child. I must have been four and a half or five. Freddie walked to the Big House and had them call the doctor. Dr. [Eugene] Durel came the next morning on horseback and give her some kind of pill. She got well."[64]

Going to the hospital was also rare. Biben recounted a frightening experience when he too broke his leg, at age fifteen, in the summer of 1949.

> Lionel [Gaines] and I were way back in the field, about a mile and a half below the cemetery. I was on my little mare horse, Dot. She turned a curve, and the ground was wet, and her foot slipped. I fell and she fell and her backbone hit my leg. I couldn't get up. My foot was turned backwards. I heard the pop; it sound like a rifle [shot]. Lionel got on the horse and went and got George [Williams], and he came and picked me up in his truck. He and somebody picked me up and put me in the front seat. I had my hand on my leg and wouldn't turn it loose.

Biben's grandmother Emma Kemp wouldn't let George take him to the hospital in New Roads until she had given him a bath, broken leg and all. "Mama scrubbed me down. She said, 'You stink. You ain't going to no hospital like that!'"

Biben was met at the New Roads Hospital by his mother and her boyfriend, Alec Labry. "Bert was at the hospital when I got there. Alec carried me in his arms." X-rays revealed that Biben had broken both the tibia and the fibula.

"They wanted to amputate the leg," he said. "A nun had my arm and her [rosary] beads and was praying over me. Dr. Morless [spelling unconfirmed] wanted to cut it off because the bone was crushed. I didn't know what 'amputate' meant. The nun explained it to me. She told me 'just below the knee.' I said, 'No, Mother.' (We called the nuns Mother.) I told the doctor, 'No, don't cut my leg!' I cried and cried. I told Bert, 'Take me to Charity Hospital [in New Orleans].'"

His mother was reluctant, because it was common knowledge that "When they take you from the quarters, if you go to New Orleans, you gon' die." But Biben prevailed. "Joe Dupas, the undertaker, got a hearse or a ambulance and they took me down there," he said. "Bert rode with me. At Charity, they just straightened it and put a cast on it. They didn't cut me. They did X-rays. I was in a cast for nine months or seven months. The cast went from below the toes almost to my privates." While he was laid up, Biben missed a year of school. "I had crutches and I used Miss Teen's wheelchair. I used the wheelchair for five or six months."

While breaking a leg was painful and frightening, some of Biben's friends had truly terrible experiences that proved fatal. Around 1941, he said, "Marshall Domino . . . was picking pecans and stuck his hand in a pecan nest and a rattlesnake bit him." Several years later, around 1948, Marshall's younger brother Walter Domino also met a premature death. "He stuck a stick in his foot and died of blood poisoning. He was about fifteen."[65]

Childbirth, attended by a midwife, could be a harrowing experience. Midwife Emma Gurley asked Ben Biben to assist when his mother gave birth to a boy, who died shortly afterward. Mrs. Gurley, who lived back by the sugarhouse, had been summoned when Albertha Bibbens went into labor, but the situation quickly got out of hand. "I think it was a breech birth," said Biben, who was a teenager at the time. "I was in the next room and the baby was coming. Miss Emma was so big and fat she couldn't help Bert. She called me to help. There was blood all over the place and I was barefoot. I had blood between my toes. It's a bad memory. Bert's head just drooped over, and I had to pick her up off the floor. She was out of it, not unconscious, but she couldn't help herself. I got her off the floor and put her on the bed and got out of there. I couldn't take it."[66] Despite such primitive and dangerous conditions, women did not remain long in bed after giving birth but instead got back to work at the earliest opportunity. Ernest Gaines said that his mother was back in the field within a week after his birth in January 1933.[67]

Biben noted that one result of midwife deliveries was that birth certificates often were filled out incorrectly. After delivering a baby, the midwife would go into New Roads and file the certificate at the courthouse. In his own case, said Biben, nearly all the information was wrong, including his name and place of birth. When he applied for Social Security, he had to hire an attorney to help him straighten out the errors.[68]

## BURYING THE DEAD

When death came to Cherie Quarters, the coffin, the funeral, and the burial were community affairs. Ben Biben said several men, including Ernest Gaines's grandfather Izel Gaines, were carpenters who made the pine casket. The body was laid in it, and men carried the open casket to the church. The wake lasted all night. "People would sing, somebody would get up and sing, then they'd get quiet for a while. The preacher would stay till about one o'clock. At daybreak, everybody would go home and take a nap and then come back for the funeral. There was always somebody with the body until daylight, then it was left alone until the funeral."[69]

Freddie Kemp went to a funeral when he was six. "Old Man Charlie Hawkins' wife died. The preacher said she was going to heaven and he did like this . . . [imitating the preacher making an upwardly spiraling motion with his hand.] But I could see that she was in the ground. I was too young to understand."[70]

Ben Biben, Freddie's nephew, said that in the 1940s they began covering the graves with concrete vaults. Before that, they simply dug a grave and buried the casket in it, often without a marker. Tending the graves meant putting fresh flowers on them and occasionally using a hoe to mound up the dirt on top of the grave. "People cleaned it and built it up. They'd build up on top of the grave like a little dome [of dirt]." After concrete vaults began to be placed atop the graves, people whitewashed them annually, usually on Toussaint or All Saints' Day, November 1.

Biben said the funerals were emotional affairs. "They used to holler and cry and stomp and want to fall in the grave. . . . We would wake all night, stay up all night with the body and sing and pray. Then a big funeral for two or three hours, then the graveyard. They would preach. No air-conditioning, no fan. It was something. It was somewhat wonderful, if you really think about it."[71]

# 8

# THE BIG HOUSE

## THE RULING FAMILIES OF RIVER LAKE PLANTATION

> I don't think the people who own the plantation understand their place is our history too.
>
> —ERNEST J. GAINES

In 1699, Pierre le Moyne, Sieur d'Iberville, led a group of French explorers up the Mississippi River, past the future sites of New Orleans and Baton Rouge, to a place where a portage of only a few hundred feet saved him from having to make an hours-long voyage around a huge loop in the Mississippi. He named the location Pointe Coupée, or cutoff point; it later became one of the oldest parishes in Louisiana. In time, the Mississippi changed course, leaving a large oxbow lake that would be named Fausse Rivière, or False River.

The land in Pointe Coupée was rich, and landowners imported slaves to plow and cultivate vast fields of indigo and cotton—and later sugar cane. Dominated by wealthy French planters, Pointe Coupée society had rigid rules of caste, class, and race. The white plantation owners, who were French-speaking Creoles, hired lower-class whites as overseers. Some were Acadians, whose ancestors had come to Louisiana after being expelled from French Canada during the French and Indian War, but others' families had come directly from France or from Belgium. At the bottom of the pyramid were the workers of color—at first slaves, later sharecroppers, and still later tenant farmers.

Along the banks of the river that was really a lake, landowners built some of the state's most historic houses, including the house fittingly called River Lake. The plantation house is on the west bank of False River in the town of Oscar, about ten miles south of New Roads, the parish seat. The house is a two-story structure with a wraparound gallery, built of brick on the lower story and timber frame and bousillage (mud and moss) above.[1]

Over the past 220-plus years, only three families have owned River Lake Plantation: the Decuir, Denis, and Major families. The house is situated on the site of a Spanish land grant issued to Isaac Gaillard around 1790 and sold to wealthy landowner Antoine Decuir in the early 1790s. Around 1795, Decuir built a raised Creole cottage on the site. The upper story was three rooms wide and one room deep, while the lower story consisted of numerous smaller rooms. The upper gallery on each side was open, while the area underneath contained small storage rooms with wooden bars on the windows.[2]

Born in 1765 in what would later become Pointe Coupée Parish, Decuir was the grandson of one of the original settlers of the parish, Albert deCuire, who had come to Louisiana from Belgium in 1720. When he built the house, Antoine was in a committed relationship with Sophie Deslondes, a free woman of color. Their first child, Terence, was born in 1790. By 1799, when their second son, Leandre, was born, Sophie Deslondes was living at the house Antoine Decuir had built at River Lake. Their twenty-seven-year relationship would produce eight children.[3]

The Pointe Coupée Parish censuses of 1807, 1808, and 1820 show Sophie still living at River Lake Plantation, now with her children. In an 1821 document dictated during an illness, Antoine acknowledged Sophie's eight children (then aged twenty-four years to five years) as his own and stated his intention that they be his heirs. Antoine's brother Joseph Decuir, who built nearby Austerlitz Plantation, also fathered children by a free woman of color, Françoise Beaulieu. Upon his death, Joseph Decuir left part of his estate to his mixed-blood children by Françoise.

But Antoine did not follow through; he did not leave River Lake to his and Sophie's children. Following his serious illness and acknowledgment of his mixed-blood children, Antoine Decuir apparently ended his relationship with Sophie Deslondes, in 1822. In 1823, at the age of fifty-eight, he married a thirty-two-year-old white woman, Louise Suzanne Beauvais, a widow with three young children. Louise was the sister of Antoine's close friend Arnaud Beauvais, who would later serve as acting governor of Louisiana.[4]

The house that Antoine built for Sophie, and from which he would later evict her and her children, however gently, so he could install his wife, is now on the National Register of Historic Places. It was nominated for listing in 1983 and was accepted onto the register later that year. The nomination notes that the house is "well detailed" and lauds it as "one of the parish's most important examples of the Creole architectural influence." It continues, "Riverlake is one of a select group of about six major Creole raised plantation houses which are Pointe Coupée Parish's largest and oldest historic structures. Taken as a whole, they are by far the most important and best known of the parish's sizable patrimony." Among its outstanding features are strap hinges, rosehead nails, board and batten shutters, French doors, and interior doors consisting of three large raised panels. The nomination form further notes, "All beams and boards are beaded on the exposed surfaces." The form states that the house "appears to have undergone three major periods of construction," around 1820, 1840–45, and 1890. Historic buildings expert Sid Gray, who examined the house three years after it was nominated to the register, believes the house was built earlier than the nomination's 1820 date of construction, placing it instead at around 1795.[5]

Gray does believe that a major renovation took place around 1820, during which time the double-pitch roof was replaced with a hip roof, portions of the encircling gallery were enclosed and transformed into rooms, and twin pigeonniers were built on the grounds of the house. These dates comply with documentary evidence that Antoine Decuir acquired the property in the 1790s and married in 1823. It seems reasonable to suppose that Antoine's 1823 marriage to Louise Beauvais motivated him to renovate the house.

Around 1845, Decuir replaced the entire roof structure, added dormer windows, and built front and rear upper galleries with enclosed sides and cabinets. He replaced the original columns on the upper gallery with Greek Revival posts with molded capitals. (It is not known whether the brick columns on the lower gallery date from this period or from the earlier period.) He replaced all of the original mantels with Greek Revival mantels. After the renovation, "Riverlake resembled many late Creole plantation houses which, because they were built well after the colonial period, had Greek Revival details."[6]

The National Register form also notes changes made during the 1890s renovation, presumably by P. C. Major, who purchased the house in 1892. Major added a two-story rear kitchen wing to the 1840–45 rear gallery and moved a set of exterior gallery stairs from the original house to the gallery of the new wing. He replaced the Greek Revival columns on the upper front gallery with Eastlake columns and balustrades. Most of the wall and ceiling surfaces on the upper part of the house were sheathed in three-inch beaded boards. Some side windows were replaced. Two upstairs mantels were replaced with "moderately elaborate" Eastlake mantels, while two 1840–45 mantels remain.

In the early twentieth century, additional changes were made: the French doors that opened onto the upper gallery were replaced with "innocuous bungalow style glass doors." The brick walls and columns of the lower portion of the house were covered in cement, as were the lower gallery floors.

River Lake's Creole features include its hall-less cabinet plan; its heavy hip "umbrella" roof, complete with the customary pair of small dormers; its basic two-story, open-galleried form; its bousillage and brick construction; its French door frames and board and batten shutters; and about half of its French doors. "In addition, [its] identity as a Creole raised plantation house is significantly enhanced by the presence of the pigeonniers."

The form notes that "the house also retains a number of historic features which, while not specifically Creole, further establish its identity as an early house in Louisiana," including the wooden bars in some of the downstairs windows, the crown moldings and baseboards, the exposed beaded beams, and the 1840 mantels.

Of the six major Creole raised plantation houses remaining in Pointe Coupée Parish, River Lake is conspicuous because of its size; it is a full five rooms wide as opposed to the usual three or four. "In addition, it is one of only two examples which retain the original pigeonniers. The latter is particularly important, because at one time almost every plantation in the parish had at least one pigeonnier." However, the form also notes the "deteriorated condition" of the twin pigeonniers built around 1820:

> The pigeonnier to the east of the house is a square, two-story structure with brick construction on the lower story and frame construction on the upper. It is surmounted by a hip roof with a finial. It is somewhat deteriorated but is more or less intact. The pigeonnier to the west was identical when originally constructed, but has since lost its upper story. . . . Despite the . . . deterioration, the pigeonniers are still of outstanding architectural importance because they are such rare survivors. . . . In any case, the east pigeonnier retains all of its essential features. Moreover, it would be possible to reconstruct the upper part of the west pigeonnier using the east pigeonnier as a model.

Unfortunately, as we saw in chapter 6, the owners did not heed these suggestions and instead allowed the west pigeonnier to crumble. By the time Sid Gray happened along in 1986, it was beyond repair.

Around the time of his marriage to Louise Beauvais, Antoine Decuir remodeled the house, according to Gray, who found evidence in the attic of a new roof dating to that period. Gray speculated that the twin pigeonniers, with brick bottoms and cypress tops, were constructed at the same time.[7]

Antoine and Louise's only child, Antoinette, was born in 1826, possibly in France, where her parents spent a good deal of their time. When Antoine Decuir died, in 1829, three-year-old Antoinette inherited River Lake—both the house and the two thousand–acre plantation. She also inherited other property owned by Antoine—and 233 slaves. Antoine's holdings were valued in excess of $200,000, making him one of the wealthiest planters in Louisiana. To his eight children by Sophie Deslondes, he left property in the Raccourci area of Pointe Coupée Parish. When Sophie died, in 1836, at sixty-two, she left an estate worth $30,000, and twenty-seven slaves. She was buried in the cemetery at St. Francis Church near New Roads; it is thought that Antoine was also buried there.[8]

A portrait of Antoine's widow, Louise Beauvais Decuir, was painted around 1840, when she was fifty years old. Attributed to the well-known French Louisiana painter Jacques Amans, the portrait was eventually inherited by Louise's granddaughter and namesake Louise Denis, who married Charles Parlange of neighboring Parlange Plantation. The painting now hangs at Parlange, just up the highway from River Lake.

## A DECUIR REUNION: JULY 21, 1996

Father Léon Lybaert raised his hand and sprinkled holy water on the small cast iron bell hanging in the rear of St. Francis Church. "Ah, oui!" he exclaimed at a whispered prompt from someone in the crowd, and gave the bell two swift tugs. The sound of the bell rang out in the century-old white wooden structure hard by the Mississippi River levee outside New Roads. With the pealing of the bell, the seventy-three-year-old Belgian priest ended his celebratory Mass commemorating the 275th anniversary of the arrival of the Decuir family in Louisiana. The priest, on his first visit to the United States, spoke perhaps twenty-five words of English, but he had no trouble making himself understood by the people in the church, though few of them spoke the French of their ancestors.

"Tout le monde sonne la cloche," he said, urging everyone present to ring the bell. One by one—young and old, Black and white, Pointe Coupée natives and people who had never been to the parish before—they stepped up, grabbed the rope, and rang the bell. Among the crowd of more than two hundred jamming the little country church were people from California, Colorado, Michigan, Ohio, Texas, Washington state, and Washington, DC. For all of them, the bell was a symbol of their heritage as descendants of Albert deCuire, the progenitor of the Decuir family of Louisiana, which has now spread all over the United States and numbers in the tens of thousands. Parish historian Brian Costello said the bell has been in Pointe Coupée for as long as anyone can remember. Thought to be a ship's bell, it is marked "1719" and "MLM." "We don't know what 'MLM' means, but 1719 is the year Albert deCuire signed a contract to come to the Louisiana colony," said Costello. "We assume the bell came over on the ship with the colonists, but we really don't know."[9]

Albert deCuire was forty-six when he came to Louisiana in response to the new French colony's advertisements for colonists to establish settlements in Louisiana. He agreed to work for six years to pay his passage to the new world. "Basically, he was an indentured servant," said Costello, a descendant of Decuir's grandson Jean Paul Decuir.

Albert deCuire sailed from France on the ship *Le Loire* in August 1720 and arrived in Louisiana on November 9, 1720. He and his wife, Marie Catherine Domer, were accompanied by four of their seven children: Anne Catherine, Jean François, Marie Marguerite Josephe, and Etienne. They were one of fifteen original families recruited to form a permanent civilian settlement at la Poste Militaire de la Pointe Coupée. They faced a hot and humid climate and various diseases as they struggled to establish themselves in their new homeland. The 1731 census of the colony shows that both Albert and his son Etienne owned slaves. Marie Catherine died within ten years of their arrival, but Albert lived until 1750. His signature on many documents, both religious and civil, attests to his position of leadership in the community. When the St. Francis church was dedicated in 1738, Albert's name was listed as sponsor for the blessing of the bell.

Albert's son Jean François, who was about sixteen when he came to Louisiana with his family, married Genevieve Mayeux in 1743 and had twelve children with her. Census records show that by 1766 Jean François had eighty head of cattle, four horses, five pigs, fourteen firearms, and thirty slaves—making him the third-largest slave owner in the area.

Jean François's sons Joseph and Antoine left a lasting mark on the parish. Joseph Decuir was born on October 30, 1752, the sixth child of his parents. Louisiana was then under Spanish rule, and he served in the Spanish militia for twenty-six years. After buying a tract of land on False River from two Indian chiefs in 1783, Joseph built the house that would later be known as Austerlitz. Joseph never married, but living with him in the house was Françoise Beaulieu, a free woman of color. In his will, Joseph acknowledged that he had fathered four children by Françoise. After Françoise's death, in 1812, Joseph fathered a daughter by another free woman of color, Claire Louise Quevain. Joseph died in February 1822, at the age of seventy-two, leaving an estate valued at nearly $1 million. Half of the estate was left to his natural children and the other half to his nieces and nephews.

Antoine Decuir was born on October 24, 1765, and like his older brother Joseph would have an extended relationship with a free woman of color, Sophie Deslondes. Also like his brother, Antoine became immensely wealthy and built an imposing house, which would come to be known as River Lake. As noted earlier, in his will dated January 6, 1821, Antoine recognized his eight children by Sophie Deslondes, and left them property near Raccourci Island, but then ultimately left River Lake to his daughter Antoinette, who was only three when Antoine died. Antoine's widow, Louise Beauvais, managed the property until Antoinette's marriage in 1850.[10]

## THE DENIS FAMILY

In 1850, Antoinette Decuir married attorney Arthur Denis and moved to New Orleans, where the Denis family included several prominent attorneys. Antoinette and Arthur used River Lake as a summerhouse, but eventually Arthur Denis gave up his law practice in New Orleans to help his wife manage her Pointe Coupée property. The couple had seven children, five of whom lived to adulthood.

Historical records suggest that Antoinette and Arthur made renovations in the original design of the house, a view supported by Sid Gray's physical examination of the building. By the time of her marriage, Antoinette had seen the addition of workers' quarters at River Lake, built by slaves in the 1840s—

twenty-five or thirty cypress cabins on brick piers. River Lake was apparently a cotton plantation until around 1855, when the sugarhouse was built, at which time it became a sugar plantation.

Arthur and Antoinette's children spent a great deal of time at River Lake. Two of them, through marriage, would form alliances with other prominent families of the lower False River area. According to historian William Reeves, Arthur Denis bought Parlange Plantation at a sheriff's sale, around 1878. When his daughter Louise Denis married Charles Parlange in 1881, Arthur sold the house and part of the land to his son-in-law, thus restoring ownership of the plantation to the Parlange family, where it remains to this day.[11]

In 1882, Arthur and Antoinette's son Charles married Anna Lancaster Hewes of New Orleans and Pointe Coupée. The Hewes family also owned a False River plantation, Pleasant View, located about a mile north of River Lake. Pleasant View, built around 1820, had been in the Hewes family since 1867, when Anna's father, Thomas Hewes, purchased it and moved his family to Pointe Coupée.

An 1881 newspaper article from the local *Pointe Coupée Banner*[12] offers insight into the opulent lifestyle of the Denis and Hewes families and their social prominence in the community. In the florid yet skimpily detailed style of the day, the author describes a ball the Denis family held in the sugarhouse at River Lake on the last day of September, perhaps as a prelude to grinding season, which ran from October through December. At the time of the ball, Antoinette Decuir and Arthur Denis had been married for thirty years, and their five children were young adults. Their son Charles Denis, twenty-eight, and his future bride, Anna Hewes, twenty-three, are mentioned in the article as members of the Merry Makers Social Club, which staged the ball. Antoinette and Arthur's daughter Louise Denis and her future husband, Charles Parlange, also attended. Guests came from up and down False River and even from St. Francisville, across the Mississippi River, arriving by horse-drawn carriage and perhaps even by steamboat.

> On Friday evening Sept. 30, we started for River Lake sugar house (Mr. Denis) to attend the ball given by the "Merry Makers" Social Club. On reaching the entrance, we were received by the members of the reception committee, ushered into the spacious hall, conducted to the dressing room in the rear. After adjusting our toilet [we] returned to the hall to make a note of the surroundings.

The spacious hall being 50 x 80 feet was splendidly illuminated. On the front end on a raised platform the musicians had already taken their seats; to the right of the music stand were the refreshment tables. The rear end of the hall being occupied by the dressing rooms. The committee on reception were busily engaged in receiving the invited guests, conducting them to the respective dressing rooms, giving the desired introductions &c, all of which they performed with becoming cordiality and courtesy so as to make their guests feel happy and at ease. The arrangement committee were engaged in decorating the refreshment tables, which were shortly laden with eatables of the daintiest kinds. They spoke very kindly of Arthur Denis, Esq., who relieved them of much work by sending his carpenters to put seats around the hall, and for the fixing of the dressing rooms. They felt flattered for having secured the popular Prof. Page and band of Baton Rouge for the occasion. . . .

At a signal from the floor managers, the band struck up a lively tune and in a few seconds all glided forth in the mazes of the waltz, followed in succession by the latest and most popular dances which the varied fashions of metropolitan life have brought forth, some of which a "matron's look might reprove," but were rendered by those who participated with such ease and gracefulness as to lose their objectionable features.

The ball during the evening presented a scene of gayety and splendor without any display of rusticity. The gracefulness of deportment, ease and elegance of manners to be found among the cultivated of the metropolis was everywhere visible. The array of feminine brilliancy whose elaborate and tastefully arranged toilets would be suitable in paying homage to his majesty, Rex [the king of New Orleans's Mardi Gras]; the whole enlivened by soul-stirring airs from the band made us feel lost in admiration, or like others who were carried off in imagination to some fairy land where one never grows old.

Not being a proficient in the terpsichorean art we refused the kind solicitations of floor managers and others of going on the floor, we could not however evade the persuasiveness of our esteemed young friend, Mr. E. F. Phillips, whose diplomacy procured us a partner in the highly accomplished Miss Belle Lobdell, of West Baton Rouge. We frankly confessed to the young lady our inability to "tip the fantastic toe." She with true politeness offered to give the necessary instructions, and safely led us through the mazy figures of the dancers, for which as well as for bearing with our imperfections we feel under many obligations. . . .

> We have never known of a more enjoyable and recherché reunion in this parish, even in the palmiest days of ante-bellum. . . .
>
> With such a company assembled the occasion could not be otherwise than one of the most enjoyable ever witnessed in this parish. Many of the company remained until the appearance of "rosy morn"; but we, warned by the fact that we had duties to attend to, left with regret at 2 o'clock, carrying with us a high appreciation of the members of the "Merry Makers Social Club[.]" . . . We hope that our sanctum may be soon gladdened by another invitation to attend such another pleasant reunion.[13]

It is a fetching picture, the beautiful young people at their ball, kindly instructing the newspaper writer in the mysteries of the newfangled dances and partying until dawn. But if you listen closely, if you read between the lines intently, you can catch the faint suggestion of an unheard and unseen presence at the ball—the people who built the "dressing rooms" and the musicians' platform and doubtless prepared the "dainty eatables" upon the tables. Did some of them lurk in the shadows to catch a glimpse of the "feminine brilliancy" and hear a few strains of the lively music? Or did they sleep in their cypress cabins just a few yards away, knowing that, come the dawn, it would be their job to clear away the remnants of merriment and prepare the sugarhouse for grinding season?

As with any plantation history, the lives of the Black workers can often be divined only by studying the lives of the white owners. Was the life of the Black residents a distorted mirror image of the white life, or was it the vast, unseen part of the iceberg, the sweat and hard work and suffering that made such merry evenings possible? In the history of River Lake, some of these questions can be answered by studying a photograph album discovered in 1993, after more than a century in obscurity.

### THE LAURA ALBUM

Research into the white and Black families that have lived at River Lake for more than two centuries has been greatly enriched by the discovery of an album containing photographs of the plantation from around 1889. Taken "on the cusp," just three years before ownership of River Lake passed from the Denis family to the Major family, they are the earliest known photographs of the plantation.

"Negro quarter at Riverlake," showing two rows of cabins behind Jean Baptiste, circa 1890. This photo depicts the earliest known view of Cherie Quarters, built by slaves in the 1840s. Photo by Anna Hewes Denis. Courtesy of Sand and Norman Marmillion.

The photograph album is owned by Sand and Norman Marmillion of New Orleans, who in 1992 began restoration of Laura Plantation in Vacherie in St. James Parish. The plantation tours focus on the lives of the women and the slaves who lived there. The Marmillions' extensive research into Laura's history led them to contact a woman in Paris, who sent them the photo album in 1993.[14]

The "Laura album" contains forty-six photographs, including photos of landscapes, buildings, and people both white and Black. Pasted onto the inside back cover is a sheet of paper with handwritten captions that correspond to the numbered photographs, which were taken in 1889 and 1890. The captions were obviously written by someone close to the people in the photos, who are identified by first names only: Arthur, Rosie, Cecil, Jean Baptiste, Martino, Millien. Even the animals are named: Kate, the donkey; Lohengrin, the cow; Bang, the dog. The houses are labeled "Riverlake," "Parlange," and "Home." Landscapes depict pastoral scenes of False River, levees, bayous, and huge oak trees, with captions such as "Bayou at Riverlake" and "Point near home."[15]

The lovingly compiled album includes posed and unposed shots of white children fishing, riding horses, celebrating a birthday, and proudly displaying a doll collection. Black workers wash clothes in huge kettles, cook in outdoor pots, or pose somberly with smiling white children. Some photographs are actually portraits of individual workers.

Sand and Norman Marmillion had no idea how an album of photographs taken in Pointe Coupée had ended up four parishes downriver—and ultimately in France. They assumed a connection between the Duparc and Locoul families, who owned Laura Plantation, and the Denis and Hewes families, who owned River Lake. The mysterious album raised intriguing questions about River Lake Plantation and Cherie Quarters.

Twenty-three years after the Marmillions received the album, in 2016, Sand Marmillion introduced me to Katy Morlas Shannon, a researcher doing work on Laura Plantation. Shannon quickly solved the mystery of the connection between the two plantations, River Lake and Laura. In an email, Shannon wrote, "In addition to being a plantation owner, Arthur Denis was an attorney in New Orleans. . . . Emile Locoul owned the downriver side of the plantation, called Laura, and his sister Aimee and her husband, Jean Flavien 'Ivan' de Lobel, owned the upriver side, called Duparc." According to Shannon, Arthur Denis's law firm handled the legal affairs of the families that owned Laura Plantation. Additionally, she said, "The de Lobel, Decuir, and Denis families were socially connected. The de Lobels were clients as well as friends of the Denis family."[16]

The first page in the Laura album contains the only photo with no caption: a head-and-shoulders portrait of a lovely young woman. The Marmillions suspected that she compiled the album and wrote the captions. But who was she? Who were Arthur, Rosie, and Cecil? Where were the houses? And who had taken the photographs?

The photos were clearly taken at two different plantations, some labeled "Riverlake" and others "Home." Pointe Coupée Parish historian Brian Costello confirmed that one of the houses was River Lake and the other Pleasant View—the place referred to in the album as "home." Thus, the person writing the captions was probably Anna Lancaster Hewes, whose family owned Pleasant View. Indeed, Pleasant View had been home to Anna until her marriage to Charles Denis, whose family owned River Lake. Anna and Charles were married on October 10, 1882, a little more than a year after they worked together to put on the ball at the River Lake sugarhouse. In 1886, Anna gave birth to their only child, Arthur Hewes Denis.[17]

Comparing genealogies of the Hewes and Denis families with the album's handwritten captions, Costello identified "Rosie" as Anna's younger sister, Rosina Dunbar Hewes, who was born in 1876, and "Cecil" as Anna's younger brother Cecil Grayson Hewes, born in 1879. "Arthur," of course, was Anna and Charles Denis's son. Costello guessed that the uncaptioned head-and-shoulders shot of a young woman was of Anna Hewes Denis herself, and he agreed with Norman Marmillion that she had probably compiled the album and written the captions. He also believed that she was the woman depicted in the photo captioned "Overseer's house at Riverlake." But who was the man in the photo with her? Her husband? Her father? And who took the photographs?

The life of the white people in the album seems pastoral and idyllic—children riding donkeys, fishing in the river, playing with dolls, gathered around a birthday cake, posing beside their Christmas presents. The contrast with the Black people is striking, in details of activities, clothing, and facial expressions. The Black people are working, or obliging the white mistress by posing for a photo. Their clothing is dark and worn, and they are often barefoot, while the white people are dressed in clean, festive-looking clothes. The white people tend to have cheerful expressions, while the Black people look somber.

As I looked at the photos, I wondered if there was genuine affection between the races—Rosie smiling proudly as she stands beside Millien; young Arthur leaning on the knee of a seated,

"Martino and Arthur," probably Martino Colar and photographer Anna Hewes Denis's young son, Arthur Denis, circa 1890. Photo by Anna Hewes Denis. Courtesy of Sand and Norman Marmillion.

white-bearded Martino. I thought of a comment Ernest Gaines had made to an interviewer: "There were certain things you had to do, a certain way of walking, a certain way of keeping your eyes, a certain direction you had to look, that black children were taught in the South at that time."[18] If that was true in Gaines's youth, during the 1930s and 1940s, how much truer was it fifty years earlier? And yet I was grateful to have these portraits of the workers, which give us at least a glimpse into their lives.

"Millien and Rosie," probably Millien, the wife of Martino Colar, and Rosina Dunbar Hewes, Anna Hewes Denis's younger sister. Photo by Anna Hewes Denis, circa 1890. Courtesy of Sand and Norman Marmillion.

The identities of the African American men and women depicted in the album were harder to pin down than those of the white subjects. One photo, captioned "Jean Baptiste of Riverlake," depicts an elderly man dressed in a white shirt and dark pants, evidently a worker on the plantation owned by the Hewes/Denis family.

Another photo, captioned "Negro quarter at Riverlake," also depicts Jean Baptiste. The photographs were evidently taken within minutes of each other; the man is dressed in the same clothing, and the objects he carries (a water jug and a basket) are identical. The double row of cabins in the background is

From an album of photographs made circa 1890 by Anna Hewes Denis. This photo is captioned "Jean Baptiste of Riverlake" and apparently shows Severin Jean Baptiste. Photo by Anna Hewes Denis. Courtesy of Sand and Norman Marmillion.

clearly the site now identified as Cherie Quarters. This is the earliest known view of the slave cabins built in the 1840s.

Jean Baptiste is probably Severin Jean Baptiste of Lakeland in Pointe Coupée Parish. Millien could be Severin's wife, Millien Cooper. But she might also be the wife of the bearded man identified as Martino. A Martino Colar, age seventy-nine, is listed in the 1900 census of Ward 8 with his wife, Millien, age seventy-four. Martino and Millien, listed as a farmer and a cook, respectively, lived next to Thomas Hewes, his wife, Anna, and their grown children at Pleasant View Plantation. They are likely the Martino and Millien depicted in the album of photographs taken by Anna Hewes circa 1890. (As noted in chapter 5, Martino Colar might be a relative of Ernest Gaines's stepfather, Norbert Colar.)

In one photo, two women are identified only as "our cook and her great grand child." They, along with Jean Baptiste, Millien, Martino, and other (nameless) African Americans depicted in the album are no doubt ancestors of Ernest Gaines and others who grew up in the quarter.

In early 1996, three years after the photo album was discovered, some of the Laura photos were published in the Baton Rouge newspaper to publicize a slide lecture that Sid Gray and I were giving on Cherie Quarters. That publication led to yet another striking discovery. A man named Charles Denis Fournier called me to say that he had two additional albums of photographs taken at River Lake and the other plantations. And he knew the identity of the photographer. She was indeed Anna Hewes Denis—his great-grandmother.[19]

## THE DENIS ALBUMS

On a cold spring Sunday in 1996, Charles Denis Fournier welcomed me to his house in the lakefront area of New Orleans. The two-story brick house was undistinguished, its small rooms crammed with old furniture that seemed to cry out for high ceilings and French windows overlooking oak allées. Fournier, a pleasant-looking but no-nonsense man of about fifty, ushered me into the den, where piles of family albums and loose photographs rested on a coffee table.[20]

Fournier again confirmed the identity of the woman who had taken the photographs in the Laura album. She was, as we had suspected, Anna Lancaster Hewes, the wife of Charles Denis—Fournier's great-grandparents. Anna and Charles Denis had traveled a lot, he said, picking up a scrapbook of photographs taken on one of their trips to California. He had letters written to Anna by her brothers in California. The Hewes family, he said, had divided its time between the two states.

Before opening the albums of photos taken by Anna, Fournier sifted through some loose photos, cartes de visite mounted on cardboard, scattered on the coffee table.[21] One of them was the same photograph of a lovely young woman that appears in the front of the Laura album—Anna. Another photo, a studio portrait of Rosina Dunbar Hewes, Anna's younger sister Rosie, revealed a sweet-faced woman of about twenty. Rosina never married. "She had a beau who went down on the *Titanic*," said Fournier, who spoke of his great-great-aunt, "Tante," with visible affection. "She was like a grandmother to me and my brother." Tante Rosina often talked about life at River Lake and Pleasant View. "She liked to ride her horse to the post office to pick up the mail."

Moving to the albums, he selected one with a lock, its pages gilt-edged and embossed. Inside were carefully posed photographs of serious-looking, well-dressed men, women, and children. The cardboard frames were stamped with the names of photography studios in New Orleans and even Paris. There were no captions in the album, but many photos had inked notations of names and dates on the back.

Finally, Fournier picked up two albums that looked homemade. Each held about fifty photographs. Some were duplicates of photos in the Laura album; others, although clearly taken at the same time, were different views. A photo captioned "Riverlake quarters Old John 1890" was the same as the photo of an African American man in the Laura album, identified there as "Jean Baptiste of Riverlake."

Fournier flipped through photos of men guarding a levee with guns, River Lake Plantation with snow on the ground, a Black woman washing clothes in the river, white people swimming in the river, men blowing up a levee, a docked steamboat. Anna's handwritten captions included, "Bathhouse in 1890," "False River from Discharge Bridge 1890," "Riverlake trees as seen from Island shore 1890," and "Levee camp at Morganza 1892." The photo captioned "Riverlake Nov. 1890" showed a family group—a man, a woman, and three children—in front of the Big House. The staircase was different from the central staircase the house now has. Instead of a single set of stairs facing the river, it had a pair of staircases that were approached from the side, similar to those at Laura Plantation in Vacherie.

The dates reveal that Anna's idyllic days at River Lake were soon to end. In January 1892, a few years after most of the photographs were taken, Anna's mother-in-law, Antoinette Denis, sold River Lake Plantation to P. C. Major for $46,000.[22]

Fournier said that some of the albums had been stored in a secretary at his mother's house. He found others in the attic after she died, in 1992. He pulled out a photo of Anna's husband, Charles Denis, as an old man holding his granddaughter, taken around 1913. Fournier said Anna had died of cancer in 1930, at seventy-two. Her husband outlived her by fifteen years, dying in 1945, at ninety-two.

He studied the handwritten captions from the Laura album, including "Arthur and Bang," which corresponded to a photograph of a blond boy of about six with his mastiff dog. Fournier had been fond of Arthur, his grandfather, who died in 1975, at eighty-nine. He remembered Arthur talking about his childhood dogs, Bang and Shot.

Fournier's namesake, Charles Denis, the man who staged a "metropolitan" ball in the heart of sugar cane country in 1881, liked the city, whereas his son Arthur liked the country and always regretted that his parents had not kept River Lake. (Arthur was six years old when his grandmother Antoinette sold the plantation.) "I always heard my grandfather talk of River Lake and Pleasant View," said Fournier, describing Arthur as "salt of the earth," a man who loved to hunt and fish, whereas his father, Charles Denis, was "more into society." Anna traveled a lot, often going alone to California to visit her brothers. She and Charles went to Europe "ten or fifteen" times. In the 1920s, they took a steamer to Alaska.

Fournier said Arthur, the solemn-faced and clearly much-loved boy in the photos, had told him stories about his childhood companion, a young Black boy about his age, the son of a worker on the place. Arthur talked often about the Civil War, although he was born in 1886, long after it had ended. "To him, they were 'damn Yankees.'"

### THE PERSAC PAINTING

The photographs and the stories were captivating, but Fournier had something even better in his cache of family treasures. On a glassed-in porch hung a painting, a large framed watercolor. Measuring about two and a half by four feet, it depicted a sugarhouse during grinding season. The two-story brick building with three chimneys was rendered in minute detail, as were the overseer astride a white horse and scores of workers cutting cane and hauling it in wagons pulled by horses, mules, or oxen.

The subject matter was fascinating, but the lower part of the painting jolted me. Inscribed along the bottom of the picture in gilt were the words "River Lake Plantation, False River, Parish of Pointe Coupee, La." The picture documented not just any plantation and not just any workers but River Lake and the workers of Cherie Quarters—some of them no doubt ancestors of Ernest Gaines. My heart gave a leap as I read the signature, "A. Persac, N.O.," in the lower right corner of the watercolor. I realized that I was face to face with a previously unknown work by an important artist, Marie Adrien Persac. This was not only a major addition to my research into Cherie Quarters but also a major event in the Louisiana art world—or it would be, when its existence was known. I knew that museum curators and collectors would be agog to hear of a "new" work by Persac, a French-born painter who flourished in Louisiana in the 1850s and 1860s.

Fournier said the picture had hung in the dining room of his childhood home in Metairie. He was no art historian, but he knew the painting was highly desirable. He had inherited it when his mother died, four years earlier. "My brother and I flipped a coin to see who would pick first, and I won the toss," he said. "This was the first thing I picked."

A few months later, Fournier took the painting to a conservator who treated it with chemicals to mitigate tannin marks created by the paper's contact with the wooden braces of the frame. Soon the word was out. "I took it for restoration work and people went crazy. We had eight or ten experts come and look at it." He contacted an auction house in New Orleans, which appraised the watercolor at $100,000—much higher than the $30,000 at which it had been appraised four years earlier.[23]

Soon the small, insular world of Louisiana art collectors and dealers was abuzz with the discovery of a previously unknown work by an important artist. People who collect Louisiana paintings jockeyed for position—just in case the Persac might be for sale. (Fournier was later offered up to $200,000 for the piece but said it wasn't for sale.) Art historian H. Parrott Bacot, then director of the LSU Museum of Art, was eager to buy the painting—or to have it donated. Bacot, who acquired several Persac paintings for the museum, had believed all the artist's works were present and accounted for. He was excited to realize that a previously unknown work had turned up after being hidden away for nearly 150 years. "The discovery of the painting is significant because it has been unknown ever since Persac painted it. Most of his works have been cataloged, which makes the discovery quite remarkable."[24]

"Persacs are extremely rare," Bacot said. "No more than sixty are known, and that's a relatively small body of work for an artist." Fournier's sugarhouse painting, he said, "is not in mint condition. It has sun damage, burn damage, and silverfish damage." Those quibbles aside, the Persac was an exciting find. "It is of great historical significance," said Bacot, who found it an atypical work because Persac more commonly painted plantation Big Houses, not outbuildings. "It is the only large painting I've seen that depicts a sugarhouse in operation and fields being worked. It illustrates the old way of harvesting sugar cane. It is part of the plantation system that has disappeared."

Bacot firmly believed that Persac is an important American artist; in fact, he and his wife spent twenty years working on a book about the man. Persac (1823–1873) was born in Saumur, in northwestern France, and came to this country in the early 1840s, reportedly to hunt buffalo. He married a Baton Rouge girl, Odile Daigre, in 1850 and spent most of his career in New Orleans as an architect, artist, and civil engineer. He made many architectural drawings, but his most famous work is an enormous and ambitious undertaking, the Norman's Chart of plantations on the lower Mississippi River, a copy of which can be found in most Louisiana libraries and museums as well as many private homes. The *New Orleans Daily Crescent* noted that the map "is a perfect picture of the windings of the Father of Waters from this city to Natchez, with every plantation on its banks drawn and colored, with the name of the owner and whatever name he may have given his plantation." (Evidently River Lake had not yet acquired that name; on the Persac map it is listed as "A. Denis," for its owner Arthur [or Antoinette] Denis.) The newspaper further noted that Persac had "descended the river in a skiff, landing at every mile, and drawing every plantation line and taking down every name and landmark on both banks of the river."[25]

In addition to his famous map, Persac did a series of gouaches of Louisiana plantations. The five years leading up to the Civil War were his most active period, during which he painted plantations and their activities in obsessive detail. Bacot said that Persac was the only painter in the Deep South doing this kind of detailed work in the mid-nineteenth century, which was more commonly found in Philadelphia or New York. Persac didn't just paint houses; he also made pictures of public buildings, a steamboat interior, and plantation complexes. Some of the latter have images of a sugarhouse in the background. Although most of Persac's plantation "portraits" depicted Big Houses, he also did illustrations of outbuildings, including a cotton gin. But the River Lake painting is the only known Persac depicting a sugar mill in detailed operation.

According to Bacot, the labeling at the bottom of the piece is unique among Persac's work. The painting was the only Persac he knew of that depicted a building in Pointe Coupée Parish. The N.O. in the signature stands for New Orleans, where Persac lived and worked for many years. Bacot said that this was one of the few Persacs to identify the artist with his place of residence. Most are signed only "A. Persac," with the date.

Unfortunately, the River Lake painting lacks a date, but Bacot guessed that the piece was done between 1855 and 1861. It depicts the "old plantation system. The workers depicted are probably slaves, and that is more rare." He initially guessed that the picture was done about the same time Persac traveled the state working on his map depicting the plantations between Natchez and New Orleans (published in 1858) and doing "portraits" of plantations along the Mississippi River and other streams, such as Bayou Teche.

Later, however, Bacot uncovered evidence to suggest that the painting might date to after the Civil War. "I think it was probably done in the 1870s, just before Persac died [in 1873]. All the prewar stuff—the dated pieces—was done on good rag paper." But another newly discovered Persac, depicting Star Plantation in St. Charles Parish, turned up at auction in 2003. Signed and dated 1872, the painting was on what Bacot called "acid-laden paper" made of pulp, not rag. "This is the same kind of paper the River Lake painting was done on, so I think it falls into the same category."[26]

It seems reasonable to suppose that Persac painted the sugarhouse shortly after it was built, so the date of construction might offer another clue. No building contract or other documentation has been found, but Bacot said the Italianate style of the building "was known before the Civil War but more popular after the war, in the 1870s and 1880s. The sugarhouse could have been built right before the war, but it equally well could have been built later."

Arthur and Antoinette Denis, who married in 1850, probably commissioned the painting, perhaps to commemorate the building of the sugarhouse. "They were probably extremely proud of it. It was a monumental investment." Did they also commission a painting of the Big House? Bacot suspected there might be a companion picture of River Lake's main house. "There must be, if he [painted] the sugarhouse." But so far none has surfaced. Bacot offered another intriguing speculation: that Persac, who was an architect and engineer, may have built the sugarhouse himself. Another missing piece of the puzzle.

Whether it was painted during slavery or Reconstruction, the painting offers interesting clues to life at River Lake Plantation and Cherie Quarters. "A sugarhouse in operation is unique. It's the only large painting I know of that depicts a sugarhouse operating and fields being worked with this kind of detail. That is highly rare and unusual." More than fifty people are working, both Black and white, men and women. Two cane wagons are pulled by four horses, each wagon with a driver astride the "southwest" horse. The wagons are painted blue—curiously, the same shade of blue that had been found on the door of one of the two surviving slave cabins at River Lake. The wagon path through the center of the cane field has ditches on either side, filled with water and crossed by plank bridges. The painting features fifty-six or fifty-seven people. "Some of the women are taking food to the men working. Seeing the workers at work makes this more interesting. It's not a typical Persac. He probably took more time and effort to do it."

Unfortunately, the sugarhouse itself is no longer standing to be compared with the painting. It was still there in 1881, when Anna Hewes and Charles Denis entertained at the Merry Makers Ball. It was still there in 1892, when Antoinette Decuir Denis sold River Lake Plantation to P. C. Major. It was still there in 1927, when several families who lived in the field behind Cherie Quarters sought in its upper story refuge from the "high water" of the great flood of the Mississippi. It was still there when young Ernest Gaines ran and played in it in the 1940s. It was still there, although already falling apart, when Charles Fournier visited as a child in the early 1950s. "It was in a ruinous state," he said. "The chimneys and the walls were still standing but in ruins. It was abandoned and in bad shape, but there were still buildings there."[27] But sometime in the mid- to late 1950s, when the sugarhouse was no longer in use and River Lake cane was being shipped elsewhere for grinding, P. C. Major's son John had it torn down, brick by brick.

### THE MAJOR FAMILY

The Major family has been in Pointe Coupée for two hundred years, but the origins of the name are not clear, for the original family name was Bosseron. Etienne Bosseron and Angelique Proteau, the originators of the family, were living in Montreal, Canada, when their son Etienne Jr. was born. Etienne Jr. married Catherine Cheval, and their son Etienne III was the first member of the Bosseron family to have the appendage "dit Major." (*Dit,* literally "said" in French, means "alias" or "known as.") How Etienne Bosseron III came to be called Major is another mystery.

Etienne served with Bernardo de Galvez during the American Revolution. In 1776, at Pointe Coupée, Etienne married Madeleine Guerin, with whom he had eleven children. One of those children, Pervis Major, was born in Pointe Coupée in 1801. He and his second wife, Marie Bergeron, had four children, of whom the oldest was a son, Jean Baptiste, born in 1834. Jean Baptiste Major married Adele David, and they had eleven children, the second of whom was a son they named Pervis Cherie, after his grandfather. P. C. Major married Marie Malvina Rougon in 1879. The Rougon family was also prominent in the parish. (The family would later purchase Austerlitz Plantation, which had been built by Joseph Decuir, the brother of Antoine Decuir, who built River Lake.) P. C. Major and Malvina Rougon had seven children. In 1892, P. C. Major bought River Lake Plantation from Antoinette Decuir Denis for $46,000.[28]

Malvina Rougon Major died in 1925. By the time Cherie Major died, in 1934, his name had become associated with the workers' quarter at River Lake, known as Cherie Quarters. In December 1933, a few months before his death, P. C. Major and his seven children filed a document donating to the school board of Pointe Coupée Parish an arpent (about an acre) of land on River Lake, to be used as the site of a school. Research to date has not determined

"Accounts Due" page from the succession of River Lake owner P. C. Major, who died in 1934. Major owed $160 to Gaines's great-aunt Augusteen Jefferson. Photo by Ruth Laney.

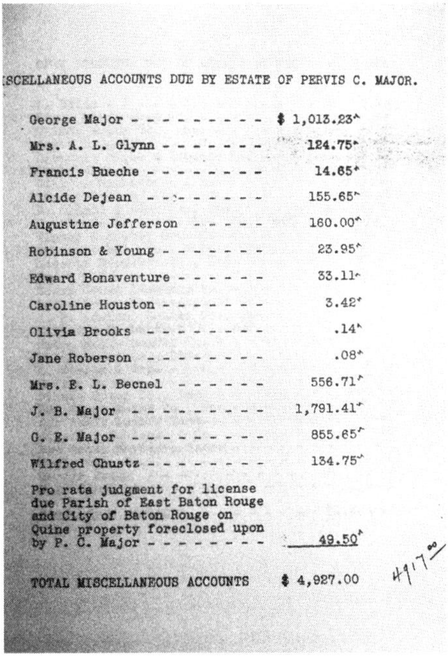

SCELLANEOUS ACCOUNTS DUE BY ESTATE OF PERVIS C. MAJOR.

| | |
|---|---|
| George Major - - - - - - - - - | $ 1,013.23 |
| Mrs. A. L. Glynn - - - - - - - | 124.75 |
| Francis Bueche - - - - - - - - | 14.65 |
| Alcide Dejean - - - - - - - - | 155.65 |
| Augustine Jefferson - - - - - | 160.00 |
| Robinson & Young - - - - - - - | 23.95 |
| Edward Bonaventure - - - - - - | 33.11 |
| Caroline Houston - - - - - - - | 3.42 |
| Olivia Brooks - - - - - - - - | .14 |
| Jane Roberson - - - - - - - - | .08 |
| Mrs. E. L. Becnel - - - - - - | 556.71 |
| J. B. Major - - - - - - - - - | 1,791.41 |
| G. E. Major - - - - - - - - - | 855.65 |
| Wilfred Chustz - - - - - - - - | 134.75 |
| Pro rata judgment for license due Parish of East Baton Rouge and City of Baton Rouge on Quine property foreclosed upon by P. C. Major - - - - - - - - | 49.50 |
| TOTAL MISCELLANEOUS ACCOUNTS | $ 4,927.00 |

if the school was designated for the Black children of Cherie Quarters, but by 1937 construction was under way on a building that would also be used as a church by the people of the quarter.

The succession papers of P. C. Major, who owned River Lake Plantation from 1892 until his death in 1934, show that his estate was valued at half a million dollars when the country was in the depths of the Great Depression. One page of the succession, devoted to "Accounts Due," includes the name "Augustine Jefferson"—the great-aunt who raised Ernest Gaines—to whom P. C. Major owed $160.[29]

After P. C. Major's death, the day-to-day operation of the plantation was taken over by his sons Joseph, John, and George. Joe Major (1891–1941) married Lillie Wilson, with whom he had two daughters, Eloise and Lillie May. According to Cherie Quarters oral history, he also fathered a daughter of mixed blood who was a favored playmate of his white children.[30] His daughter Eloise married Alcide "Bub" Bouanchaud, who followed in his father's footsteps by serving as sheriff of the parish for four years. When he died, in 1956, Eloise was appointed to serve out his term; she was later elected to a second term. Their only child, Madeleine Bouanchaud Caillet, would inherit the Big House, one half of the Cherie Quarters cabins, and the church/schoolhouse.

George Major, who married Eola Bertonnier around 1940, had one daughter, Melodie, who was about a year old when George Major died of heart disease at the age of forty-six.[31] As we have learned, he also fathered a son by one of the Black women of Cherie Quarters, Albertha Kemp. George had a paternalistic attitude toward the people of the quarter, sometimes paying their doctor bills or bailing them out of jail. He owned the houses on the right side of Major Lane, while his brother Joe owned those on the left. In the 1940s, George Major installed running water on his side of the quarter, so that every house had an outside pipe with a faucet, served by a well on the grounds of the Big House. Water was never installed for the houses on the left side of the lane. Right up until the last tenant left, in 1993, the people who lived on that side of the lane had to cross the road with buckets to get water from a neighbor's pipe.

John Major, who was unmarried, lived in the Big House with his brother George and George's wife and daughter. According to Ben Biben, George's wife had been expected to marry John: "George Major stole Miss LaLa [Eola Bertonnier] from John Major. John went out with a few women, but he never came to the quarters looking for women [as George did]. We thought John Major would marry LaLa after George died. He split the land right away. John took the quarters, and the land up to a point, and Miss LaLa took the rest."[32]

After George died, his widow and child left and John lived alone in the Big House. He ran the plantation store where the people of the quarter were paid after harvest and where they bought groceries, using scrip money color-coded for people who couldn't read. John Major destroyed many of the buildings in the quarter, including the sugarhouse, the plantation store, and several slave cabins. "The sugarhouse was beautifully built," said Malvina Pickett, John Major's niece. "Uncle John tore it down. . . . He was afraid someone would get hurt and sue him." He tore down the store, she said, shortly before his death in 1974. An interesting feature of the plantation store was its huge ledger books, in which the purchases of plantation workers were recorded.[33]

Ben Biben recalled a story about John Major. "George Hebert told me that John Major told him to 'get off the damn place.' John Major wanted him to work on the plantation, but George had a little job at the Standard Oil plant in Baton Rouge and lived with his daddy, Joe Hebert, in the quarters. John Major met him at the head of the quarters and told him he couldn't live here. He left with fear."[34]

Biben told a similar story about Ernest Gaines's great-uncle Horace McVay, using his nickname. "Mom-sun had a pasture where he kept his mule. He heard that John Major wanted to farm that land, so he got Willie Aaron and George Hebert to help him tear the fence down. John Major started cussing and made him move."

Another story Biben told suggests that John Major was the model for Frank Laurent in "Bloodline" and Jack Marshall in *A Gathering of Old Men,* two Gaines characters notable for sitting on the gallery and drinking. "John Major drank and stayed drunk all the time. He done his work, he was smart, but he'd just drink all the time. Every night he'd go down to the little bar Will Chustz used to run [near River Lake]. He'd get drunk and drive home going ten miles an hour. We used to trot along with him."[35] Biben later added details even more reminiscent of Gaines's characters: "John Major, at noon he'd drink and go to sleep. Then wake up at two and open the store. Then [after closing the store, he'd] get in his car and go to a bar for whites with a side bar for Blacks. He'd get almost drunk and drive home around ten miles an hour, get in people's way."[36]

Madeleine Caillet told me, "My bachelor uncle [actually great-uncle] John Major was an alcoholic. My mother would take care of him. Toward the end, he accused her of stealing. He would misplace things."[37]

Madeleine Bouanchaud Caillet, granddaughter of Joe Major and great-granddaughter of P. C. Major, now owns River Lake. Her son Craig and his wife, Colleen, raised their family in the Big House and continue to live there. They and their children are the fifth and sixth generations of the Major family to inhabit it, making River Lake one of very few Louisiana plantations to remain in the same family for more than a century.

# 9

# TIME IS THE ENEMY

## THE FRIENDS OF CHERIE QUARTERS

> Preservation historically has had little to do with common people, especially those who are black. . . . Just as African American history has been relegated to a sidebar in the history books, the historic preservation movement has rarely devoted critical attention to African American resources. . . . Many were quietly obliterated as plantation homes were interpreted without reference to the slave economy that supported them.
>
> —PATRICIA WILSON, "Historic Preservation and the African American Community: A Measure of Commitment to Cultural Diversity"

> They were in the heart of the quarters now[.] . . . Most of the houses on the left had been torn down and had been replaced by patches of corn and sugar cane. The houses that still remained looked so worn and dilapidated that Jackson knew it would be only a matter of time before they would be torn down also.
>
> —ERNEST J. GAINES, *Catherine Carmier*

Over many years of studying the life and work of Ernest Gaines, I gradually recognized the crucial role of Cherie Quarters. Ironically, just as work on the television documentary took me to the quarter and brought its importance into focus, its long slow demise suddenly speeded up. Soon after completing work on the documentary, in late 1992, I learned that historic buildings expert Sid Gray was directing the removal of four slave cabins from River Lake Plantation to Magnolia Mound Plantation in Baton Rouge. As we saw in chapter 6, Gray had discovered the cabins when he was hired by owner Madeleine Caillet to restore a pigeonnier on the property.

Gray learned that the ownership of River Lake was complicated by how the land had been divided after the deaths of P. C. Major and his heirs. Mrs. Caillet owned the tract of land upon which the Big House sat; she also owned the left side of Major Lane, upon which two cabins were located. Her first cousins Pervis Cherie Major II and Marjorie Major Broome owned four cabins on the right side of the lane. When Gray discovered that P. C. Major II planned to bulldoze the cabins and plant sugar cane on the site, Gray persuaded him to donate the cabins to the Baton Rouge Recreation and Parks Commission, which owns Magnolia Mound.

While moving the cabins to Baton Rouge in the spring of 1993, Gray had a change of heart. Although hauling them away was preferable to seeing them destroyed, he realized that the cabins decreased in historic value when they were moved off site. Mrs. Caillet, the owner of the last two cabins on the left side of the road, had also planned to donate them to BREC. Gray telephoned me in April 1993 to say, "I think those last two cabins should be left where they are."[1]

While making the documentary, we had videotaped footage at Cherie Quarters. Shug Edwards lived in one of the cabins. Red gladiolas bloomed in her front yard, and Shug attended services in the church every other Sunday. I first saw the other cabin, last lived in by Reese Spooner, on the cold February day in 1982 when photographer Philip Gould and I accompanied Ernest Gaines to his home place to shoot photos for a magazine story. Gaines introduced us to Spooner, who talked about the fourteen hogs he owned and was followed about by a small, white, three-legged dog.

Having met people who lived in them made the cabins more than an abstract group of Slave Cabins That Should Be Preserved. They were houses people had lived in and had made into homes. So when Sid called to say the last two cabins should be preserved on site, I immediately agreed. I was new to the idea of historic preservation, but I already regretted the removal of the cabins to Magnolia Mound—both because of their historic value and because of their Ernest Gaines connection. The actual cabin Gaines lived in had been torn down years earlier, but I agreed with Sid that we could still learn much from the final two structures, which were exactly like it. We realized that these rare surviving cabins, and their connection to an esteemed American author, made Cherie Quarters a unique site in Louisiana—and, indeed, in the country. The buildings, we felt, should be preserved in their cultural and historic context.

Together, Sid and I formed the idea of preserving, on site, the last two cabins, the 1937 church, and the small shed next to the church. We envisioned a heritage site that would pay tribute to Gaines's unique contribution to American letters and also honor the hundreds of people who had lived at Cherie Quarters and now lay in its cemetery, most in unmarked graves. As we talked, I grew excited about the possibilities. In the four hundred yards of empty space between the two cabins, I thought, we could erect a visitors center—a new structure that looked like the slave cabins on the outside. But inside would be a large open space in which we could create exhibits about the quarter and Ernest Gaines.

The one-hour documentary, *Ernest J. Gaines: Louisiana Stories,* had been edited from sixty hours of raw footage, much of it filmed in the quarter, including interviews with Gaines and other former residents. We had videotaped family photographs. I envisioned a center where visitors could view the finished documentary and parts of the actual footage. We could enlarge still photos and create panels from them; we could do the same with key passages from Gaines's work. With no knowledge of museums—except that I had visited a lot of them—I suddenly found myself planning to create one! Cherie Quarters, the place and the people, would be memorialized in photographs, documents, oral histories, but primarily by preserving the two cabins, the church, the shed, and even the graveyard—the last physical remnants of Cherie Quarters.

The most important "artifact" of the museum would be the two slave cabins that had been continuously occupied from the 1840s until the late twentieth century, preserved on their original site. "Such cabins are increasingly rare," we declared in the mission statement we wrote to explain why we were creating a nonprofit organization. "Their historic value cannot be overstated. Preservation and proper documentation of these buildings is extremely important, because they offer an opportunity to study the slave/worker quarter in a sugar-plantation complex, which offers insights into the workers' community and their lives. The site also offers insight into the work of Ernest Gaines, who has made lasting contributions to American literature with his novels and short stories."[2]

I was strongly influenced by Dorothy Spruill Redford's 1988 book *Somerset Homecoming* and by hearing a talk the author gave in Louisiana. Redford, a Black woman, researched her family history and discovered that her ancestors included the white owners of Somerset Place, a plantation in North Carolina. At first she resisted the idea of her white ancestry. "I could not bear the idea that I might have white blood inside me," she wrote. But she eventually accepted it and, inspired by watching Alex Haley's *Roots* on television, began researching both her African and Caucasian ancestors. From her home in another state, Redford organized a reunion of more than two thousand descendants at the plantation and eagerly anticipated seeing the slave quarters where her Black ancestors had lived. She finally arrived at the plantation in 1986, only to find that all traces of the quarters were gone. She found only a sign reading "Site of Slave Quarters."

A photograph in the book shows Redford and her daughter, Deborah, standing beside the sign. That photo haunted me. How awful it would be for descendants of Cherie Quarters' inhabitants to go looking for the quarter and find nothing but a sign—if that. Redford's story was a cautionary tale, a warning not to allow the past to be eradicated.

Redford later became manager of the Somerset Place State Historic Site. Her first order of business was to replace the long-gone buildings with replicas, including the overseer's house, the hospital, and slave quarters. "The cabins will come first, built slowly, one by one, of the same size and shape and on the same spots where they originally stood," she wrote. "People will walk into them . . . and they will know who lived here. . . . They will know the work these slaves did and how they did it—the sweat and the skill of these men and women."[3]

In 1994, Sid and I incorporated the Friends of Cherie Quarters, a nonprofit organization dedicated to preserving what was left of the workers' quarter at River Lake. We held the first meeting of our advisory board, which included Ernest Gaines as president and Madeleine Caillet as vice president. In January 1994, some months after the cabin was moved to Magnolia Mound, I spoke to Mrs. Caillet on the phone. She told me that her cousin had donated four cabins because "he got nervous about liability." She said she was being pressured to donate the last two cabins.

> Bill [Palmer of BREC] called last week and was really pushing me. He said, "I have a crew of sixty men with nothing to do." I've held him off as long as I could because of the people living there. Shug's son is living there [in Shug Edwards's house] without water. I have to tell him he has to move. Willie [Aaron] asked if he could move into that shed next to the church. I told him no because the national news would be down there. I told Bill I would donate my cabins. I would get a tax credit. He's really pushing me. I really need the tax break. I told Magnolia Mound they could have them, and I hate to go back on my word.

Returning to the idea of donating the cabins to the Friends of Cherie Quarters, Mrs. Caillet asked me, "Would I have to donate the land? Who handles the upkeep? There are a lot of legal and practical considerations." As these were questions her attorney could answer, I reminded her that we were willing to meet with him. But she deflected that idea and told me, "Get some answers for me. I don't have time to pursue any of it." She concluded by saying, "From my grandmother on down, we've made a lot of sacrifices to hold on to it and let the people live in peace. It has meaning to me."[4]

That same month, Sid and I visited New Roads businessman Humphrey T. "Bubber" Olinde, who owned a furniture store and was a lifelong resident of the town. He was active in civic affairs and was president of the Pointe Coupée Historical Society. Hoping he could help, we told him of our desire to preserve the two remaining cabins at River Lake and of our organization, the Friends of Cherie Quarters. A few months later, in mid-May, I was startled to see an article in the *Baton Rouge Advocate* about a fundraiser for the historical society—a jazz brunch to be held at River Lake Plantation the following Sunday. The charge to attend the brunch was sixty dollars. The article quoted Mr. Olinde saying that one of the society's projects "is restoring the last two cabins left at the Riverlake Plantation site."[5] Olinde also told the reporter that "writer Ernest Gaines was born on that plantation and wants to be buried there." He gave wrong information about Magnolia Mound Plantation in Baton Rouge, which planned to restore one of the four cabins removed a year earlier. "There were five cabins there, but Magnolia Mound grabbed three," Olinde said. "They tried to get the other two, but we blocked them."

That was inaccurate. There had been six cabins, not five. Madeleine Caillet's cousin P. C. Major II had donated four to Magnolia Mound, only one of which was to be reconstructed on the site. Mrs. Caillet had agreed not to donate her two cabins to Magnolia Mound so that the Friends of Cherie Quarters could preserve them on site. For Bubber Olinde to claim that he and his group had "blocked them" was hyperbolic, not to mention untrue. The newspaper story was illustrated with photos, including one of Shug Edwards's house with the caption, "The society wants to restore this cabin on the grounds of the former [*sic*] Riverlake Plantation, birthplace of writer Ernest Gaines."

Olinde had co-opted our one and only project and added it to his own lengthy list of ambitious preservation plans throughout the parish. I called

Sid and told him about the article. We were stunned at what appeared to be an act of outright opposition, not to mention backstabbing. Had Bubber Olinde stolen our project? It certainly looked that way. We were also puzzled about why Mrs. Caillet had not mentioned this turn of events. I wrote to her, noting, "Back in January, Sid and I approached Bubber Olinde and told him of our desire to preserve the cabins at River Lake. I see in the paper that he has added the cabins to a long list of projects of the Pointe Coupée Historical Society. We hope that he will make a portion of the money from the jazz brunch available to us, so the Friends of Cherie Quarters can begin working."[6]

I told Ben Biben about this act of hostility, as I perceived it, and learned that Olinde was notorious in the African American community for selling people furniture on the installment plan. If customers missed payments, Olinde would sue them. Ben said that Olinde had acquired several people's property that way. "Everybody's afraid of Bubber Olinde. Even back of town. 'He beat so-and-so out of his money. Sold him more furniture than he could pay for just to get his property.' They whisper."[7]

In mid-May 1994, the Friends of Cherie Quarters group visited River Lake. I wrote to thank Mrs. Caillet for allowing us to visit, adding:

> I have a vision of a day in the not-too-distant future when we hold our opening ceremony for the Cherie Quarters heritage site. It's a beautiful spring day, with glorious weather, a fresh breeze, birds singing. Everyone gathers for a service in the church, perhaps conducted by Bill Robillard or Forrest Zeno. Then everyone walks down to the graveyard for another service to remember the friends and relatives buried there. Then we stroll over to Reese's cabin, which has been restored and stabilized. Ernest Gaines makes a little speech and cuts the ribbon across the front door, and we all go inside. Inside the cabin are blow-up photographs of the people of the quarters, as well as pictures of P. C. Major and his family. Written panels on the walls tell the stories of Cherie Quarters—the place and the people. There's a VCR and monitor where people can see E. J., Ben Biben, Ada Mae and Lionel Gaines, and others reminisce about life in Cherie Quarters. There are also audiotapes with headsets, where people can listen to stories. We all drink coffee and wine and munch on tea cakes and "plarines" and remember life in Cherie as it used to be. This vision is very real to me. I believe it can and will happen.[8]

That same month, Mrs. Caillet told me, "The cabins really are getting kind of bad. I don't want them to fall down. They go down real fast." She mentioned, "The historical society here is having a fund-raiser to restore the Poydras school and do some other things. I think they got panicky because I had told Magnolia Mound they could have [the cabins]. I feel the same way and hate to see them leave the parish." She then veered to discussing the cemetery, saying, "Right now you can't get in the graveyard. The church used to take care of it as long as they had the church. Somebody tried to go back there to take pictures and couldn't get in there [because of overgrown weeds]."

She also mentioned her relatives the Thibauts, saying, "They have mixed feelings about E. J. My memories are exactly the same as his. Pigeon [Thibaut, her aunt] feels like he's putting down the family. Some Black folks think they know who he's talking about [in his fiction]. My mother said 'nigger' one time, and she was not allowed to use that word. We were all taught to be respectful."[9]

In July 1994, Sid and I met with Mrs. Caillet to show her the images from the Laura photo album. She remembered a fence around the Big House, and she remembered the overseer's house, which she thought was built before the Big House. "My grandmother tore it down when I was in college in the 1960s," she said. "You can still see where the brick pilings were." She recalled when each house in the quarter had a yard planted with flowers. She remembered the dirt road before it was graveled and later paved, and she remembered the dirt path leading to the store in 1940s and 1950s. She said the store was torn down while she was in college and that she had salvaged a thread holder from it.[10]

A few months later, in October 1994, in another telephone conversation with Mrs. Caillet, she told me, "I had a dream the other night. Black women make the best pralines. I dreamed all this [the remaining cabins] was restored. I had a gift shop with books and I was selling pralines." I realized that Mrs. Caillet shared our vision on some level, even if only subconsciously. But she also said, "I'm in the middle of a bank merger[11] and [planning her son's] wedding and I don't need this." She repeated the idea that Gaines's work had stirred ill feelings. "I wonder if Black people would feel like we're trying to make a buck off them. I know Black people here who consider Ernest Gaines a terrible person, like he's exposing them to danger." She added, "Sid believes rumors he's heard that I'm floating around in money."[12] As with many of our conversations, we touched on a number of topics but never seemed to move forward.

In early December of 1994, I spoke briefly to Mrs. Caillet, who told me, "I took a group of LSU students who are reading *A Gathering of Old Men* to see the quarters. They were all excited about it."

In 1995, with Mrs. Caillet's cooperation, we submitted the last two slave cabins for listing on the National Register of Historic Places, and they were accepted. We began to gather artifacts related to Gaines and other residents—we called these artifacts, rather optimistically, the Cherie Quarters Collection.

In some ways, our timing was fortuitous. There had recently been a national symposium in Washington, DC, where preservationists from all over the country had met to address the fact that African American landmarks were being lost at an alarming rate. The Friends' mission to preserve Cherie Quarters was partly inspired by our reading about that meeting. By saving the quarter, we hoped to help correct the imbalance in the historical record. We believed the wider community would share our interest in Cherie Quarters and understand our desire to save it from the ravages of time. We hoped that seeing the place would help visitors understand the people who had lived there.

We knew that some people would question the political wisdom of preserving "slave cabins," but we hoped that most would share our view that slavery is best dealt with in the light of day, not by destroying every remnant of it. As painful as it was, it is part of our history. We sought reactions and support from members of Louisiana's African American and preservation communities, such as Gerri Hobdy, the state historic preservation officer; Charles Siler of the Louisiana State Museum, a friend of Ernest Gaines; Kathe Hambrick of the River Road African American Museum; and Gregory Osborn of the African American Resource Collection at the New Orleans Public Library. All supported our efforts to save the cabins. Some made site visits and immediately grew excited about preserving the cabins in their historic context. Most important, we had the support of former residents of Cherie Quarters, such as Ben Biben, who agreed to serve as treasurer of the Friends group, and his sister Barbara Overstreet, who would later become its president.

Throughout 1995, the Friends of Cherie Quarters continued to have regular meetings at the Oxbow Restaurant that overlooked False River near River Lake Plantation. Ernest Gaines would drive in from his home in Lafayette to attend the meetings, often treating the entire group to dinner and drinks. At one meeting, he showed up with large color photos of himself with Reese Spooner, taken by Philip Gould on our visit a few years before Reese's death, and gave them to the board members. At another meeting, Gaines and his wife Dianne pledged funds for carpentry work on Reese's cabin, which needed immediate stabilization.[13]

That summer, Sid and I met with Ann Reilly Jones, a state official who was a fan of Gaines's work. She was sympathetic to our cause and later spoke to two state senators who agreed to sponsor a line item of $60,000 in that year's budget. The funding was approved, and we were excited about the possibility of making immediate repairs to the cabins. Unfortunately, as often happens, the item was later cut from the budget. Jones had warned us that the state could not release the money unless Mrs. Caillet agreed to donate the cabins to our nonprofit organization. As she told us succinctly, "It is illegal to spend state money on private property."[14]

Mrs. Caillet deferred making the donation and referred us to her attorney. We wrote to him, outlined our mission, and offered to go to his office to discuss it with him. But he told us that he couldn't meet with us without her permission. That permission was never granted. We realized that we were perceived by the community as outsiders. Meanwhile, our visits to Cherie Quarters revealed that the cabins were continuing to disintegrate.

Sid Gray said the cabins were in dire need of immediate stabilization and restoration. The frames were built of durable cypress, but other parts were secondary wood, such as gum, which had deteriorated more rapidly. Reese's cabin, with part of the tin roof gone, had been extensively damaged by rain, accumulated moisture, encroaching vegetation, and animals such as rats. The concrete piers had deteriorated and needed repair. Shug's cabin was in much better condition but also needed extensive repair to protect it from the elements and from human predators who removed cypress boards, shutters, and other materials.

The church was structurally sound but its roof, doors, and windows needed stabilizing. The shed had also had part of its roof torn away and needed extensive repairs. Former residents maintained the graveyard and kept the grass cut, but we agreed that steps must be taken to protect the cemetery and to ensure that those with ties to Cherie Quarters could continue to bury their dead there. The only brick tomb was in immediate need of repair, and we wanted to establish a history of the graveyard and a list of the people buried there. We discussed the construction of a memorial that would include all their names, perhaps engraved on a brick walkway. Our primary concern was to create a suitable memorial that would blend in with the rural surroundings.

The short-term plan was to physically preserve the two cabins, the church, the shed, and the graveyard at Cherie Quarters; to have the church listed on the National Register of Historic Places (although technically not old enough to qualify for the register, the church was eligible owing to its function as a school and its role in Black education); to provide maintenance for the site, including grass cutting and building repairs; and to continue collecting oral histories and otherwise documenting the history of the quarter.

In March 1996, Sid and I presented a slide lecture on Cherie Quarters at the Louisiana State Archives. We showed photos dating from the 1880s to the 1990s, showing many quarter residents, some living, many now dead. At the end of the lecture, which was attended by about one hundred people, I asked for everyone with ties to Cherie Quarters to stand. Half the audience rose to its feet.[15]

In June of that year, Barbara Overstreet had a family reunion for the Lovely, Kemp, and Horton families. Sid and I provided the "entertainment" by giving our slide lecture. Again, it met with great enthusiasm; some people walked right up to the screen, pointed out people they knew, and told stories about living in the quarter. Several brought pictures of ancestors, which we photographed for later inclusion in our slide collection.

In late 1996, the Friends agreed that furniture and other items stored in Reese's cabin should be removed. We wanted to preserve the furniture and other artifacts for later inclusion in the Cherie Quarters Collection and to remove the clothing and unsalvageable furniture that were soaking up water and preventing the cabin from drying out after a rain.

Ernest Gaines spent most of 1996 in France as writer in residence at the William Faulkner Foundation in Rennes. During this time, he and his wife, Dianne, formed a separate corporation, the Mount Zion River Lake Cemetery Association, focused on acquiring ownership of the Cherie Quarters graveyard. Gaines had often expressed the wish to eventually be buried there.

## THE POSSUM AND THE POCKETBOOK

In the Friends organization, one person stood out for his commitment to the preservation of Cherie Quarters. Ben Biben was born there in 1934, lived in the quarter until 1954, and had remained a close friend of Ernest Gaines. Of all the former residents of the quarter, Ben most seemed to "get it." He owned several small businesses in Baton Rouge, traveled regularly to toy shows to replenish stock for his Rak-Rite Toy, and always seemed to have too much to do, but he was a willing participant in the Friends' activities—going to meetings, donating money, pitching in to help clean up a cabin.

On a cold, sunny day in January 1997, Ben and I drove to Cherie Quarters, arriving just after noon. As Ben parked his large white truck in front of Reese's cabin, we noticed that the left front door, the right-side window, and the right rear door were all wide open, although we had always left them shut following our visits. We entered the cabin through the right rear door, because the front room on the left was missing some floorboards and it did not appear safe to walk in. This was the first time I had been inside the house in a year, and I was shocked at how badly it had deteriorated. Large pieces of the roof were missing from above the left front room, and bricks had begun to fall from the top of the chimney. One of the large beams running from front to back on the right side of the house had broken in two and hung at a precarious angle. Several floorboards were missing in the other rooms.

We were soon joined by Ben's sister Barbara Overstreet, who by that time was the president of the Friends group. Like Ben, Barbara had a busy schedule—she worked full time in Baton Rouge and was raising a granddaughter—but she was always willing to help with Friends projects. The three of us spent several hours in Reese's house, moving cautiously to avoid dislodging bricks or boards.

We decided that the first step in cleaning out the house should be removing large pieces of furniture—two armoires of dark wood and a white-painted wooden cabinet. This took us nearly three hours, because the drawers of the armoires were filled with detritus. Rats or possums had pulled cotton batting from a mattress or sofa and made nests in all the drawers. We removed cotton, twigs, plastic bags, food wrappers, corncobs, and other material from the drawers. Then we pulled out the drawers, most of which fell apart; they would have to be repaired. After clearing out all the debris, we started to lift one armoire and heard a scrabbling noise inside it. Suddenly we realized that it contained a live possum! We dropped the armoire and the possum dashed for daylight. Barbara theorized, half seriously, that the possum was the ghost of Reese, the last person to live in the house.

With towels, we cleaned spiderwebs, dirt dauber nests, and other material from the outside of the furniture. Lacking brooms, we cleaned the insides of the armoires with a broken crutch we found in the house and a feather duster Ben had in his truck. We loaded the three large pieces of furniture into the truck, along with the drawers, several nails, a hammer, a bullet, and a chain Ben found under the house—all potential artifacts for the Cherie Quarters Collection.

Our most notable find, and the one most urgently in need of immediate attention, was the large amount of clothing and carpeting inside the house. The floor had been covered in carpet, which was either glued to or simply laid on top of the wooden floor. The armoires had contained some clothing, which we stored in plastic garbage bags, and there was a plank nailed across the left front wall, from which hung wire coat hangers with clothing on them. Clothes were also strewn about the floor. These items retained moisture in the house, especially during rainy seasons, and we agreed to remove them as soon as possible to stem the tide of destruction. The house also contained numerous worthless furnishings—old mattresses, bedsprings, couches, and television sets—that should be cleared out.

We agreed to organize a cleanup day and estimated that it would take a crew of ten an entire day, perhaps longer, to remove all the items from the house. We agreed to designate boxes for potentially valuable items such as letters, bills, and dishes, which we would catalog and store for potential inclusion in the Cherie Quarters Collection. After removing all debris from the house, we agreed, we would try to make the most urgent repairs to slow the demolition by neglect. Lacking funds, we decided to ask local lumber companies to donate materials. Although we did not own the cabins, we felt that these emergency measures could not wait any longer.

After securing the doors and windows of Reese's house, we visited the graveyard. The homemade sign that Ben had nailed to a pecan tree, asking visitors to mark the names of their loved ones on the graves, was gone, but we noticed that somebody had written names on several graves. A handsome marble marker had been affixed to Reese Spooner's tomb, and two other marble markers commemorated other Spooner family members. (We later learned that the Thibaut family, relatives of Madeleine Caillet, had provided the markers.) Other tombs had been marked with paint, stating the names of those buried in them.

We discussed our hope that one day we could erect a sort of rural version of the Vietnam Veterans Memorial wall, listing every name we could find of those buried there. As Ben pointed out unmarked graves and recalled who was buried where, I realized we needed to do a walk-through and record his recollections. We could also do that with older people who attended burials there.

In February 1997, about a month after the January cleanup of Reese's house, several members of the Friends returned to complete the project. It had been raining heavily in recent days and the smell of mold was strong in the cabin. Wearing hard hats, gloves, and dust masks, we laboriously pulled up the carpet in the right front room. The task was onerous; the carpet literally fell apart in our hands as we yanked it up. Rather than pulling up sections of carpet, we were tugging on strings. We ripped it all out, plus as much of the foam underpad as we could remove, shoveling up the crumbling foam and tossing it into an existing trash pile outside the right rear door. It was filthy, backbreaking work. We stuffed old clothing into plastic bags and tossed them, too, except for a few pieces we saved for the collection. We salvaged medicine bottles, letters, and other items with Reese Spooner's name on them.

Two weeks later, on a Saturday afternoon, Ben, Willie Aaron, Sid, and I drove to Cherie Quarters to continue cleaning out Reese's cabin. Willie, in his seventies, had been one of the last residents of the quarter, sharing a house with Carrie Hebert until it was dismantled and moved to Magnolia Mound. He had been good friends with Reese and recalled a visit during which a rattlesnake, curled in a corner of Reese's "parlor," caught their attention when it rattled. "I'm not afraid of snakes," Willie said as we gasped. Reminiscing about Reese, Ben recalled, "Reese's mule didn't like light-skinned people. He would run away from them."

Reese had agreed to store furniture and other belongings of Ben's mother, Albertha Bibbens, who had left Cherie Quarters in the 1970s. "When Bert moved to Rougon, my sister Barbara took everything to Reese's," Ben said. "He probably expected them to come back for it."[16]

The left front room of the cabin contained several pieces of furniture that Ben recognized as his family's, including a stuffed chair that had belonged to his grandmother, Emma Lovely Kemp. There was also a small handmade wooden footstool, painted green, that had replaced the missing leg of an armoire.

Ben found several tools, including handmade hoes and axes, an ax handle, and a homemade hay fork. We found a blinder or bridle for a mule, sheer fabric with hand embroidery on it, and ladies' dresses that looked homemade. Among the clothing, Ben made the most exciting find of the day: a lady's handbag that had belonged to his grandmother Emma Kemp. The black purse had evidently been used as a portable file cabinet; it contained numerous pieces of paper folded into tiny rectangles and carefully stashed inside. Many were handwritten receipts for house rent for Sam and Emma Kemp, dating from 1941 until 1951, in amounts ranging from two to five dollars, each signed by a member of the Major family that owned the plantation. (Mrs. Caillet had told us the tenants were never charged rent.)

A postcard addressed to Samuel Kemp notified him of a free dental clinic, with the penciled notation "July, 1939"; another postcard was about Sam's application for a war ration book. A 1941 postcard informed Emma Kemp that her son Freddie had been assigned to Fort Leonard Wood, Missouri; a 1943 postcard from the War Department notified her of Freddie's change of address.

There was a handwritten receipt to Emma Kemp for a 1945 church donation and a 1945 form letter from the Office of Dependency Benefits in New Jersey regarding Freddie's pay. She had saved a 1947 receipt from the Southern National Insurance Company of Little Rock, Arkansas, and two utility bills from the Gulf States Utilities Company, dated 1949 and 1952, in the amounts of $1.98 and $2.16.

A handwritten letter to Sam Kemp from his brother Eddie Kemp Sr., postmarked Houston and dated May 28, 1948, informed him of Eddie's upcoming trip to Louisiana. Ben, who was about fourteen at the time, remembered when his grandfather received that letter, and he remembered the subsequent visit. "It was the first time we met Eddie Kemp. We had a home baseball game, and I pitched and done real well."[17]

Emma's pocketbook also contained miscellaneous empty envelopes, including one addressed to Freddie Kemp with a return address for Mr. Anthony

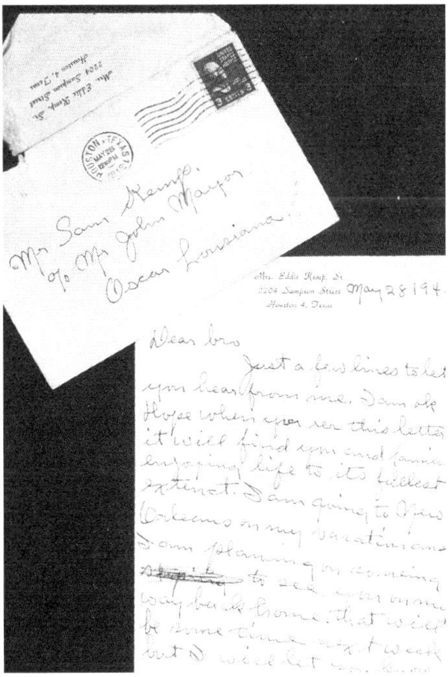

Mr Sam Kemp.
c/o Mr John Major
Oscar Louisiana.

Mrs. Eddie Kemp, Sr.
2204 Sampson Street
Houston 4, Texas

May 28 194

Dear bro
Just a few lines to let you hear from me. I am ok
Hope when you see this letter it will find you and famil
enjoying life to its fullest extent. I am going to New
Orleans on my vacation and I am planning on coming
to see you on my
way back home. that will
be some time next week
but I will let

Letter to Sam Kemp from his brother Eddie Kemp in Houston, dated May 28, 1948. The letter was discovered in 1997 as members of the Friends of Cherie Quarters cleaned out Reese Spooner's house. The letter, along with other papers, had been carefully kept in a purse that belonged to Sam's wife, Emma Lovely Kemp. Photo by Ruth Laney.

Cochran, 1346 Pelopidas Street, New Orleans, dated March 1952. Ben said Cochran was Freddie's older half brother. There were numerous undated papers, including a Social Security card for Freddie, a postcard addressed to Emma from the US Census Bureau regarding her request for a search of records, and a gray envelope addressed to Emma and marked "Freddie Kemp / retake D. 34," possibly an envelope that had once held photographs.

Several papers related directly to Ben and his mother, including a 1943 postcard addressed to "Alberta Bibbin" from the War Department, concerning the change of address of Robert Hornsby, A/C, the father of two of Bert's children. There was a 1950 bill for "Albertha Bibbin" from Dr. Eugene G. Durel in New Roads, marked "$6.00 paid." Among the papers relating to Ben were two US Army meal cards; three men's ration books from Japan; a Selective Service card; a Red Cross membership card dated 1956; two receipts from the Fort Chaffee, Arkansas, exchange; a receipt from Louie's store in Fort Smith, Arkansas, for clothing; a receipt from the Misawa Airmen's Open Mess in Japan, dated 1956; a bedding card; and miscellaneous army-related receipts. A card with the address of Jack Kernohan of Cleveland, Ohio, reminded Ben of a "white fella" who befriended him in the service and stayed in touch with him for years afterward.

A 1951 handwritten note from Reverend O'Neal Bouie, who for many years preached Sunday services at Mount Zion church, was addressed to "Mamy [*sic*] Williams" regarding "Mr. Ginn," possibly a relative of Ernest Gaines. A printed or typed card from Mt. Zion Benevolence Association, Inc., from the 1940s, listed the names "Rev. O'Neal Bouie, Pres.; Joe William [*sic*], V. Pres; John Bolden, Tres.; Henry Paul, Sect." and bore the handwritten signature of Revel Domino. Ben thought the benevolence association was a burial society whose members paid dues toward their funeral services.

There were numerous blue-green papers that appeared to be money orders or postage receipts, a blank check from the Bank of New Roads from the 1940s, a 1941 receipt for insured mail, part of a stamp book with the legend "Save Time—Use Air Mail," a piece of paper money from Mozambique, a small sheet of tablet paper with a penciled notation of money amounts totaling $8.46, two business cards from the Brooklyn Bargain Store on Rampart Street in New Orleans, and miscellaneous other papers. The purse also contained a key that had been twisted to a point, a wad of string, and a broken rubber band. There was even an item that could have once belonged to Ernest

Gaines himself: a coupon from the St. Augustine Church fall festival of 1947, when Gaines attended the Black Catholic school.

Also found in Reese's cabin that February day, though not in Emma's purse, was an envelope addressed in pencil to Emma Kemp, with the return address to John Lovely at "R1 Bx 140" in White Castle, Louisiana, postmarked March 29, 1957, and bearing a three-cent stamp. Inside was a two-page letter, written in pencil on lined paper, from Emma's brother, which included the information that John's wife, Lucinda, was the only member of the family "a little sick at this time." There was a "Final Notice" addressed to "Albertha Bibbin" in Lakeland, apparently for gas service, for $19.08, dated May 16, 1957. There was an envelope postmarked Lakeland, May 19, 1958, and Oscar, May 20, 1958.

Emma Kemp's battered black pocketbook was an archive. Each little piece of folded paper told a story. We carefully saved the purse and the papers for the Cherie Quarters Collection. Ben said he had never known that the owners charged rent until he got out of the service and returned to the quarter in the 1950s. As we examined the pocketbook archive, I wished I had known Emma Lovely Kemp. I was intrigued by her instinct to save these documents. Did she act out of mistrust of the white owners? (If so, it was no doubt warranted.) Had she kept the rent receipts as proof? By creating this archive, Emma had been exerting control over her life—and leaving a legacy.

## THE LAGNIAPPE TOUR

In April 1997, I called Madeleine Caillet to ask permission for the Foundation for Historical Louisiana to take a group to visit the quarter and the graveyard. "Please don't go in the houses," she said. "There is drug dealing going on down there. My little grandchildren were camping out and found a gun and bullets at Shug's house on the porch." Mrs. Caillet told me there had been "drive-by shootings and gangs" in New Roads, Rougon, and Batchelor, and that Major Lane was now a public road. "People go up and down at all hours of the day and night. I live here, my family is here. I'm not comfortable at all." As for the cabins, she said,

> I'm going to have to move them. It's dawning on me that it's not a good idea to have empty buildings. I'd like to donate them to a museum or historical society. I would really like them to stay in the parish. The police jury [the main administrative and legislative body in many Louisiana parishes] would

probably say, "We don't have the money." The historical society is probably the most interested. The parish ought to want them. It's a shame they don't. I cannot afford to run a private museum. It's time to go to another plan. The police said to get rid of the empty buildings. My insurance agent says they need to be gone. I don't have much choice.

I suggested that the Friends meet with her insurance agent. "I'm tired of talking," she said. "They are unsafe, empty buildings in the middle of nowhere."[18]

That was discouraging, but a month later we did a test run on Cherie Quarters as a tourist attraction. On a fresh and breezy spring Friday, Lagniappe Tours took a busload of twenty-five people to River Lake and nearby Parlange Plantation. The group left Baton Rouge at 9:00 a.m. and headed across the old Mississippi River bridge to Oscar. In our roles as "step-on tour guides," Sid Gray gave background information about the landscape, particularly the 1927 flood, and I sketched Gaines's early life in the quarter that had furnished material for his fiction.

When the bus pulled on to Major Lane, Ernest and Dianne Gaines were waiting in their car, having driven over from Lafayette. They climbed aboard the bus and everyone burst into applause. "This is one of the most important tours I have ever done for the foundation," said the enthusiastic young tour director, Briana Bramlette. "It is really special to be at Ernest Gaines's birthplace and to have him here with us."

Our first stop was the Mount Zion Baptist Church. Gaines took the microphone to tell the group about attending school in the church as a child. "About fifty of us would be in the school at once," he said. "The older ones taught the younger ones." He said female teachers from Baton Rouge would board with his grandmother, returning to Baton Rouge on weekends. He recalled playing baseball in the churchyard/playground. "I thought this was the biggest yard in the world at one time." He also described a small cemetery behind the church, with three or four graves. He was twelve years old when he was baptized in False River. "We washed our souls in the river, and we washed our clothes in water drawn from the river. We did a lot of washing in that river for the last hundred years."

Next, the bus stopped at the first of the two slave cabins still standing. Sid explained that the cypress cabins were originally built as two-family dwellings, the two rooms separated by a "privacy wall." Later, many occupants built "shed additions" across the back of their houses. Deep front galleries ran across the houses, each of which had two front doors.

The second surviving cabin had last been occupied by Reese Spooner. Gaines said that the "old people" called him "Ré-zis" (*Ray-ZEES*), giving it a French or Creole pronunciation. "My Aunt Octavia spoke Creole. Many of the old people did."[19] The cabins were "all exactly alike"; although they originally had roofs of cypress shingles, they had tin roofs when he lived there. When rain pattered on the roof, "that sound was beautiful to listen to." He remembered playing in the attics of the cabins as a child.

Sid explained why he dated the construction of the cabins to the 1840s and noted that they were rare survivors of the antebellum period. "There are probably only fifty slave cabins left in the entire state," he said, noting that at one time River Lake Plantation alone had that many cabins, as did many other large plantations in south Louisiana. "These cabins are important because they are part of a place which played a significant role in the history of south Louisiana," he said. "As part of the larger context of the sugar plantation, they provide the opportunity for people to learn about this part of history. It's important to know that there was a time when people could live in these meager dwellings, raise families, and lead productive lives, even into the twentieth century."

Our final stop was the graveyard, where, the visitors learned, seven or eight generations of Gaines's family and friends were buried, including his grandmother Julia McVay and his great-aunt Augusteen Jefferson. With the wind soughing through the oak and pecan trees and the bamboo surrounding the cemetery, the group sauntered among the graves, studying inscriptions on the stones. "For every marker you see here, there are probably ten people buried without markers," said Gaines.

Ernest and Dianne Gaines joined the group for lunch at the Oxbow Restaurant, sitting at tables overlooking False River as we devoured trout and pecan pie. The tour then continued to Parlange Plantation, just up the road, where "Miss Lucy" Parlange led us into the house. Staring mournfully down from a parlor wall, dressed in widow's weeds, was Antoine Decuir's widow, Louise Beauvais, painted by the noted French Louisiana artist Jacques Amans. The portrait was a poignant reminder of River Lake Plantation's past. Although Antoine Decuir had built the plantation for his mistress of color, Sophie Deslondes, she had been displaced when Antoine married Louise, a young widow who bore his only white child, Antoinette. Antoinette's daughter Louise Denis would marry Charles Parlange; she apparently took the portrait of her grandmother and namesake with her when she moved to Parlange.

We bid Ernest and Dianne Gaines goodbye and climbed aboard the bus for the trip back to Baton Rouge. The Friends were greatly encouraged by this experiment in visiting Cherie Quarters as a "tourist attraction." The fact that twenty-five people had paid sixty-five dollars apiece to tour the quarter renewed our determination to preserve the site. From the proceeds, the foundation donated two hundred dollars to the Friends, which we designated for urgently needed repairs to Reese's cabin. Tour leader Briana Bramlette later said that foundation members hoped to conduct another trek to Cherie Quarters. "We heard fabulous comments from everybody who went on the tour. We were on a high for days afterward."[20]

A week later, the Friends held a "carpentry day" to replace a missing column on the front porch of Reese's cabin. Ben, Sid, and I used part of the foundation's donation to buy lumber and replaced the right front column on the porch, propping up the roof with two-by-six boards. We also made note of other repairs needed on both cabins.

Daniel Carey of the National Trust for Historic Preservation made a site visit to Cherie Quarters in April 1997 and urged its preservation as part of the "River Road corridor." Although we had warned him about the poor condition of the cabins, he said, "This is not as bad as I expected."[21]

A few months later, in September 1997, Oprah Winfrey announced the selection of *A Lesson Before Dying* for her book club. In October, her producers visited River Lake Plantation with an eye toward possibly videotaping the book club segment there. I furnished the producers with a history of the plantation and of Cherie Quarters as well as videotape and photographs of former residents. A few weeks later, Oprah herself came to the plantation, and the author's dinner was taped inside the Big House, with four guests chosen from among readers of the book. Owner Madeleine Caillet, whose son and daughter-in-law and their children lived in the Big House, said friends and relatives had convinced her to allow the shoot there because "It's Oprah!" Winfrey was videotaped visiting the two slave cabins, the church, and the graveyard. The show aired on October 27, exposing Cherie Quarters to millions of viewers.

## THE BRICK TOMB

In 1998, concerned about preserving tombs in the graveyard, the Friends sought the advice of the Save Our Cemeteries organization in New Orleans. Executive director Louise Fergusson agreed to make a site visit, along with board member Cynthia Seward. They left New Orleans early on a Sunday morning in June and drove to Baton Rouge to meet me, Ben, and several others. They followed us to Cherie Quarters.[22]

At the graveyard, we showed Louise and Cynthia the L. J. Johnson tomb from 1924. Although there were doubtless many earlier burials there, the Johnson tomb is the earliest tomb with a marker. It also is the only brick tomb in the graveyard, which in itself is interesting to speculate about. Who in 1924 had the money to build a brick tomb, one that must have stood out in size and grandeur? Did Johnson have a special relationship with the Majors that inspired them to memorialize him? Another mystery of Cherie Quarters. Now three-quarters of a century old, the tomb had deteriorated; a number of bricks had come loose and there was a hole through which we could see into the vault. Cynthia noted vines growing in the mortar and recommended spraying them with weed killer. "Don't pull them out while they are still alive, because the roots will damage the mortar and bricks. Clip the vines, and pull out only what you absolutely have to."

Louise pointed out that most of the damage to the tomb was on the top layer. A previous repair of the tomb had been made using Portland cement, which "does more harm than good." She recommended replacing the cement with plaster, which would drain off the rain. "Don't do anything drastic, just stabilizing and preventive maintenance."

She cautioned against tearing down the tomb and rebuilding it. "There is no reason to do that. It's old and historic. Once you tear it down and rebuild it, it's not the same tomb any more, and it loses its historic value." Louise said the top layer of brick should be removed and replaced with a new layer. Cynthia recommended matching the bricks, which were machine or factory made, not slave made. "You mostly need a good brick mason. The mortar is soft, which is good. You want the tomb to look old, because it *is* old." Louise suggested that Save Our Cemeteries oversee the project. "We can come out and be sure our suggestions are followed correctly," she offered.

At this point, Durrell Domino from New Roads and his friend Fred Sam arrived at the graveyard. Domino, who grew up in Cherie Quarters, said he had talked to a man who quoted an estimate of $1,800 to replace the top layer of bricks and to level the tomb. But Louise and Cynthia warned against leveling it. "One good reason not to is that it is probably on top of previous graves and bodies that are decomposing," said Cynthia, who agreed that a fee of about $2,000 was reasonable. "Once you take the top of the tomb off, move as quickly as possible to finish the job."

Driving back to Baton Rouge, Ben and I discussed ways to raise money to repair the tomb, adding yet another item to our Things to Do list.

## PRESERVATION VERSUS PRIVATE PROPERTY

Since founding the Friends of Cherie Quarters in 1994, we had spent hours of our time, driven countless highway miles between Baton Rouge and Oscar, and talked to many people about saving and restoring the cabins. We had held numerous meetings. But our most urgent project remained exactly the same as the day we began: to repair and stabilize the two slave cabins that remained at Cherie Quarters. The Friends had encountered many obstacles in conserving the site, owing to the lack of cooperation by the owner and the resultant lack of funding.

We realized that preservation is a complicated thing, particularly when it comes to an operating sugar plantation owned by several family members of different generations. Madeleine Caillet, the owner of the Big House and of the cabins we were trying so hard to save, often stated that she valued Ernest Gaines's work and recognized the historic significance of his birthplace. But she had to weigh many other considerations in deciding whether to preserve the remaining buildings. She also was protective of her rights as owner and was not inclined to welcome the opinion of outsiders as to how she managed what was, after all, private property.

One conversation showed me that inheriting the property could be a burden. It was almost as if just owning a "plantation" made one suspect. The comments of Madeleine's daughter-in-law Colleen Caillet illustrated the point.

A few months after the Oprah show aired, I called Colleen to ask if we could photograph one of the store ledgers for our slide lecture. Colleen was a high school English teacher (and later principal) who had taught Gaines's work in her classes. She and her husband, Craig, and their children had moved out of the Big House when the Oprah crew came to shoot the Gaines segment. Their living room had been cleared of furniture and a dining table set up there so that Gaines, Oprah, and four guests could eat and talk about *A Lesson Before Dying*. Colleen said she would check with Craig and Madeleine about my request. "If they say no, it's because of the way we were treated by Oprah," she said.[23]

I had been at River Lake that day, and everyone seemed to be in a good mood. Ernest and Dianne Gaines chatted on the back gallery with Madeleine as the crew readied for the shoot and Oprah's chef prepared the meal. The producers got regular walkie-talkie updates on Oprah's imminent arrival. By the time her limousine pulled up, all eyes were on it. Oprah exited wearing dark glasses, her two cocker spaniels in tow. She marched up the stairs of the Big House. I was on the front lawn, too far away to see what happened up on the front gallery.

"Oprah snubbed Miss Madeleine," Colleen told me. "Madeleine was waiting at the top of the stairs. She extended her hand and said, 'Miss Winfrey, I'm Madeleine Caillet. Welcome to River Lake Plantation.' Oprah's shoulder brushed Miss Madeleine's shoulder and she brushed past her. Madeleine was speechless. She's never been treated like that."

Colleen said the family had declined to appear in the episode "because we were unsure of the angle it would take." They felt that "we were personally held accountable for a hundred and fifty years of oppression." When the crew returned the next day to shoot the church and the cane, "Oprah still never spoke to us."

The family had agreed to the shoot out of respect for Gaines. "We did it for him. As an English teacher, I know he has the critical acclaim but not the popular acclaim. Now he's closer to it."

That conversation helped me understand some of the issues facing the owner. One issue—private property ownership—ultimately proved to be the Friends' biggest obstacle. After four years of meetings that ultimately came to naught, we reluctantly admitted that the single biggest cause of the preservation problems at Cherie Quarters was the owner. While she said she wanted to preserve the site, her actions—or rather, inaction—said otherwise. Her continued procrastination and raising of seemingly irrelevant issues as obstacles finally forced the Friends to conclude that the owner did not want to save Cherie Quarters and was willing—perhaps eager—to let it die a slow death by neglect.

There was ample evidence to support this belief. Recent history showed the owner's apparent lack of appreciation and respect for the historic property in her care. In 1983, when the Big House was nominated to the National Register, there were two 1820s pigeonniers on the property, one of them in extremely poor but salvageable condition. Instead of repairing the historic pigeonnier (a building type that, like the slave cabins, was and is an endangered species in the state), the owner allowed it to collapse. If not for the intervention of Sid Gray, the second pigeonnier would also have been lost. (See chapters 6 and 8.)

Other historic artifacts in Caillet's possession were also threatened. Record books of the plantation store, dating back about a century, were at the Big House. In October 1997, during the videotaping of the Oprah Book Club sequence, I had paged through one of the books, dated 1906, which had a section recording the purchases made by Ernest Gaines's great-grandmother Susan Jones McVay. The large ledger book was open, resting on a wooden lectern in one of the downstairs rooms, which is covered overhead but open to the elements on the sides. Such conditions are far from ideal for the preservation of a book that contains information of vital interest to parish historians, preservationists, and descendants of the people of Cherie Quarters. I learned that perhaps a dozen ledger books exist, most of them stored in the River Lake attic—another environment not conducive to preservation. The potential danger from fire, heat, damp, and insects should alarm anyone interested in the history of the plantation.

In the fall of 2003, I went to Cherie Quarters with a friend who wanted to see it. As we drove up Major Lane, we saw Madeleine out walking, getting her exercise. We stopped and I introduced her to my friend. "She wants to see Cherie Quarters," I said. Madeleine was cordial but told us, "It's all gone." She said Shug's house would either be "moved or torn down" because "I can't keep an eye on it." She told us not to go inside because the floor was in bad shape.

I asked her if it might be possible to come and look at the ledger books from the store, which I had never seen, save for that one brief glimpse. She seemed amenable to the idea but said, "First I have to find them." I asked her about the possibility of putting them in a library or museum and she seemed open to the idea.

The record reveals other examples of the owner's poor track record when it comes to preservation. Around 1990, she and her husband obtained a grant from the Louisiana Division of Historic Preservation to paint the Big House. But they delayed putting the project out for bids, as required by state law, until it was too late to meet the grant's one-year deadline, and they were forced to give up the grant money. The owner had shown that she was not inclined to repair her property and was unwilling to spend money on it. Her procrastination also prevented others from saving the cabins. By refusing to turn the cabins over to preservationists, she effectively handed down a death sentence on the structures. As we had been told back in 1995, most government bodies or other granting institutions will not give funds to improve private property.

One result of the owner's inability to share the vision of the Friends was the lack of support from the wider community of Pointe Coupée Parish. Given Mrs. Caillet's well-established ambivalence toward the site, and the lack of true interest among local preservationists such as Bubber Olinde, community involvement was unpredictable at best. Olinde had muddied the waters and interfered with the Friends' efforts to save the cabins by offering to remove them to the town of New Roads. The owner of another local plantation had responded with anger when I expressed the desire to study the store ledgers at River Lake, telling me, "Madeleine will do what's right with them when the time comes!" The parish is racially divided, and the white people with the power to save Cherie Quarters either did not recognize its significance or did not care to save it. ("To me, they are just shacks," confessed one woman.) The Friends believed that, left to their own devices, neither the owner nor the citizens of the parish would ever take the necessary steps to preserve the Cherie Quarters complex. At this point, the Friends felt that only the attention of a broader community could save Cherie Quarters.

We strongly believed that somewhere out there were people who shared our vision. Many former residents still cared, despite strong evidence that we were fighting a losing battle. Strangers also cared—the Friends had received donations from people in other states who read of our preservation efforts in the *Southern Register Quarterly* or heard about them on the *Oprah* program. If we could obtain ownership of the complex, we believed, we could overcome the apathy of the local community through a combination of education and fund-raising. Our slide lecture and field trips were ample proof that we could attract interested people, and recent tours of African American sites by the Preservation Resource Center of New Orleans had sold out, demonstrating a strong interest in sites related to Black history. With the added attraction of Gaines's work and reputation, Cherie Quarters was a "natural" as a tour destination—or so we liked to think.

Sid Gray in Reese Spooner's abandoned cabin, May 1999. Built in 1840 and abandoned in 1985, the cabin had become unsalvageable. Photo by Ruth Laney.

Desperate to save the cabins, the Friends finally asked Mrs. Caillet to sell them to us. She stated that she was willing to donate them but then cited "liability" concerns. She failed to come up with the requested donation document and/or lease agreement. Meanwhile, the rain was falling and the cabins were falling apart.

It wasn't just the elements that threatened the cabins. In October 1998, Sid Gray noticed that the original cypress ceiling boards, about thirty in number, had been removed from Shug's cabin. We reluctantly admitted that if we were going to save the cabins we would probably have to move them off site. But even that possibility was uncertain, given the owner's habit of procrastination—a way of performing demolition by neglect.

As we looked back, we realized that 1998 was a turning point. That was the year when we concluded that our efforts to save Cherie Quarters were probably doomed. But like many preservationists, we did not want to admit that our efforts were futile. (I told Sid, "They need to come up with a new branch of psychiatry to treat 'preservation psychosis.' Because if you love old buildings, it *will* make you crazy.")

Ernest and Dianne Gaines at the annual cemetery cleanup at Cherie Quarters, 2014. Photo by Philip Gould. Copyright © Philip Gould.

In 1997, Barbara Overstreet held another Kemp–Lovely–Horton reunion in Baton Rouge. Sid and I gave our Cherie Quarters slide lecture at Magnolia Mound Plantation, four years after the Cherie Quarters cabin had been moved there. Again, the lecture attracted a crowd of about a hundred, including most reunion attendees, Ernest and Dianne Gaines, and members of the English department at the University of Louisiana at Lafayette, where Gaines taught. After the lecture, we toured the cabin that had been moved to Magnolia Mound. Sid pointed out some mistakes made when the house was reassembled by Baton Rouge Recreation and Parks Commission workers, such as raising the house too high off the ground and painting it a blinding white instead of leaving the weathered gray cypress in its natural state. But at least the cabin was *there;* it had been saved. People walked through the house—including Ernest Brooks, who as a child had lived in that very cabin. By now we realized we were probably going to fail, but it was hard to look at the enthusiastic crowd and not hope for a miracle.

By the fall of 1997, Ernest and Dianne Gaines were well on their way to acquiring ownership of the graveyard, at least. With the help of a New Roads attorney, Ralph Chustz, they had formed a nonprofit corporation to oversee the cemetery. Several people owned the land the cemetery was on, and Chustz had secured verbal agreements that each would donate his or her portion of the graveyard to the Mount Zion River Lake Cemetery Association. "The problem is, the graveyard is in the exact middle of the plantation, and five or six people each own about twenty feet of it," Ernest Gaines said. "We had to get an agreement with each of those people that it will always be maintained as a cemetery." Gaines said that preserving the cemetery, both for the hundreds already there and for people like him who wanted it to be their final resting place, "has been my one and only obsession for the last five years. . . . My ancestors have been buried there for more than a hundred years. No one wants to plow that cemetery over now, but I want to make sure that can never happen."[24]

In the fall of 2000, Ernest and Dianne Gaines bought two pieces of property on False River. One was a fishing camp, a trailer house with a pier on the river. The other was a plot of land across Highway 1, a quarter mile or so from the Big House, where they planned to build a house.

In July 2001, Ben Biben drove over to visit Ernest Gaines at his camp and drop off paperwork related to the cemetery association the Gaineses had formed, of which Ben was treasurer. Then he drove to Cherie Quarters, as he usually did when he was in the area. Parking in front of the church, he was shocked to see the door open and one of the benches lying across the threshold. Jumping from his truck, he glanced inside the church and saw that most of the benches were gone; of the dozen or so left, about half had been "torn to pieces" and their backs removed. Perhaps half a dozen were still intact. Stunned by what he had seen, Ben drove back to the fishing camp to tell Gaines, who followed Ben back to the church to see the damage for himself. They were mystified as to who would do such a thing—and why.[25]

In a 2003 interview, Gaines said that he now owned the graveyard. As for the quarter, he said, "There are only about two old shacks remaining in the quarters and I have no input there at all."[26]

In October 2001, the Friends held a garage sale to raise money and try to attract favorable publicity, a last-gasp effort to keep our project alive. We raised about four hundred dollars and garnered favorable newspaper coverage, but that would turn out to be our last hurrah. By then it was clear that the owner did not plan to cooperate and that an alternative plan, such as moving the structures, was unlikely. Even Ben, who for so long had kept his hopes up, was despondent. "I give up," he told me. "I can't fight them. I just don't have any more energy."[27]

Asked to assess the "progress" of the project, Sid Gray commented, "In six years, the only thing the owners have done is put up a NO TRESPASSING sign and a padlock at Shug's cabin and cannibalize boards from the houses.

They haven't made any noticeable effort to preserve the houses. The [second] owner [P. C. Major II] bulldozed the other side of the road. He saw the short-term economic value more than the long-term archaeological value. [On the positive side], archaeology was done and the houses were put on the National Register."[28]

In May 2003, Gaines secured permission from Madeleine Caillet to move the Cherie Quarters church/school onto the property where he was building a house. He installed a few benches salvaged from the church. He told Ben that he had asked Mrs. Caillet to let him buy the shed and Shug's cabin but she had refused, saying she planned to use the structures; perhaps she would make the cabin into a hay barn and the shed into a pool cover. (By early 2005, the shed was in ruins. The surviving cabin was still intact.)[29]

River Lake continued to function as a sugar plantation, with the two owners, Madeleine Caillet and her cousin P. C. Major II, leasing much of the land to sugar cane farmers. It was clear that they were determined to remove the last two cabins. The only way to "save" Cherie Quarters was to document its existence by talking to those who had lived there; preserving their photographs, furniture, and tools; and researching the history of their ancestors.

River Lake may have been a typical Louisiana sugar plantation of its time, but it has been forever set apart by the fact that a major American writer memorialized the place in his fiction. When Ernest Gaines left False River, the plantation, and especially Cherie Quarters, he took it all with him. Most of his stories are set in the Louisiana he left behind, and the Cherie Quarters of his childhood is a major character in them. The fields, the trees, the bayous, the river, the sky—the place and especially the people—all have been re-created in his work.

Gaines wrote from a sense of place, but also from an elegiac sense that the place from which he sprang was dying. Like his character Rufe in *A Gathering of Old Men,* he was, in a way, "the last one left." He was a witness to the life that once flourished in Cherie Quarters and is now dead. The little cabin where he grew up long ago fell to the tractor. Other houses slowly met the same fate. By the time of his death in 2019, the last two houses, Shug's and Reese's cabins, had vanished without a trace. Even the graveyard where he is buried feels as if the surrounding fields of cane are closing in. But when all the plowing under is done, there will still be his books, bearing witness.

# ACKNOWLEDGMENTS

My first and greatest thanks goes to Ernest Gaines, who preserved the quarter in his fiction and proved that you can go home again. And his wife, Dianne, who helped him save the graveyard where he is buried.

David Biben generously shared detailed memories of Cherie Quarters and truly cared about saving it when few others did. Ben began as a helpful source and over the years became a beloved friend. He wanted this book out in the world, and I'll always regret that he didn't live to see it.

Sam Bibbens supplied fascinating anecdotes of both Louisiana and California and puzzled over several versions of the bird's-eye view of Cherie Quarters to be sure we had everyone in their rightful places.

Barbara Overstreet Hardy welcomed me to her family reunions and carried on the great Cherie Quarters tradition of good cooking.

Former residents of Cherie Quarters, and their kin, talked about life there: Deidra Biben-Glynn, Jerry Brooks, Tony Cador, Norbert Colar Jr., Ernest Gaines II, Levert Kemp, Alma Robinson, Ruby McVay Simmons, Lois Gaines Young.

Those gone but not forgotten shared their memories: Ernest Brooks, Frankie Christopher, Adrean Colar, Ada Mae Gaines, Lionel Gaines, Freddie Kemp, Bill Robillard, Eliza Robillard, Joe Williams.

Linda Lawrence and her daughter Roz Arbel shined a light on Ernest Gaines's life in San Francisco and made pilgrimages to Cherie Quarters to see for themselves the place Gaines had memorialized.

Sid Gray shared his knowledge of and passion for old buildings and taught me to see them as valuable.

Madeleine Bouanchaud Caillet, owner of River Lake Plantation; her son Craig and daughter-in-law Colleen; and her late aunt Malvina Becnel Pickett shared photos and stories.

Decuir descendant Julie Eshelman-Lee and Pointe Coupee historian Brian

Costello shared the fruits of their research. John Kelly and Brendan Riley were tireless in their pursuit of California information.

The late Gerry Anders first read the manuscript and urged me to publish it. Subsequent readers made helpful suggestions: John Easterly, Barbara Nielsen, Amy Reynolds, the late Robb Forman Dew, and Pamela Dean. Writer and photo expert Charles East, who introduced me to Ernest Gaines so long ago, contributed greatly to the early stages of the book.

Alyssa Trosclair's organizational and whiteboard skills helped me launch this project. Coach Verda Lester encouraged me to keep my eye on the prize and talked me off a few ledges. Sallie Randolph, fellow member of the American Society of Journalists and Authors, made sense of publishing mysteries.

The staff of the State Library opened its treasures to me, starting with Virginia Smith and Judy Smith; after they retired, I got help especially from Charlene Bonnette and Marc Wellman. At the East Baton Rouge Parish Library, Melissa Eastin's Baton Rouge Room personnel, especially Emily Ward and Ammon Marshall, were always willing to offer guidance. Aftin Gaddy, archivist at the Louisiana State Penitentiary (Angola), supplied invaluable information.

My thanks to Sand and Norman Marmillion, who shared their 1890s photographs of River Lake Plantation, and to researcher Katy Morlas Shannon, who discovered the connection between Laura and River Lake Plantations. Photographer David Humphreys helped turn old photos into even more compelling images. Artist Mary Lee Eggart displayed patience and sensitivity in creating the map and the bird's-eye view of Cherie Quarters.

I am pleased that LSU Press is publishing this book, as the press was the site of my introduction to Gaines and his work. Thanks to Jenny Keegan for her encouragement, Neal Novak for his enthusiastic support, Todd Manza for his careful copyediting, Sunny Rosen for her markeing savvy, Barbara Bourgoyne for brilliant design work, and to James Wilson for his many helpful contributions.

My husband, Jerome Ducote, visited Cherie Quarters and nearby graveyards with me and listened patiently to stories about people he'd never met. He lent valuable perspective while fighting to keep his business (and himself) alive through the coronavirus pandemic. He also kept me laughing, fed, and supplied with binge-worthy TV series.

The Louisiana Endowment for the Humanities funded my initial work on the book with a research-and-publication grant and underwrote several slide lectures about Cherie Quarters.

# NOTES

## INTRODUCTION

1. Ruth Laney, "A Conversation with Ernest Gaines," *Southern Review* 10, no. 1 (Winter 1974): 1–14. This interview was reprinted in John Lowe, ed., *Conversations with Ernest Gaines* (Jackson: University Press of Mississippi, 1995).

2. *Ernest J. Gaines: Louisiana Stories,* produced by Rick Smith and Ruth Laney (Baton Rouge: Louisiana Public Broadcasting, 1993), 55 min.

3. Visit to Cherie Quarters and New Roads with Gaines and Gould, February 25, 1982. All quotations in this section are from that visit. Notes in possession of author.

4. David Biben, telephone conversation with author, February 9, 1992.

## 1. THE LAST ONE LEFT: THE AUTOBIOGRAPHER OF *MISS JANE PITTMAN*

1. Ernest Gaines, remarks made during appearance at Fanfare festival, Southeastern Louisiana University, Hammond, October 25, 1990. Notes in possession of author.

2. Jim Crow laws were state and local statutes that legalized racial segregation. Named for a Black minstrel show character, the laws—which were in effect for about one hundred years, from the post–Civil War era until 1968—served to marginalize African Americans by denying them the right to vote, hold jobs, get an education, or pursue other opportunities. Anyone who attempted to defy Jim Crow laws often faced arrest, fines, jail sentences, violence, or death. During slavery, there were numerous restrictions to enforce social control: slaves could not be away from their owner's premises without permission, could not assemble unless a white person was present, could not own firearms, were not to be taught to read or write, and could not transmit or possess "inflammatory" written materials.

3. Ernest Gaines, audiotaped interview with author and Jane Bonin, Baton Rouge, November 20, 1983.

4. David Biben, telephone conversation with author, December 28, 2003.

5. Ernest Gaines, interview with author and Sid Gray, Lafayette, November 4, 1993.

6. Norbert Colar Jr., videotaped interview with author, San Jose, May 30, 1992.

7. Gaines, interview with author and Sid Gray, Lafayette, November 4, 1993. After examining the Cherie Quarters cabins, building historian Sid Gray concluded that some occupants built additions to the two-room cabins, usually for bathrooms or kitchens.

8. David Biben, telephone conversation with author, October 22, 1992.

9. Ruth Laney, "A Conversation with Ernest Gaines," *Southern Review* 10, no. 1 (Winter 1974): 2.

10. David Biben, telephone conversation with author, December 2, 1998.

11. Laney, "Conversation," 2.

12. Ada Mae Gaines, videotaped interview with author, Baton Rouge, October 3, 1992.

13. David Biben, telephone conversation with author, December 2, 1998.

14. Norbert Colar Jr., videotaped interview with author, San Jose, May 30, 1992.

15. Lois Gaines Young, videotaped interview with author, San Jose, May 30, 1992.

16. David Biben, telephone conversation with author, December 2, 1998.

17. Lois Gaines Young, videotaped interview with author, San Jose, 1992.

18. Barbara Overstreet Hardy, telephone conversation with author, March 14, 1996.

19. Ernest Gaines, "Miss Jane and I," *Mozart and Leadbelly* (New York: Alfred A. Knopf, 2005), 5.

20. David Biben, telephone conversation with author, December 2, 1998.

21. Laney, "Conversation," 3.

22. James Brooks, interview with author, Baton Rouge, February 28, 1992.

23. David Biben, telephone conversation with author, December 2, 1998.

24. Lionel Gaines, videotaped interview with author, Baton Rouge, October 3, 1992. This remembrance by his brother appears in the television documentary about Ernest Gaines.

25. Ernest Gaines, videotaped interview with author, Oscar, Louisiana, December 13, 1991.

26. Ernest Gaines, "Three Men," *Bloodline* (New York: Vintage Contemporaries, 1997), 152; Gaines, *In My Father's House* (New York: Vintage Contemporaries, 1992), 102; Gaines, *A Lesson Before Dying* (New York: Vintage Contemporaries, 1994), 20.

27. Ernest Gaines, audiotaped interview with author, Baton Rouge, December 7, 1984.

28. Steve Culpepper and Mary Broussard, "Writer Draws on Pointe Coupée Childhood," *Baton Rouge Sunday Advocate,* December 4, 1988.

29. James Brooks, interview with author, Baton Rouge, February 28, 1992.

30. Ada Mae Gaines, videotaped interview with author, Baton Rouge, October 3, 1992. This remembrance by his sister-in-law appears in the television documentary about Ernest Gaines.

31. Margaret R. Knight, "He Must Return to the South," *Baton Rouge Sunday Advocate,* April 7, 1974.

32. Ernest Gaines, videotaped interview with author, Oscar, Louisiana, 1992.

33. Ernest Gaines, interview with author and Sid Gray, Lafayette, November 4, 1993.

34. Ernest Gaines, videotaped interview with author, Oscar, Louisiana, 1992.

35. Ernest Gaines, audiotaped interview with author and Jane Bonin, Baton Rouge, November 20, 1983.

36. Ernest Gaines, interview with author and Sid Gray, Lafayette, November 4, 1993.

37. Freddie Kemp, interview with author, Oscar, Louisiana, April 23, 1993.

38. Malvina Pickett, interview with author, Baton Rouge, October 29, 1992.

39. Ernest Gaines, conversation with author, Oscar, Louisiana, October 28, 2000.

40. Ernest Gaines, interview with author and Sid Gray, Lafayette, November 4, 1993; Gaines, interview with author, December 7, 1984; Gaines, comments made after receiving Louisiana Writer Award from Louisiana Center for the Book, Baton Rouge, October 27, 2000.

41. Ernest Gaines, audiotaped interview with Jane Bonin and author, Baton Rouge, November 20, 1983; Gaines, interview with author, Oscar, Louisiana, January 7, 2015.

42. James Brooks, interview with author, Baton Rouge, February 28, 1992.

43. David Biben, interview with author, Baton Rouge, February 22, 1996; Biben, telephone conversation with author, Baton Rouge, October 8, 2014; Biben, telephone conversation with author, December 2, 1998.

44. Ernest Gaines, videotaped interview with author, Oscar, Louisiana, December 13, 1991.

45. James Brooks, interview with author, Baton Rouge, February 28, 1992.

46. Ernest Gaines, conversation with author, February 25, 1982.

47. Ernest Gaines, interview with author, Oscar, Louisiana, January 7, 2015.

48. Ernest Gaines, telephone conversation with author, October 23, 1993.

49. Gaines read from the novella at the Gaines Center on September 25, 2013. Notes in possession of author.

50. Ernest Gaines, audiotaped interview with Jane Bonin and author, Baton Rouge, November 20, 1983.

51. Ernest Gaines, videotaped interview with author, 1992.

52. Frank Spooner, conversation with author, New Roads, Louisiana, May 3, 1997.

53. James Brooks, interview with author, Baton Rouge, February 28, 1992.

54. Adrean Colar, videotaped interview with author, San Jose, May 30, 1992.

55. Ernest Gaines, interview with author, March 3, 1983.

56. Ernest Gaines, interview with author and Sid Gray, Lafayette, November 4, 1993.

57. David Biben, telephone conversation with author, August 14, 2009.

58. David Biben, telephone conversation with author, June 26, 1998.

59. Ernest Gaines, interviews with author; David Biben, telephone conversation with author, January 20, 1997. According to the National Archives database *US World War II Army Enlistment Records, 1938–1946,* Manuel Gaines enlisted in the army in November 1942.

60. Divorce document, Pointe Coupée Parish Courthouse, New Roads, Louisiana. Adrean Jefferson, aged fifteen and a half, married Manuel Gaines, who had just turned twenty, on December 3, 1931. A little more than a year later, when she was sixteen and a half, Adrean gave birth to her first child, a son she named Ernest James Gaines. About a year and a half later (July 1934), she gave birth to a second son, Lionel, and she had more children in rapid succession: Eugene born in October 1935, Lois in March 1937, Charles (Mitchell) in 1939, Norbert Jr. in 1940, and (after a six-year gap) Joseph "Mack" in 1946.

In December 1945, after fourteen years of marriage, Adrean had Manuel served with divorce papers, which were accepted in his absence by a woman with whom he was apparently living, Angelina Zenon. In Adrean's petition for divorce, she states that she and Manuel had married in 1931 and separated "on or about" the year 1935, "and since then have been continuously living separate and apart." She states that she has been living continuously in Pointe Coupée Parish and that Manuel is "a resident of the Parish of Orleans . . . but is now temporarily residing" in Pointe Coupée Parish. Adrean states that two children were born of the marriage—Ernest, age twelve, and Lionel, age eleven—and that she "is entitled to the complete care, custody and control of said minor children." Manuel was served with papers on December 19, 1945, and apparently made no response to them; at least, none is on file in the Pointe Coupée courthouse. A divorce was granted to Adrean on June 28, 1946, and she was granted full custody of Ernest and Lionel Gaines. Adrean Jefferson and Norbert Colar were married in New Orleans on December 6, 1946. He was thirty-three and she was thirty.

What is interesting about Adrean's divorce petition is that it makes no mention of Ernest and Lionel's four siblings: Eugene, born in October 1935, Lois in 1937, Charles (Mitchell) in 1939, and Norbert Jr. in 1940. (Her sixth child, Joseph Mack, was born June 4, 1946.) Norbert Jr. was five or six years old by the time his parents married.

In the divorce petition, the names Gaines and Ginn are used interchangeably. Throughout the Petition for Absolute Divorce, the typed name "Gaines" is appended with the inked parenthetical annotation "(Ginn)." In the judgment, Adrean Jefferson Ginn is granted a divorce from Manuel Ginn and granted custody of Ernest Ginn and Lionel Ginn. Gaines 62, 18th JDC, 2889, Gaines Adrean Jefferson v. Manuel Gaines, 1945, Pointe Coupée Parish Courthouse, New Roads. (The word "annulment" also appears on this document.)

In his license to marry Clara Zeno, Manuel Gaines stated that his "preceding marriage" had terminated in 1945 in Pointe Coupée Parish. See Certificate of Marriage, license no. 5094, for the year 1948, Pointe Coupée Parish Courthouse, New Roads, Louisiana. Manuel and Clara married on May 15, 1948, just a few months before Ernest Gaines would leave for his new life in California.

According to oral histories from several contemporaries of Gaines, Adrean had children with several fathers. It is generally acknowledged that, although his mother was married to Manuel Gaines when she gave birth to Ernest, he was not in fact Manuel's son but the son of Freddie Kemp, another man who had lived at Cherie Quarters since childhood and had had a relationship with Adrean. (He also was a friend of Manuel Gaines.) It was generally agreed that Lionel was the son of Manuel Gaines, and in fact the resemblance between them was marked. David Biben, in a conversation on August 14, 2009, said that Manuel knew that Ernest was not his son "but he went along with it."

Their brother Eugene was also generally acknowledged not to be Manuel's son, although he went by the name Gaines throughout his life. His father was widely accepted in the quarter as Walter "Salute" Zeno (the father of Clara Zeno). According to David Biben, Salute was in the habit of roaming the quarters at night naked, in search of women who were easy prey. Whether Adrean was raped by Salute or had a consensual relationship with him is unclear, but many Cherie Quarters residents believed that Eugene was Salute's son. Eugene died of cancer in 1997. At his funeral service, his step-siblings passed out a sheet of paper that read, "In loving memories of our dear brother Mr. Eugene Gaines Zeno," stating that he was the son of "Mother: Adrine G. Collard [*sic*]" and "Father: Walter Zeno" and was "Survived by 4 brothers and 5 Sister [*sic*] from his father," listing their names, including Forrest Zeno and Clara Zeno Gaines, Manuel Gaines's wife. When Manuel Gaines died two years later, Eugene was not mentioned in his obituary as having predeceased him. (Copy of funeral handout in possession of author.)

A longtime resident of Cherie Quarters stated that Lois, Adrean's first daughter, and Charles, also known as Mitchell, were not Manuel's children either but were fathered by a man remembered only by his last name, Johnson.

Norbert, Adrean's sixth child, did not go by the name Gaines but by Colar; he was named Raphael Norbert Colar Jr. after his father, Adrean's second husband. He was born in 1940, five years before his mother divorced Manuel Gaines.

One might think that the next six of Adrean's twelve children were all fathered by Norbert, but there is some doubt even about that. There is a six-year gap between Norbert's birth in 1940 and the birth of Joseph Mack Gaines, known as Mack, in June 1946. Among those who grew up with the children, it was believed that Mack, too, may have been the son of Freddie Kemp. Whoever his father was, Mack was treated differently from Adrean's other children. According to David Biben, Mack was "given" to another woman, Lucille Martin, to raise. He eventually moved to California after growing up in Louisiana as part of another family. In adulthood, he and Ernest Gaines maintained a friendly relationship. Mack died in August 2021 in Vallejo, California; he was memorialized in services in both Vallejo and Baton Rouge and was buried in Cherie Quarters. His obituary mentions "his parents Henry and Lucille Martin Queen."

61. David Biben, telephone conversation with author, February 23, 2010.

62. David Biben, telephone conversation with author, June 11, 1994.

63. David Biben, telephone conversation with author May 10, 2005.

64. Marcia Gaudet and Carl Wooton, *Porch Talk: Conversations on the Writer's Craft* (Baton Rouge: Louisiana State University Press, 1990), 84.

65. Adrean Colar, videotaped interview with author, San Jose, May 30, 1992. This comment by Gaines's mother appears in the television documentary.

66. Ernest Gaines in Ruth Laney and Rick Smith, *Ernest J. Gaines: Louisiana Stories* (Baton Rouge: Louisiana Public Broadcasting, 1993). Gaines made similar comments in a conversation with the author, Baton Rouge, October 17, 1983; and in an audiotaped interview with author, Lafayette, July 8, 1993. David Biben later described how some of their contemporaries died. "Harry Domino got his head shot off from the nose on up. His brother Rudolph killed himself in California; a guy beat him so bad his head swoll and then went back down too small. His brother Revel died of a heart attack; they found him in his house in California. Louis Simon was an alcoholic; he was found dead of a heart attack in New Roads. Henry Marcellin had a kidney problem from drinking. Griffin Domino drank himself to death; his stomach was ate up." David Biben, telephone conversation with author, December 2, 1998.

67. Ernest Gaines, interview with author, 1992.

68. Ruth Laney, "The Last One Left," *Baton Rouge Sunday Advocate Magazine,* October 30, 1983, 7.

69. Ernest Gaines, audiotaped interview with author and Jane Bonin, November 20, 1983.

70. Brendan Riley, "Solano Chronicles," *Vallejo Times-Herald,* August 2, 2020.

71. Ernest Gaines, interview with author, Oscar, Louisiana, January 7, 2015. The 1949 Franklin Junior High School yearbook includes photos of faculty member Miss Fidella Legg, apparently a member of the science department. Prankster Gilbert Crane is a student, as is Ernest Gaines; his class photo may be the earliest known photograph of Gaines.

72. Laney, "Conversation," 4.

73. Riley, "Solano Chronicles."

74. Adrean Colar, videotaped interview with author, May 30, 1992.

75. Laney, "Conversation," 4. Norbert Colar's World War II draft card, issued when he was twenty-seven, lists his height at six feet and his weight at 196 pounds.

76. Ernest Gaines, audiotaped interview with author and Jane Bonin, Baton Rouge, November 20, 1983; typescript in possession of author.

77. Ruth Laney, "Gaining Knowledge: Road to Author's Fame Wound Through Libraries," *Baton Rouge Advocate,* May 5, 1997, 3B. Gaines was the keynote speaker at a fundraiser for the Pointe Coupée Parish library, the very place he would not have been allowed to enter as a child. The event was held at the Scott Civic Center in New Roads.

78. Ibid.

79. Ernest Gaines, audiotaped interview with author, October 28, 1972.

80. Angela Noel, "Plantation-Raised Ernest Gains [*sic*] Loves to Write about Louisiana," Associated Press article syndicated in *Baton Rouge Sunday Advocate,* April 24, 1977.

## 2. I WANTED TO READ ABOUT THE SOUTH: BECOMING A WRITER

1. Ernest Gaines, Fanfare festival, Hammond, Louisiana, October 25, 1990.

2. Ernest Gaines, audiotaped interview with author and Jane Bonin, Baton Rouge, November 20, 1983; typescript in possession of author.

3. Ruth Laney, "Gaining Knowledge: Road to Author's Fame Wound Through Libraries," *Baton Rouge Advocate,* May 5, 1997, 3B.

4. Adrean Colar, videotaped interview with author, San Jose, May 30, 1992.

5. Ruth Laney, "Bard from the Bayou: At Sixty, Writer Ernest Gaines Enjoys the Rewards of a Long Career Filled with Struggle," *The World and I,* October 1993, 308. This article was reprinted in John Lowe, ed., *Conversations with Ernest Gaines* (Jackson: University Press of Mississippi, 1995).

6. Ernest Gaines, comments made in creative writing class, University of Southwestern Louisiana, Lafayette, March 2, 1982.

7. Ernest Gaines, audiotaped interview with author, December 7, 1984.

8. Ernest Gaines, interview with author, Oscar, Louisiana, January 7, 2015. Miss Melba Olsen is depicted in the Vallejo High School yearbook as a member of the commercial department, where she taught typing and possibly other courses.

9. David Biben, telephone interview with author, December 2, 1998.

10. James Brooks, interview with author, Baton Rouge, February 28, 1992.

11. Ruth Laney, "A Conversation with Ernest Gaines," *Southern Review* 10, no. 1 (Winter 1974): 5. This interview was reprinted in John Lowe, ed., *Conversations with Ernest Gaines* (Jackson: University Press of Mississippi, 1995).

12. James Brooks, interview with author, Baton Rouge, February 28, 1992.

13. Ernest Gaines, comments made in creative writing class, University of Southwestern Louisiana, Lafayette, March 2, 1982.

14. Norbert Colar Jr., videotaped interview with author, San Jose, May 30, 1992.

15. Ruth Laney, "A Conversation with Ernest Gaines," *Southern Review* 10, no. 1 (Winter 1974): 5.

16. Augusteen Jefferson's death certificate is on file at the Louisiana State Archives in Baton Rouge. Her date of birth is given as April 5, 1892, and her place of birth as Lakeland. Lionel Gaines was the "informant"; her parents are listed as "unknown." This information may not be accurate.

17. Ada Mae Gaines, videotaped interview with author, Baton Rouge, October 3, 1992.

18. Adrean Colar, videotaped interview with author, San Jose, May 30, 1992.

19. David Biben, telephone conversation with author, December 2, 1998.

20. Samuel Bibbens, audiotaped interview with author, June 1996.

21. Ernest Gaines, videotaped interview with author, Oscar, Louisiana, May 19, 1992.

22. Adrean Colar, videotaped interview with author, San Jose, May 30, 1992.

23. Laney, "Conversation," 5.

24. Ernest Gaines, interview with author, 1973.

25. Ernest Gaines, interview with Jane Bonin, Lafayette, 1983; typescript in possession of author.

26. Laney, "Conversation," 5.

27. Ernest Gaines, interview with author, October 28, 1972.

28. Ernest Gaines, talk at Deep South Writers' Conference, University of Southwestern Louisiana, Lafayette, September 19, 1981.

29. San Francisco State College, *Transfer* 1, no. 1.

30. Ernest Gaines, interview with Jane Bonin, Lafayette, 1983; typescript in possession of author.

31. Ernest Gaines, videotaped interview with author, San Francisco, May 1992.

32. According to her Social Security application form, Dorothea Amalie Oppenheimer was born on November 14, 1918, in Berlin.

33. Jane Bonin, telephone conversation with author, January 11, 1984.

34. Marcia Gaudet and Carl Wooton, *Porch Talk: Conversations on the Writer's Craft* (Baton Rouge: Louisiana State University Press, 1990), 115–16.

35. Ernest Gaines, "The Boy in the Double-Breasted Suit," *Mozart and Leadbelly* (New York: Alfred A. Knopf, 2005), 88.

36. Laney, "Bard from the Bayou," 308.

37. Ernest Gaines, interview with Sid Gray and author, Lafayette, November 4, 1993.

38. Ernest Gaines, audiotaped interview with author, Baton Rouge, December 7, 1984.

39. Laney, "Conversation," 5–6.

40. Ernest Gaines, audiotaped interview with author, Lafayette, March 3, 1982.

41. Eloise Dungan, "He Walks His Own Line," *California Living (San Francisco Examiner* Sunday magazine*)*, July 12, 1970, 27.

42. Ernest Gaines, audiotaped interview with author, Baton Rouge, October 28, 1972.

43. Ernest Gaines, interview with Jane Bonin, Lafayette, 1983; typescript in possession of author.

44. Diane Manuel, "Tending a Legacy: Mary Page Stegner on Life and Work," *Stanford Today*, March/April 1996, https://web.stanford.edu/dept/news/stanfordtoday/ed/9603/9603mps01 .html. Stegner died of complications from injuries received in an automobile wreck in 1993.

45. Ibid.

46. Mary Stegner recalled the conversation as taking place at dinner and that Ned Jones asked Stegner to write him a letter outlining his need for funds. Stegner biographer Philip L. Fradkin wrote that the conversation took place over lunch and that Richard Jones approached Stanford administrators for approval of the idea. Fradkin, *Wallace Stegner and the American West* (Berkeley: University of California Press, 2008), 113.

47. Rick Dodgson, *It's All a Kind of Magic: The Young Ken Kesey* (Madison: University of Wisconsin Press, 2013), 74.

48. Unbeknownst to Stegner, Strucinski had done time in federal prison for burglary, larceny, mail fraud, and forgery. At Stanford, he lifted several books and documents from the university library and sold them. The thefts were discovered when a Woodrow Wilson letter turned up in a Manhattan bookseller's catalog. Elmer Robinson, the former mayor of San Francisco, had donated it and many other documents to Stanford. He spied it in the catalog and contacted the university. Strucinski was eventually arrested and served time.

49. News release on Scowcroft's death. Stanford News Service, "Scowcroft, Former Creative Writing Director, Dies at 85," October 16, 2001, https://news.stanford.edu/pr/01/scowobit1017.html.

50. Wendell Berry, telephone interview with author, February 26, 2004.

51. Michalene Busico, "Bringing It All Back Home: Ernest Gaines Is a Southern Writer with a Northern California Address," *San Jose Mercury News,* January 16, 1994, AB15.

52. Jackson J. Benson, *Wallace Stegner: His Life and Work* (New York: Viking, 1996), 261.

53. Berry recalled Gaines visiting him in Port Royal in 1980 and said he and his wife, Tanya, visited Ernest and Dianne Gaines at their house on False River in 2007.

54. Laney, "Conversation," 5–6.

55. Gaudet and Wooton, *Porch Talk,* 129.

56. Leslie Sowers, "Bayou Born," *Houston Chronicle,* June 2, 1993, D1.

57. Ernest Gaines, comments made at Deep South Writers' Conference, Lafayette, September 19, 1981.

58. Gaudet and Wooton, *Porch Talk,* 115.

59. Gaines, "Miss Jane and I," *Mozart and Leadbelly: Stories and Essays* (New York: Knopf, 2005), 16.

60. Ibid., 24–25.

61. David Biben, telephone conversation with author, December 2, 1998.

62. See chapter 5 for details about Mamie's brother Freddie Kemp and his family moving to Baton Rouge.

63. Sam Bibbens, telephone interview with author, July 11, 2020.

64. David Biben, telephone conversation with author, December 2, 1998.

65. David Biben, videotaped interview with author, Baton Rouge, October 3, 1992.

66. Norbert Colar, videotaped interview with author, San Jose, May 30, 1992.

67. David Biben, telephone conversation with author, February 9, 1992.

68. Ernest Gaines, interview with author, Oscar, Louisiana, January 7, 2015.

69. David Biben, conversation with author, Port Allen, Louisiana, June 28, 1998.

70. Ernest Gaines, comments made in fiction workshop, Deep South Writers Conference, Lafayette, September 19, 1981; notes in possession of author. Gaines often quoted the line, changing it slightly from Hopkins's original, "Keep out of the graveyard, I'll save you from the pen."

71. David Biben, telephone conversation with author, September 11, 2003.

72. Ernest Gaines, audiotaped interview with author, July 8, 1993.

73. In an interview in 1982, Gaines revealed that he had originally planned to spend that time in New Orleans. "I've never lived in New Orleans," he said. "I wanted to live there in '63, but my uncle persuaded me to live in Baton Rouge." Jeanie Blake, "Interview with Ernest Gaines," *Xavier Review* 3, no. 1 (1983).

74. Gaudet and Wooton, *Porch Talk,* 113.

75. Ernest Gaines, interview with author, Oscar, Louisiana, January 7, 2015. Atheneum Books was established in 1959 by Alfred A. Knopf Jr., Simon Michael Bessie, and Hiram Haydn.

76. "I'd hate to tell you how many magazines sent back ["Sky"] before it was published in *Negro Digest,*" Gaines told an interviewer in 1980, when the film version was scheduled to be shown. Joseph McLellan, "Gradual Gaines," *Washington Post,* March 10, 1980. *Negro Digest,* later renamed *Black World,* was a magazine for the African American market, founded in 1942 by John H. Johnson of Johnson Publishing Company in Chicago.

77. Gaudet and Wooton, *Porch Talk,* 127.

78. Laney, "Conversation," 6.

79. Gaudet and Wooton, *Porch Talk,* 112.

80. Ernest Gaines, interview with author, Oscar, Louisiana, January 7, 2015.

81. Ernest J. Gaines, *Catherine Carmier* (New York: Vintage, 1993), 190–91.

82. Ibid., 102.

83. James Baldwin, "The Price May Be Too High," *New York Times,* February 2, 1969. The comment appeared as a blurb on the front cover of the Bantam paperback issued in 1972.

84. Ernest Gaines, interview with author, Oscar, Louisiana, January 7, 2015.

85. Linda Lawrence, telephone conversation with author, October 2, 2013.

86. *Of Love and Dust* was published on October 31, 1967.

87. Linda Lawrence, telephone conversation with author, October 2, 2013.

88. Roz Arbel, telephone conversation with author, September 21, 2013.

89. Roz Arbel, telephone conversations with author, June 5, 2016, January 15, 2015.

90. Jim Larimore, "Clean Language, Perfect Stories: Author of 'Bloodline' Visits His Sister Here," *San Jose Mercury News,* September 1, 1968.

91. Laney, "Conversation," 6–7.

92. The couple had a daughter, Rebecca, in 1969. Walker and her husband divorced in 1976.

93. Linda Lawrence, email to author, March 8, 2011.

94. *The Denisonian,* May 9, 1969, 1, 4.

95. Roz Arbel, telephone conversation with author, September 21, 2013.

96. Under the title "Native Author May Become Image-Making Faulkner for Rural Louisiana's Negroes," the syndicated article ran in the *Baton Rouge Morning Advocate* on August 8, 1968.

97. Ernest Gaines, videotaped interview with author, Oscar, Louisiana, December 13, 1991.

98. Ernest Gaines, interview with author.

99. Pinkie Gordon Lane, conversation with author, New Roads, Louisiana, May 3, 1997.

100. I had first heard about the murder in 1992, just as I began work on the documentary about Gaines. One of our first projects was calling people in Pointe Coupée Parish, both Black and white, seeking photos and people to interview. Lucy and Walter Parlange Jr., who owned Parlange Plantation, were the first to mention it. Shortly thereafter, David Biben told me "Norbert Colar was shot by one of his younger sons in California." Lucy Parlange left me a phone message that included the words, "Norbert [pronounced *Nor-BARE*] was a wonderful man. He helped form that child's [Gaines's] life. He was a fine man. It's tragic that he got killed." We did not pursue this line while making the documentary, fearing that it would shut us down just as we were getting started.

101. Roz Arbel, telephone conversation with author, January 15, 2015.

102. Paul Avery, "A Zodiac-Like Ambush," *San Francisco Chronicle*, November 25, 1969, 1.

103. Ernest Gaines II, telephone conversation with author, April 18, 2021. (Ernest Gaines II, born March 10, 1954, the son of Eugene Gaines, had recently moved to Vallejo from Louisiana. His uncle Lavern Colar was born July 8, 1956.)

104. County of Napa, Certificate of Death no. 950. The certificate states that Colar was in Queen of the Valley Hospital in Napa for twenty-seven hours and that his death was being investigated as a homicide by the sheriff's office coroner.

105. Linda Lawrence, telephone conversation with author, March 22, 2021. Jules Colar (1920–2000) was born in Louisiana and, like his older brother, joined the merchant marine and moved to California. According to news reports, Jules Colar had gone with Norbert earlier in the evening to visit a third brother (probably Murphy Colar) at a veteran's home. According to Avery, "A Zodiac-Like Ambush," Norbert had dropped Jules off at his house a few blocks away before returning home and being shot.

106. "Detention Hearing for Vallejo Youth," *Vallejo Times-Herald*, July 17, 1970.

107. A 1974 newspaper account states that Leonard had been sentenced to the California Youth Authority and "later was paroled from CYA to the Oakland area." In April 1974, at age twenty, he was arrested in Oakland for assault with a deadly weapon but was released when the victim refused to testify. "Ex-Vallejo Youth Held in Assault," *Vallejo Times-Herald*, April 23, 1974; "Witness Mum, Suspect Goes Free," *Oakland Tribune*, May 7, 1974.

108. Linda Lawrence, telephone conversation with author, April 25, 2009.

109. Linda Lawrence, telephone conversation with author, March 22, 2021. In *The Autobiography of Miss Jane Pittman*, Ned is about three when he accompanies ten-year-old Jane as they try to make their way to Ohio. He carries a rock and a piece of iron with which to start a fire at night.

110. Linda Lawrence, telephone conversation with author, April 25, 2009.

111. Linda Lawrence, telephone conversation with author, October 2, 2013.

112. Roz Arbel, telephone conversation with author, June 21, 2016.

113. Eloise Dungan, "He Walks His Own Line," *California Living (San Francisco Examiner* Sunday magazine*)*, July 12, 1970, 26.

114. Roz Arbel, telephone conversation with author, January 15, 2015.

115. Dungan, "He Walks His Own Line," 28.

116. Ibid., 24.

117. Ibid., 26, 28.

118. Ruth Laney, "Gaining Knowledge."

119. Ernest Gaines, from talk delivered at Deep South Writers' Conference, University of Southwestern Louisiana, Lafayette, September, 22, 1978.

120. Ernest Gaines, comments made in fiction workshop, Deep South Writers Conference, Lafayette, September 19, 1981; notes in possession of author.

121. Ernest Gaines, from talk delivered at Deep South Writers' Conference, University of Southwestern Louisiana, Lafayette, September 19, 1981.

122. Gaines's photographs have been published in several journals and books. A selection of his photos taken in and around Oscar, Louisiana, was published in the journal *Callaloo,* which devoted an entire issue to Gaines. *Callaloo* 1, no. 3 (May 1978).

123. Ernest Gaines, from talk delivered at Deep South Writers' Conference, Lafayette, September 19, 1981.

124. Gaines, talk delivered at Louisisana State University, Baton Rouge, April 16, 1982. Notes in possession of author.

125. Gaines, interview with author, Lafayette, March 3, 1982.

126. *Denisonian,* January 15, 1971, 3.

127. Ellen Nibbelink, email message to author, April 12, 2021.

128. William Nichols, telephone conversation with author, April 9, 2021.

129. William Nichols, "Performance Becomes Something Like Therapy," *Valley News,* March 27, 2021.

130. Ellen Nibbelink, email message to author, April 12, 2021.

131. Ronald E. Santoni, whose main focus was Jean-Paul Sartre and existentialism, taught at Denison from the 1960s through the 1980s, twice serving as chairman of the philosophy department.

132. Julia McVay died on April 11, 1970, in San Francisco and is buried in the graveyard at Cherie Quarters.

133. William Nichols, email to author, July 24, 2021.

134. *Ernest J. Gaines: Louisiana Stories.* For more information about James McVay's leaving, see chapter 5.

135. Gaines told writer Bill Ferris, "Some people have asked me whether or not *The Autobiography of Miss Jane Pittman* is fiction or nonfiction. It is fiction. When Dial Press first sent it out, they did not put "A Novel" on the galleys or on the dust jacket, so a lot of people had the feeling that it could have been real. . . . I did a lot of research in books to give some facts to what Miss Jane could talk about, but these are my creations. I read quite a few interviews performed with former slaves by the WPA [Works Progress Administration] during the thirties and I got their rhythm and how they said certain things. But I never interviewed anybody." Ferris, "A Conversation with Ernest Gaines," *Humanities* 19, no. 4 (July–August 1998).

136. Ernest Gaines, remarks made during appearance at Fanfare festival, Southeastern Louisiana University, Hammond, October 25, 1990. Notes in possession of author.

137. S. I. Hayakawa was acting president of San Francisco State College in 1968 when there was a student strike and demonstrations demanding a department of Black studies and other changes. Hayakawa relented on December 6, 1968, and announced the creation of a Black studies program at the university. Although he agreed to that demand and started a department of ethnic studies, Hayakawa, who was president of the college from 1969 to 1973, became popular with conservative voters after he pulled the wires out of loudspeakers on a protesters' van at an outdoor rally. He was elected senator in 1976 and served until 1982.

138. Beverly Beyette, "Quiet, Sincere—or Not Black Enough?," *Baton Rouge Sunday Advocate,* May 8, 1983.

139. John Semien, "Author Says New Issues Face Young Black Writers," *Baton Rouge Morning Advocate,* April 16, 1982.

140. The Ten-Point Program is a set of guidelines that states the Black Panther Party's ideals and ways of operation, a "combination of the Bill of Rights and the Declaration of Independence." The document was created in 1966 by the founders of the party, Huey P. Newton and Bobby Seale, who were influenced by Marxism and Black nationalism. The Ten-Point Program comprised two sections. "What We Want Now!" described what the party wanted from the leaders of American society. "What We Believe" outlined the philosophical views of the party and the rights that African Americans should have but were denied. Two of Gaines's younger brothers were members of the party for several years.

141. Ruth Laney, "Ernest Gaines: A New Approach for Black Writers," *Baton Rouge Sunday Advocate,* April 17, 1977, 2E. This was a theme Gaines had addressed earlier. "I think I have a lot of protest in . . . the story 'Just Like a Tree,'" he said in 1972. "After all, a woman dies because she is moved out of her home. It's nothing more than that. But she's uprooted. The bombings going on—well, you could go into a long, long dialogue about things like that. But I think one gets the message, one gets the *feeling* from it. And if I cannot move you by dramatizing a situation like that, then I'm not going to try to move you by all the rhetoric in the world. I just am not that kind of person." Laney, "Conversation with Ernest Gaines," 12.

142. Melvin Maddox, "Root and Branch," *Time,* May 10, 1971. Cited in Mary Ellen Doyle, "Ernest J. Gaines: An Annotated Bibliography, 1956–1988," *Black American Literature Forum* 24, no. 1 (Spring 1990): 125–50.

143. Wallace Stegner, who had retired from the creative writing program at Stanford, published the novel *Angle of Repose* in 1971 and won the Pulitzer Prize in fiction for it, beating out his former student.

144. Linda Lawrence, telephone interview with author, April 25, 2009; Roz Arbel, telephone interview with author, June 5, 2016.

145. Linda Lawrence, telephone interview with author, October 2, 2013.

146. Roz Arbel, telephone interview with author, June 5, 2016. In the opening scene of the story, six-year-old Sonny's mother wakes him up and tells him to "get up and wee-wee." Ernest Gaines, *A Long Day in November* (New York: Dial Press, 1971), 4.

147. Ernest Gaines, interview with author, Baton Rouge, March 8, 1985.

148. Ernest Gaines, interview with author.

149. McLellan, "Gradual Gaines."

150. Linda Lawrence, telephone interview with author, April 25, 2009.

151. Roz Arbel, telephone interview with author, September 21, 2013.

152. Anne Price, "Miss Jane Pitman Author Set to Resume Work on Next Novel," *Baton Rouge Morning Advocate,* February 22, 1974.

153. Ruth Laney, "A New Approach for Black Writers," *Baton Rouge Sunday Advocate,* April 17, 1977, books section.

154. Roz Arbel, telephone interview with author, June 5, 2016.

155. Linda Lawrence, telephone interview with author, October 2, 2013.

156. Blake Green, "Going Away to Write About Home," *San Francisco Chronicle,* April 29, 1976.

157. Linda Lawrence, telephone interview with author, October 2, 2013.

158. Green, "Going Away."

159. "Genevieve Stuttaford, "Somebody Back There Had Strength to Survive," *San Francisco Examiner,* April 25, 1971, 36.

160. Roz Arbel, telephone interview with author, June 5, 2016.

161. Linda Lawrence, telephone conversation with author, March 22, 2021.

162. Linda Lawrence, telephone conversation with author, October 2, 2013.

163. Jeanie Blake, "Interview with Ernest Gaines," *Xavier Review* 3, no. 1 (1983). Gaines said much the same thing when I interviewed him for the magazine *50-Plus* in 1984. "I'd give anything just to have a twenty-seven-year-old daughter, just to cry on her shoulder sometimes," he said, adding, "She would be there to see that the holes in your socks were sewed up and that your food was properly prepared." Gaines, audiotaped interview with author, December 7, 1984. Editor Anne Heller suggested we delete the quote because it made Gaines sound "selfish." Heller, telephone conversation with author, April 29, 1985; notes in possession of author.

164. Roz Arbel, telephone interview with author, June 5, 2016.

## 3. THE HOUSE AND THE SCHOOL: WRITER IN RESIDENCE

1. "Ernie and I looked at one of those famous Victorians on Steiner Street opposite Alamo Square, with an idea to purchase. I told Ernie that I did not think the neighborhood was a good place to raise a girl." Linda Lawrence, Facebook message to author, October 10, 2021.

2. Linda Lawrence, telephone conversation with author, October 2, 2013. Gaines had met Linda's father shortly after he met Linda, when they all attended a party together. Linda recalled her father "buttonholing" Gaines and talking to him about sports.

3. Linda Lawrence, telephone conversation with author, March 22, 2021. In *The Autobiography of Miss Jane Pittman,* Jane lives on "Master Bryant plantation." Bryant is the cruel slave master whose wife beats Jane because she "sassed her in front of the Yankees." Richard Dysart played the role of Bryant in the TV version.

4. Roz Arbel, Facebook comment, September 11, 2012.

5. Linda Lawrence, telephone conversation with author, October 2, 2013.

6. Roz Arbel, telephone interview with author, June 5, 2016.

7. Roz Arbel, telephone interview with author, September 21, 2013.

8. Linda Lawrence, telephone conversation with author, October 2, 2013.

9. Roz Arbel, Facebook message to author, November 17, 2019.

10. Roz Arbel, telephone interview with author, September 21, 2013.

11. Linda Lawrence, telephone interview with author, April 25, 2009.

12. Roz Arbel, telephone interview with author, September 21, 2013.

13. Roz Arbel, telephone interview with author, August 29, 2009.

14. Charles Rowell, "'This Louisiana Thing That Drives Me': An Interview with Ernest J. Gaines," *Callaloo* 1, no. 3 (May 1978): 40.

15. Ernest Gaines, audiotaped interview with author, Baton Rouge, September 26, 1978. Dorothea Oppenheimer suggested that Gaines leave Dial Press and sign with Knopf because she felt that Dial did not do enough to promote his books. In a talk at Louisiana State University in April 1982, Gaines said that the novel "never sold to paperback" to explain why he had accepted a teaching position at the University of Southwestern Louisiana.

16. Ernest Gaines, audiotaped interview with author, Baton Rouge, September 26, 1978.

17. Ernest Gaines, interview with author, Lafayette, March 3, 1982.

18. Ernest Gaines, interview that accompanied the film of "The Sky Is Gray"; notes in possession of author.

19. Ernest Gaines, comments made in creative writing class, University of Southwestern Louisiana, Lafayette, 1981.

20. Jane Bonin, undated letter to author.

21. Jane Bonin, letter to author, May 26, 1982.

22. Ernest Gaines, audiotaped interview with author, December 7, 1984.

23. Linda Lawrence, telephone conversation with author, October 2, 2013.

24. Ernest Gaines, telephone conversation with author, September 18, 1983.

25. Ibid.

26. Stacey Courville, "Gaines' Writing Inspires Couple to Donate a House," *Lafayette Daily Advertiser,* September 25, 1983.

27. Ruth Laney, "Echoes of a Southern Childhood," *50 Plus,* July 1985, 70.

28. Larry McMurtry, eulogy for Irving "Swifty" Lazar delivered at memorial service, Los Angeles, January 6, 1994. Reprinted in Cyrus M. Copeland, ed., *Farewell, Godspeed: The Greatest Eulogies of Our Time* (New York: Harmony Books, 2003), 242. McMurtry won the Pulitzer Prize in fiction for *Lonesome Dove.*

29. John Callahan, telephone conversation with author, February 17, 1992.

30. The location of Oppenheimer's papers is unknown.

31. Jane Bonin died in July 2016, three and a half years before Ernest Gaines.

32. Dorothea Oppenheimer to Jane Bonin, November 21, 1983; copy in possession of author.

33. Jane Bonin, telephone conversation with author, January 11, 1984.

34. Twayne did eventually publish a book on Gaines by writer Valerie Babb, in 1991. Gaines liked it, saying, "She interprets things very well," although he noted a couple of factual errors in its biography. (Gaines's mother's name is incorrectly cited as Adrienne J. Colar Gaines instead of Adrean Jefferson Gaines Colar. The date of the airing of the CBS Television movie of *A Gathering of Old Men* is listed as 1984; it was filmed in 1986 and aired in 1987.) Gaines commented about the Babb book in a telephone conversation with the author on March 9, 1992.

35. Ernest Gaines, remarks made during appearance at Fanfare festival, Southeastern Louisiana University, Hammond, October 25, 1990. Notes in possession of author.

36. Ernest Gaines, audiotaped interview with author, Lafayette, July 8, 1993. Gaines stated that, despite having won the MacArthur money, he had assured department chairman Doris Meriwether that he was committed to teaching at the University of Southwestern Louisiana. "I'd like to stay ten more years if I live that long," he said. In fact, he stayed longer, officially retiring from USL (which had been renamed the University of Louisiana at Lafayette) in late 2004.

37. Ernest Gaines, audiotaped interview with author, Baton Rouge, December 7, 1984.

38. Ernest Gaines, audiotaped comments made during school visit, December 7, 1984. All quotes in this section are from that event.

39. The AmEx "Do You Know Me?" ad campaign ran from the mid-1970s through the mid-1980s.

40. Ruth Laney, "A Gathering of Old Men: Another Ernest Gaines Work Converted to Film," *Baton Rouge Sunday Advocate,* April 26, 1987, 4–5. Details not in the article are from author's notes.

41. Oppenheimer died on May 7; the premiere was held on May 10. Oppenheimer obituary, *New York Times,* May 12, 1987, D31.

42. Jeff Gerecke, email to author, February 24, 2022.

43. David Biben, telephone conversation with author, February 9, 1992.

44. The Carnegie Public Library, on the corner of Virginia and Sacramento Streets, opened in 1904 and was demolished in 1969. Jerry Bowen, "Temperance, Taxes Part of Library's Past," *Historical Articles of Solano County,* August 29, 2004, http://www.solanoarticles.com/history/index.php/weblog/more/temperance_taxes_part_of_librarys_past. It was replaced in 1970 by the John F. Kennedy Library on Santa Clara Street. In 1992, when the documentary crew visited Vallejo, the Kennedy Library staff showed us several large photos of the old Carnegie Library that gave good views of both the interior and the exterior. The photographs appear in the documentary.

45. Ernest Gaines, "Miss Jane and I," *Mozart and Leadbelly* (New York: Alfred A. Knopf, 2005), 42.

46. Marcia Gaudet and Carl Wooton, *Porch Talk: Conversations on the Writer's Craft* (Baton Rouge: Louisiana State University Press, 1990), 112.

47. Adrean Colar, videotaped interview with author, San Jose, May 30, 1992.

48. Alice Walker, "The Black Writer and the Southern Experience," in *In Search of Our Mothers' Gardens* (New York: Harcourt, Brace, Jovanovich, 1984), 19.

49. Rod Dreher, "Long-Ago Times Never Far from Gaines' Heart," *Washington Times,* April 14, 1993, E3.

## 4. THE RELATIONSHIP I DREAMED OF: GETTING MARRIED, COMING HOME

1. Ernest and Dianne Gaines, audiotaped interview with author, Lafayette, July 8, 1993.

2. Gaines was on medical leave the following fall, owing to back surgery, but he continued to give readings and make other appearances on behalf of the school. He officially retired from the University of Southwestern Louisiana (which had been renamed the University of Louisiana at Lafayette) in December 2004. ULL threw a retirement party for Gaines on January 15,

2005, his seventy-second birthday. Many of his out-of-state relatives and friends from Cherie Quarters attended the event.

3. After learning how serious the surgery was, Gaines put it off. In a phone call in January 1994, a couple of weeks after his sixty-first birthday, he told me, "The back surgery was [said to be] serious, high risk, [involving the] brain stem. Dianne and I decided to do further investigation and find the best there is in the country." He told me that he did have carpal tunnel surgery to regain the use of his hands. "My thumbs are numb. Right now it's impossible to write, tie my shoes, cut food with a knife. I'm all bandaged up [with hands that look like] a big old snowball, my arm in a sling."

4. Ernest and Dianne Gaines, audiotaped interview with author, Lafayette, July 8, 1993.

5. Ruth Laney, "Gaining Knowledge: Road to Author's Fame Wound Through Libraries," *Baton Rouge Advocate,* May 5, 1997, 3B.

6. Ernest Gaines, interview with author, April 21, 1999.

7. Ruth Laney, "The Oprah Effect," *Baton Rouge Sunday Advocate Magazine,* November 16, 1997.

8. Ibid.

9. Ernest Gaines, telephone conversation with author, April 21, 1999.

10. R. Reese Fuller, "Going Home," *Times of Acadiana,* March 5, 2003.

11. Ernest Gaines, comments made after receiving Louisiana Writer Award from Louisiana Center for the Book, Louisiana State Library, Baton Rouge, October 27, 2000.

12. "The Sky Is Gray," art exhibit brochure, in possession of author.

13. When I viewed the film of "The Sky Is Gray" at the University of Southwestern Louisiana in 1982, there was a short interview with Gaines appended to the film. I took notes on his comments, a copy of which is in my files. The interview segment was not attached to the film when I viewed it online in 2021.

14. Ruth Laney, "A Conversation with Ernest Gaines," *Southern Review* 10, no. 1 (Winter 1974): 12.

15. Clarence Major, *The Dark and Feeling: Black American Writers and Their Work* (New York: Third Press, 1974), 58.

16. Carleen Brice, "Buy a Book for Someone White This Holiday," *White Readers Meet Black Authors,* blog, November 18, 2008, http://welcomewhitefolks.blogspot.com/2008/11/buy-book-for-somebody-white-this.html.

17. Rebecca Gross, "(National Medal of) Art Talk with Ernest Gaines," National Endowment for the Arts, September 13, 2013, https://www.arts.gov/art-works/2013/national-medal-art-talk-ernest-gaines.

18. Marcia Gaudet and Carl Wooton, *Porch Talk: Conversations on the Writer's Craft* (Baton Rouge: Louisiana State University Press, 1990), 72.

19. Continuous positive airway pressure (CPAP) therapy is a common treatment for obstructive sleep apnea. A CPAP machine, used when sleeping, has a hose connected to a mask or nosepiece to deliver constant and steady air pressure to help with breathing while asleep.

20. The Ernest J. Gaines Award for Literary Excellence recognizes young African American fiction writers. The award was initiated by the Baton Rouge Area Foundation in 2007. The foun-

dation is nationally recognized for enhancing the visibility of emerging African American writers and expanding the audience for their fiction. The cash prize enables the writer to focus on writing.

21. Gaines actually received $2,000 for the Joseph Henry Jackson Award. The Gaines award, presented annually, was later increased to $15,000.

22. In fact, Gaines's own family was "like that."

23. David Biben told me how some of their contemporaries died. "Harry Domino was shot to death; his brother Rudolph killed himself after having been badly beaten; his brother Revel died of a heart attack; Louis Simon, an alcoholic, was found dead of a heart attack; Henry Marcellin had a kidney problem from drinking; Griffin Domino drank himself to death." David Biben, telephone conversation with author, December 2, 1998.

24. Roz Arbel, telephone conversation with author, June 5, 2016.

25. Roz Arbel, Facebook message to author, November 30, 2019. Within a few months, both of the houses she saw had been torn down.

26. Lois Young, telephone conversation with author, November 6, 2019.

27. David Biben, telephone conversation with author, June 2, 2009.

28. Roz Arbel, Facebook message to author, November 30, 2019.

## 5. EVERYBODY WAS EVERYBODY'S CHILD: THE PEOPLE OF CHERIE QUARTERS

1. Sam Bibbens, audiotaped interview with author, Baton Rouge, June 16, 1996.

2. Certificate of Marriage, license no. 642, February 14, 1926, Pointe Coupée Parish Courthouse, New Roads, Louisiana. Appended to the certificate is a handwritten statement by Dr. C. G. Devron of Lakeland that reads, "I, Cyril G. Devron, being a legally licensed physician, do certify that I have this fourth day of February, 1926, made a thorough examination of Isaih Ginn, of Oscar, Louisiana, and believe him to be free from all venereal diseases."

3. Certificate of Marriage, license no. 1565, December 3, 1931, Pointe Coupée Parish Courthouse, New Roads, Louisiana. Adrean filed for divorce on December 10, 1945. Manuel was served with papers on December 19, and Adrean was granted the divorce on June 28, 1946. Petition 2889, 18th Judicial District Court, Parish of Pointe Coupée, on file in the parish courthouse, New Roads. Another document at the Pointe Coupée courthouse adds another layer of mystery: a marriage certificate for Manuel Ginn and Annie Boberton, dated October 30, 1930. It is not clear if this was the same Manuel Ginn who would marry Adrean Jefferson just over a year later. Certificate of Marriage, license no. 1384, October 30, 1930, Pointe Coupée Parish Courthouse, New Roads, Louisiana.

4. Ancestry.com, accessed on December 11, 2021.

5. Ernest Gaines, interview with author and Sid Gray, Lafayette, November 4, 1993.

6. Mack Gaines was raised by a woman named Lucille Martin, a cousin of Norbert Colar. Lucille married Henry Queen. When Mack, who had spent his adult years in Vallejo, died in 2021, he was buried in the Cherie Quarters graveyard. His obituary named his Gaines, Colar, and Queen relatives and stated that he was preceded in death by Henry and Lucille Martin Queen. "Joseph Mack Gaines," *Advocate,* August 20, 2021, https://obits.theadvocate.com/us/obituaries/theadvocate/name/joseph-gaines-obituary?id=21726751.

7. Ada Mae Gaines, videotaped interview with author, Baton Rouge, October 3, 1992.

8. Certificate of Marriage, Manuel Gaines and Clara Zeno, license no. 5094, for the year 1948, Pointe Coupée Parish Courthouse, New Roads, Louisiana; R. Reese Fuller, "Going Home: The Transcript," http://www.reesefuller.com/articles/going-home-the-transcript.

9. According to her obituary, Bernice Joyce Jefferson, born April 12, 1920, moved to Wichita, Kansas, in 1944, shortly after marrying Ambrose Price Woodard Jr. (1919–1972), who had served in Africa during World War II. Her husband was a lawyer who briefly served as Wichita's first Black mayor (1970–1971) . Bernice worked as an elementary school librarian and was a board member of the National Conference of Christians and Jews. Her daughter, Susan Woodard Bragg (1949–2005), served as an Oklahoma City judge. Bernice and her husband were also the parents of a son, Ambrose Price Woodard III. Adrean Colar was still alive when her sister died, on December 17, 1990, and was mentioned as a survivor in the obituary. But apparently the sisters were not close and did not maintain contact. Census records show Bernice living with Julia Cross, age twenty-three, in 1920, when Bernice was a year old. In 1930, Bernice, age eleven, and Julia Cross, age thirty-two, are both listed as "roomer" in the household of Frank and Clara Johnson in Alexandria, Louisiana, some ninety miles north of Oscar. In 1940, Bernice, now twenty-two, was back in Pointe Coupée Parish, living with "Julia Cron." It is unclear who Julia Cross or Cron was and whether she was in fact Julia McVay. Suzanne Perez, "Bernice Woodard Served Quietly: Mayor's Wife Met All Commitments," *Wichita Eagle,* December 20, 1990; Judge Susan Woodard Bragg obituary, *Oklahoma City Oklahoman,* July 21, 2005.

10. David Biben, telephone conversation with author, January 22, 2005.

11. Census records; oral history interviews; Adrean Colar, videotaped interview with author, San Jose, May 30, 1992.

12. Marriage license no. 2123, State of Louisiana, Parish of Pointe Coupée, 18th Judicial District Court, July 16, 1873.

13. David Biben, telephone conversations with author, December 2, 1998, and May 2, 2003. Man Jefferson was sent to Angola State Prison in May 1922 on a charge of forgery committed in DeRidder, Louisiana, in the northern part of the state. Prison records show that he was discharged on May 25, 1924, at age twenty-nine. According to the Social Security Death Index, he died in 1973 in New Orleans.

14. Adrean Colar interview, May 30, 1992.

15. Sixteen years later, her son Ernest Gaines would die two months shy of eighty-seven.

16. I would like to thank Vallejo resident John P. Kelly, who photographed the graves and emailed the photos to me.

17. David Biben, telephone conversation with author, July 21, 1998.

18. Marriage Certificate no. 962, Pointe Coupée Parish Court House, New Roads, Louisiana.

19. David Biben, telephone conversation with author, November 28, 1993. Biben said he was told this information by Adrean, Ernest Gaines's mother.

20. David Biben, interview with author, January 20, 1997; Adrean Colar, videotaped interview, May 30, 1992.

21. Ernest Gaines, videotaped interview, May 1992.

22. Ruby McVay Simmons, telephone conversation with author, October 6, 2021.

23. David Biben, telephone conversation with author, July 31, 1998. In a later conversation, on February 13, 2001, Biben said McVay left because of the Ku Klux Klan. "I know the Klan ran him away," he said. In an earlier conversation, on June 11, 1994, Biben had told me, "James McVay killed a man about his wife [Susan Jones McVay]."

24. Ada Mae Gaines, videotaped interview with author Baton Rouge, October 3, 1992.

25. Sam Bibbens, audiotaped interview with author, Baton Rouge, June 16, 1996.

26. Matthew Jefferson died in 1973. According to Ruby McVay Simmons, Julia McVay sent her daughter Bernice to Leland College in Baker, Louisiana. Simmons, telephone conversation with author, October 6, 2021.

27. David Biben, telephone conversation with author, March 12, 1996.

28. David Biben, telephone conversation with author, April 19, 1996.

29. Ruby McVay Simmons, telephone conversation with author, October 8, 2021.

30. Adrean Colar, videotaped interview with author, San Jose, California, May 30, 1992.

31. David Biben, telephone conversation with author, November 24, 1993.

32. Marcia Gaudet and Carl Wooton, *Porch Talk: Conversations on the Writer's Craft* (Baton Rouge: Louisiana State University Press, 1990), 72.

33. Ernest Gaines, audiotaped interview with author, Baton Rouge, December 7, 1984.

34. Susan Jones's death certificate is on file at the Louisiana State Archives.

35. Gaudet and Wooton, *Porch Talk,* 42.

36. Sam Bibbens, audiotaped interview with author, Baton Rouge, June 16, 1996.

37. Ibid.

38. David Biben, telephone conversation with author, June 11, 1994.

39. David Biben, telephone conversation with author, November 2000.

40. Sam Bibbens, audiotaped interview with author, Baton Rouge, June 16, 1996.

41. Both David Biben and George's grandson Anthony Cador told me that George was arrested for cutting hair without a license and actually was booked into jail for the offense.

42. Freddie Kemp, interview with author, Oscar, Louisiana, April 23, 1993; David Biben, telephone conversation with author, December 2, 1998.

43. Charity Kemp's death certificate is on file at the Louisiana State Archives.

44. David Biben, telephone conversation with author, December 2, 1998; January 2, 1999.

45. Freddie Kemp, interview with author, Baton Rouge, April 30, 1996.

46. Ernest Brooks, audiotaped interview with author, Baton Rouge, June 13, 1996.

47. Freddie Kemp, interview with author, Baton Rouge, April 30, 1996.

48. David Biben, interview with author; Biben, telephone conversation with author, March 18, 2001.

49. David Biben, telephone conversation with author, February 17, 1997; August 24, 2014.

50. David Biben, conversation with author, Oscar, Louisiana, May 10, 1997.

51. Ernest Brooks, audiotaped interview with author, Baton Rouge, June 13, 1996.

52. David Biben, telephone conversation with author, January 2, 1999.

53. Ernest Brooks, interview with author, June 13, 1996.

54. David Biben, telephone conversation with author, June 11, 1994.

55. Freddie Kemp, interview with author, Baton Rouge, April 30, 1996.

56. David Biben, interview with author, Baton Rouge, April 30, 1996.

57. Hark Bibbens's name on his 1936 marriage license to "Alberta" Kemp is given as "Harkie Bevins." Marriage license no. 2423, State of Louisiana, Parish of Pointe Coupée, 18th Judicial District Court, May 14, 1936. The name appears on his gravestone as "Hawkins Bibens / Dec 23, 1913 / Nov 28, 1963." David Biben said that only his next-younger sister, Rosemary, was the child of Hark Bibbens. Biben was the son of plantation owner George Major. Sam and Frankie were the children of Robert Hornsby; Barbara the daughter of Percy Brooks; Alma the daughter of Alec Labry; and Albert James the son of Richard Isaac. David Biben, telephone conversation with author, September 2, 1996.

58. Frankie Christopher and Barbara Overstreet Hardy, conversation with author, Oscar, Louisiana, October 31, 2009.

59. Joe Williams, audiotaped interview with author, Baton Rouge, June 10, 1996.

60. David Biben, telephone conversation with author, October 19, 2003.

61. Freddie Kemp, interview with author, Baton Rouge, April 30, 1996.

62. Ernest Gaines, audiotaped interview with author, October 28, 1972.

63. Ernest J. Gaines, *The Autobiography of Miss Jane Pittman* (New York: Dial Press, 1971), 113.

64. Levert Kemp, telephone conversation with author, August 7, 2021.

65. According to a newspaper notice, Freddie paid $1,300 for the house at 1419 Orange Street in June 1952. *Baton Rouge State-Times,* June 19, 1952.

66. McKinley High School, built in 1927 at the corner of East Boulevard and Louise Street, was the first high school for African Americans in the state. Housed in a two-story building, it offered vocational and college preparatory courses, including Latin, math, chemistry, and music. Its campus included science labs, a building for shop classes, and a library. Students came from all over the state, and even from out of state, to attend it. In 1950, a new school was built on McCalop Street; it functioned as both a junior and a senior high school until 1961, when the present McKinley Senior High School was built on East McKinley Street. See Petra Munro Hendry and Jay D. Edwards, *Old South Baton Rouge: The Roots of Hope* (Lafayette: University of Louisiana at Lafayette Press, 2009). The book includes quotations from *In My Father's House* that mention East Boulevard.

67. The Brooks Park pool was established by the United Negro Recreational Association in 1949 to give Black children a safe place to swim. (Several children had drowned swimming in unsafe places, including flooded streets, borrow pits, and creeks infested with water moccasins.) Although it was immensely popular, it was closed when the Baton Rouge mayor ordered all pools in the city closed as a response to desegregation.

68. According to David Biben, the house was owner financed by Dr. Curtis J. Gilliam (1922–1995), who had previously lived there. Biben recalled that Gilliam had an office in the area, at East Boulevard and Louise Street. Gilliam was a longtime civil rights activist and the first Black optometrist in Baton Rouge. A former president of the Baton Rouge chapter of the NAACP, he participated in the 1953 Baton Rouge bus boycott. In 1956, he helped to organize and file a desegregation lawsuit against the East Baton Rouge Parish school board. The Louise

Street house would remain in the family for sixty years. When Joe Williams died in 2001, his nephew Anthony Cador inherited the house. His cousin Frankie Christopher lived there until her death. Cador, who lives in San Francisco, eventually sold the house.

69. Anthony Cador, telephone conversation with author, August 15, 2021.

70. Freddie Kemp, interview with author, Oscar, Louisiana, April 23, 1993. Ethel Ferdinand Kemp is buried alongside her husband at Port Hudson.

71. William "Bill" Robillard, videotaped interview with author, Oscar, Louisiana, May 19, 1992.

72. Ada Mae Gaines, videotaped interview with author, Baton Rouge, October 3, 1992.

73. David Biben, telephone conversation with author, June 11, 1994.

74. Bill Robillard, videotaped interview with author Oscar, Louisiana, May 19, 1992; Ada Mae Robillard Gaines, videotaped interview with author, Baton Rouge, October 3, 1992. Bub Bouanchaud married Eloise Major, the granddaughter of P. C. Major. Their daughter, Madeleine Bouanchaud Caillet, is the present-day owner of the Big House.

75. Bill Robillard, videotaped interview with author, May 19, 1992.

76. Freddie Kemp, interview with author, Oscar, Louisiana, April 23, 1993.

77. Ada Mae Gaines, videotaped interview with author, Baton Rouge, October 3, 1992.

78. Information about Zeno's birth date and place is difficult to pin down. Census records show him as age three, living in Assumption Parish in 1900, the son of Francis Zeno and Octavie Comeaux. By 1930, he was in Oscar, age thirty-nine, with his wife Mary, age twenty-six, and five children: Verda, twelve; Forrest, ten; Clara, nine; Angelina, four; and Margaret, one. Whether he was unaware of his exact birth date or gave false information, in 1940, still in Oscar, he is age forty-three, with his wife Lelona, age twenty-seven, and five children: Verad [*sic*], twenty-two; Forest [*sic*] twenty; Clara, seventeen; Elvise, two; and Wilbert, ten months. Apparently, Zeno left his first wife between 1930 and 1940, a fact supported by my 1994 interview with his son Forrest. His gravestone in the Cherie Quarters cemetery reads "Aug. 15, 1895 / June 4, 1978."

79. Bill Robillard, videotaped interview with author.

80. Ernest Gaines, interview with author and Sid Gray, November 4, 1993.

81. Gaines, remarks made during appearance at Fanfare festival, Southeastern Louisiana University, Hammond, October 25, 1990. Notes in possession of author.

82. David Biben, telephone conversation with author, June 11, 1994.

83. Sam Bibbens, telephone conversation with author, July 11, 2020.

84. David Biben, telephone conversation with author, January 11, 1996.

85. David Biben, telephone conversation with author, September 6, 2003.

86. David Biben, telephone conversation with author, June 11, 1994.

87. Gaines told this story many times, including at a gathering at the state library to present him with an award from the Louisiana Center for the Book on October 27, 2000.

88. There is some question about whether Walter Zeno was born in 1895 or 1897. Census records state that he was born "about 1897," but his tombstone in the graveyard at Cherie Quarters reads "1895–1978." Thanks to Ammon Marshall at the East Baton Rouge Parish Library for locating Zeno's Angola record. Photocopy in possession of author.

89. Forrest Zeno, interview with author, Oscar, Louisiana, April 28, 1994.

90. Forrest Zeno lived to be ninety-eight, dying in 2017, and is buried in a veterans cemetery in Zachary, Louisiana.

91. Census records. A lodger was generally someone who paid to live in the house and was not a member of the family.

92. David Biben, telephone conversation with author, December 28, 2003.

93. Jerry Brooks, conversation with author, Baton Rouge, July 3, 2002.

94. Jimmy Brooks was able to "read and write a little" and Pearlie was unable to read or write. James Brooks, interview with author, Baton Rouge, February 28, 1992.

95. Ernest Brooks, interview with author, Baton Rouge, February 22, 1996.

96. Census records; Pointe Coupée Parish Catholic records.

97. Adrean Colar, videotaped interview with author, San Jose, May 30, 1992.

98. Interview with Ernest Gaines, 2003. R. Reese Fuller, "Going Home: The Transcript," http://www.reesefuller.com/articles/going-home-the-transcript.

99. Ernest Gaines, interview with author; Norbert Colar Social Security application form, copy in possession of author. Adrean's divorce from Manuel Gaines became final in June 1946; she and Norbert married on December 6, 1946.

100. Adrean Colar, videotaped interview with author, San Jose, May 30, 1992.

101. Michael was born in 1949; Lavern on July 8, 1956.

102. Ernest Gaines, letter to Hiram Haydn, April 1964, on file at Ernest Gaines Center, University of Louisiana at Lafayette.

103. David Biben, telephone conversation with author, June 11, 1994.

104. David Biben, telephone conversation with author, March 2, 1999.

105. David Biben, telephone conversation with author, August 30, 1994.

106. David Biben, telephone conversation with author, August 8, 1993. Mary Gehman notes that such coded spelling was common in New Orleans, beginning in the Spanish period (1763–1802). "Generally, illegitimate children of color were acknowledged by their white father and given his last name, but there are cases where it appears that only the white father's first or middle name was adopted. Sometimes . . . a letter or two in the white man's surname was changed to denote his children of color." Gehman, *The Free People of Color of New Orleans* (New Orleans: Margaret Media, 1994), 41–42.

107. David Biben, telephone conversation with author, March 2, 1999.

108. Ernest Gaines, telephone conversation with author, October 25, 1993.

109. Biben recalled one time when he did ask his white kinfolk for help. In the 1960s, when he was living in Baton Rouge, he asked Eloise Major Bouanchaud, his cousin, to lend him a small sum. "I went to her and asked her for money one time. I wanted to open a parking lot downtown. All I needed was the first month's rent. She said, 'I don't have any money.'" Biben said such stinginess was a family trait. "Her mama, Lillie [Wilson Major], wouldn't give God a prayer. Oh, she was tight. I worked for her for two days and she give me a dollar. I wouldn't go back. I was seventeen or eighteen, painting their house. She paid me a dollar a day. I said, 'I can go to Triple Arch [restaurant] and make more than this.' She was tight, Lord. She'd stand over you while you were working and push you." David Biben, telephone conversation with author, February 25, 2005.

110. David Biben, telephone conversation with author, June 11, 1994.

111. George Major's death certificate is on file at the Louisiana State Archives.

112. David Biben, telephone conversation with author, August 8, 1993.

113. David Biben, telephone conversation with author, June 11, 1994.

114. David Biben, telephone conversation with author, May 2, 2003. Biben said that Williams shot and killed a man who was having an affair with Williams's wife. "He was E. J.'s uncle. They called him Bro Son, like Brother Son. He was a Ginn." Biben said that, years later, his godfather Clinton told him "I want to talk about what happened with your daddy [George Major]." But Ben never got to hear Clinton's story. "He went back to Seattle and had a heart attack and died." Again, I asked Aftin Gaddy at Angola to check her records. She sent me a scan of an index card stating that on October 28, 1938, Clinton Williams of Pointe Coupée Parish had been convicted of manslaughter and sentenced to one to four years in the state prison. Through FamilySearch, I found that Clinton Williams had been imprisoned on May 24, 1939. "Louisiana State Penitentiary Records, 1866–1963," https://familysearch.org, accessed September 26, 2020. Clinton, who was born in February 1914, is enumerated with his family in Oscar in the 1920 and 1930 censuses of Ward 8, Pointe Coupée, but in 1940 he is at the "State Penal Farm" in West Feliciana Parish—Angola. The Social Security Death Index shows that he died on October 27, 1990, in Seattle. This scenario may have inspired Ernest Gaines's *Of Love and Dust,* in which Marcus is bonded out of jail by the plantation owner, although in the novel Marcus is obliged to work on the plantation in exchange for being freed from prison.

## 6. GONE BACK IN TIME: THE HOUSES OF CHERIE QUARTERS

1. Sid Gray, interview with author, Baton Rouge, January 6, 2004. All quotes from Gray in this chapter are from this interview, unless otherwise noted.

2. The Louisiana Purchase of 1803 transferred the territory of Louisiana from France to the United States. The portion that is today's Louisiana achieved statehood in 1812.

3. Malvina Pickett, conversation with author, Baton Rouge, November 26, 1993.

4. Pervis Cherie Major II and Marjorie Major Broome wrote letters to superintendent Eugene Young on December 1, 1992, donating the four cabins to the Baton Rouge Recreation and Parks Commission. Copies in possession of the author.

5. Laurie A. Wilkie and Paul Farnsworth, "Riverlake Plantation, Louisiana," *African-American Archaeology* 9 (Winter 1993), 5–6. This article was also published in *The Society of Historical Archaeology Newsletter* 26, no. 3 (October 1993), 27–28.

6. Laurie Wilkie, "Childhood in the Quarters: Playtime at Oakley and Riverlake Plantations," *Louisiana Folklife 18* (1994), 14, 17–18.

7. Eliza Robillard, interview with author, Oscar, Louisiana, February 27, 1993. All comments by Mrs. Robillard are from this interview.

8. David Biben, interview with author, Oscar, Louisiana, February 27, 1993.

9. Ibid.

10. James O. Breeden, ed., *Advice Among Masters: The Ideal in Slave Management in the Old South* (Westport, CT: Greenwood Press, 1980).

11. Ibid., 128.

12. Ibid., xi.

13. Ibid., xviii.

14. Sid Gray, "Description of Slave Cabins at River Lake Plantation," typescript, 1995, unpaginated. Copy in possession of author.

15. John B. Rehder's dissertation was eventually published as Rehder, *Delta Sugar: Louisiana's Vanishing Plantation Landscape* (Baltimore: Johns Hopkins University Press, 1999).

16. Ernest Gaines, interview with Sid Gray and author, November 4, 1993. All of Gaines's comments in this chapter are from that interview, unless otherwise noted.

17. David Biben, telephone conversation with author, November 8, 1997.

18. Gaines was mistaken about the demolition of the overseer's house. David Biben later found a 1973 aerial photograph of River Lake Plantation that shows it still standing.

19. Ernest Gaines, remarks made during appearance at Fanfare festival, Southeastern Louisiana University, Hammond, October 25, 1990. Notes in possession of author.

20. Freddie Kemp, interview with author, Oscar, Louisiana, April 23, 1993. Item no. 1 in the succession names River Lake, noting that P. C. Major had bought the plantation on January 4, 1892. "There is deducted from the above plantation that certain lot containing one square arpent of land donated by the late P. C. Major and his children to the Pointe Coupée Parish School Board by act before Geo. R. Kearney, Notary Public, on December 15th, 1933, and recorded under Entry No. 2016 of Book 'I' of the Conveyance Records of the Parish of Pointe Coupée, Louisiana."

21. David Biben, telephone conversation with author, January 25, 2004.

22. Sid Gray, telephone conversation with author, December 8, 1998.

## 7. OF LOVE AND DUST: DAILY LIFE IN CHERIE QUARTERS

1. Ada Mae Gaines, telephone conversation with author, February 26, 1992.

2. David Biben, telephone conversation with author, December 28, 2003.

3. Ibid.

4. David Biben, telephone conversation with author, January 4, 2004.

5. Bill Robillard, videotaped interview with author, Oscar, Louisiana, May 19, 1992.

6. Forrest Zeno, interview with author, Oscar, Louisiana, April 28, 1994.

7. Freddie Kemp, interview with author, Oscar, Louisiana, April 23, 1993.

8. David Biben, interview with author.

9. David Biben, telephone conversation with author, January 25, 2004.

10. Joe Williams, telephone conversation with author, April 4, 1993.

11. Ernest Brooks, audiotaped interview with author, June 13, 1999.

12. David Biben, telephone conversation with author, January 25, 2004.

13. David Biben, interview with author, Oscar, Louisiana, February 27, 1993.

14. Ernest Gaines, interview with Sid Gray and author, Lafayette, November 4, 1993.

15. David Biben, conversations with author, Oscar, Louisiana, May 10, 1997; October 28, 2000.

16. Freddie Kemp, interview with author, Oscar, Louisiana, April 23, 1993.

17. Sam Bibbens, audiotaped interview with author, Baton Rouge, June 16, 1996.

18. Barbara Overstreet Hardy, conversation with author, Oscar, Louisiana, October 28, 2000.

19. David Biben, telephone conversation with author, December 28, 2003.

20. David Biben, telephone conversation with author, September 28, 2004.

21. David Biben said his mother, Albertha Bibbens, got her first icebox when she worked at Triple Arch restaurant; the owners got rid of it and gave it to her. "It was like a refrigerator with a door at the top and a door at the bottom," he said. "The ice would go in the top and the food in the bottom. Bert would buy a hundred pounds of ice and it would last two days."

22. Bill Robillard, videotaped interview with author, Oscar, Louisiana, May 19, 1992.

23. Ernest Gaines, interview with author, Oscar, Louisiana, October 28, 2000.

24. Freddie Kemp, interview with author, Oscar, Louisiana, April 23, 1993. Asafoetida is the fetid gum resin of various plants of the carrot family, used in medicine as an antispasmodic and in folk medicine as a general prophylactic against disease. It is said to have a strong odor and taste of garlic.

25. David Biben, telephone conversation with author, January 25, 2004.

26. Lois Young, videotaped interview with author, San Jose, May 30, 1992.

27. Ernest Gaines, interview with author.

28. David Biben, conversation with author, Oscar, Louisiana, February 27, 1993.

29. James Brooks, interview with author, Baton Rouge, February 28, 1992.

30. David Biben, videotaped interview with author, Oscar, Louisiana, 1992.

31. David Biben, interview with author, Oscar, Louisiana, February 27, 1993.

32. David Biben, telephone conversation with author, January 4, 2004.

33. James Brooks, interview with author, Baton Rouge, February 28, 1992.

34. Adrean Colar, videotaped interview with author, San Jose, May 30, 1992.

35. David Biben, telephone conversation with author, January 4, 2004; Bill Robillard, videotaped interview with author, Oscar, Louisiana, May 19, 1992.

36. David Biben, telephone conversation with author, June 11, 1994.

37. Norbert Colar, videotaped interview with author, San Jose, May 30, 1992. This account by his brother appears in the television documentary about Ernest Gaines.

38. Ernest Gaines, audiotaped interview with author and Jane Bonin, Baton Rouge, November 20, 1983.

39. Freddie Kemp, interview with author, Oscar, Louisiana, April 23, 1993. As noted in chapter 6, P. C. Major had donated the lot to the parish school board.

40. David Biben, telephone conversation with author, December 2, 1998.

41. Ernest Gaines, audiotaped interview with author and Jane Bonin, Baton Rouge, November 20, 1983.

42. O'Neal Bouie (1901–1974), a native of Oscar, was the son of George Bouie and Harriet Ranson Bouie. He married Ophelia Ross (1903–1960) and is buried alongside her in the cemetery at Cherie Quarters.

43. James Brooks, interview with author, Baton Rouge, February 28, 1992; David Biben, telephone conversation with author, May 11, 2016.

44. Lois Young, videotaped interview with author, San Jose, May 30, 1992.

45. James Brooks, interview with author, Baton Rouge, February 28, 1992.

46. Malvina Pickett, interview with author, Baton Rouge, October 29, 1992.

47. David Biben, interview with author.

48. Ada Mae Gaines, telephone conversation with author, February 26, 1992.

49. David Biben, telephone conversation with author, January 4, 2004.

50. Eddie Phillips (1918–1973) is buried in the Cherie Quarters graveyard. His service in World War II is noted on his tombstone.

51. James Brooks, interview with author, Baton Rouge, February 28, 1992; Malvina Picket, interview with author, Baton Rouge, October 29, 1992; David Biben, telephone conversation with author, October 29, 1997.

52. Steve Culpepper and Mary Broussard, "Writer Draws on Pointe Coupée Childhood," *Baton Rouge Sunday Advocate,* December 4, 1988.

53. James Brooks, interview with author, Baton Rouge, February 28, 1992.

54. Freddie Kemp, interview with author, Oscar, Louisiana, April 23, 1993.

55. Forrest Zeno, interview with author, Oscar, Louisiana, April 28, 1994.

56. David Biben, interview with author, Oscar, Louisiana, February 27, 1993; Ada Mae Gaines, telephone conversation with author, February 26, 1992.

57. Ernest Gaines, comments made during Lagniappe Tours visit to Cherie Quarters, Oscar, Louisiana, 1997; Ada Mae Gaines, videotaped interview with author, Baton Rouge, October 3, 1992; James Brooks, interview with author, Baton Rouge, February 28, 1992; David Biben, interview with author, Oscar, Louisiana, February 27, 1993; Bill Robillard, telephone conversation with author, March 17, 1992.

58. James Brooks, interview with author, Baton Rouge, February 28, 1992.

59. Ernest Gaines, comments made during Lagniappe Tours visit; James Brooks, interview with author, Baton Rouge, February 28, 1992; David Biben, interview with author, Oscar, Louisiana, February 27, 1993.

60. State Department of Education of Louisiana, Division of Administration and Finance, *Ninety-Second Annual Report for the Session 1940–41,* 90, 92.

61. Steve Culpepper and Mary Broussard, "A Struggle in Pointe Coupée," *Baton Rouge Sunday Advocate,* December 4, 1988.

62. David Biben, conversation with author, Oscar, Louisiana, February 27, 1993; Barbara Overstreet Hardy, interview with author, Baton Rouge, September 16, 2000.

63. Freddie Kemp, interview with author, Oscar, Louisiana, April 23, 1993.

64. David Biben, telephone conversation with author, August 27, 2009.

65. David Biben, telephone conversation with author, January 20, 1997.

66. David Biben, telephone conversation with author, January 4, 2004.

67. Ruth Laney, "A Conversation with Ernest Gaines," *Southern Review* 10, no. 1 (Winter 1974): 1–14.

68. David Biben, telephone conversation with author, January 24, 1994.

69. David Biben, telephone conversations with author, January 4, 2004; January 12, 1997.

70. Freddie Kemp, interview with author, Baton Rouge, April 30, 1996.

71. David Biben, telephone conversations with author, December 28, 2003; July 2, 1994.

## 8. THE BIG HOUSE: THE RULING FAMILIES OF RIVER LAKE PLANTATION

1. Donna Fricker, "Riverlake," National Register of Historic Places inventory/nomination form, Louisiana Division of Preservation, Baton Rouge, February 22, 1983.

2. Julie Eshelman-Lee, "Antoine Decuir and His Legacy: River Lake Plantation," unpublished article, 1998. Copy in possession of author.

3. Ibid., 6–8.

4. Ibid., 14–18.

5. Fricker, "Riverlake"; Sid Gray, interview with author, Baton Rouge, January 6, 2004.

6. Fricker, "Riverlake."

7. Sid Gray, interview with author, January 6, 2004.

8. Eshelman-Lee, "Antoine Decuir," 23–31.

9. Brian Costello, conversation with author, July 21, 1996.

10. Eshelman-Lee, "Antoine Decuir," 22.

11. William Reeves, personal communication.

12. Established in 1880 by Judge L. B. Claiborne, the *Banner* continues to be published today. Brian J. Costello, *A History of Pointe Coupée Parish, Louisiana* (Margaret Media, 2010), 153.

13. "The 'Merry Makers' Ball," *Pointe Coupée Banner,* October 8, 1881. Photocopy in possession of author.

14. Sand Marmillion, telephone conversation with author, August 10, 2016.

15. On May 13, 1994, at the invitation of Sand and Noman Marmillion, Pointe Coupée Parish historian Brian Costello and I drove to Laura Plantation to examine and photograph the album. Within a few days, Brian had determined the identities of the people in the album.

16. Katy Morlas Shannon, email communications to author, August 2016. Shannon also noted, "It's interesting the Denis family sold out in 1892. [Antoinette Decuir Denis sold River Lake Plantation to P. C. Major in January 1892.] That was also when the Locouls and de Lobels sold Laura Plantation. I also believe the connection went further back than that. Louis Duparc sold a slave to Emile Tanneret (Antoinette Decuir's half brother), Emile Tanneret sold property in New Orleans to Flagy Duparc, and a 'Mr. Tanneret' is mentioned once in a family letter. Laura's great-grandfather Guillaume Duparc, founder of Laura Plantation, was commandant of Pointe Coupée; many of the ties the family formed during their time there remained long after they moved to St. James Parish."

17. Brian Costello, telephone conversation with author, May 1994.

18. Michaline Busico, "Bringing It All Back Home," *San Jose Mercury News,* January 16, 1994.

19. Charles Denis Fournier, telephone conversation with author, March 1996.

20. Charles Denis Fournier, conversation with author, Metairie, Louisiana, March 24, 1996.

21. The carte de visite was originally a calling card, especially one with a photographic portrait mounted on it. Patented by Parisian portrait photographer André Adolphe-Eugène Disdéri in 1854, it was immensely popular in the mid-nineteenth century.

22. Land sale, Louise Antoinette Decuir Denis to Pervis Cherie Major, conveyance entry 16254 of the year 1892, Pointe Coupée Parish Clerk of Court, New Roads, Louisiana.

23. Charles Denis Fournier, telephone conversation with author, March 15, 2005.

24. H. Parrott Bacot, telephone conversation with author, May 1, 1996.

25. H. Parrott Bacot et al., *Marie Adrien Persac: Louisiana Artist* (Baton Rouge: Louisiana State University Press, 2000), 58.

26. H. Parrott Bacot, telephone conversation with author, March 13, 2005.

27. Charles Fournier, conversation with author, Metairie, Louisiana, March 24, 1996.

28. Judy Riffel, ed., *A History of Pointe Coupée Parish and Its Families* (Baton Rouge: La Comité des Archives de la Louisiane, 1983), 254–57; land sale, Louise Antoinette Decuir Denis to Pervis Cherie Major, conveyance entry 16254 of the year 1892, Pointe Coupée Parish Clerk of Court, New Roads, Louisiana.

29. P. C. Major succession no. 1583, 18th Judicial District Court, Parish of Pointe Coupée, located in parish courthouse, New Roads, Louisiana. Copy in possession of author.

30. David Biben, telephone conversation with author, December 2, 1998.

31. The exact date of their marriage is unknown, but the 1940 census of Ward 8 in Pointe Coupée Parish shows George, age forty, enumerated with his wife, Marie E[ola], thirty-seven, and brother John B., forty-five.

32. David Biben, telephone conversation with author, March 12, 1996.

33. Ibid. The ledgers are kept in the attic at River Lake; in 1997, I viewed one that listed the purchases of Ernest Gaines's great-grandmother Susan Jones.

34. David Biben, telephone conversation with author, January 20, 1997.

35. Ibid.

36. David Biben, telephone conversation with author, December 13, 1998.

37. Madeleine Caillet, telephone conversation with author, May 3, 1985.

## 9. TIME IS THE ENEMY: THE FRIENDS OF CHERIE QUARTERS

1. Sid Gray, telephone conversation with author, April 21, 1993.

2. Mission statement, Friends of Cherie Quarters, in possession of author.

3. Dorothy Spruill Redford with Michael D'Orso, *Somerset Homecoming: Recovering a Lost Heritage* (New York: Doubleday, 1988), 29, 244–45, 261.

4. Madeleine Caillet, telephone conversation with author, January 27, 1994.

5. Chris Frink, "Pointe Coupée History: Sunday Jazz Brunch Scheduled to Raise Funds for Historic Places," *Baton Rouge Advocate*, May 16, 1994, C1.

6. Author to Madeleine Caillet, copy in possession of author.

7. David Biben, telephone conversation with author, April 19, 1996.

8. Author to Madeleine Caillet, copy in possession of author.

9. Madeleine Caillet, telephone conversation with author, May 11, 1994.

10. Madeleine Caillet, conversation with author and Sid Gray, Oscar, Louisiana, July 27, 1994.

11. Like her uncle John Major; mother, Eloise Bouanchaud; and great-grandfather P. C. Major, Mrs. Caillet was a member of the board of directors of the Bank of New Roads, which merged with Regions Bank on March 31, 1995. As part of the merger, she was immediately appointed a member of the Regions Bank advisory board of directors.

12. Madeleine Caillet, telephone conversation with author, October 13, 1994.

13. Minutes of meetings in possession of author.

14. Ann Reilly Jones, conversation with author and Sid Gray, Baton Rouge, June 23, 1995. Notes in possession of author.

15. Notes from lecture presented on March 17, 1996, in possession of author.

16. David Biben, telephone conversations with author, May 22, 1998; September 16, 1999.

17. David Biben, telephone conversation with author, February 17, 1997.

18. Madeleine Caillet, telephone conversation with author, April 8, 1997.

19. Gaines said the terms "Creole" and "French" were used interchangeably on the plantation. Telephone interview with author, January 19, 1996.

20. Brianna Bramlette, telephone conversation with author, May 14, 1997.

21. Daniel Carey, conversation with author, Oscar, Louisiana, April 18, 1997. Carey was the Southern Regional Coordinator for the National Trust for Historic Preservation.

22. Notes from Save Our Cemeteries visit in possession of author.

23. Colleen Caillet, telephone conversation with author, February 11, 1998.

24. Cindy Urrea, "Small Cemetery Serves as Source of Inspiration," *Lafayette Advertiser,* October 26, 1997.

25. David Biben, telephone conversation with author, July 23, 2001.

26. Rose Anne Brister, "The Last Regionalist? An Interview with Ernest J. Gaines," *Callaloo* 26, no. 3 (Summer 2003).

27. David Biben, telephone conversation with author, October 29, 2001.

28. Sid Gray, conversation with author, October 8, 2000.

29. David Biben, telephone conversation with author, May 21, 2003.

# BIBLIOGRAPHY


## WORKS BY ERNEST GAINES

### Books

*Catherine Carmier,* Atheneum, 1964.
*Of Love and Dust,* Dial Press, 1967.
*Bloodline,* Dial Press, 1968.
*The Autobiography of Miss Jane Pittman,* Dial Press, 1971.
*A Long Day in November,* Random House, 1971.
*In My Father's House,* Alfred A. Knopf, 1978.
*A Gathering of Old Men,* Alfred A. Knopf, 1983.
*A Lesson Before Dying,* Alfred A. Knopf, 1993.
*Mozart and Leadbelly: Stories and Essays,* Alfred A. Knopf, 2005.
*The Tragedy of Brady Sims,* Vintage Contemporaries, 2017.

### Short Stories

"The Turtles." *Transfer,* 1956.
"Boy in the Double-Breasted Suit." *Transfer,* 1957.
"Mary Louise." *Stanford Short Stories,* 1960.
"The Sky Is Gray." *Negro Digest,* August 1963.
"Just Like a Tree." *Sewanee Review,* Autumn 1963.
"A Long Day in November." *Texas Quarterly,* Summer 1964.
"My Grandpa and the Haint." *New Mexico Quarterly,* Summer 1966.
"Jesus Walked Down Market Street." *Mozart and Leadbelly,* 2005.

### Published Articles

"Home: A Photo-Essay." *Callaloo* 1, no. 3 (May 1978): 52–67.
"Miss Jane and I." *Callaloo* 1, no. 3 (May 1978): 23–38.
"Auntie and the Black Experience in Louisiana." In *Louisiana Tapestry: The Ethnic Weave of St. Landry Parish,* ed. Vaughan B. Baker and Jean T. Kreamer. Lafayette: University of Southwestern Louisiana, Center for Louisiana Studies, 1982.

"A Very Big Order: Reconstructing Identity." *Southern Review* 26, no. 2 (Spring 1990): 245–253.
"The Autobiography of Mister Ernest Gaines." *Cultural Vistas,* Spring 1990: 4–6, 15–16.
"Mozart and Leadbelly." *Phi Kappa Phi National Forum* 78, no. 1 (1998): 11–16.

### *Unpublished Talks*

"Obsession," a talk about his desire to preserve the Cherie Quarters graveyard. Copy in possession of the author, undated.
"Three Meetings—Sterling Brown." Copy in possession of author, undated.
Talk delivered at the Deep South Writers' Conference, 1981. Copy in possession of author.
Comments made in creative writing class, University of Southwestern Louisiana, Lafayette, March 2, 1982.
Talk delivered at Southeastern Louisiana University, Hammond, October 25, 1990.
Keynote speech, Society of Southwest Archivists, University of Southwestern Louisiana, Lafayette, May 29, 1998.

### *Works Made into Films*

*The Autobiography of Miss Jane Pittman,* CBS Television, 1974.
*The Sky Is Gray,* American Short Story Series, PBS, 1980.
*A Gathering of Old Men,* CBS Television, 1987.
*A Lesson Before Dying,* HBO, 1999.

## BOOKS AND ARTICLES ABOUT GAINES AND HIS WORK

Anderson, Ed. "Support Black Talent, Writer Urges." *New Orleans Times-Picayune,* February 11, 1987.
Babb, Valerie Melissa. *Ernest Gaines.* Boston: Twayne, 1991.
Baudoin, Richard. "The Importance of Being Ernest." *Times of Acadiana,* July 14, 1993.
Beavers, Herman. *Wrestling Angels into Song: The Fictions of Ernest J. Gaines and James Alan McPherson.* Philadelphia: University of Pennsylvania Press, 1995.
Beyette, Beverly. "Quiet, Sincere—or Not Black Enough?" *Baton Rouge Sunday Advocate Magazine,* May 8, 1983.
Blake, Jeanie. "E. J. and His Miss Jane." *New Orleans Times-Picayune,* February 28, 1982.
———. "Interview with Ernest Gaines." *Xavier Review* 3, no. 1 (1983).
Brister, Rose Anne. "The Last Regionalist? An Interview with Ernest J. Gaines." *Callaloo* 26, no. 3 (Summer 2003).
Brown, Dale. "A Lesson for Living." *Sojourners Magazine* 31, no. 5 (September–October 2002): 30–33.

Buchan, Bliss S. "Negro Plight, Progress from Freedom to Now." *New Orleans Times-Picayune,* May 30, 1971.

Busico, Michalene. "Bringing It All Back Home." *San Jose Mercury News,* Arts and Books section, January 16, 1994.

Callahan, John F. "One Day in Louisiana." Review of *A Gathering of Old Men* by Ernest J. Gaines. *New Republic,* December 26, 1983: 38–39.

Carlson, Thomas. "The Class of 2087." *Southern Magazine,* March 1987.

Carmean, Karen. *Ernest J. Gaines: A Critical Companion.* Westport, CT: Greenwood Press, 1998.

Carter, Tom. "Ernest Gaines." *Essence,* July 1975.

Clark, Keith. *Black Manhood in James Baldwin, Ernest J. Gaines, and August Wilson.* Urbana: University of Illinois Press, 2002.

———. *Navigating the Fiction of Ernest J. Gaines: A Roadmap for Readers.* Baton Rouge: Louisiana State University Press, 2020.

Courville, Stacey. "Gaines Writes About the South He Grew Up In." *Lafayette Daily Advertiser,* September 25, 1983.

Crockett, Lane. "Ernest Gaines Given Literary Medal by Centenary." *Shreveport Times,* April 15, 1992.

Culpepper, Steve, and Mary Broussard. "A Struggle in Pointe Coupée." *Baton Rouge Sunday Advocate,* December 4, 1988.

———. "New Roads Activist Says Races Don't Mix." *Baton Rouge Sunday Advocate,* December 4, 1988.

———. "Writer Draws on Pointe Coupée Childhood." *Baton Rouge Sunday Advocate,* December 4, 1988.

Deruisseaux, Paul. "Ernest Gaines: A Conversation." *New York Times Book Review,* June 11, 1978.

Doyle, Mary Ellen. *Voices from the Quarters: The Fiction of Ernest J. Gaines.* Baton Rouge: Louisiana State University Press, 2002.

Dungan, Eloise. "He Walks His Own Line." *California Living Magazine* (*San Francisco Examiner* Sunday magazine), July 12, 1970.

Estes, David C., ed. *Critical Reflections on the Fiction of Ernest J. Gaines.* Athens: University of Georgia Press, 1994.

"Gaines Says Decade Shaped Modern History." *Natchitoches* (Louisiana) *Times,* March 3, 1977.

Gaudet, Marcia, ed. *Ernest J. Gaines: Conversations.* Jackson: University Press of Mississippi, 2019.

Gaudet, Marcia, and Carl Wooton. *Porch Talk with Ernest Gaines: Conversations on the Writer's Craft.* Baton Rouge: Louisiana State University Press, 1990.

Green, Blake. "Going Away to Write About Home." *San Francisco Chronicle,* April 29, 1976.

Gremillion, Jeff. "Down the Quarter." *The Times of Acadiana,* May 19, 1999, 26–28, 30.

Hogan, William. "Growing Up on the Plantation." *San Francisco Chronicle,* World of Books column, November 11, 1971.

"House Donated for Writers-in-Residence." *The Vermilion* (University of Southwestern Louisiana student newspaper), September 2, 1983.

Hustmyre, Chuck. "Gaines Stops by LSU for Story Time." *Baton Rouge Advocate,* February 21, 2005.

"Jane Pittman Author Wants to Avoid Films." *Baton Rouge State-Times,* February 22, 1974.

Karem, Jeff. *The Romance of Authenticity: The Cultural Politics of Regional and Ethnic Literatures.* Charlottesville: University of Virginia Press, 2004.

Knight, Margaret R. "He Must Return to the South." *Baton Rouge Sunday Advocate,* April 7, 1974.

Laney, Ruth. "Bard from the Bayou." *The World & I,* October 1993.

———. "Can Birthplace of Ernest Gaines Be Saved from Bulldozer?" *Preservation in Print,* September 1994.

———. "Cherie Quarters: The Place and the People." *Preservation in Print,* August 1999.

———. "Clan Returns to Graveyard: Family Recalls Sacrifices, Life in Pittman's Autobiography," *Baton Rouge Advocate,* June 10, 1996.

———. "A Conversation with Ernest Gaines." *Southern Review,* Winter 1974.

———. "Echoes of a Southern Childhood." *50-Plus,* July 1985.

———. "Ernest J. Gaines: A Great American Author Pays It Forward to a New Generation of Black Writers." *The Root,* January 22, 2015.

———. "Ernest J. Gaines: A Life in Words." *Cultural Vistas,* Spring 1993.

———. "Ernest J. Gaines: The Autobiographer of Miss Jane Pittman." *Louisiana Life,* July/August 1982.

———. "The French Connection: Louisiana Author Ernest Gaines Will Teach Writing in France." *Baton Rouge Sunday Advocate Magazine,* February 18, 1996.

———. "Gaining Knowledge: Road to Author's Fame Wound Through Libraries," *Baton Rouge Advocate,* May 5, 1997.

———. "A Gathering of Old Men: Another Ernest Gaines Work Converted to Film." *Baton Rouge Sunday Advocate Magazine,* April 26, 1987

———. "The Last One Left." *Baton Rouge Sunday Advocate Magazine,* October 30, 1983.

———. "A Lesson Before Dying: Ernest Gaines Novel Becomes HBO Event," *Baton Rouge Sunday Advocate Magazine,* May 16, 1999.

———. "A New Approach for Black Writers." *Baton Rouge Sunday Advocate,* book section, April 17, 1977.

———. "The Oprah Effect." *Baton Rouge Sunday Advocate Magazine,* November 16, 1997.

———. "Preservationists Organize Friends of Cherie Quarters." *Louisiana Cultural Vistas,* Fall 1995.

———. "Remembering Ernest Gaines: A Friendship Founded on a Love for Words." *Country Roads Magazine,* December 2019.

———. "Southern Sage Savors His Rise to Success." *Emerge,* May 1994.

———. "Writers in Residence: Eminence Grise Ernest Gaines and Rising Star Olympia Vernon Are Inextricably Linked—to Louisiana and to Each Other." *Country Roads Magazine,* January 2008.

Lightfoot, Linda. "Black Author Cites La. 'Soul.'" *Baton Rouge State-Times,* April 14, 1982.

Lowe, John, ed. *Conversations with Ernest Gaines.* Jackson: University Press of Mississippi, 1995.

Lowe, John Wharton, and Herman Beavers, eds. *Approaches to Teaching Gaines's* The Autobiography of Miss Jane Pittman *and Other Works.* New York: Modern Language Association, 2019.

McClatchey, Walter, Jr. "Writers Seminar Is the Best One to Date." *Baton Rouge Morning Advocate,* September 22, 1981.

McLellan, Joseph. "Gradual Gaines." *Washington Post,* April 7, 1980.

McMurtry, Larry. "Reverend Martin's Son: Review of *In My Father's House.*" *New York Times Book Review,* June 11, 1978.

Mulhern, Mike. "Novelist Returns to State." *Baton Rouge Sunday Advocate,* October 11, 1981.

"Native Author May Become Image-Making Faulkner for Rural Louisiana's Negroes." *Baton Rouge Morning Advocate,* August 8, 1968.

Noel, Angela. "Plantation-Raised Ernest Gains [*sic*] Loves to Write About Louisiana." *Baton Rouge Sunday Advocate,* April 24, 1977.

Ramsey, Alvin. "Through a Glass Whitely: The Televised Rape of *Miss Jane Pittman.*" *Black World,* August 1974: 10, 32–36.

Semien, John. "Author Says New Issues Face Young Black Writers." *Baton Rouge Morning Advocate,* April 16, 1982.

Simpson, Anne K. *A Gathering of Gaines: The Man and the Writer.* Lafayette: University of Southwestern Louisiana, Center for Louisiana Studies, 1991.

"Southern Authors to Speak." *Baton Rouge Sunday Advocate,* September 9, 1973.

Stuttaford, Genevieve. "Somebody Back There Had Strength to Survive." *San Francisco Examiner,* April 25, 1971.

Summer, Bob. "Ernest J. Gaines." *Publishers Weekly,* May 24, 1993.

Thames, Kathleen. "Lessons from Ernest Gaines." *La Louisiane,* Fall 1993.

Urrea, Cindy. "Reaching New Heights with Ernest." *Lafayette Sunday Advertiser,* October 26, 1997.

———. "Small Cemetery Serves as Source of Inspiration." *Lafayette Sunday Advertiser,* October 26, 1997.

West, Hollie I. "Memories of Childhood on Plantation at Oscar Inspire Author." *Baton Rouge State-Times,* February 5, 1976.

Wright, Dick. "Author Discusses Bestseller at SU." *Baton Rouge Morning Advocate,* March 16, 1972.

"Writer E. J. Gaines to Appear." *Natchitoches* (Louisiana) *Times,* February 24, 1977.

## RELATED READING

Bacot, H. Parrott, Barbara SoRelle Bacot, Sally Kittredge Reeves, John Magill, and John Lawrence. *Marie Adrien Persac: Louisiana Artist.* Baton Rouge: Louisiana State University Press, 2000.

Benson, Jackson J. *Wallace Stegner: His Life and Work.* New York: Viking, 1996.

Botkin, B. A., ed. *Lay My Burden Down: A Folk History of Slavery.* New York: Dell, 1973.

Breeden, James O., ed. *Advice Among Masters: The Ideal in Slave Management in the Old South.* Westport, CT: Greenwood Press, 1980.

Copeland, Cyrus. *Farewell, Godspeed: The Greatest Eulogies of Our Time.* New York: Harmony Books, 2003.

Costello, Brian J. *C'est ça yé dit: Creole Folk Tales, Superstitions, Remedies, Customs, Nicknames, and Linguistic Peculiarities of Pointe Coupée Parish, Louisiana.* New Roads, LA: New Roads Printing, 2004.

———. *From Ternant to Parlange: A Creole Plantation through Seven Generations.* Self-published, 2002.

———. *A History of Pointe Coupée Parish, Louisiana.* Margaret Media, 2010.

Ellis, Clifton, and Rebecca Ginsburg, eds. *Cabin, Quarter, Plantation: Architecture and Landscapes of North American Slavery.* New Haven, CT: Yale University Press, 2010.

Foley, Albert S., S.J. *God's Men of Color: The Colored Catholic Priests of the United States 1854–1954.* New York: Farrar, Straus & Co., 1955.

Gaines, Ernest II. *Three Ws: Tears of Pain and Joy.* Bloomington, IN: Archway, 2019.

Gold, Herbert. *Bohemia: Where Art, Angst, Love, and Strong Coffee Meet.* New York: Simon & Schuster, 1993

Gore, Laura Locoul. *Memories of the Old Plantation Home and Creole Family Album, with Commentary by Norman and Sand Marmillion.* Vacherie, LA: Zoe Company, 2007.

Hahn, Steven. *A Nation Under Our Feet: Black Political Struggles in the Rural South from Slavery to the Great Migration.* Cambridge, MA: Harvard University Press, 2003.

Hendry, Petra Munro, and Jay D. Edwards. *Old South Baton Rouge: The Roots of Hope.* Lafayette: University of Louisiana at Lafayette Press, 2009.

Hilliard, David, and Lewis Cole. *This Side of Glory: The Autobiography of David Hilliard and the Story of the Black Panther Party.* Boston: Little Brown, 1993.

Kern, James E. *Vallejo.* Mount Pleasant, SC: Arcadia, 2004.

McGriff-Payne, Sharon. *African Americans in Vallejo.* Mount Pleasant, SC: Arcadia, 2012.

Middleton, Ernest J. *History of the Louisiana Education Association.* Washington, DC: National Education Association, 1984.

Olmert, Michael. *Kitchens, Smokehouses, and Privies: Outbuildings and the Architecture of Daily Life in the Eighteenth-Century Mid-Atlantic.* Ithaca, NY: Cornell University Press, 2009.

Redford, Dorothy Spruill. *Somerset Homecoming: Recovering a Lost Heritage.* New York: Doubleday, 1988.

Reeves, William. *From Tally-Ho to Forest Home: The History of Two Louisiana Plantations.* Bayou Goula, LA: D. Denis Murrell and David R. Denis, 2005.

Rehder, John B. *Delta Sugar: Louisiana's Vanishing Plantation Landscape.* Baltimore: Johns Hopkins University Press, 1999.

Riffel, Judy, ed. *A History of Pointe Coupée Parish and Its Families.* Baton Rouge: Le Comité des Archives de la Louisiane, 1983.

Riley, Brendan. *Lower Georgia Street: California's Forgotten Barbary Coast.* Mount Pleasant, SC: Arcadia, 2017.

Sexton, Richard, Randy Harelson, and Brian Costello. *New Roads and Old Rivers: Louisiana's Historic Pointe Coupée Parish.* Baton Rouge: Louisiana State University Press, 2012.

Starr, Kevin. *Golden Dreams: California in an Age of Abundance, 1950–1963.* New York: Oxford University Press, 2009.

Walker, Alice. *In Search of Our Mothers' Gardens: Womanist Prose.* New York: Harcourt, Brace, Jovanovich, 1984.

Wilkie, Laurie. "Childhood in the Quarters: Playtime at Oakley and Riverlake Plantations." *Louisiana Folklife* 18 (1994): 13–20.

———. *Creating Freedom: Material Culture and African-American Identity at Oakley Plantation, Louisiana, 1840–1950.* Baton Rouge: Louisiana State University Press, 2000.

Wilkie, Laurie A., and Paul Farnsworth. "Riverlake Plantation, Louisiana." *African-American Archaeology* 9 (Winter 1993): 5–6. Also published in *The Society of Historical Archaeology Newsletter* 26, no. 3 (October 1993): 27–28.

## DOCUMENTARY

Laney, Ruth, and Rick Smith. *Ernest J. Gaines: Louisiana Stories.* Baton Rouge: Louisiana Public Broadcasting, 1993.